MONTAUK:
The *LIGHTNING* Chance

Dr. Julio Antonio del Marmol

"THE CUBAN LIGHTNING"

© 2020 Dr. Julio Antonio del Marmol
All rights reserved. No part of this publication may be reproduced, stored in a retrieval system, or transmitted, in any form or by any means, electronic, mechanical, photocopying, recording, or otherwise, without the written prior permission of the author.

ISBN: 978-1-68588-028-6 (sc)
ISBN: 978-1-68588-027-9 (hc)
ISBN: 978-1-68588-029-3 (e)

Because of the dynamic nature of the Internet, any web addresses or links contained in this book may have changed since publication and may no longer be valid.

Any people depicted in stock imagery provided are either drawn from historical archives, the author's own private collection, or models and such images are being used for illustrative purposes only.

Cuban Lightning Publications, Int

Hypocrisy Destroys Itself: 2030

The powerful, totalitarian Oriental hypocritical Beast, full of hatred and thirst for power and not caring even for its own people or humanity at large, will throw in his rage indiscriminately a ball of fire trillions of times more powerful than Hiroshima and Nagasaki. This ball of fire from the sea that the unscrupulous Beast plays with will burn himself, destroying all of humanity and at the same time his dreams and ambitions of global control. He will not only fail to control the world, but he will also manage to destroy it along with his people and himself.

This can be stopped, yes, if we open our eyes. We have to destroy the Beast before he possesses this extraordinary power. We can stop him from creating this horrible cataclysm that only a few will survive. It is in our hands to not let it become our final reality.

The Vision of Bejasmin Cesar Loubus, imparted to Dr. Julio Antonio del Marmol

MONTAUK: THE LIGHTNING CHANCE

PROLOGUE

We all come into this world without knowing what's going to happen in the future or what is going to happen next. Some of us when something negative or bad happens, ask ourselves "if I only knew this is how it would be, I wouldn't proceed." Most of the time, however, after that bad period passes, something great happens afterwards. The good, the bad, and the ugly actually is what makes life a box of surprises, makes us dream of a better future while we're experiencing bad times; and when we're in the bright, great moments of happiness, we can be a little afraid of what will happen next. All these emotions, compiled, create the beauty of life. I ask myself if you have the chance to know ahead every single minute, hour, day, week, and month ahead of your life, and predict every one of them, would you take it? From my point of view and experience, life would be very boring, monotonous, and sometimes horrifying if you did. That is why they say to be careful what you wish for. What you think will be the greatest and happiest thing, to know your future, can actually be the worst curse that you could ever imagine, especially when you can even predict it before having a conversation with someone and knowing what that individual will say to you and what that conversation will lead to. That is why I say "Give me a balanced knowledge with certain limitations in life about everything. Then, only then, will you have a balanced life."

I have been in the position to see with great description sometimes what will occur the next days or weeks of my life. To me, it doesn't bring any happiness, only anxiety, uncertainty, and sometimes is scarier than what they really are. That is why I tell my audience to read this book with an open mind. Don't be sorry for the knowledge that you don't have. Be curious, be alert, and always be prompt to digest what life brings to you at all times. Avoid excess, because no excess can bring anything good to you or anyone. Live life to its maximum plentitude as if you are going to be gone in the next minute, day, or month. I decided to share my experiences and I want you to choose what route you are going to take in your life. Sometimes it's very lucrative, and for some people it might be great to know ahead of time what the next day can bring, rain or sunshine. To me, it's a blessing to go to sleep not knowing if maybe the next day I'm not going to wake up. Taking this out of your mind will take the greatest flavor that life and God can provide.

CHAPTER 1: THE LIGHTNING CHANCE

A Man's Best Treasure

A man has three great treasures that he should never compromise: his principles, his moral values, and his freedom. If he loses any one of these treasures, he becomes a shadow of a lost soul in the dark night, for the rest of his life.

Dr. Julio Antonio del Marmol

February 6, 1972

I had just returned to California, where I had been relocated following my arrival in the United States in Miami. The previous three months had been the most miserable in my life, as I had been sequestered in a basement at MIT providing the intelligence community with all I knew about Cuban experiments in cloning. For a young tropical bird, the winter months in Massachusetts were pretty brutal.

O'Brien and I sat in canvas deck chairs on an opulent yacht berthed in the Balboa Bay Club marina. I was having a mimosa while O'Brien held a bottle of Lowenbräu as we sat watching the procession of luxury yachts and smaller boats pass by us in the harbor. O'Brien put his bottle down on the deck, picked up his briefcase, and pulled out a file.

"Well," he said, "the highest levels of our intelligence have gone through your file. They discovered something that, though I didn't know about it I have to say I'm not surprised. You have natural, extremely potent psychic powers. Is that how you survived all those attempts on your life in Miami? And how you survived so deep in the Cuban communist system for over a decade, undetected? You saw them coming before the events actually happened?"

I scratched my chin as I thought about it. "Well, you're never 100% sure. Premonitions, signals in your brain, but I also hate to be a pessimist. I fight pessimism with optimism. I've been told since I was a little boy that I was born under a shining star and could see things happen far away with my mind. I don't know if this is a gift; sometimes, I think it's a curse. To see what other people have in their mind is no joke. It can be very disturbing."

O'Brien smiled and shook his head. "I think it's a gift, but I see your point that it can sometimes be a curse. Some of the stuff here in your file that we just acquired shows you've done some unbelievable things in the past. It now makes sense to me how you could survive so many traps in Cuba. They want to send you to Montauk, where we have one of the finest facilities available at this time. We have people there that specialize in psychic powers, and they will work only with people like you, who have natural gifts. They can help you channel those abilities not just as weapons, but also as a powerful means of defending yourself. Believe me, whatever training you had in Cuba for intelligence will in no way match what you'll learn in this facility. They'll enhance your natural gifts so that you can protect yourself, be disarming, and if necessary, how to put your adversaries down using only the power of your mind and a few fingers of one hand. In some situations, you'll be surprised at what you can do with that secret weapon you've carried inside you for so long."

I frowned skeptically. "Who are these people? Are you telling me that Houdini and Einstein, two of the most brilliant minds in history, aren't really dead, but teaching there as professors? Isaac Newton, too?"

O'Brien smiled and chuckled. "Well, I think Houdini is a suckling baby compared to the people we have in this facility. As for Einstein and Newton, we have a few of them, too. But I'm not going to ruin your surprise. I can only tell you to tighten your seat belt—of course, if you're willing to go."

"Absolutely! I'm always open to new ideas and experiences, especially of this kind. When are we leaving?"

"The next couple of days. Make whatever arrangements you have to with your friends, tell them you'll be out of the state for a few months, and we'll put you in the intensive course. That way I can bring you back to do what you're good at doing as soon as possible."

"How long do these courses normally take?"

"It all depends on your abilities and willingness to learn. It varies, between 6 months and a year."

"Do I have to worry about any money or any expenses?"

"Don't worry about it, everything is on us. You won't have to worry about that for a long time-we're indebted to you. Remember, Uncle Sam's not paying you for anything you do or whatever you did in the past because you declined it." He shook his head. "God as my witness, it never even crossed my mind to do something like that. But I know you are a very rare species of animal. Don't worry, we'll take care of everything for you. As a matter of fact, we'll keep our eyes on your friends and make sure they don't need anything as well until you guys adjust."

"Thank you, I really appreciate that."

"By the way, since we're talking about money...." He leaned over and took a large manila envelope out of his briefcase. He handed it to me. "This is a credit card with an unlimited balance."

"Really? You mean I can buy a yacht like this?"

"You didn't know that this one is already under your mother's name?"

"Really?"

"Since we have a slip here, and I'm good friends with the owners, we docked it here for you."

I was a little skeptical at this. It sounded too good to be true. "You're not screwing with me?"

"If you don't believe me, check the registration there in the flybridge by the helm."

I got up and went to the helm. I looked at the registration and saw that it was made out to B. R. I turned to O'Brien. "I know you guys know everything, but how the hell did you know my mother's second name?"

"A little research, my son. A little research."

I sat back down in my chair and picked up my mimosa. "Well, easy come, easy go."

"You're too skeptical."

"I'll feel better when I pay for it out of my own pocket."

"You already did."

I looked at O'Brien in astonishment. "What do you mean?"

"Where do you think that credit card came from?"

"Where? The government?"

"No, the government has nothing to do with you. Remember, you don't work for us."

"OK. Can you please explain, then?"

O'Brien leaned back and took a sip of his beer. "Well, since you consider me your second father here in the US, I took all the money deposited in your account that you didn't want and put it under your mother's name. I didn't think you would decline that, since when they come here, you'll need to support them and sponsor them. It's your dream for the future, after all. I set up automatic payments to that credit card to your trust."

"Hmm. I think you tricked me, old man. You're corrupting me; not just that, you're bribing me! That will be my wildest dream coming true, to see my parents secure here. I won't sleep a single night thinking the communists could do harm to them or any other member of my family."

"No, no, my son—I'm just looking after you. But Uncle Sam did do something for you. You'll find it in that folder as well a green card. That is your first step to validate you in the United States of America. I also took the liberty of opening an account with Downey Savings on 17th Street in Costa Mesa. It's more discreet, not such a fancy city like Newport Beach. You're going to go whenever you have the time and visit a gentleman that's a branch manager there, Mr. Laden. Introduce yourself and tell him that a mutual friend sent you to him and mention my name. He will give you the keys for the safe deposit box that you'll have there, where you will find a Brazilian-made 9mm pistol and several different passports. That is courtesy of Uncle Sam-you don't pay for those."

"Thank you."

"Let's go back to the initial subject. In reference to the people you will meet in this

facility, I want to give you a piece of advice. There will be different kinds of

people in this course, from different nations. I don't have to tell you this, but keep your

distance from everyone. Whoever appears to be your best friend could be your worst enemy."

I smiled. "Thank you. It's nice to know I have a second father in this nation. Believe me, I'm very grateful."

Montauk: The Lightning Chance

"I know you are." We both stood up and said our farewells for the time being. I had much to do to prepare my team for my lengthy absence.

A couple of days later, as O'Brien had promised, we were in a private jet flying to Montauk, New York. I tried not to think about the cold that would greet me there. We landed and deplaned to find a minivan waiting for us. In a repetition of my departure from Guantanamo Base, I was covered with a blanket and lay in the back seat. O'Brien turned to me.

"Are you comfortable?" he asked.

"Sometimes I forget I'm on US soil. I feel like I'm back in Cuba."

"We did it for a different reason in Cuba than we're doing it here. We've got sophisticated satellites that can identify a man from orbit, and we don't want anyone to know what kind of training you're going through and so alert our enemies."

The security of the compound was the highest I had ever seen. O'Brien and I both had to have full-body image scans as well as retinal scans for future access to the facility. This security was so tight that, when I would have later occasion to return after a mission with a new scar, I had to go through a new full-body scan to account for the change to my body. Even the slightest variation would trigger the security system there. Even the doubles of Lee Harvey Oswald would not be able to infiltrate this facility to impersonate that patsy.

We went inside to an office. It looked fairly standard as far as US military offices went, based on my previous experiences at Guantanamo. O'Brien introduced me to Mike Thompson, who was a tall, pale mulatto in his 40's with a beard and mustache. He took my hand to shake it, but did not let go, instead staring into my eyes.

"You've been going through a lot for your age, eh?" he asked me.

"In which circle? In the circle now, or in past circles? I've been told I was a very old man since I was 5. My father called me his Little Old Man."

"No. You've been going through a lot from this circle."

"Yes, I think so."

"You don't even know what is coming. There's a lot. Do you think you can handle it?"

"If I've been able to handle it up to now, I think I can handle it for the rest of my journey."

Mike nodded. "Welcome to our facility. We will bring the best out of you and prepare you so that your future is a lot easier for you. We will enhance your gifts. That way you can handle any situation that is thrown at you."

"I'm ready."

Mike looked at me curiously, a half-smile on his face. "Did you know a lady who has an Asian look but is not completely Asian back in Cuba?"

"I know many people. What about it?"

"Well, her last name is Xiang." I smiled. Despite O'Brien's endorsement, I didn't completely trust Mike. Steffan had O'Brien's endorsement, as well, and he proved to be a double agent for Cuba. I didn't want to acknowledge knowing Chandee to him yet. "She is supposed to be working with our intelligence in there, but we never knew under who she had been working until very recently. I believe that she crossed your path a few times in Cuba. Is that one of your secret contacts you never revealed to anyone?"

I shook my head. "I don't think those details are relevant to the reason O'Brien brought me over here. Whatever is in your file, let's leave it alone so it doesn't end up in our enemies' hands."

Mike grinned broadly at O'Brien as he jabbed his thumb in my direction. "No doubt that this guy has been well-trained; in intelligence, the less you say the better. You never know who is working for the enemy until it's too late and your head gets blown off." He turned back to me. "All I want to know is if it's possible that she knows you."

"Anything is possible," I replied. "I will let you know eventually when I see her face."

"OK, fair enough."

"It's even possible for me to recognize someone without that person apparently recognizing me. That's the way we played the game in Cuba. My team in Cuba was very small, but I had a group that had grown up with me, with very few exceptions. Some I even knew from birth. That's one reason I was able to survive for so long undetected in that complicated world of espionage and intrigue. I always relied on trusting everyone without trusting anyone."

Mike stood up with a slight smile, holding my file. "Yes, yes-I don't have to say anymore." He shook the file as if he had something verified. "You have a very impressive and unique record, not only for your integrity, loyalty, and patriotism, but also for your unselfishness, without caring about money in the slightest. To me, it is a great pleasure and an honor to have somebody of your standards here. I can tell my grandchildren later on that I had the Cuban Lightning in our facilities as my student."

I smiled. "Let's hope you don't attribute to yourself what belongs to others. Thank you for your compliments and your welcome. You make me feel great, especially after leaving all of my family behind in that small island. Remember-don't believe anything in writing and only half of what your eyes can credit." I tapped the folder with my right hand.

O'Brien said, "I told you, Mike. I've brought you a jewel. Make sure that you make him shine more-don't take anything away. I not only have a professional attachment with him, but I also have a personal and emotional attachment with his uncle. He's part of our family."

Mike nodded. "That's good to know, O'Brien. You're leaving him in good hands. You can go anytime and be at peace."

I said, "I don't want any extra privilege or anything like that. They say the Devil loves his son so much that he will poke his eyes out. If you show me favoritism, the others could develop feelings of animosity and resentment against me, and that could interfere with both our training. It will also make my life here not very pleasant, which I am not looking for. I've had enough of that in the past."

O'Brien put his hand on my shoulder. "Don't worry, my son. We are good enough spies to treat you specially without anyone noticing."

"OK, I cannot say no to that."

We walked back out into the corridor. O'Brien and I embraced in farewell. As O'Brien left in one direction, Mike led me in a different direction, folder still in hand. "Let me show you the more important places in this facility. It's only a few places, because the facility is huge. It will take you months to see every single research facility in this place."

"Do you have a restroom nearby?" I asked.

He pointed down the hall. "Yes, right over there. I will be in room B1." He pointed towards a door opposite the restrooms he had indicated. "Meet me there."

I walked the few steps down the hall towards the sign indicating the restrooms. I looked at the steel walls and reinforced concrete on the base. I thought to myself how ultra-secret an intelligence facility this had to be. I felt truly privileged to be shown this level of trust, to be provided the opportunity not many people could be offered of seeing the place. I realized they must really have deeply researched my background.

I walked into the bathroom. I saw an Asian man with an unkempt beard who must have been in his early twenties. He looked me up and down appraisingly. His demeanor was unfriendly as he spoke to me. "Who are you? The new arrival? You don't look like you belong here. You're too well-dressed and too clean."

I replied, "Thank you for your welcome. I didn't know that, in order to belong here, you need to be filthy and ill-dressed. My handler must not have known, or he would have had me cut holes in my pants, not have a haircut, and look scuzzy and disheveled." The man smirked. I looked at him in an assessing manner. His clothes were very stained, what beard he had was scraggly with a Fu Manchu mustache. He finished washing his hands in the sink. "If you don't mind, I'm going to do my business." I walked towards a urinal.

"No, no, go ahead." I started to discharge my weapon. "So, what is your extraordinary gift? What are your abilities?"

"I don't know. You have to have one to get here?"

"I believe so. I have, and I've been talking to everyone else here and they all have one or two. I have mastered six martial arts, and I can do things with my mind, move objects and stuff like that."

"Good to know."

"Yeah, I only let these gringos know a little bit. They believe all the shit we tell them. We are the superior race-you can believe me or not, but we Japanese are the best. Samurai, martial arts, we created all of it. I don't trust anyone, especially not intelligence."

I raised an eyebrow sardonically. "That's probably why your ancestors enjoyed the Nazis in World War 2–they also thought they were the superior race. Remember, no one is superior. You can find a bullfrog under a rock and get a big surprise by it peeing in your eyes and blinding you. My friend, you're in the wrong place if you don't trust intelligence. Can you keep a secret?"

He looked a little intimidated, but answered, "Of course."

"I'm not still alive after multiple assassination attempts because I'm a blabbermouth, but if you don't like these gringos, what are you doing in this country, let alone this facility? You're walking in a mine field."

"Ha! Like you've walked in a mine field before and know from experience, huh?"

I glanced at him and smiled. I know a little bit about that."

"You don't look like you know much. You don't look older than 16. What kind of experience? The only people who knew about walking in mine fields were in World War 2 like my father."

"Really? I don't think you've been exploring too much out of your country's boundaries. And you say you're Japanese, but you look Korean to me."

"Yeah, I was born in Japan, but we left for Korea and got caught up in all the bullshit there. As for those boundaries, there are mine fields in North Korea, the country I was raised in, but they don't walk in them unless they want to blow their asses up. My name is Hiro. What's your name?"

"You have a noble name. You should work hard to maintain that status. My name is not important, but I'm J. Anthony or Dr. del Marmol."

"Doctor?! OK, I've heard enough. Whatever I've heard about you, and I don't know if it's true or not, but I don't think you look like enough of a fool to go walking in mine fields."

"Thank you."

Hiro walked towards the exit. "Bye."

"See you later."

Hiro grunted in irritation and left. I finished, washed my hands, and left the men's room. I opened the door and found a Chinese girl in her mid-20's waiting for me in the corridor. I, of course, would have known her anywhere—it was Chandee.

As I walked out, she gasped excitedly. "No! It's you?"

Remembering where we were, I asked, "You want to be recognized?"

Chandee embraced me, reminding me acutely that her slim, willowy frame belied how strong she was. "Of course! Oh, my God!! This is unbelievable. I've only been here one month, and I've learned so much. You're going to have fun." Hiro stood at one end of the corridor, scowling at us. Chandee turned towards him and threw her hands out in exasperation, exaggerating a feigned curiosity, but there was a challenge in her voice. "What? What?? Can I help you?" She turned back to me. "This guy is the worst scum and has the biggest ego I've ever seen in a man." Hiro kissed the palm of his hand mockingly and left. "He is jealous of everything. He's got a crush on me, and I don't want to have him within ten miles of me. I did a reading of him immediately knew that he was a zero."

"I just met this Japanese guy who thinks his crap is gold and knew that he was a triple zero. And you've been around him for a month! We should thank God for that natural ability we have to detect zeroes."

"Ha! He's not even Japanese! He's from North Korea; he's got this big ego because his ancestors came from Japan."

"That does not surprise me at all."

She laughed. The bell summoning students to class rang. "I have to go. I'll see you later in the dining room. I don't know where they're going to put you."

I looked at my watch. "Oh! I have to go, too. Mike has been waiting for me. It's great to see you! We'll catch up later."

"Great to see you, too! Don't miss lunch-I want to see you, OK?"

"Are you kidding? I haven't even breakfasted-only some oyster crackers on the plane."

We waved to each other as Chandee rushed off to her class. I turned and saw Mike standing there. He said, "I was about to leave but saw you through the door. I guess you met Miss Xiang?"

"Yes, what a coincidence."

"No coincidence at all-I told her you were here, and she was waiting for you."

"You spoiled it all! I thought God sent her to me again, like in the past in Cuba."

"I'm sorry-but she asked me, and I knew it would be a pleasant surprise for you."

"I'm just kidding. Thank you."

"You're welcome. OK, let's take you to the classes. I want to introduce you to the gentleman who will be in charge of one of the portions of your training."

We walked through the extensive corridors lit by long florescent lamps in the concrete ceilings, going through several metal hydraulic doors. They were incredibly thick, like bank vault doors. Mike used an ID swipe card on a lanyard around his neck at each door. I thought about the security I had to go through just to get *inside* the base and marveled privately about this added layer of protection.

We got to an elevator that looked like a mine elevator in design and took it down five levels. There were racks of hard hats with a green line along the right side of the elevator car and another holding hard hats with a yellow line on the left. Mike took one for himself and handed the other to me.

I said, "I didn't know we would be mining."

Montauk: The Lightning Chance

Mike replied, "It's a safety measure."

We reached our floor and got out. Mike took me on a small tour, showing me various labs of highly advanced design for scientific experiments and sophisticated technological development. The last two we came to involved robotics and another with numerous microscopes, electron microscopes, and advanced scanning equipment along with caged animals.

He pointed at this last and said, "This is your expertise. We're cloning animals."

I asked, "What are you cloning?"

"Organs. I think you know a little about that."

"A little."

His tour had taken us in a loop back to the elevator. We entered the elevator and went back up two levels. We got out and walked by several different rooms that resembled lecture halls. "You've seen some of the parts where we develop the various toys for the intelligence community, as well as applications of various theories. You, however, are here for something else, and this floor is, as you can see, where all of the instruction occurs." He stopped by one door and entered the room. I followed him inside.

A Greek man of Russian descent with white hair on the temples, around his early 50's stood at a podium. He wore coke bottle glasses and was very well-dressed in a suit and tie. The name plate on his desk read Nicholai Marchenko. There were around fifteen or twenty people in the room, ranging from 18-25 years of age. Four girls sat in the front row together; one of them is Chandee. The rest of the class were males.

We stopped by the door and Mike said to me, "Julio Antonio, wait for me here." I waited by the door as Mike headed down the aisle. As he gestures to Nicholai, Chandee turned to me and smiled. Nicholai and Mike had a quick conversation, and Mike turned to me to beckon me down. "Nicholai, this is Dr. Julio Antonio del Marmol. This is Nicholai, one of the most important of your instructors. He is a Professor in Parapsychology."

Nicholai shook hands with me. "It is an honor to have you in my class. I know what you went through in Cuba from a couple of ladies that teach here. You will, I'm sure, meet them later." That statement made me very curious, but I remained silent. "Let me introduce you to the rest of the class. I'm going to step out for a few minutes; Mike wants to show me some things in his office, and you can become acquainted with your classmates in that time."

I replied, "Thank you."

"You're very polite. You say thank you for everything."

"Yes. Thank you is the magic word that opens all the doors in life, even the heavy steel doors you have here."

Nicholai smiled as he patted my shoulder. "Oh, we have a great philosopher with us, too!" He brought me down to the podium. "I have the honor and pleasure to introduce you to this young man, who has dedicated almost all of his life, since he was twelve, to defending freedom, democracy, and God. It's almost cost him his life multiple times, as well as several friends and family, but he never fell. He took it upon himself to attempt to pull down the communist leader of that country, Fidel Castro—an attempt which cost the life of one of his best friends. For 10 years, undetected, he exposed all the plans of the Castro government around the world, communist infiltrations, terrorist attacks, you name it, until his cover was accidentally blown by our own politicians. With a small group of his friends he used the only alternative they had, to leave his country. They went through mine fields, in which he lost yet another friend who unfortunately disobeyed his orders by straying from the path. They then swam for over 12 hours in the freezing October waters into the Guantanamo base to come not only to the United States and freedom but to save hundreds and thousands of our clandestine agents with encoded music that he kept sealed in a shoe polish can in his shorts. I have nothing else to add but to say that you all should be proud to call this man your friend. And now please give a welcoming hand to Dr. Julio Antonio del Marmol.

The class applauded, some politely, others near Chandee a little enthusiastically. It was clear she had told some her friends about me. "And now I'm going to step out for a few minutes to get an updated file on him from Mike. While I'm gone, please be on your best manners and make him welcome as a new member to our family." I stepped down from the podium. Nicholai puts his arm around my shoulder. "Go introduce yourself to everyone. I'll be back in a little while."

Mike said to me, "See you later in the dining room. We have to do your biometrics to add to your file later."

As Mike and Nicholai left, the others crowded around me to introduce themselves, Chandee among them. She turned to them and said proudly, "He was my teacher in Cuba."

One of the girls introduced to me was named Niurka, a blonde Russian girl with a pretty face and unusually vibrant green eyes. I also met Sharlyn, a beautiful Creole from New Orleans around 19 years of age with long wavy hair, full lips, deep green eyes, and olive skin; Inca, of Peruvian descendant of the Incas, an exotic beauty in her late 20's; Ray, a tall, handsome man with curly black hair and beard in his early 20's; and Bolgary, a man of Russian descent 17 years of age.

Niurka asked, "Really? It must be great for you guys to reunite here now."

Chandee said, "Yes. All I know I owe to him. Julio Antonio, these are my friends Niurka, Sharlyn, Inca, Ray, and Bolgary."

They all shook hands with me. Hiro was also in that class and had been scowling at all the attention lavished on me. "Oh, look at all of you idiots! I don't believe a single piece of shit he's spewed: walking in mine fields? Swimming for 12 hours? What is he, a submarine or a mutant half-fish?"

I looked at him calmly, controlling myself. "I told you already earlier in the restroom that no one is superior. What I didn't add was that an attitude like yours covers a sense of inferiority. You want to parade your inferiority complex? Don't do it with me." I turned away from him.

But he was not to be deterred and persisted. "And 'Doctor'? What are you, 18? How did you get your degree? Who did you screw?"

I turned back and pointed at him as I furrowed my eyebrows. I said sternly, "You just crossed a line. I'm going to leave now, because on my first day here I don't want to bloody anyone up. Do you want to be humiliated in front of everyone here, urinate in your pants, and cry your eyes out?" I started to walk away, my ears red with anger.

Hiro said mockingly, "Ooooh, I'm so afraid! Is that why Chandee is all over you? Was she your tramp in Cuba?"

I turned back. "Now you have reached my limit! Leave her out of this, or you will regret this. I guarantee you that."

"You want to see what I can do??" He concentrated. Before I could turn to leave again the buttons on my shirt pulled out and popped off, one after another, by themselves. One at a time, they rolled back down into the classroom. "You want me to do your trousers next and show the color of your underwear to everyone here?"

I calmly walked down, picking up the buttons one at a time and putting them in my shirt pocket. Hiro stepped on the last on intentionally, a challenge in his eyes. I looked up at him, locking eyes with him. I calmly reached out and felt for the right nerve and tendon area, like a concert pianist placing his hands on the keyboard before playing. The point located, I gripped the hamstrings in Hiro's legs so hard that cords bulged on my hands and arms. Hiro's eyes began to flutter rapidly. His face began to spasm as he lost control and went limp. Tears began to stream down his face. I decided to share with him one of my private nightmares, the old one of Che Guevara, but putting him in my place. He saw his own head cut off by Che, rolling down into the fire at the center of the ritual area around which demonic figures danced. Only Chandee and I could see clearly the flickering of the flames reflected in his eyes. We glanced at each other. Chandee nodded in approval to what I had put in Hiro's mind. Regaining eye contact with Hiro, I slowly controlled Hiro's collapse and eased him down onto one of the seats. Hiro urinated in his pants as tears continued trickling down his cheeks.

I said very softly to him, "I told you I didn't want to humiliate you. You asked for it, you got it."

Chandee leaned over Hiro and whispered, "You messed with the wrong man."

Niurka crouched behind me, close to Chandee. The smile faded from her lips and her eyes showed momentary surprise and a little fear. She said in a satisfied, sarcastic whisper, "This is great—this is a lesson this bully has needed for a long time. Now he is in reality, not how he sees himself within his superiority complex." Chandee and Niurka exchanged satisfied looks and gave each other a high five. Niurka's look changed to one of sorrow and pain. "This degenerate bully almost raped me the first day I came to this facility. Fortunately, Chandee was in the bathroom that day. If it hadn't been for her coming to my defense, he would have. He ripped my blouse and bra as it was. And in nothing classier than one of the stalls in the women's bathroom—so glamorous!"

Chandee nodded her head corroboratively. I shook my head, understanding more than ever what kind of bully Hiro was. I said, "That makes me feel a little better. I feared my actions might have been a little extreme, that the lesson I tried to impart might have been a little over the top."

Seeing that Hiro had enough, I relaxed my grip. Hiro jerked spasmodically, as if awakening from a bad nightmare. He opened his eyes in shock, tears still blurring his vision. He looked at me in panic, his arrogance completely deflated. He looked down for a moment in humiliation.

At that moment, the door in the back of the classroom opened. Nicholai came back into the room. He quickly realized from the silence

Montauk: The Lightning Chance

and reading the students' faces that something has happened. He demanded, "What is going on here? Is everything OK?"

Chandee answered, perhaps just a little too quickly, "Yes, yes, Professor. Dr. del Marmol had the courtesy to give us a little demonstration of how you can use the power of your mind and physical strength to disarm and utterly neutralize an attacker."

"Oh, really?" The entire class nodded and voiced support of Chandee's account. "I would like to see that myself one day."

As he walked by everyone to continue the class, Hiro stood up awkwardly and said, "Excuse me, Professor. I have to go to the restroom."

"OK, go." Hiro rushed out, holding his hands over his groin in an attempt to conceal the tell-tale moisture in his pants. "OK, let's continue the class. My subject today is fear: how you can use it to control your enemies, avoid confrontations, how with your mind you can inflict so much damage to an adversary without a weapon that you can petrify that individual. All you have to do is project the worst fear you have ever experienced telepathically into his or her mind. That is the greatest power any human being can have. This is one of the reasons we want to teach you to control those powers without damaging yourself. There is an exceptionally fine line between inflicting that devastating effect into someone's mind and experiencing that same outcome yourself."

I sat down with the group. They looked at him. My face was sweaty, and I was clearly trying to control himself. I said quietly to Chandee, "I need a few seconds. I need to control the temperature of my body and cool my mind down."

She asked, "Why are you even here? You already know how to do that."

I stroked my chin, smirked, and shook my head. I wiped the sweat from my face with a handkerchief. Nicholai closed the book and signaled to the projectionist. The lights went down and slides and film clips were shown providing examples of people moving objects with their minds by telekinesis, levitating people, and people changing emotional states rapidly beyond the subject's ability to control themselves. The last bit of footage showed a woman and man eating at a table. Both got onto the floor and begin crawling around all fours like dogs. They crawled over to lap water out of a dog's bowl on the floor. Each subject had numbers—no names were listed. The whole class laughed at the scene.

Nicholai said, "We will have more details and techniques from those who already have these gifts developed at the highest level. Your abilities will become so refined that you can excite the molecules of an object to heat it up so that your opponent must drop it."

The bell for dismissal rang. Mike came walking towards me as Chandee said, "I'll see you in a couple of hours in the dining room."

Mike said, "Come on, Julio Antonio, we need to scan you and then I'll show you to your quarters." I accompanied Mike to the Processing Center where I was fingerprinted, my blood pressure taken, and my height and weight measured. They then had me step once more into the full body scanning device. Mike then took me out of the room. We walked along several corridors until he brought me to a specific door. "This will be your quarters while you're here."

I must have been more stressed than I thought, as I took an extra-long shower in order to relax myself. I noticed that they had already unpacked my luggage and put my clothes away, which I felt was very accommodating of my hosts. A plate of food was also sitting there for me. I looked at my watch and realized I must have missed dinner. I changed clothes, ate, and then headed to the dining room.

When I got there, I saw Chandee was still there, sitting with her friends. I walked over and said, "I'm sorry I missed lunch. Mike brought me something to eat. It took longer than I thought it would for them to process me."

Chandee smiled and said, "It's OK, you're here now. You'll have to come with us into town some evening. There are some great movie theatres, even swimming pools and bowling alleys, and the food at the restaurants is fabulous!"

"OK, it will be a pleasure for me to join you guys sometime."

We chatted for a while, and I got to know her friends a little better. I made certain that I left them early enough to get a good night's sleep. I wanted to be fresh after the flight, recuperate following my unexpected need to confront Hiro, and expected a full day of activity starting early the next morning.

I wasn't exaggerating. The next several days were intensive, as I received training in many approaches to using my mind I had never considered. To my joyful surprise, two of my professors were ladies I had literally known all of my life—but more about them will come later in this book. I worked very hard to master these new techniques with my usual discipline and focus.

Around two months later, I received a visit during one of my training sessions from Mike. He beckoned me out of the class and said, "I have O'Brien in my office. He needs to speak with you."

I nodded. It would be a pleasure to see him again. "Of course. I'm at his immediate disposition."

I accompanied Mike to his office where O'Brien waited, seated in a chair. He stood up as we entered the office. As we shook hands, he said, "Great to see you, Julio Antonio. Mike, do you mind if I have a moment alone with him?"

Mike nodded. "Of course. I'll be just outside if you need me."

O'Brien waited until Mike left the room and shut the door. He turned to me and said, "Julio Antonio, I'm sorry to interrupt your training, but we have a situation in Vietnam. Some of our kids, prisoners of war, are being tortured and then brainwashed to become Viet Cong. It's not a Russian or Chinese soldier doing it—we think it's a Cuban. We need you to infiltrate them and identify him for us."

"OK, when do we leave?"

"Right now. The plane is waiting for us. But first, you need to put this on." He tossed down an olive-green uniform with a medic's red cross armband.

I looked at it distastefully. "Oh, no! I promised myself that I would never wear that kind of crap again—I had enough of that in Cuba!"

"I'm sorry, Julio Antonio, but there is no way you can be there as a civilian, not in a war zone. By disguising you as a medic, you should be able to move around freely. You have to blend in."

"OK, for you, I will break that promise to myself."

I quickly changed into the uniform he had given me, and we left the base to board the plane. We flew to Thailand, refueled, and then on to land at the US Air Force base in Saigon. Before we deplaned, O'Brien stopped me and handed me a work helmet.

I looked at him in astonishment. "You've got to be kidding me!"

"Please. It's for your safety. The North Vietnamese are making a major push south, and you should keep your head protected."

"No blanket this time?"

O'Brien chuckled as a large, burly black man came in. He wore the uniform of a sergeant, reminding me irresistibly of a cowboy from the two .45 pistols he sported in his web belt. O'Brien replied, "No—no blanket this time. You can sit openly in the back of the car. This is Sergeant Major Johnson. He will make sure you get to your destination in one piece. I'll see you back in the States. This shouldn't take more than a week or two. Remember, don't get too involved. We need you back as soon as possible. You're here on just one mission—identify those people. We need you back in that training."

Accompanied by Johnson, I got off the plane in my medic's uniform. There were three cars waiting for us, reminding me once more of unpleasant experiences in Cuba. We got into the middle of the three cars and drove off the tarmac.

We drove through the streets of Saigon. The signs of recent explosions were still evident. Dead animals littered the area: dogs, a horse still attached to a wagon, even cattle. Vietnamese soldiers coordinated with civilians to move the animals out of the way of traffic.

An ambulance sped by the convoy, followed by a transport full of Vietnamese soldiers, nearly cutting us off. We passed a heavily damaged building flying a red cross flag. A plane flew low overhead and dropped a bomb not 150 feet away. The explosion caused the lead car to flip into the air. It soared over our car and came crashing down on the rear vehicle.

Our car swerved as the driver tried to maintain control. It careened onto a sidewalk, taking out several cafe chairs and tables, and stopped just before it hit the building. The weakened roof structure collapsed onto the front of the car. A steel bar nearly cut the driver in half, while a concrete support crashes down on the front passenger side, pancaking that soldier.

Some Viet Cong were crossing the street, approaching the car. They fired their AK-47s indiscriminately, shooting the Vietnamese soldiers and civilians, even the ones trying to move the horse.

I was trying to open my door, but concrete debris blocked my attempts. Johnson handed me a .38 pistol. "Here. Take this. Under no circumstances let them capture you alive. They like doing things like shoving bamboo splints under your fingernails, in your testicles, in your penis, everywhere to get you to talk. Now get out on my side!"

I climbed out of the car, followed by Johnson. A small girl of about six was crossing the street with her mother. The mother's leg was bleeding, as if she gotten injured in the bomb blast. We joined the pair and began to run. One of the Viet Cong spotted us and opened fire. The Viet Cong had stopped to scavenge the produce from the wagon. The other Viet Cong joined in.

We ran along the street towards the ruined hospital, using concrete columns and other forms of hard cover to duck behind. I saw one Viet Cong lifting an RPG, a guided shoulder-mounted missile. I yelled, "Oh, God! Watch out! Watch out!"

I grabbed the little girl, hugged her to my chest as I dove down to cover her with my body. The mother embraced both of us protectively. Johnson ran across the street, yelling, This way! This way!" The RPG fired. The rocket screamed over our heads and hit the ambulance, killing its occupants, and catching the transport in the blast. We held our position for a few seconds. Fragments of bodies rained down on us. The girl and her mother started to scream.
Johnson motioned down an alley. "This way!"

The little girl grabbed his arm, shook her head, and pointed in the opposite direction, saying, "No, no!!"

I yelled, "Johnson-this way!"

"Are you kidding? You trust them? They're probably Viet Cong!"

"They're wounded—do you think they'll take us to anywhere other than where wounded get treated?"

"OK. You're the boss."

The two Vietnamese took us to another small alley off of the street. The little girl moved a piece of corrugated aluminum fencing and motioned inside. It was clear she spoke no English.
We followed her directions and went through. She put the aluminum section back into place. Looking up, I could see that it was attached to the fence by a single screw. We crept past the broken washing machines and driers, into a room with boilers to heat water for sterilizing clothing. The boiler also is broken. The little girl opened the door, and we entered the room. There was a large hole in the wall from large caliber machine gun fire, and we could see the entire hospital. We peered through it. We could see Viet Cong entering the ruins. There were bodies piled up like sandbags in the hallway due to the lack of room. A Vietnamese nurse walked around the corpses as she did her job, while blood-covered doctors worked on the living patients. The Viet Cong moved in, clearly searching for someone.

The little girl touched my shoulder, her finger to her lips motioning for silence. She ran a finger over her throat and then pointed at the Viet Cong. We lay hunkered down for a couple of hours. Exhausted, I fell asleep.

The little girl shook me gently and pointed at the hole. "American! American!"

Dr. Julio Antonio del Marmol

I looked through the hole and saw American soldiers in the hospital. I touched the little girl and motioned to myself. "Anthony." I pointed to her. She looked at me uncomprehendingly. I repeated, this time including Johnson. "Anthony. Johnson." I pointed to her again.

Comprehending, she pointed to herself. "Zuyen." She pointed to her mother. "Bian." She crossed herself, and then crossed me before patting my ear. She clasped her hands before her and bowed slightly. "*Cám ón bạn.*[1]"

I nodded. "Thank you." I pantomimed by pointing upwards and pointing at each of them. "God bless you both."

We entered the hospital. Doctors started treating the mother's wound, while Johnson made contact with the American soldiers. They offered the use of one of their jeeps, and Johnson and I said our farewells before we left. I gave Zuyen a card with my contact number. I looked up and saw Johnson gesturing to me to come with them.

We followed the group of soldiers to some underground bunkers. After they made sure that both of us were uninjured, they took us to a colonel dressed in civilian clothes. He wore dark glasses, a Hawaiian shirt, sandals without socks. He introduced himself as Patrick. "They tell me you almost didn't make it, man."

"They didn't tell me this was a literal war zone," I said kiddingly.

"The bastards are getting closer and closer. Those morons in Washington aren't even sending us beer anymore. I hear they want to end the war and make us run like chickens after all the work we've done! One thing only I asked O'Brien. I'm sorry I interrupted your training, but I want to see if you can identify the motherfucker who's been destroying our kids. Some of them commit suicide, others are renouncing America as their homeland. Douse those lights and switch on the projector." Slides appeared on the screen of young soldiers with Viet Cong tattoos on their faces burning the American flag. He pointed to a blurry image in the frame. "This is their torturer. Or brainwasher, if you prefer. He's very sneaky. We can't ever quite capture him. The last time we got close to him, he killed six of our intelligence guys."

I said, "Give me a close up of that picture." The image grows larger. It was grainier, but a little clearer for me. I still couldn't quite make out enough to solidly identify him. "Do you have any other picture from a different angle?"

---

[1] "Thank you" in Vietnamese

"Yes, but it's kind of blurry. It's a picture of him at a younger age, when he was a cadet lieutenant in Cuba."

"Can you please show me that?"

"OK. I don't think you're going to get anything out of it. Corporal, get that photo out of that #1 SOB we're looking for."

The corporal rummaged around and found the photo. He put it up, expanding the image. I examined it. "No—it cannot be!" I moved closer. "That is Lieutenant Lenin. He made my life miserable in the military service. Listen, I'm not sure, but I would say that it's 90-95% likely this is that guy. I would never forget that face."

Patrick smiled. "How about you look at him in person? You're about my size. You can dress like me, go to the bar he goes to twice or three nights a week, and maybe you can identify the son of a bitch? We'll have ten guys there. You don't have to get involved. Just tell me if it's him, and we'll take care of the rest."

"This is going to be shorter than I imagined. Tonight? OK, let's go for it."

"OK, take a shower, refresh yourself. I'll see you at 2100 hours. We're going to have fun. Do you like margaritas?"

"I prefer piña coladas or orange daiquiris."

"OK, we'll have a few of them."

Johnson asked, "Colonel, can I dress like that and come with you guys?"

Patrick nodded. "Of course. You're his personal custodian. You have to make sure he gets back to the States in one piece. You fail in that, and it's your ass in the sling."

I took a shower and a nap. When I woke up, I dressed in my borrowed clothes of white pants, white shoes without socks, and a blue and white floral Hawaiian shirt, and headed to the officer's mess. When I got there, I went up to the counter.

The mess hall cook asked, "What would you like, sir?"

I looked at the available options. "I'd like a Ruben, please."

"Yes, sir. Would you like bell peppers on that?"

"Yes, please."

Johnson walked in, got his food, and sat down with me. We were both dressed like Hawaiian playboys. After we got done, we went to meet the colonel. We all of us piled into four cars and drove through the night scene of Saigon. The other cars were filled with Green Berets. When we arrived, the group gathered around Patrick by his car.

He said, "Let's not all of us go in at once. The bird will fly. Julio Antonio and Johnson go in first. I'll come in casually and join you. The rest of you come in gradually and sit in various places. Just make the signal when you see him and are positive who it is."

I asked, "What is the signal?"

"Light a cigarette."

"I don't smoke."

"That's OK. All you have to do is light a cigarette. Then just get up and leave." He handed me a pack of Lucky Strikes.

"You don't have them in menthol?"

"You're too fancy for this!"

Johnson chuckled. "This is the Cuban Lightning. You never heard the stories from GTMO?"

I asked Patrick, "Do you have a hat?"

"A hat?" he asked in puzzlement.

"I can cut a little piece of the border of this shirt and sew it on as a bandana."

"I have some ladies who can do that."

"That's fine. But I don't want him to see my face. This way there's no chance of him recognizing me. If we're going to catch a big fish, you need a jumbo shrimp as bait. If I wear sunglasses it will look strange."

"Done! Give me your shirt. Hey, Oscar—take this to Jane. Tell her cut off a piece of it and attach it like a bandana to the hat."

The man he had called Oscar took a look at it. "Oh, Jane will do that in ten minutes. It's not a big deal at all."

I said, "OK, I will feel very good then."

True to their estimate, they brought the hat to me ten minutes later. Johnson and I went inside the bar, walking very casually. We ordered some drinks and got a table. A few minutes later, Patrick joined us. A few minutes later, one of the Green Berets drifted in and settled in nonchalantly in another corner of the bar.

Two and half hours passed. All the Green Berets by now had entered the bar and were strategically positioned near all of the exits. It was clear that things were dragging out longer than expected. Patrick began to grow anxious.

He said, "Maybe he's not going to show tonight."

I asked, "Do you think his sources warned him off?"

Montauk: The Lightning Chance

"Anything's possible. I did mention that he comes here 2-3 nights a week, not every night. It's possible we simply picked the wrong night."

"Well, maybe then this will take me a little longer than I had hoped. Excuse me, I need to use the restroom."

I got up and walked toward the restrooms near the front entrance. Just as I crossed in front of the front door, Lenin walked in. We stared at each other. It was clear that he was wondering if he knew me from some place. I immediately recognized him and saw the glimmer of recognition in his eyes. I continued on into the men's room. Johnson followed me but was distracted by a beautiful prostitute's attentions.

I no sooner got done in the restroom then Lenin came in behind me. He put a pistol to the back of my head. He snarled, "Who the fuck are you? I know you from someplace. *Hablas Español?*

I replied, "Nope."

"Where the fuck do I know you from?"

"I don't know."

"Where are you from? You're not American."

"I'm French. *Comment allez-vous, monsieur?* Can I shake my wee wee now? Will you take that pistol from my neck?" As soon as Lenin took the pistol away, I spun and kneed him in the groin, snatched the pistol from his hand, and then tagged him in the neck with my ring. "Welcome to justice, you filthy animal!" Lenin began to convulse and shake. He tried to draw another pistol from a leg holster. He began to gasp, and I took that gun from him as well. Lenin's legs gave out and he crumpled in a quivering heap. I pulled off the hat. "Remember me? Yes, from Cuba." Two men tried to enter the bathroom, but I spun and cocked one of the pistols. "Back off! The restroom is out of order!"

The door closed immediately only to open again five seconds later to admit Johnson. I trained the pistol on him. He threw his arms up. "Hey, it's me! They told you that you didn't have to do that. What did you do to him?"

Lenin was beginning to pass out, indicating his time was growing very short. "We have two choices. I can give him the antidote and you can then do with him as you will, or we can let him die now. I would rather give him the antidote."

"OK. Let me go and get the Colonel. Let him make the decision. How long do we have?"

"At most 10-15 minutes. After that, we get brain damage. Go get the Colonel."

Johnson popped out to get Patrick. When they returned, they had three or four men with them. Patrick said, "Give him the antidote. I want to interrogate this son of a bitch. I want to give him the same courtesies he's given our POWs. Letting him die like this is too easy." I administered the antidote and let the men drag Lenin out of the bathroom. I walked out, Patrick following. "Thank you very much. You don't know how valuable this is. You've done in a single day what we've been trying to do for years."

"That's the reason I don't want to take any chances. I know I wasn't supposed to be involved, but I reacted out of necessity. If he's so dangerous, I couldn't take any chances. He had a pistol at my neck."

"No kidding me!"

"Yes, he came in behind me. He knew he recognized me from somewhere. As soon as he took the pistol away, I put him down. I disarmed him, and he had a second pistol concealed in a leg holster. I took that from him as well."

"God is with you, man. No doubt about it. This man is extremely dangerous." By way of thanks, Patrick ordered a bottle of champagne. Everyone toasted me and the success of the operation. They left to take me back to the barracks so I could change and get on the next flight back to the States. My meeting with Lenin brought back old, unpleasant memories, which brought me to reflect on the turmoil my poor Cuba had experienced for so many years. It didn't start with Castro. My uncle had left me extensive notes, and I knew that my homeland's troubles started long before I was even born, long before even Batista had seized power.

Figure 1 Montauk Air Force Base

Montauk: The Lightning Chance

In December 1933, in a huge Spanish colonial salon, with a big long wooden table in the center, kerosene lamps along the walls cast flickering light, the evil, demonic cult, advised by the Devil himself, reorganized their global tactics for the future. Because it was winter, a fire burned in a vast stone and mortar fireplace. Twelve men were dressed as members of some sinister cult in black, hooded robes. Gathered around that long table at a secret location in the Cuban town of Guane in the province of Pinar del Rio, they developed new tactics and techniques, informed by their many failures. One appeared to be the leader of the clan, his hood and robe blood-red in contrast with the others. A tuxedoed man in a top hat served what appeared to be red wine to the members from a jar. The leader stood after everyone had been served and raised his cup. The others clinked their glasses in toast with each other.

The leader said in a solemn voice, "Let's cheer for the first union between the ultra-Right Nazi, or National Socialist Party, and ultra-Left Marxist Communist Party. For too long have we been divided; now we shall be unified for the common benefit and interest of having within our grasp the power to control the world. We will swear by our lives and blood from this day forward our loyalty to the man we have all selected to lead our movement to pave the way through history until the chosen one arrives and takes the bridle of global control."

The others stood, raised their glasses, and chanted, "Hooray, hooray, hooray." All the men's facial expressions were joyful. Only one man whose face, obscured by shadow, showed discontent, and he stroked his beard with a hand bearing the caduceus symbol of a medical school graduation ring.

The leader said, "Anyone who refuses to join with us will die." The cultists all stood and embraced in a sinister group, their hands touching across the table over their heads in a symbolic gesture of agreement with their heads bowed beneath their upraised arms. They drank from their cups and threw them into the fireplace. The kerosene lamplight once more shone in the dark on the caduceus symbol of the man's ring.

Everyone returned to their chairs as the man in formal dress turned off the kerosene lamps one at a time. Then he turned a projector on. The image on the wall near the end of the table that appeared was that of Adolf Hitler, delivering his famous speech before the German parliament and his first speech as Chancellor for the Nazi Party in 1933. The speech lasted four minutes, thirty-nine seconds. When it was finished, every man stood up as a solemn gesture of respect and applauded. They raised their right arms and exclaimed in unison like they were worshiping God in a temple, "Together we will conquer the world! Hoorah, hoorah, hoorah!"

CHAPTER 2: CLAUDIA AND ZOFIA—TIME TRAVELERS OR ANGELS?

In 1933, the 5th President of Cuba, Gerardo Machado y Morales, was nearing the end of his second term. One of the generals of the Cuban War of Independence, he had initially been elected with massive popular support; however, he had pledged to serve only one term, and his popularity waned and vanished. He had been the leader of the Liberal Party in Cuba, he began to curtail free speech and as protests and rebellions became more strident began to use repressive, brutal police tactics against his opponents. His principal political opposition were members of the Conservative Party, and they bore the brunt of his attempts to exterminate all resistance in a bloody campaign of torture and death of any who dared demonstrate against his regime.

1933 was also the year that the Nazis of Germany, joined in their thirst for power with the Communist Party (which supported Machado's Liberal Party) to destroy all democratic institutions in Cuba. The pact they made was in support of Machado as well as the others in Central and South America who embraced their doctrine.

The Conservative Party had been fighting Machado for several years, and their forces in Guane were commanded by a tall, dark man named Nolberis and my father, the Grand Master Mason Leonardo del Marmol, under the disguise of being the intellectual leader behind the opposition. They were marching peacefully in the streets to protest. Everything was going well until military and police vehicles blocked them, issuing orders for them to disperse and started to beat aggressively the crowd with batons. My father was totally against violence but could not control the crowd in the face of this aggression by the authorities.

The crowd, already gathered to express frustration, began to throw rocks. As party members started to drive their cars alongside the government vehicles to protect the crowd, others began to climb up on the trucks and cars, yelling at the authorities. "*Esbirros! Lacayos!*[2] Death to tyranny! Liberals go to Hell, restore our freedom!"

Intimidated, the police and soldiers began to retreat. The soldiers continued to use their batons to beat the protestors nearest them on the neck, arms, and legs as they tried to control the protestors. Instead of calming the crowd, it incited them to even greater violence. This abusive treatment caused the crowd to push forward in spite of the beatings. The government agents put their vehicles in reverse and began to back up. Seeing this, the crowd yelled triumphantly and began to chant "Freedom! Freedom!"

Their joy turned quickly to tears as they turned the street corner. Before them they saw a double rank of military vehicles. The soldiers had their weapons trained on the crowd. A lieutenant colonel who was leading the soldiers addressed the crowd with a megaphone. "If you do not stop, we will open fire!" He had a hideous face, with a nasty scar running down from the empty socket of his right eye, across his cheek, and down to his lips. He had an aggressive, nasty attitude. He repeated his demand, "You all back off now, or you will all die!"

There was silence for a few seconds. One member of the crowd yelled "Freedom or death!" The rest of the crowd picked up and began chanting it. Men, women, and children began to move forward once more. The grotesque officer repeated his demand more urgently. Seeing that the crowd would not stop, he gave the command for his soldiers to open fire. Bullets rain into the crowd. Killed and wounded drop, but the crowd continued in vain, even as blood soaked the pavement. The screams of anger turned into those of pain. The crowd broke up, running in different directions, but the hail of bullets continued. Some running away fall, shot in the back. Everyone was gunned down without mercy.

The soldiers and police then started to go door to door, pulling people out of their houses. Some were arrested by the police and put into the paddy wagons. Others, however, especially those that showed

---

[2] Minions! Mercenaries!

any signs of being recently wounded, were executed by the soldiers in front of their families on the spot.

At House #12, Jose Marti Street, the del Marmol house, Leonardo helped his friend, Nolberis Guerero, who had been shot in both the arm and the leg. Camila, the family's housekeeper, opened the door to let them in. The entire household descended to quickly clean up all traces of blood and take the wounded man into the basement. Leonardo went to the bedroom and quickly changed into his bathrobe.

Just in time, as it turned out, as the expected knock came at the door. Soldiers burst into the house and began to search the premises, forcefully pushing Verena, Leonardo's wife, out of their way. A police captain, Heraldo Mojica, pushed his way in behind them and reprimanded their behavior. "No! These people are well-respected, and Mr. del Marmol isn't involved in politics." He turned to Verena and spoke respectfully to her. "Mrs. del Marmol, could you please let your husband know I would like to ask him some questions?"

She said, "He is in the library, officer, but he is very busy."

The soldier brushed past her and burst into the library, where Leonardo was seated in his favorite recliner, blankets covering his legs as if to protect him from the winter cold, looking at a file in his hands. He looked up. "Come in. Can I help you?"

Verena came in behind the soldier. "I told you—my husband is busy." She noticed that in his rush, Leonardo had not removed his two-toned shoes and donned slippers; additionally, she saw that the shoes were bloodstained. She quickly went over and adjusted his blanket to cover his shoes.

Heraldo walked briskly into the library. Glaring at the soldier, he said sternly, "I told you to leave this man alone!" He forced the soldier from the room, apologized to Leonardo and Verena for the rudeness and improper treatment of the soldiers, and for all of the searchers leave the house. "I'm sorry. This is not my police. It's the new lieutenant colonel from the army they sent from the capital to push back against the political opposition by the Conservatives. He commands an army that is crazy and bloodthirsty." He crossed himself. "So many people have already died unnecessarily this night." With an apologetic salute, he turned and left the library.

Verena went onto her knees before the image of Christ on the wall and looked up prayerfully, tears in her eyes. "Thank you, Lord Jesus, for saving my husband's life!"

Leonardo got up and went into the bathroom. Removing the blanket, he noticed the large bloodstain covering the stomach of his undershirt and his blood-covered arms. He turned and said to Verena as he began to wash himself in the sink, "Please, remain calm. There's no need to panic and no time to waste. Everything is fine. Go and tell Camila to get my brother, Emilio. Nolberis is bleeding too much; he needs urgent medical attention."

A little while later, Emilio arrived. He took one look at Nolberis' injuries and shook his head gravely. He quickly opened his medical bag and got to work. After several minutes, Nolberis was growing visibly paler and Emilio looked up at Leonardo. "This is bad, my brother. He's losing blood much too rapidly. We can slow his blood loss, but I need to give him more blood, anticoagulants, and several other things. It will be much too dangerous to keep him here in Guane. Even if they weren't actively searching for him, just getting the kind of medical supplies I need to help him would not go unnoticed in a small town like this. We must take him to Havana. I have contacts from my university days who are completely trustworthy. One of my best friends that's been working with the resistance against the dictator, Mr. Xiang, will help us. He has the perfect location not only in terms of garage access to his house and for keeping Nolberis to stay out of sight until he gets better and we can get him out of Cuba. Any supplies I need can be obtained from several different pharmacies across the city. That way we won't attract any attention."

Leonardo looked worried. "How can we get him past the security checkpoints without them searching the car?"

Emilio shook his head. "I don't know. That will be a big problem, especially if, as we're assuming, they're looking for him."

Leonardo said, "I have an idea—one of my brother Masons owns a funeral home. We can get a coffin from there, bandage his face—just in case—and put him inside, and then if we see any check points, they'll think we're transporting a deceased family member."

"Sounds workable. Let's do it."

"OK. Let's go and get the coffin."

Leonardo drove his Ford Woody Station Wagon to the mortuary and gained the cooperation of his friend. He helped them load the coffin into the back of the car, and they drove back to Leonardo's house. They parked in the garage. Leonardo cleared the tools off of his worktable and the two of them unloaded the coffin, putting it on top of the table. Bandaging Nolberis' face and arranging him as if he were a corpse with

Montauk: The Lightning Chance

the aid of Verena and Camila, they carefully put him into the coffin and the four of them loaded it back into the station wagon. Leonardo kissed Verena and thanked Camila for their help.

Verena crossed herself. "Please—please, remember your children. Please, both of you take care of yourselves and be very careful. Remember, these people have no scruples; they'll kill anyone."

They drove down the road towards San Luis, and as expected, they had to slow down for a check point. The sergeant came up to the driver's side window.

Leonardo put on a mournful face. "May we pass, Sergeant? My brother died, and we're taking his body to our family in Havana."

The sergeant nodded. "Of course. Pass on through, I'm very sorry for your loss."

They drove into the city of Pinar del Rio, and Emilio had Leonardo pull into a pharmacy. There he purchased some snacks for the two of them and some glass bottles filled with plasma and some anticoagulants to keep Nolberis alive until they reached the capital, Havana.

As they drove to Havana, Leonardo put the radio on, and they listened to the news updates. As Emilio had feared, the bulletins named Nolberis as the leader of the opposition party in Guane and that the soldiers were searching for him all over the nation. They entered Havana after a couple more checkpoints.

Leonardo asked, "Where will we take him? I don't want to get your friend in any trouble."

Emilio sighed. "My brother, I think it's a time for me to make a confession to you. There's nothing to worry about for Mr. Xiang—he owns an antique store, and people come and go all the time. But I need to tell you something, and you must not ever tell anyone, not even your wife."

Leonardo glanced at him in confusion. "Don't tell me, after all these years of criticizing me for being involved in this rebellion, you've been lying to me and have been doing it yourself!"

Emilio replied, "Remember, I'm your older brother. It's my duty to keep you out of trouble. Especially since you have three kids now. I could never forgive myself if something happened to you. But my involvement is a lot bigger and more dangerous than what you've been doing. I've admired your courage for being involved in the fight against the tyrant. You have your grandfather Donato's blood, same as I do. That's why we del Marmols are so crazy."

"What could you be doing that's crazier and more dangerous than what I've been doing? Or is it like always you're taking bigger credit than me? What's crazier than what we're doing today, transporting a body in a coffin to the capital?"

Emilio put a hand on Leonardo's shoulder with a sarcastic smile. "My brother, like I said before, you cannot repeat this to a soul. I've been a spy since my youth in the university, protecting our part of the Western hemisphere, South and Central America and the Caribbean Islands, against the penetration of the Nazis and communist totalitarian ideas."

Leonardo glanced at him incredulously. "For the Americans?"

"Yes, the American intelligence as well as others."

Leonardo frowned. "Is that the reason you've traveled so much to Berlin and Spain? And the British colonies?" Emilio said not a word but nodded. "I always *knew* that you were doing something much crazier than what I've been doing, but it never even crossed my mind that you're a real spy. I'm very proud of you, my brother!" He clapped Emilio on the shoulder.

"Remember, don't tell a soul, unless you want to see your brother in one of those." He jerked his thumb back towards the coffin.

"My, my, my—it's true what our mother said. God protects me from the calm waters, because from the rough waters I can protect myself."

Emilio could not hold it any longer and burst out laughing. "You mean I'm the calm water?"

"Yes, you've been telling me all this time how crazy I've been, and you're really the crazy one!"

They reached Mr. Xiang's antique store. Emilio directed Leonardo to park in front of the store. It was almost midnight. "Go into that alley and wait in front of the only green garage doors in the middle of the alley. I'll wake Mr. Xiang up and open the gate for you."

He got out and went to knock on the door while Leonardo followed the directions he had been given. Leonardo stopped before the green doors that his brother had described. After a few minutes he grew nervous and checked his watch. Emilio appeared with a young Chinese man. Both of them opened the doors and motioned for him to drive inside. As soon as he was in, they closed the doors to the interior courtyard. Emilio introduced Leonardo to his friend, Mr. Xiang, who unfolded a canvas stretcher while Leonardo and Emilio took Nolberis out of the coffin. They carefully laid him out on the stretcher, Leonardo

Montauk: The Lightning Chance

taking the front, Mr. Xiang taking the rear, while Emilio kept the plasma bottle elevated. They went through a cigar packaging factory beneath the dim lights of the long hallway. They came to a small door. Mr. Xiang nudged the door open with his foot and they brought Nolberis into a small room inside the gift shop, trying hard not to make too much noise and disturb Mr. Xiang's terrified wife, who nervously watched the parade.

Mr. Xiang said, "To avoid any embarrassing questions, let me get you a dark blanket to cover that coffin. I guess you already have an answer prepared in your mind if you have to show that to anyone."

"Yes, of course," Leonardo replied.

They made Nolberis comfortable while Emilio put in a fresh bottle of plasma. Emilio looked at Leonardo. "You can go home now or in the morning if you're too tired. We don't want to get too much attention in Guane with people missing you there. If anyone asks, you tell everyone that I came to visit Mom and Dad here in the capital. I'll spend a few days here."

"OK, my brother."

"Are you OK to drive back? Why don't you stay the night in our family home? That way you'll be rested and leave in the morning." Emilio noticed that his brother was fatigued as he watched Leonardo yawn.

"No," Leonardo said, "It will be less noticeable if I leave tonight. Say hello to Father and give Mom and our sisters a kiss for me."

"OK. I'll stay with Mr. Xiang tonight and make sure our friend has everything he needs before I lay down and rest for a while."

Emilio walked Leonardo back through the corridors to the courtyard and opened the gate for him. The two brothers embraced and said goodbye after Leonardo said goodbye to Mr. Xiang.

After a while, Leonardo stopped at a Shell gas station to refill his car's tank. There was a bus terminal at this gas station, and a silhouette in the darkness walked up behind him and clapped a hand on his shoulder, shaking it firmly. Leonardo whirled and exclaimed, "Menelao! My cousin! You scared me half to death—I nearly dropped the gas nozzle on the ground."

Menelao grinned and said, "I'm just testing your nerves, cousin."

"What are you doing here in the middle of the night?"

"Shh, I'm bringing weapons to the FEU[3]. I had to travel by bus to keep a low profile, but I unfortunately missed the bus, and the next one isn't until early in the morning."

"I'm going back to Guane right now. I could easily drop you at your house in San Luis."

"Bless you, my cousin! God always has an additional salvation for us when we don't expect it."

Leonardo finished pumping the gas. They got into the car. Menelao noticed the covered object in the back.

"What is that, my cousin?"

Figure 2 FEU Student Protests

"That is a long story. They sent a bloodthirsty lieutenant colonel to Guane. Nolberis was badly injured in the attack, my brother needed to bring him here to treat him. He had an arterial wound that nearly caused him to bleed to death."

"You del Marmols are crazy! No wonder they look for equals, because us Moras follow only a step behind you, winding up in trouble trying to fix that which is broken. There's always a hole in the wall or the street!"

---

[3] *Federacion Estudiantil Universitaria*, the Federation of University Students

Montauk: The Lightning Chance

They drove to through the city. Leonardo said, "Do you mind if we stop at a bakery? I need to stop and get Verena some pastries."

"Oh! That's a great idea! That way my wife won't grouse so much when I come home so late."

Leonardo drove to a Cuban bakery on the way out of the capital to do what he always did whenever he came to Havana: to purchase some delicious pastries that Verena and the rest of his family loved so much. He filled the tray and brought it to the register. The young lady boxed it up for him, and he saw two very refined, distinguished looking women bringing their pastries over as well for boxing. The way they dressed caught his attention; they looked rather upper class, but the style was outdated. Both were beautiful. One was a brunette, the other with auburn hair, and both had very pale skin. He couldn't date the fashion for certain, but there was something odd about their attire that he couldn't place. They certainly seemed to be very wealthy and well-educated women. He was nearly finished paying for the pastries as they approached, and he could smell their perfume was quite exquisite and probably expensive.

The more attractive one, the brunette, said, "You probably don't remember me. Do you still live in San Luis, or have you moved back to the capital?"

He looked at her in surprise. He had never seen either of them before. He replied, "No to both questions." He grew suspicious at her open friendliness or her physical nearness to him.

The other woman said, "What a small world this is, for us to come to the same place to buy our favorite pastries, only to encounter someone we know from the past!"

Leonardo frowned but smiled politely. "All right, ladies, you have a great evening. I have many miles to cover, almost all the way to the end of the island." He picked up his box and walked out.

While the red head was paying at the register. The brunette tapped her on the shoulder, and exclaimed, "My God, Zofia, there's no way you'll be able to eat all those pastries!" She then walked out behind Leonardo. She followed Leonardo and Menelao out to the parking lot; then he opened trunk of the car to put the pastries inside. He was caught by surprise when he heard her say immediately behind him, "I don't think you should drive all the way to Pinar del Rio with that coffin in the back of your car."

Leonardo turned around with a surprised smile on his face. "What? What are you saying?"

She smiled. "Listen—I'm your friend. Don't make me explain to you in details. Just listen and please do what I tell you to do."

Leonardo furrowed his brows. "Yes, OK? What do you want me to do?"

"We're here to protect you. If you don't listen, you will be arrested and probably tortured and killed in the next seventy-two hours. I don't think that coffin is worth that. You either throw that behind the next ruined building you find. If you want, we'll help you. I know it's probably a little too heavy for you to do that by yourself. If you don't want to do that here in the city, wait until you get onto the highway. Pull over onto a dirt road and get rid of it there."

He stroked his chin in wonderment. "Who are you? You're assuming what I have in my car. How do you know what I have? Do you work with Machado's repressive secret police, and you're looking for another victim? Even if what you say is true, I don't see that there's any law in this country that prohibits one from transporting a coffin from a dead relative or friend from one town to another in Cuba."

She smiled again. "You see? That is your major problem. Where are you going to produce the dead body you brought in that coffin? With this dictator, you have to be very prompt to give him the right answer if you don't want to wind up tortured and dead at the side of the road with your mouth full of ants."

The other woman was coming out of the bakery with the box in her hand. She said loudly, "I told you he wouldn't believe you. We should do what we're supposed to do." She put the box of pastries on the roof of the black and burgundy 1933 Ford Roadster parked right next to Leonardo's car. Leonardo shot her a dirty glance. She turned and smiled at him. "It's nothing personal, Leonardo. But I told my friend Claudia not to waste her time. I wouldn't believe her, either."

Leonardo spread his hands in puzzlement. "Who are you, ladies? How do you know my name?" Both women had been talking to Leonardo, completely ignoring Menelao as if he didn't exist.

Claudia smiled once more. "I told you—I've known you for a long time. You might not remember me. All we're trying to do is to keep you alive so that you can keep going on and have all the six children you will have. If you listen to us and not waste your life by being a hardheaded chauvinist by not listening to a couple of women with your best interests for you and your family in mind, you'll be fine. By the way, where is your brother Emilio?"

Montauk: The Lightning Chance

Leonardo shook his head. He held up his hands. "You had better explain better. I'm a very, very understanding, polite, and courteous, not just with women but with everyone. You're reaching the border of my patience. I don't know how you know all the things you're telling me. I've never seen either of you before, and you keep telling me things and now you're asking me about my brother. I've asked you once, and I'll ask you again: do you work with Machado's secret police? If you will speak plainly to me, and if you actually do have my best interests at heart, then kindly answer my questions. Do you want money?" He reached around for his wallet. "I have plenty of money. But if you do *not* work with the secret police, how do you know all these things about me? Where are you pulling them from? If you will answer my questions, I'm sure we can reach some kind of accommodation or understanding."

Sofia interjected, "Leonardo, please listen very carefully. If we explain to you where we come from or how we know all these things, you'll not only freak out, but you'll also think we should drive to Mazorra[4]. You're an intelligent man. All we want you to do is understand that we're trying to help you. The most important reason we came here and approached you is because if we couldn't get in touch with your brother Emilio beforehand and something happens to us, tell him not to go to Berlin much less Madrid, or he and some of his friends will get killed.

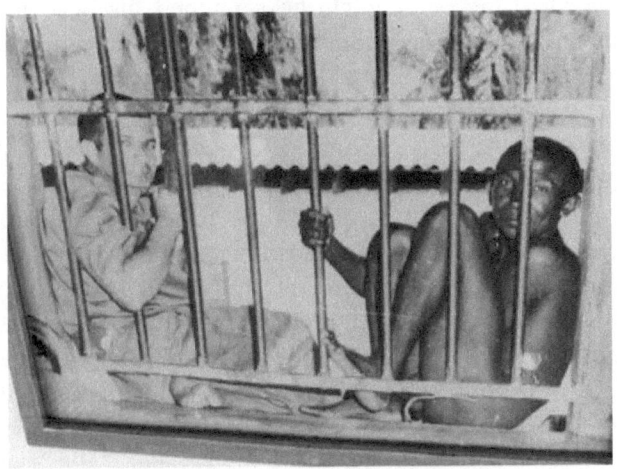

Figure 3 Mazorra Psychiatric Hospital

---

[4] Mazorra Psychiatric Hospital

"Also, let him know that he has to be alert because the Nazis have the vaccine for these diseases and intend to spread their virus of typhus and polio in several nations they intend to invade. They already have the vaccines. They will be immune. Since your brother is a doctor and a very intelligent man," she reached inside her purse and pulled out two glass tubes labeled *typhus* and *polio*, "this can save thousands if not millions of lives if he reproduces these formulas." She opened an envelope and showed it to Leonardo. "The formulas are right here." She handed them all to Leonardo. "What we're telling you now is too difficult to understand for any normal individual, even the most intelligent, like you. Your brother probably won't understand either, but you will see eventually with your own eyes that what we're telling you is the truth. You will have several children. You already have one boy; you will have two more boys. One will be born in 1947, and he will grow up to be a specialist in genetics. It's very important that you remember this: if that boy dies, it will be a catastrophe. It will be in his hands to save the genes to save thousands if not millions of lives. He will be working with your brother, even if it's against your will because he will not sympathize with your political ideology. I cannot tell you more because you will neither remember nor understand what I tell you. If you're willing to help us, we will assign the task of giving this envelope to your brother, he will know what to do."

Menelao had been listening to the entire exchange without saying a single word. Once in a while he scratched his head in confusion, holding his box of pastries under his left arm. His puzzlement reflected openly on his face.

Leonardo said, "I have no problems giving this to my brother. I don't believe a word you're saying. Unless you are witches, nobody can tell what will happen tomorrow. Only the Supreme Architect of the Universe knows what will happen in the future. I'm an open-minded man, but you've done nothing to harm me, and I hope at the end of this conversation I will be able to return to my family safe and sound. That will convince me, more than anything, that you guys aren't working for the dictator and trying to deceive me. What else can I do for you? If you don't have anything else, I need to keep going because I have a long trip and many problems I have to resolve when I get back to my town." He turned to Menelao. "OK, let's go, my cousin. I don't want the sun to catch us—I want to get home while it's still dark."

Claudia smiled. "That is why we're telling you to drop that coffin in the nearest place you can find. The authorities and Machado's secret

Montauk: The Lightning Chance

police are waiting for you right at the entrance to the town of Guane with a lot of questions you had better have answers for. They want to know why you left town after all that violence and what you did with your friend, Nolberis, that they've been looking for all over the island."

Leonardo's surprise is evident. "Honestly, are you not working for Machado? How do you know all these things?"

Zofia answered and pulled out a hypodermic needle. "We were supposed to use this and put everything in writing. You're a Mason and very hard-headed, and it would be difficult to accept everything we're telling you. We decided it wasn't necessary to do that. We don't think it's fair to drug you up. But let's hope that you give your mind the time to reflect. By the time you reach Guane and these things we're telling you happens, you'll start to take into consideration the things we're telling you now. Believe it or not, we're here to help you, to help your brother, to help your family, to help your country, and to help the world."

A flash of twin bolts of lightning burst down from the sky, seeming to strike both women. Both of them disappeared. He stepped back in panic and put his back against the car, expecting to be hit next. The lightning returned and struck their car. The only thing that disappeared this time was the box of pastries. It took him a few minutes to regain his composure, the envelope clutched in his shaking hand. He leaned his head against the roof of the car. "I should have listened to my brother and gotten some sleep before making this trip. He knows better, he's a doctor. I'm going out of my mind."

Menelao replied, "You're not the only one, my cousin. Can you explain to me what's going on?"

"I have to explain it to myself first, but I'm glad you're with me to witness this madness."

The night was silent. The lights in the bakery turned off. Darkness enveloped the parking lot. His eyes adjusted to the starlit night. Employees of the bakery came out in wonderment. They looked around, and every light in Havana was out. After he pulled himself together, he opened the door to his car, put the envelope in the front seat. He sat down in the driver's seat and started to close the door.

Menelao said, "If I hadn't seen this with my own eyes, I would never believe it. What are you going to do with that beautiful car? We need to at least check it out, see what they have in there."

Leonardo, the door still half opened, thought for a few seconds. "OK, let's go see what's behind all of this, something that will explain who those two crazy women were. Was it an extraordinary phenomenon, or were they extraordinarily crazy?"

He went to open the front door of the Ford. He could hear Menelao behind him repeating once more, "Even if someone told me a thousand times, I swear I would never believe my eyes."

Leonardo discovered the door was unlocked. This was surprising. As he opened the door, the dome light turned on. An 8x10 envelope was in the front seat with the car keys on top. His name was written in large letters. As if this weren't a large enough surprise for him, his astonishment grew in scale when he saw the title for the car was in his name. The beautiful luxury car had been registered in his name just a few days before. He turned and held it out to Menelao, who got close to the dome light to read it. Leonardo opened the envelope and started to read the handwritten notes left for him. He shook his head and sighed sadly. He reached inside the glove compartment.

"Well, if we're taking this car, we'd better make sure there's nothing compromising in it." He opened the trunk and told Menelao to check to see if the car was clean while he continued searching the glove compartment. He found a cherry wood box with a beautiful Lugar with a silencer inside. It fit the barrel of the Lugar perfectly. There was another note under the pistol which read, *You might need this pistol to defend yourself. Keep this in a secure place.* After he finished searching, he found two boxes of ammunition for the pistol. He put a box in each pocket and the pistol in his waist.

Menelao came back and shook his head. "Nothing back there. Just a travel bag with some women's clothes, and the engine is so clean that I don't think this car has been used for very long." Leonardo sat down in the passenger's seat. He sighed. "What's the matter?"

Leonardo replied, "Nothing. This is so ridiculous and goes against everything I've believed as a Mason until now that I feel like an idiot getting a wake-up call. To be more extreme, the call came from two women who say they know me, and I've never seen either of their faces in my life. This has no explanation at all to a logical mind, and I'm not a man who likes to assume anything. The most proper step to follow is that you will drive my car with that coffin. We'll store it in your garage at your house, far away from Guane, and I'll drive this clean car in case I get stopped for any reason. No matter who these two ladies might be or where they came from, it makes no difference to me. I only have to do the logical thing. They convinced me completely that they mean no harm to me, they left behind something very valuable like this car, not counting this beautiful weapon. Like they say, you cannot see God, you cannot feel Him, but you can hear Him. Maybe this time, we didn't see Him, but we heard Him. Maybe a being from another dimension came to prevent me from losing my life before my time. That is the reason I will do exactly what they told me to without a single protest. But I need your help, and God probably put you in my path because of that."

"Name it, my cousin. We are not together just in blood but also in the cause. I risk my life every day for the freedom of Cuba, why not once more for my cousin and his family?"

"OK. The first thing we're going to do is go back where I left my brother. I need to deliver what these ladies asked me to give him and I also need to bring you as a witness. My brother will go nuts when I tell him what happened. Even though I know he respects me very much, this that I will tell him now will push him too far. But when he hears it from you as well, knowing what kind of man you are, he'll have no choice but to do as these ladies instructed. I will explain in greater detail to you, but my brother is involved in something bigger than we are; this could have international repercussions. Let's leave my car here in the parking lot and go back."

"No problem. Let's go."

They locked Leonardo's car and got into the Roadster and drove back into Havana. As they drove from the bakery, Leonardo pointed to the dash. "Look at this—they even left it with a full tank of gas."

Menelao shook his head. "No doubt in my mind, from the moment I saw them, I thought they were the goose with the golden eggs."

They drove to Mr. Xiang's house. Leonardo opened the door and got out. "Wait for me here." He went up and rang the bell for the store. Mr. Xiang opened the door. "I'm sorry, Mr. Xiang, to bother you at this hour...."

"Did anything happen?" he asked anxiously.

"No, no—just something I forgot to tell my brother, and it's something I don't want to say to him over the phone."

"Of course! Come in, come in."

"No, no—please have him come out here. It won't take long."

Mr. Xiang left the door open, and Leonardo could hear him waking Emilio up. Emilio came out at once. "What's happened?" he asked anxiously.

"Don't worry, it's OK. Leave the door open. I need to talk to you."

He continued asking questions in concern but stepped outside. "Did the police stop you?"

"I wish it were the police. What I have to tell you is a lot crazier than the police stopping and questioning me."

After a few minutes of hearing Leonardo's story, Emilio put his hand to his balding forehead. "Leonardo, if this came from anyone else, I would be laughing right now. But coming from you, a Master Mason, and you're on the border of being an atheist in the past, it's very hard to decide if I want to cry, laugh, or scream, 'What on Earth are you telling me?' It makes absolutely no sense." He spread his arms. "And poof! The ladies disappeared." He shook his head and noticed Menelao. "Who is that guy in the car, and where is *your* car?"

"I told you—that's not the whole story. That was just an appetizer to prepare you for the rest."

"Oh, my God! Don't tell me you're going to give me a CMQ soap opera[5] at 1 o'clock in the morning! At least let me sit down."

Figure 4 CMQ Television Station

"Come my brother, sit down. You remember my cousin, Menelao, who works with the FEU? He's part of their movement."

Menelao got out of the car and shook hands with Emilio. "Hi, my cousin, how are you?"

Emilio spread his hands. "Are you a witness to all of this?"

Menelao shook his head. "Yes, yes."

"And the ladies just vanished, poof?"

"Yes, yes, they did."

"No trace, not even the pastries? Not just the one box, but two?"

"No, no!" Leonardo exclaimed. "Not *my* pastries—they left that. Apparently, they like exquisite pastries wherever they come from."

---

[5] CMQ was a television station in Havana

Montauk: The Lightning Chance

Emilio looked at the other two men. "You realize that we cannot tell anyone about this. If we do, they'll put us in straightjackets and send us all to Mazorra."

Menelao said, "I don't know what I can tell you. If I wasn't there, like I said to Leonardo, even if someone swore to me one thousand times, I would never believe it."

Emilio said, "And this beautiful car—the registration, can I see it, please?" Leonardo handed it to him. "This is very strange—this is dated four days ago, and four days ago, Leonardo, you weren't here. You were with me, remember?"

"Yes—and this is where it really gets strange."

Emilio started as if struck by lightning. "You mean there's *more*?!" He clasped the paper to his chest and looked up and down the street. "Would you please lock the car, Menelao? Let's take a walk." They locked the car and walked down towards the alley. "Did you ever think this might be something from the secret police?"

"That's what I thought, and I confronted them with that. But no harm has befallen us, and they told me they were here for my benefit as well as yours. If they are the secret police, what is the reason to go through all this elaborate deception. This car is expensive, probably nearly $2,000! I could almost buy a house for that! Why would they go through all of this for us? We're not big leaders or anything like that of this movement. We're from a little town from the hind end of the entire island."

Emilio threw his hands up. "Don't take me wrong, I believe you. The worst part of this is that we can't tell anyone. OK, guys. You say there's more?"

"Yes. They told me that you should not go to Berlin or Barcelona, because you will be killed."

"How in hell did they know where I'm going? Nobody knows that, not even my wife! I haven't even told you!"

Leonardo held up his hands defensively. "My brother, that's what I asked them—how did they get this information? They said that if they told me that I would not understand. They repeatedly told me that. But there's more."

"More?"

Leonardo pulled the envelope out of his jacket pocket and handed it to Emilio. "They wanted me to give this to you."

"What is it?"

"It's the vaccine for the viruses the Nazis are going to spread all over the world: polio and typhus."

"Oh, my God!" Emilio opened the envelope and saw the glass tubes. He pulled out a small visor light and put it on his head. He held the glass tubes. After a few minutes. "Whoever these women are, they are angels. You know, Leonardo, I'm not too religious, but I believe, after tonight, if you have any doubts about the existence of God, I don't want ever to hear anything of that nature from you."

Leonardo held up his hands. "I have no problem. I never had any doubts. I've always told you that there's a Supreme Being out there, and after today I have no doubts anymore. Whatever this is has to be close to God. If these are women from the future or the past or whatever, they have to be from God. The Devil just wants people to die, he doesn't want to save anyone."

The three men looked at each other, Emilio holding the tubes in one hand and the slip of paper with the formula in the other. Tears welled in his eyes. "Do you guys realize what this is? This is the future of humanity—the future of humanity. They put in our hands the way to stop evil on this Earth." Tears welled in Leonardo and Menelao's eyes as well. They embraced. "OK, my brother. Go and do what you need to do and save your family. Make sure you leave a clean trail behind you. I will leave right now with Mr. Xiang to wake up our young brother Francisco. He will be your alibi, that he bought that car for you. Just in case there's any government inquiry."

Leonardo explained to Emilio what he had in mind to do with the car and the coffin. Emilio agreed. "Excellent idea. That justifies why you came here with the other car and returned with a different car. You tell your brother Mason from the funeral home what happened, and if need be, we'll reimburse him any financial loss he incurs from that coffin's absence."

They said their farewells and left. They drove back to the pastry shop. Menelao got into Leonardo's car and they drove out of the capital en route to Pinar del Rio. A few hours later they arrived at Menelao's house in San Luis. They hid Leonardo's car in his garage. Menelao insisted to come with Leonardo all the way to Guane in order to be a good alibi in case of questioning by the authorities. Leonardo was reluctant to have his cousin go through the hassle of going an extra hour out of the way, but Menelao insisted.

"OK, maybe it will be a good idea. I can bring you back tomorrow or the next day after things calm down."

Montauk: The Lightning Chance

Around 5 am, they arrived in Guane. It was still dark. They could see as they entered the town a barricade with soldiers manning it in the distance. Bodies hung from the light poles on both sides of the street, suspended by ropes beneath their arms. There were around thirty corpses, and a sign on each one read, *They hurt three of our soldiers, we kill thirty of yours.* When they reached the barricade, the grotesque lieutenant colonel was sitting in a jeep. Leonardo explained to the soldiers that they had just arrived from the capital.

Just as the soldiers were about to pass them through, the lieutenant colonel stood up and stopped them. He walked around the car and patted his hand on the roof. Leonardo rolled the window down. "You're the famous Leonardo del Marmol, the Master Mason of this town? The honorable man? Or are you the main intellectual brain behind all this insurrection and sedition? Who are you, Mr. del Marmol?"

Leonardo tried to open the car door. "Excuse me," he said as he pushed the door open. Menelao, seeing Leonardo getting out, did likewise on his side. "I've been taught that dignified men, when they speak, should look each other in the eyes." He held his hand out to the lieutenant colonel. He smiled in a friendly fashion and said in a strong but pleasant tone, "Yes, I am Leonardo del Marmol. In that, we are in complete agreement, and it's a pleasure to meet you. But I believe we must have a little disagreement with that 'famous.' I don't deserve that title because I don't believe in attributing to yourself distinctions which don't fit your personality or character, or that you haven't earned. In my vocabulary this word is more adequate to political representatives and presidents of our republic, those I try to keep my distance from. I don't like politicians or politics. So much corruption exists in those institutions, especially in our republic."

The lieutenant colonel didn't care for what he heard. He grimaced in discontent. His expression was confused and surprised by the integrity and self-confidence at this man telling things to his face that he wasn't accustomed to hearing without any fear of retaliation. He hesitated for a few seconds, but then with a cynical smile and completely ignoring the extended hand replied, "It's refreshing to meet a man like you. I am Bruno Menocal, the new lieutenant colonel. The President sent me to this town to re-establish that order we need to maintain our status from the government. The citizens around this country, especially in this town, have lost all respect for the local authorities." There was slight sarcasm in his voice as he spoke. In a more intimidating tone he continued, "I am very well-known around this country from one corner to the other, for the nickname of 'Bruno the Brutal.' For sure, wherever I put my boots," he raised his pants and tapped his shiny boot with a leather riding crop in his right hand with a cynical smile, "I leave the opposition long and unforgettable memories for the rest of their lives for those who preserve their lives before I leave at the end of my military mission. Wherever the President sends me to re-establish respect and order for our government. I believe that our enemies should be smashed, exactly as we do with the cucarachas. Don't you believe so, Mr. del Marmol?" He then finally took Leonardo's hand.

Leonardo took Menocal's hand in a very firm grasp. He smiled slightly and replied, "I don't believe in violence. It never brings good results and always leaves a line of bad consequences behind wherever it's executed. We can corroborate this with the course of history, how dictators end their lives most of time, like Julius Caesar, killed by his own followers, betrayed by his best friends, and dragged through the streets of Rome."

Colonel Menocal, in a reaction that took Leonardo by surprise, took his crop and sharply slapped Leonardo's hand with it. He let go of Leonardo's hand abruptly and dismissively.

Leonardo, as he recovered from his surprise, rubbed the back of his hand. He looked up indignantly, not showing any pain. He held the eyes of Colonel Menocal continually, even as he rubbed the red mark on his hand. The colonel didn't say a word but leaned down and acted like he was picking something up off the ground, something imperceptible in the darkness of the night. He raised it up as if he were showing it to Leonardo. To Leonardo's even greater surprised, he tossed it over his shoulder carelessly. "You had a bee over your hand. I'm sorry if I inflicted any pain on you with my crop. They've been telling me ever since I arrived in this town that there is a kind of killer bee that, if it stings you, can put you into a coma and even kill you."

Leonardo's demeanor changed at the apology, even though he didn't believe it. He managed to give the colonel a half-smirk, knowing that it could all be just an excuse to justify his violent act. Just as a bully who as a boy had a toy taken away from him, Leonardo's disagreement with his theories that glorified violence was something he didn't like as a weapon to make political opposition submit protected by this fanatic colonel. Leonardo shook his head disbelievingly. "Thank you," he muttered.

Montauk: The Lightning Chance

Colonel Menocal said loudly, "You're welcome." He pointed to Menelao with his crop, who stood next to Leonardo in shock at what he had seen and watched the proceedings with discontented expression. He also didn't swallow the story of the invisible killer bee. "Who is this individual with you? Your bodyguard?"

Leonardo replied this time with a big smile, "No, Colonel. I don't need any bodyguards. As I told you before, I'm a man that loves peace, and respect everyone, even the few enemies I have. I don't live a life that builds them; being a peaceful man prevents me gaining enemies."

Menelao stepped forward. "I am Menelao Mora Morales. I'm the cousin and attorney of Leonardo, my Colonel."

"Attorney, hey?" He said with a mocking nod.

"Yes," Menelao said with pride and conviction in his voice, "and the First Secretary of the FEU."

Colonel Menocal nodded. He held Menelao's hand and said mockingly, "Ah ha, ah, ha!"

Menelao snatched his hand out of the colonel's grip. The colonel didn't expect that, and it took him by surprise as he looked askance at Menelao. Menelao put his right hand on his chin, smiled, and said, "I think I saw a bee in your hand in the darkness, flying, and I didn't want to hit your hand. That's why I jumped, so it would go away."

"Ah," Menocal said, unconvinced. "And I guess, as is logical, neither one of you guys knows where the leader to this insurrection, Nolberis Guerero, happens to be right now?" Both Menelao and Leonardo shook their heads. Menocal smiled sarcastically. "Of course. You are both men of peace and could never have an association with this violent rebellious agitator."

Menelao said, "Of course not."

At that moment, one of the men hanging on the light pole nearest them moaned pitifully, "Water—please, water. Have mercy on us."

Menocal turned and pointed at him. "You see? It will only be a matter of time. Today, tomorrow, whenever, but one of these men will crack. And when they do, the knitting yarn will be unraveled, and I will know all the names, including the hypocrites pretending not to be involved in this rebellious sedition." He leaned in intimidatingly. "When we have every single name, we will kill them *all*. Even those who cover themselves as being people of peace." He pointed again at the people hanging. "Look at them. Maybe in the next week or two, we'll have a new batch with the real leaders of all this insurrection. Now, please—get out of here." He turned away angrily.

Leonardo and Menelao got in the car. Menelao said, "I will volunteer. We have to eliminate these men in the next seventy-two hours. I hate taking any man's life, but this man has no scruples. He will kill you, your family, me, and my family, and go on killing in this town, and the next, and the next."

Leonardo took the pistol out of his waistband and put it on the center divider. "Calm down, Menelao. You see all this violence and this braggart of a man? This is fear—they fear what we're doing because they see the end is very near. We will discuss this with my brother Masons tomorrow. Let's rest for what's left of this night. We'll take a vote. Drastic situations in drastic times, and maybe a drastic solution is in order. Maybe you're right—we have to put this man down before this regime collapses because of the damage he could do, and we don't want to see any more widows and orphans. I agree with you that this man is a sadist, and what he's done to our brothers in this street is inexcusable."

The next day, the whole family sat down together for breakfast. Leonardo was the first to finish, and he rushed to make several emergency telephone calls to his brother Masons to meet immediately. He also called his closest friends who, though not Masons, were involved in the clandestine fight against Gerardo Machado, who had cost so many innocent lives of the Cuban people. After he got done, he said goodbye to Verena and his two daughters, Elda and Disa, and his son Luis. As he was leaving the dining room on his way to the garage, he turned his head and said to Verena, "Don't wait for me at lunch. I will try to be home for dinner, but I'm not sure. I'll be very busy all day long, so if I'm not back, don't wait on me. Just save a place for me and a couple of those exquisite chocolate-covered napoleons. That way we don't miss on that great pleasure—one for me and one for my cousin."

Verena smiled. "Hm. In other words, it's not just for me and the kids like you said earlier this morning when you gave me that box of pastries." Everyone laughed.

Menelao patted Leonardo on the shoulder. "My cousin, she caught you but good!"

After they went into the garage, Leonardo started the car to warm up the engine. He and Menelao made small talk while they waited. They then left the house in the Ford Roadster. They drove around,

Montauk: The Lightning Chance

visiting several businesses of Leonardo's in town to make sure everything was still running in good order. They arrived at the last business, a beautiful mixed product store of imported clothing and shoes from Italy for all ages, the largest of his businesses in town. Leonardo gave his manager in charge of this store instructions, assured himself that everything was in order, and the two cousins left and drove across town. Every eye in town was on them, admiring the car they were driving, curiously wondering who was in it. They drove to the Bataclan Country Club. It was a banquet hall combined with a social meeting space for different types of gatherings. Leonardo usually called meetings there that were large enough that the Masonic Lodge could not accommodate everyone. They drove up to the main gate and identified themselves. The enormous gates opened to admit them, and they drove past the elegant gardens lining the drive into that place. Leonardo pulled up to the main entry to the club and tossed the keys to the valet. The young man's face lit up with admiration and said, "If I had this car for just a day, I would have all the most beautiful ladies in town at my feet."

Leonardo grinned at the youth. "It's possible, but you have to remember, young man, that you should not get one of those ladies to be your spouse unless they went out with you before in your old car."

The teen nodded in agreement. He pursed his lips thoughtfully. "Thank you for your wise advice, Mr. del Marmol. You always give me the best counsel."

Leonardo smiled in satisfaction and waved his appreciation to the valet as he entered the club. Leonardo and Menelao continued through the main lobby in the beautiful place. Menelao could not control his admiration of all the luxury, craning his neck around as he looked at the beautiful décor.

Menelao said, "It's been a long time since I've been to Bataclan. Everything looks very different, extremely beautiful."

"Yes, we just finished remodeling the whole place. Even the bathrooms are either solid marble or granite."

"I see, I see." Menelao continued walking along in open admiration. "This must have cost a fortune! But that doesn't surprise me, with members like you and your friends. You all own very profitable and prosperous businesses. I'm not surprised at all that behind this place the owners are all you guys."

Leonardo smirked. "I assure you that if we didn't have this kind of corrupt political dictatorship stealing from our national treasury every year, every single Cuban could be living at the same level of prosperity and even luxury. You know I don't consider luxury necessary to live a decent life with happiness, peace, and harmony—it's good, it's nice, but it's not necessary."

Menelao nodded in agreement with what his cousin just said. "I agree with you one hundred percent, because I know for a fact you mean what you say."

A man with a pronounced receding hairline approached them with a huge smile of greeting. He held his hand out to Leonardo and they shook hands. "Let's go, let's go in. Almost everyone is here, waiting for you." He ushered them into the conference room. He extended a hand to Menelao. "I am Bernavet Valdivia. It's a pleasure to meet you."

"The pleasure is all mine. I'm Menelao Mora Morales, Leonardo's cousin and his legal advisor."

A large multitude of around twenty or twenty-five well-dressed businessmen were gathered in the room. They were chatting noisily, but immediately subsided into silence as Leonardo walked into the room. One of them put a sign in the hallway which read, *Conference in session. Do not disturb.* Two men stood outside the door while two more stood on the inside of the door. The rest of the gathering sat around a beautiful cherrywood table with the Masonic symbol of the compass and square in the center. Several attendants served hors d'oeuvres and carafes of wine on silver platters for self-service and then the tuxedoed men, towels draped over their arms, left the room. Two remained outside the doors in case services were needed.

Leonardo walked over to the podium that was set up before the table near the front of the room. Bernavet said, "You don't need to be introduced to our Master Mason. I just need to say that we've been asked to convene this emergency meeting because things are deteriorating rapidly in our country. As members of this community, we have a duty to stop evil in every way or form from harming members of our family and community. Leonardo will explain in greater detail. Mr. Leonardo del Marmol, the Master Mason of our Lodge."

He stepped back and the others stood and applauded. Leonardo acknowledged their ovation humbly and gestured for them to resume their seats. Once silence and peace had returned, Leonardo spoke. "I have to begin by thanking everyone here today for your beautiful and cordial welcome to me. This is a crucial time as our friend Bernavet said, not just for our town but for all our country, possibly even for the rest of the world. We have been surrounded by very bad, evil people who through intimidation, persecution, and even assassination of our defenseless brothers have been changing daily the good lives we have enjoyed before, who were peacefully protesting merely for fair reforms in our political system. Our voices are being suffocated by violence and this has to end today. You and I know that in the last twenty-four hours there have been several deaths in our community. Many mothers and many brothers and sisters are crying today.

"This virus is like a mutated infectious disease that if it isn't stopped here and now in this little place will spread to every inhabitant of the planet in which we live today, infecting and killing without mercy or respect for race or religion of everyone. I have to admit that, for me, as a personal experience, even some of you or perhaps a lot of you, this vile virus has changed my way of thinking and maybe opened my eyes in an exorbitant manner as a hammer hits your head violently, putting right in front of my conscience and my eyes the extreme evil that men are capable of creating in their minds against his brothers and sisters. Its sole object is to take power and force the majority to submit to a handful of a minority.

"We will not try today to understand man's evil, greed, and tyrannies; today we will try to prepare ourselves as dignified men in order to defend our families, our country, our religions, and established institutions, and possibly the rest of the world from this horrendous contagious virus that corrupts the minds and is capable of destroying all of us. Maybe in the process it can destroy itself—but in the end, it could be too late for us if we don't do what is right at the right time. As they used to say in our country, sometimes, to fight fire we have to use fire." He turned around. "Well, I just came here to tell you a bit about what we plan to do but will leave the rest to my cousin who is my legal advisor and right arm in the fight against this dictator in our country. He is also a man of action who doesn't hesitate to do what is necessary when the time comes to stop evil and halt the bullies that have been growing by the minute in our country. Gentlemen, my cousin, Menelao Mora Morales. He will be coordinating with you the plan of action that we have prepared and have to follow in the next few days."

The men applauded and stood up again. Bernavet came over to Leonardo and whispered in his ear, holding Leonardo's right shoulder. Evidently this was not pleasant news as Leonardo grimaced. He said to Bernavet, "Tell Menelao I will be outside when he finishes." He rushed from the conference room as Menelao started his discussion with the others.

Dr. Julio Antonio del Marmol

The attendant opened the door, and one of the men outside escorted him to the telephone booths. The other man was holding the receiver out for him. Leonardo took it from the man, entered the booth and closed the door behind him. He spoke into the receiver. "Yes, this is Leonardo del Marmol. Who do I have the pleasure to speak with?"

A familiar, creepy voice answered, raising the hair on the back of Leonardo's neck. "Ah ha. Like a man of peace, eh? Do you know who is talking? This is Lieutenant Colonel Menocal, and you, Leonardo del Marmol, are a royal hypocrite. You and your lying, traitorous cousin that is only a student at the Havana University and calls himself an attorney because he spends all his time organizing student riots and violence."

Leonardo could not contain his rage at hearing this moron express his views about the dignified Menelao, knowing that his cousin had graduated three years previously from the law school. That part was a dirty lie. "Look, you illiterate, imbecilic minion—instead of talking that way about my cousin, go to your master, put your coffee cup below his penis and drink the urine of his hatred—which must be muriatic acid—wash your hands, and rinse your mouth at the same time. My cousin has graduated with a Doctor of Civil Law in 1930. The only liar and traitor to his country is you."

Menocal laughed hysterically for several seconds. "There it goes—that is the way I like it! Leonardo del Marmol, I knew you could comport yourself like a man with hair on your testicles. Bravo, bravo! Let's see how long you can keep those hairs there when I tell you that I have your beautiful wife and three children right here with me in my compound. I also have a witness that assures us that you know where Nolberis is. According to this witness, Nolberis is only the front of the whole seditious rebel insurrection we have in this town and around the country. The intellectual leader of this entire province is *you*. What about that? Who has got the loudest voice now?" Leonardo was struck mute, petrified at hearing the words about his wife and children being in the hands of such a killer. His face grew livid. He was silent for several seconds. Menocal's voice said, "Are you still there?" It was clear that he was enjoying Leonardo's confusion immensely. "Ha, ha, ha! I think the hairs on your tongue have gotten braided with your hair."

Leonardo shook himself out of his confusion and spoke in a calm voice. "What you just told me I know for a fact is another lie. My wife and kids are at my house. All you're doing is trying to intimidate me with your lies and maybe add another crime on the long list against you. I've checked you out and very soon you will pay for all of this at

Montauk: The Lightning Chance

the hands of the people you have been oppressing. The crimes you have committed all these years—I know you haven't got the power to arrest my family, including my kids who are underage, and bring them to your compound. We have a system in place, and you need a judge giving you a warrant to do that, and I know perfectly no judge would go along with this, especially not the Provincial Magistrate, who happens to be a friend of mine."

"Leonardo, you really don't know my power. Just wait for a few seconds."

Leonardo put the receiver down and began to sweat, fearing the worst. He brought the receiver back up when he heard Verena's voice screaming on the other end.

"I will say whatever I want to say, not what *you* want me to say!" she screamed.

Leonardo called her name a couple of times. "Calm down. Don't worry about it. Everything will be OK."

She replied, "I will tell you the same. Don't let this lowlife intimidate you. We're all OK. Don't even think of coming over here. That's what this sadist wants so that he can torture and hurt you."

Verena's yelling receded into the background. The kids yelled about being kicked, and Menocal's voice returned as he said, "That is not what I told you to say, you bitch! Take them back to their cells—they will learn discipline, by the whip if necessary!"

Two tears of frustration and agony ran down Leonardo's face. He yelled "Verena! Verena!"

Menocal answered, "Your Verena is not beautiful anymore. She has a black eye and a broken tooth. If you don't get your ass here in the next half hour, you probably bring a dentist to fit her for dentures, since she won't have any teeth left. She has a worse mouth than you. Remember—I *am* the law and order in this country. The sooner you understand this, the better. I want you to tell your cousin that he is wanted all over the nation for killing one of our officers. I'm looking forward to meeting him again. Half an hour, Leonardo del Marmol, or kiss your wife and children goodbye."

"Wait! Wait!"

"What?"

"Wait. I want to tell you something, and I want you to impress this on your brain. I will cut you into pieces. If I don't do it with my own hands, I will have someone do it for me."

"What? What did you say?"

In a stronger voice, Leonardo repeated, "It doesn't make any difference where you go. I will get you and make pieces out of you. Today your criminal career is finished. Wait for me. There it goes, I'm coming for you now." He slammed the receiver down and continued slamming it repeatedly against the shelf until the casing shattered, tears streaming down his face. Pieces rolled down onto the floor of the booth.

The attendant noticed the violence and saw Leonardo pull the Lugar out and begin to screw the silencer onto the muzzle. He held up his hands. "I hope you had a nice call," and without comment began to meekly sweep the shattered pieces into a dustpan.

Leonardo started to walk towards the conference room. The doors were open, and people were leaving, indicating that the conference was finished. He hid his pistol under his coat. He saw Menelao and walked over to him, waving goodbye to Bernavet and the rest of the crowd. He said to Menelao "We need to get out of here and quickly. I'll tell you on the road what just happened."

They walked out and got the car from the attendant. As they drove off, Leonardo said, "Menocal has Verena and the children," and then he explained the phone call as quickly as he could.

Menelao shook his head. "Oh, no! I'm sorry!"

While traveling on the road, they passed a truck full of soldiers and two jeeps. He looked into one of the jeeps and saw Menocal sitting in the passenger side and their eyes met. Leonardo could clearly see in the rear mirror Menocal's jeep make a U turn, followed by the other jeep, but the truck continued on its way. It was clear that Menocal considered eight men enough to take Leonardo and Menelao, while the truck continued to arrest the other men.

Both jeeps tried to speed up to catch them, but the Roadster had a more powerful engine. Leonardo pressed the pedal to the floor, and rapidly the jeeps were left behind. A few miles further, they came to a cutting where the road was constructed through some hillier countryside. The cutting was recently expanded as construction crews began to prepare to widen the highway at that point. Leonardo pulled sharply over onto the dirt expanse for water runoff, and he and Menelao quickly got out, leaving the doors open to make it look like control had been lost and an accident occurred.

Leonardo asked Menelao, "Are you armed?"

Menelao opened his black suit jacket to reveal two beautiful shoulder holsters with two .38 pistols in them. He smiled. "All the time, my cousin. Always prepared to make *chicharrones*[6] from the skin of this dictator. Never again will these degenerates touch me. They tortured me and pulled my nails out because they caught me unprepared and unarmed. This time, if I get arrested again, I will make *chicharrones* out of their own skins." He looked satisfied and smiled mischievously. He pulled what appeared to be two short wooden poles out of his jacket pockets.

Figure 5 Pork skin vendor

"What are those?" Leonardo asked.

"What do you think? Grenades! We're at war, my cousin." He pulled two out of his jacket pockets and two more out of his pants pocket. "A war against oppression. We'll blow the testicles off this degenerate lieutenant colonel."

They climbed to the top of the hill, leaving the "accident" below them. A few minutes later, the jeeps arrived. They cocked their guns. Both jeeps stopped, one a little further away from the location of the Roadster. Immediately, out of the blue, the heads of two grenades plopped out of the sky, one on the floor of the first jeep, the other in the lap of one of the soldiers. The soldiers scrambled to get out of the jeep, but before they could the grenades exploded, sending the corpses flying through the air. Two more grenades fell on Menocal's jeep, but the soldier next to Menocal in the back managed to throw his out, and it exploded harmlessly in the roadside, but the one that landed in front blew, sending the corpses of the two soldiers flying.

---

[6] Pork skin snacks

In dazed confusion, the soldier and Menocal rolled out with their weapons out, but bullets rained down from above. The soldier was killed, but Menocal was hit in the right arm and leg. He tried to escape from the ambush, dragging himself along the road.

Leonardo and Menelao rushed down the cliffside. They made sure the soldiers were dead, disarming the weapons by dropping them into the runoff of the construction side. Even those soldiers still living were mortally wounded, and Leonardo followed Menocal. He blocked the colonel's escape, disarmed him, and pointed the Lugar with its silencer in his face.

Leonardo said, "I hope to God that my wife and kids don't have even a little scratch on their body, or you will lose one piece of your body for each scratch inflicted on them."

The colonel looked up at Leonardo in panic. His previous arrogance and pretension had evaporated, and he resembled more the cockroach he liked to kill. "Please, have mercy. I'm only following the orders I was given by my superiors. I also have a wife and kids waiting for me at home."

Leonardo looked at him in disgust. "You should have thought of that before you ordered your soldiers to shoot into a multitude of men, women, and children who were defenseless. You are a murderer, the worst of the worst of the human race. And in addition, I now see you are a coward." Even though Menocal was wounded, Leonardo forced him to limp forward, shoving him ahead of them. They walked up to Menelao, who was filling the trunk of the Roadster with the weapons they had seized, making sure that they hadn't missed any of the soldiers. Suddenly, the truck full of soldiers rounded the corner perhaps one thousand feet away. There was no time to think about anything.

Before they could do anything, Menocal screamed joyfully, "Ah ha! Here are my reinforcements! Let's see who's in charge here now—you or I!" He bent down, and with his left hand tried to pull a small pistol he had tied to his right leg under his pants.

Fast as lightning, Leonardo aimed his Lugar and shot the pistol. With an agonized scream, the colonel clutched his hand as the pistol flew into the air and landed at Leonardo's feet. He rushed over, cocking the small pistol as he went, giving both cousins two pistols each. He trained both pistols on the truck, which was now slowing down. Menelao grabbed the colonel by the scruff of his neck, pointing one pistol at his head, training the other pistol towards the truck.

Montauk: The Lightning Chance

To both their surprise and the lieutenant colonel's disappointment, Bernavet shouted out, "Leonardo, Menelao—don't shoot, it's us. We're just dressed as soldiers. We tied up the soldiers who wanted to carry out these orders and left them at the club and brought these men with us."

Leonardo and Menelao literally jumped for joy at this, while the other men poured out to celebrate the accomplishment of the two cousins. Leonardo took Bernavet to one side to inform him of what had happened with Verena and the children. They quickly sketched out a plan to not only free Leonardo's family but also any other prisoner that had been taken in town. Once they determined how to proceed, they sat Menocal in the still-intact jeep in his usual place in the front, Leonardo and Menelao in the back. Leonardo kept his pistol on the colonel's neck. Bernavet got in the driver's seat, while one of the other brother Masons got into the Roadster. The three vehicles caravanned back to the town.

The group took the sergeant in charge of the hostages hanging from the light poles by surprise. Menelao managed to turn the sergeant to their side.

The sergeant said, "I'm fed up with the abuses of Lieutenant Colonel Menocal and the general way this regime has been treating the population. I don't want to be with them anymore—if you will let me, I'll work with you from now on."

Five of the six soldiers crossed the line to the side of the rebels; only one remained loyal to Machado. After the prisoners were released, that soldier was hung up on the pole for his devotion.

All of this happened before the astonished eyes of Menocal, who could not comprehend how it seemed so easy to convince these soldiers to mutiny against him, but he said no word. He was clearly concerned about his own future at that moment.

The citizens of the town had by now arrived, the gossip traveling like wildfire, drawing them. This time, however, they arrived with machetes, hunting rifles, and pitchforks. It was an angry crowd gathered there, men and women yelling, demanding that any soldier that insisted on serving the colonel should be hung by the neck, not the arms.

Menelao stepped up on the jeep. "We need Lieutenant Colonel Menocal for us to be able to take over the military headquarters. Once we do that and liberate all the prisoners held there. I promise you for sure that you can have him to do whatever you think is appropriate. All I ask of you is half an hour. That is enough for us to complete our plans. We want to take the headquarters over with as little bloodshed as possible." The crowd, for the most part, was in agreement, but isolated voices demanded Menocal's immediate death.

Menelao raised his arm high to signal the caravan to move forward. Leonardo did not move his silenced Lugar from Menocal's neck. He said, "Well, well—thanks be to God or the Supreme Architect of the Universe, I've had a great experience these past few days, and I will never doubt Your existence. And now Menelao will give me the opportunity to cut this scum I have in front of me into pieces. All the families, victims of this man's crimes, will do justice for me. That is why I thank You once again, Lord." Menocal was sweating profusely and tried to turn his head back to speak, but Leonardo forced him to face forward once more by jabbing the silencer into his neck. "If you don't want to die right now, before you get to the Regiment, don't move your neck again until we get there. If you make any unpleasant gesture, you will have your brains in your lap. Remember, my finger is on the trigger—it could be slippery. If you move, there could be an accident, not because I want to kill. But perhaps I want to—you'll never know."

Menocal replied, staring straight forward. "Your wife and kids are in good health. I didn't do anything wrong to them, only roughed them up a little bit."

Leonardo said, "You have to remember what I told you. If you roughed them up and I see any scratches on their bodies, you will pay for it. Maybe I won't do it myself, these people will do it for me."

"I didn't mean them any harm. I just wanted you to rush to meet me."

"*Claro, chico*[7]—you wanted me to come to you to torture me and pull my nails out, like all of you do to your prisoners as good *secarios*."

"I am a military officer, and I only obey the orders from the highest places. Those are the people you have to punish and kill, not me. I'm only a little, tiny potato in a basket full of big potatoes."

Leonardo grew upset. "I assure you that if I gave this pistol to you, and your superiors commanded you to put it to your head and blow your brains out, that you would not obey that order. I would even bet a million to one on that one. Eh?" Menocal didn't answer.

They approached the gates to the headquarters compound. The guards on the gate immediately recognized the lieutenant colonel and opened the gate. After they came in, the soldiers jumped out of the truck and rounded up the gate guard. Those that were willing to join the

---

[7] Of course, man

rebellion climbed into the truck, the others were tied up and left in the guard shack. They closed the iron gates and proceeded into the compound towards the barracks where Menocal had indicated the cells for the prisoners were. There were fifty people, as it turned out, held in the cells, men, women, and even children. Among them, Leonardo was reunited with his wife, two daughters, and only son. All three kids embraced their father, weeping, and Verena cried uncontrollably. She had a black eye, a burst lip, and bruises on both arms revealing where she had been roughly handled. They freed the prisoners, and Leonardo brought his family out to where Menelao and Bernavet held the lieutenant colonel, Bernavet training a large .38 on Menocal. Leonardo forced the sinister man out of the jeep and forced him on his knees to ask Verena for forgiveness. When he did, Verena spat in his face with tears in her eyes. They also then discovered the truth about the three injured soldiers: one had a scratch on his head requiring a few stitches, another had a scratch on his leg, and another one had a slight bruise on his arm from the thrown rocks.

The crowd by now had reached the gate, yelling for justice. Menelao asked, "What are you going to do with him? Don't stain your hands with blood. That's all I ask you."

"No, I won't," Leonardo answered. He held up the Lugar. "Remember those two ladies? They said it would save my life, but I think it saved yours, too."

"Yes, that's right—that's what she said. She even wrote it down on that note."

Verena exclaimed, "What women?"

Leonardo said, "I'll explain it to you later. I don't know if you'll believe it or not, but I will tell you the whole story."

Menelao said, "OK. Let's go and finish this mission. Let's give the people what we promised."

Menocal said, "Please, no! These people are ignorant, they have no idea that I've gone to the military academy!"

Leonardo said, "Explain that to them yourself." He and Menelao flanked Menocal, and forced him to march towards the crowd, each kicking his leg forward from behind to compel him forward. Menelao signaled to Bernavet to bring the jeep forward after they had walked around a hundred feet. Menocal frequently fell to the ground, and each time they dragged him back up to his feet. He blubbered and begged for mercy the entire way.

Bernavet drove to the gate, and Menelalo got up on the hood. "This is the man who ordered the soldiers to shoot your husbands, wives, and children only two days ago. The bodies that you have either in your house or the funeral home, this man is responsible for them. Now you are the judges. You decide what to do with him." He signaled to the man on the gate, who cranked it slowly open. They then shoved Menocal out to the crowds, who immediately began chopping the evil man to pieces.

In the midst of this chaos, three police cars arrived with their lights and sirens going. Captain Heraldo got out of one of the cars. He said, "I need to speak with Mr. Leonardo del Marmol."

"I'm right here, Captain Heraldo. Come on in."

The police got out of their cars, but none of them reached for a weapon. "What can I do for you?"

"I just wanted to let you know that I have nothing against you at all. This government is on the verge of collapsing, but until that happens, you have to be careful. They sent six military brigades that are on their way here from the capital. They called me to facilitate whatever they need here. I have to be completely honest," he pointed at the pieces of Menocal, where members of the crowd were fixing his head on a pole, "that man deserves that and a lot more. I sympathize with everything you've been doing. But I have to advise you to take your family away from here until things calm down or we see what happens in this political climate."

Leonardo nodded. "OK." He looked at Menelao. "I can't put Verena and the children in the Roadster—it only has two seats."

Heraldo said, "Menocal had an Excalibur. Menelao can take that car home after he relocates your family and put it in his garage at home, but I advise you to disappear immediately. Now please let me talk to this crowd to get them to go home. I don't want any more deaths in this town on my watch. Now let's go—let me show you." Bernavet, Menelao, Leonardo, Verena, and the children followed Heraldo to where there was a motor pool for the compound. He opened what appeared to be a special hanger, revealing a Cessna airplane, helicopter, two Mercedes Roadsters, and the Excalibur stored inside. The keys were all hanging on a pin board on the wall. Heraldo walked over and tossed the keys to the Excalibur to Leonardo. "My contribution to the new republic. Don't waste any time—even if you want to hang around, get your family out of here." He pointed at Verena and the kids. "They are your weak spot in your armor."

Montauk: The Lightning Chance

Figure 6 1933 Excalibur

Menelao walked to one of the closets which contained several unworn colonel's uniforms in plastic bags. "Wait for me here a moment, Leonardo. I'll be back in a few minutes."

Leonardo replied, "OK. Let me talk to the crowd to tell them to disperse and go home. I'll meet you back here in a few minutes."

Bernavet said, "OK, I'll start the car and warm the engine up for you, brother."

Leonardo, followed by his family, Bernavet (after he had started the car), and Captain Heraldo, got on top of the jeep Menelao had used. "Please, everyone—give me your attention. Please!"

The crowd began to calm down. Someone had put Menocal's head on top of the roof of the guard shack.

Leonardo pointed to Heraldo. "This man is a very decent man and we are very lucky to have him as our Police Captain in this town. Captain Heraldo Mojica should always be re-elected to that position in this town, no matter what happens with the dictator. He came here to warn us of an approaching military force to repress us more. Don't resist—don't give them any excuse to spill more blood than they already have. The monster is wounded and will die soon. Let us handle that. Go back to your homes, mourn your dead, and celebrate the triumph we had today. We can call the town of Guane today a town free of tyranny."

Everyone applauded and began to disperse. Captain Mojica embraced Leonardo. "Thank you. Believe it or not, you just saved many lives. Now get the hell out of here—I don't want to see you suffer any more than you have already." He pointed at Menocal's head. "Seeing what that monster did to your wife enraged me more than I ever thought possible. How anybody could be so sadistic is beyond me. But that is the end of all brutality. These men do not ever learn. They do the same thing, all throughout history."

There was a honking of a horn. They turned and saw the Excalibur. Menelao got out, dressed in a lieutenant colonel's uniform. He saluted Leonardo and said, "Mr. President, your car is ready." Everyone laughed in relief at that.

Verena said, "Let's go home. I have to put some things together for the children, Leonardo, and then we'll go wherever you want to go."

Menelao said, "I've got a nice 50' powerboat in the port of La Coloma in Pinar del Rio with a very trustworthy captain who can take you to a very secure place, anywhere you want."

Leonardo clapped Menelao on the shoulder. "Thank you, my cousin."

"You don't have to thank me; you're my brother." They embraced.

Bernavet said, "Leonardo, don't worry. I'll take care of your businesses. Go. We'll watch out for everything, but you are *two* targets—your face will be all over the nation, just like your cousin's. Heaven knows what that sadistic criminal, Lt. Col. Menocal, sent by way of report to the capital. By now it's in the hands of the dictator. Go now."

Leonardo breathed deeply. "I'll think about it. If I don't return, it means you're in charge of my businesses." They shook hands.

Bernavet said, "Be very quick thinking about it, so you don't regret it later on. Look after your children. I will drive the Roadster behind you guys to leave it at your house, so no suspicions arise."

Captain Mojica said, "We'll provide an escort and pick you up from there. In fact, we'll provide an escort all through town to make certain no harm comes to any of Leonardo's family."

Verena looked at Leonardo. "I don't want to leave if you don't come with us."

Leonardo accepted fate. "OK, Verena. I'll come with you."

They drove home, escorted by the three police cars as escort, one in front and two behind. People in town did a double take, wondering if the President indeed was in town.

Montauk: The Lightning Chance

As soon as they reached home, Verena took the children to quickly pack some necessaries. Leonardo went to his safe and pulled out several bundles of money and filled up the bottom of a travel back, packing some underwear and socks on top of the cash. He zipped it closed, he unscrewed the silencer from the Lugar, put both weapon and silencer into the cherry wood box, and put them back into the safe. He scrambled the numbers, picked up the bag, and walked out to the rest of the family. "OK, let's go."

Captain Mojica escorted them to the edge of town, taking them to the limit of safety. They pulled over and everyone got out of their respective cars. Bernavet, the Captain, and Leonardo all embraced. "Good luck," Bernavet said.

They drove to the town of Mendoza and encountered a barricade erected by the soldiers. They saluted at the sight of Menelao's uniform and waved them through. Menelao laughed. "Mr. President, we have a green light through these check points. These idiots aren't even bothering to check and see who is inside the car."

As they drove along the highway, they saw the promised military caravan: two jeeps with more officers in front of six trucks, followed by a flatbed truck with a tank on it bringing up the rear. It was coming the opposite direction and as soon as they saw them in the rear-view mirror, Menelao wiped his forehead as if wiping away sweat.

The children fell asleep as they continued their way to the town of San Juan y Martinez, and but before they reached it a tire blew out. Menelao got out to change the tire, but there wasn't a wrench. He came around and said, "Stay here with the car. The town is not more than two miles ahead, so I'll walk in to find what we need there."

Leonardo disagreed. "Menelao, it's very late. You're very tired, I am, let's just sleep here in the car. Let's rest here and deal with this in the morning. The way you're dressed, and with the kids, nobody will bother us."

Menelao didn't like that idea. "Remember, your face and mine is known. We can't just stay here in the open. Let's pull off the side of the road where we won't be so obvious, and *then* it will be OK. You're right about one thing—I'm very tired."

Verena and the children were already beneath blankets and sound asleep. They managed to get the car pulled off the road behind some bushes, pulled out some blankets themselves, and got some rest.

Leonardo fell asleep and had a strange dream. He dreamed of the two women telling him, "Go to the next town. You're free. You're free. You can go home now." The two ladies walked over to him and embraced him.

He then saw the head of Menocal, and the same lightning that caused the ladies' disappearance caused it to vanish. He started, awakening at that moment.

He looked around the car and saw everyone still sound asleep. He got out, left his blanket on his seat, and walked around to the trunk. He pulled out a canteen of water and washed his face from it. He heard a truck approaching and looked up. He peered through the bushes and saw a Shell gasoline truck drive by. He walked back to the car and wrote a note to leave behind: *Don't worry. I just decided to walk ahead into town. I will be back soon.* He went into his travel bag and pulled out a couple of bundles of cash. One of them he put inside his suit and cracked the windows to give them some fresh air.

As he approached the town limits, he saw a Shell gas station. Right next to the Shell was, to his astonishment, a pastry shop. The garage was still closed. He checked his watch and saw it was still 6 am, and the sign said that it would open at 8 am, but that there was a mechanic on duty. He also saw a tow truck. There was a black man there as a night watchman.

"Hi, how are you doing? My name is Leonardo del Marmol Mora."

"Tomaso. What can I do for you, Mr. del Marmol?"

"Oh, I had a blowout just up the road, and I need to change the tire."

"Don't worry about it, they'll be here any minute. They say eight, but they're usually here by seven."

"Is that a pastry shop next door that smells so good?"

"Oh, yes—a Cuban pastry shop, the most famous in the world!"

"I didn't know there was one here—I thought they were only in Havana and Pinar del Rio."

"Oh, no, they're the best here!"

"Tomaso, are you on commission with them?"

Tomaso laughed. "No, no."

Leonardo went into the shop, filled up a tray full, and went to the cashier. As he was paying, a beautiful fragrance caught his attention.

Montauk: The Lightning Chance

It was familiar. He turned around and saw the two ladies, Zofia and Claudia. He smiled at them. "Oh, ladies! Thank you very much!"

They looked at him in puzzlement. "Do we know you?" Zofia asked. She looked at Claudia.

"You don't remember me?"

Claudia said, "No, but you're a handsome man. We have the same tastes—we also came in to buy pastries."

Leonardo looked at them skeptically. "Do you live in this town?"

Zofia said, "No, we live in San Luis."

Leonardo smiled. "And you don't remember me."

Zofia said, "I'm sorry, honey. You look familiar, and you're very handsome...." She looked at Claudia. "Do you remember him? But I have great news for you!" She pulled out a newspaper from her bag, *El Mundo*. The front-page headline read, **Army Rebels Against Machado, Forces Resignation. Machado Leaves for Bahamas; The Tyranny Is Over.** Another headline read, **Huge Outbreak of Typhus and Polio in Argentina and Other South American Countries**.

Figure 7 Geraldo Machado

While Zofia was paying at the register, Claudia tapped her on the shoulder, and exclaimed, "My God, Zofia, there's no way you'll be able to eat all those pastries!"

Leonardo was walking out of the store with his pastries and said over his shoulder, "Well, you have a great day, ladies."

65

Claudia "Did you give your brother those vaccines?"

Leonardo froze at that one. The two women walked past him, and each winked at him. As she passed by him, Zofia asked, "Have you been enjoying the Roadster?"

Leonardo was struck mute in shock as he watched them as they walked across the street. A bus was stopped there, and they quickly walked in front of it. As soon as they were clear, the bus pulled away. As it cleared them, Leonardo looked, as there was no time for them to have boarded the bus. But they gone.

Leonardo, full of frustrated curiosity and simultaneous shock, shook his head still holding the box of pastry. He wondered why Zofia and Claudia had denied any knowledge of him. He had so many questions that he had wanted to ask after their first meeting in Havana that he had been dying to see them again. Now, he blamed himself for not being firm enough and allowing this opportunity to slip through his fingers. For all he knew, he would never have an opportunity like this again. But it was water under the bridge. It taught him once more that an opportunity lost might never come again. Determined to be an optimist, he said to himself, "I'll see them again. I won't let this bother me." He was so happy with the news that he had in his hand to show his family and cousin that the dictator had left the country. He started to dance a little, chanting "The dictator is out of Cuba" on his way back to the gas station.

Right in front of the gas station the driver for the tow truck was revealed to be Tomaso, who smiled at him in greeting. Leonardo said, "This is for my family, but I want you to have one."

"Ah, no, man," Tomaso objected, "I couldn't do that."

"Yes, please, I insist. Take some. I bought more than we normally eat, because they are so delicious, and this is closer than the bakeries I normally get them from in Pinar del Rio or Havana."

Tomaso grinned and took one of the pastries. Leonardo saw a Coca-Cola vending machine in front. "I'm going to get some drinks for my family. What would you like?"

"No, no, man, that's OK."

"Please—what flavor do you like? I'm going to get one for you anyway, so you may as well tell me what you like."

"OK, man. Orange is my favorite."

Leonardo bought several of the small bottles, getting an assortment of different flavors: orange soda, Coke, root beer, grape soda, and *jupiña*[8]. He put all the bottles into the paper bag Tomaso offered him, and he gave the driver an orange soda.

"Thank you, my friend," Tomaso said, smiling so broadly that he displayed his white teeth.

"You're welcome." Leonardo started to joke with him. "You play most of the instruments of the orchestra here. You do everything!"

"Mostly, mostly. The owner trusts me, and I feel bad for the others, but I do the best I can to earn *una buena billetisa*[9] and be able to support my family in a decent way."

"There it goes—that is a good way to think, my friend. One day you will probably own this gas station. Hard work, decent living, no abuses, and no more dictators!"

Tomaso grinned again. "Amen to your words, my brother. Amen to that."

They arrived at the car. It was still early. Everyone was still asleep save for Menelao. When he saw Leonardo with the box of pastries in his hand, he smiled.

Leonardo called out, "Rise and shine! Room service is here with pastries and sodas!" Tomaso immediately got to work changing the tire.

Leonardo gave the newspaper to Menelao. He took one look at the headline and let out a scream of joy and started dancing. Leonardo joined him. Every time they came near the window, Menelao pounded on the window. The kids woke up, and Verena said, "Have you guys gone crazy? What are you doing?" Menelao showed her the headline and it was her turn to scream as she got out of the car. "Kids, wake up, wake up! The dictator is gone, we can go home now!"

All the kids piled out of the car and joined hands, dancing around the adults like playing a game. They chanted, "We can go home, we can go home, the dictator is gone, the dictator is gone!"

---

[8] Pineapple soda
[9] A handful of cash

CHAPTER 3: FROM THE UNKNOWN TO THE UNEXPECTED

May 21, 1947
Small town of Guane, Province of Pinar del Rio

My father had by now completely remodeled our plantation house on the outskirts of town by the river. A hurricane was raging this particular night, and my mother was in bed, screaming with a very difficult labor. She had already lost a lot of blood. The black midwife, Majito, was sitting at the end of the bed. She told my father, "This is not good. She has lost a lot of blood." My father was standing on the other side of the bed, dressed in an impeccable white suit. He rushed from his business as soon as he was told that my mother was in labor. Majito continued, to my mother, "Come on, my lady...push hard, please! Push hard, we're almost there. I can see his head."

My mother was exhausted and pale from all the blood lost, her flawless beauty still reflected in her stunning eyes, even through her perspiration. She gave a last strain, and her final push.

"Yeah!" Majito exclaimed, full of joy. "Yes. Fair skin, pure like a coconut. Red hair like a fighter. He is going to be a blessing for this family." She wrapped the baby in white linen, turned to my mother, and said, "Good job, my lady. Beautiful baby. I will be right back. I will take him, because he must be protected."

My father scowled in anger and reached out his hand to Majito. "No," he said as he tried to take the baby away from her. "No. I don't believe in that voodoo garbage. Don't take my son to do that."

Montauk: The Lightning Chance

Majito's face grew sad, and obediently started to hand the baby to him. My mother, compassionate and lovely (even though she didn't believe in these things, either), said, "Take him. If you believe in that, it won't hurt him. I know you mean well. Bless him in your own way." My father looked at my mother as if he were about to deny this again, but she looked at him so appealingly, and he halted. "Please, Leonardo," she said, "let her do this. It won't hurt him, and she's been taking care of all our babies." Her look of appeal was so moving, and his concern of her loss of blood worked on him that he finally relented. My mother said to Majito, "Go on, take him, protect him. But get back quickly."

Majito's face lit up like the sun, and she held the newborn child closely as she scurried out. She had been preparing for this ritual for weeks. She went out into the courtyard, ran through the partially covered hallways, fighting her way through the hurricane winds which were still blowing wildly. Lightning illuminated the corridors in the black night sky, illuminating the beautiful water fountain in the center of the garden. Leaves and branches flew in the violence of the furious hurricane winds. The lightning struck a huge ceiba tree.

Figure 8 Ceiba Tree

The lightning struck in one of the tree's healthiest branches, cutting it like a sharp machete cuts sugar cane. The enormous branch swung down with tremendous speed due to the weight of the massive limb. Majito froze, her eyes wide with panic. She thought she saw the death of both herself and the baby in her arms inevitably swinging towards them, so she screamed in desperation and horror, hugging the small baby to her in an attempt to protect it. She raised her head high in resignation to her apparent death in that dark night during the hurricane. She said softly to herself, "Protect us, Lord."

In that fraction of a second, as the torrential rain and the whistle of the angry winds whipped at her, two lights, surrounded around the border with a celestial blue glow and shaped like human hands, appeared in the sky. Faster than the lightning which flickered continually in the sky, they pushed the large branch forward. It missed her completely and crashed into the wall a few feet in front of her, creating a hole in the brickwork and sticking there. Pieces of concrete flew and spattered over her. Though she felt the impact of the concrete, she was unhurt.

Majito embraced the baby and looked towards the sky as the light disappeared. She smiled. She crossed herself with her right hand as best she could with her arms full encumbered by the baby she held. This time, she said in a voice loud enough for anyone to hear, she shook her head and said, "No—no, nobody will believe me if I tell them what just happened, and I was witness to. Even Verena, who is a loyal and fervent believer, would never believe it."

She moved around the branch to continue crossing the courtyard. A sweet woman's voice spoke behind her and a hand took her by her right arm. The woman was dressed all in white, and the water did not touch her, as if she were holding an umbrella. It was a woman Majito had never seen before. It was Leonardo's old mysterious acquaintance, Claudia. She said, "Verena will believe you when you tell her what occurred here tonight, especially when you tell her that I gave you this crucifix to put around the neck of her new baby boy."

Majito kept looking at the woman. Her white clothing was not of the fashion of that time. The clothing was very well tailored and elegant. She handed Majito a beautiful crucifix made of gold. It shone under the reflected light of the display of lightning. She took it and looked at the strange woman in confusion. She asked, "I'm sorry, my lady, but this crucifix belongs to Verena."

Claudia smiled and nodded. "Yes. It's identical to the one she has, but this is a new one for her baby." Majito's thoughts ran in circles, trying to process this. "Don't worry—you will understand eventually. Verena still has her crucifix around her neck that Leonardo gave her the day she had given him his first baby boy. She is sleeping soundly right now."

Majito shook her head in confusion. It only grew greater when another feminine voice spoke on her left side on the other side of the branch. She began to freak out a little more at this turn of events. *Where on Earth did these women come from?* She wondered. They were both dressed in white and looked a little like ghosts. The personal information about Leonardo and Verena was the sort of thing that only she knew after all the years of service she had performed for the household.

Zofia, the new arrival, broke Majito's train of thought by saying, "Tell everything you see tonight here to Verena and Leonardo."

Majito started and with difficulty crossed herself again. "Verena, yes! Leonardo? Hell no! I'm sorry, my ladies," she added quickly. "Leonardo almost ripped my arm and nearly gave himself a heart attack in taking this baby out of my arms when Verena told him that I wanted to bring this little creature to my altar to protect it."

Claudia and Zofia looked at each other and smiled. Claudia said, "The dog is not so bad because he barks loudly. Leonardo is not what he seems to be. That creature you hold in your arms has a name: Julio Antonio Donato, for his grand uncle and great-grandfather, respectively. That is what Leonardo will name him. All we ask you to do for us, please, as the saviors of that baby and your lives, is to not to ask any questions. You will not understand the answer we would give you now. Only tell Leonardo whatever you've seen with your own eyes and show him in the morning that huge tree branch stuck in that wall that nearly cost the lives of you and his son. And send our regards to him, Menelao, and his brother, Emilio."

The light that was shining in the sky appeared once more, that blue celestial glow, but this time it came like a bright beam from powerful searchlights, embracing both women, and then they vanished before Majito's astonished eyes. She got onto her knees on the rough pieces of brick and wood. She looked up towards the sky as she held the baby boy still wrapped in his blankets. She held him up above her head, murmured a prayer in her African dialect, and then brought him back down, saying "Thank you, Lord, for sending this beautiful new life and this celestial gift to this humble home. Thank you, Lord, because thanks to Your interventional gift of Providence, our family will be full of happiness, joy, and divine peace in this home. Blessed are you, Julio Antonio del Marmol."

She ducked into a doorway and went inside. She descended some stairs into the servants' quarters and went into her small room. In the room were a small bed and a strangely decorated altar. Another black lady was there, cleaning the altar. Majito said, "Camila, come here quickly." Camila ran to Majito's side. "Quickly," Majito continued, "help me."

Together, the two women unwrapped the baby and placed him on a small table surrounded with candles. Camila asked, "Leonardo let you take the baby?"

Majito replied, "Shh! Let us do this quickly. I'll explain to you later."

She opened a glass jar, and the two women rubbed the baby with different oils and lotion. At the same time, Majito chanted something in an African dialect. She took three bottles of blood from the altar, each of a different shade of red. Camila watched closely, fascinated. Majito took the first bottle and poured some of the blood onto her fingers.

In a very deep voice, Majito intoned, "Yemaya! Blood of the bull! Give strength and power to the little creature I bring to you now." She dabbed some of the blood on the baby's forehead, chest, and legs. After that, she took a second bottle and poured more on her fingers. "Chango! Blood of the fox, give intelligence to this newborn." She once more dabbed the blood on the baby's forehead, chest and legs. She reached for the third bottle, poured more blood. "Elegua! Blood of the peacock, enlighten, cleanse, and give beauty to the soul of this baby."

She took a mouthful of rum from a bottle, held it for a moment, and then blew it out over the baby and the candles. The flames ignited the rum and erupted in a flash of fire. She did this three times. In the meantime, the baby had fallen asleep and lay there quietly.

She then took a colorful rooster from a cage and quickly beheaded the bird with a small hatchet. She went over to a small fireplace and let most of the blood from the rooster drip into the fire. She then turned to the baby and dripped blood in the sign of the cross on the baby's chest. The warm blood made him awaken, and he started to smile. Majito looked at Camila, and said, "Look, Camila—he is smiling, like he knows we're trying to protect him! What a beautiful boy." She looked up and prayed, "God, let the blood from this rooster protect him for the rest of his life."

Montauk: The Lightning Chance

The two women washed the baby and wrapped him in clean white linens. Majito quickly left her quarters to rush him back to the house. She entered the room, where my mother received her with a big smile, while my father looked relieved at the return of the baby. Majito said, "My lady, he is protected now forever."

My mother held her hand, looked into her eyes, and said, "Thank you, Majito."

My father came over, took the baby, and held him up. "We shall name him Julio Antonio Donato del Marmol. Julio Antonio, for the son of my great grandfather, killed by the Spanish soldiers in the War of Independence. Donato for his great grandfather, the Major General, del Marmol because he is my son. The pride of our family goes with him."

Yes, this baby was me.

My mother smiled with pride and watched Leonardo with the baby in his hands. That, according to Majito and my mother, is how I was born.

By about 10:00 the next morning, the hurricane had blown past, bringing a beautiful, sunny day in its wake. In the street not too far away, a car with large loudspeakers on top drove by blaring a political message with music. The lyrics for the music sang "Ae ae, Ae La Chambelona!" The message followed: "Vote for Noriega! Vote for Noriega for Alcalde and you will have new roads and new schools for your children."

A small crowd of people with political signs followed the car, cheering, "Arriba Noriega!"

My father walked out onto the porch to join Mima. He shook his head. "Politicians are like monkeys: if they don't hear the coins in the can, they don't dance. They're all the same."

Mima said, "It's OK, Leonardo. Let's just enjoy the music."

Guane
1950
Three Years Later

Dr. Julio Antonio del Marmol

Figure 9 Guane, Pinar del Rio Province, Cuba

    Very early that morning I jumped out of bed and dressed in my favorite clothing: my Havana baseball team jersey and cap. I was ready to see what this day brought in the way of new things for us. With no knowledge of what the new day would show out of the unknown but full of enthusiasm and expectations of what this beautiful day could bring, I had in my mind the hope to convince my big brother Leonardo, Junior ("Leo" as we called him) to take me to the baseball game they played in our town every Sunday. This day, so far, had been wonderful. The temperature that end of May was around 70 degrees. My mother and my father had left town the day before towards the capital of Havana to take my older sister Elda to her routine annual checkup at the pediatric hospital where she had been taken care of for many years, since she was born. She had been born with a cardiac deficiency she inherited from my mother.

    Even though the previous day it had been raining, the sun shone high in the sky. At this time of year, normally by 10 am it was near 80 degrees. Everything looked like the day would be a spectacular summer day of 1950. Our parents had left us in the charge of Majito and Camila, like they normally would whenever they took one of these trips to the capital. The ones left behind in the house, even though we put on a sad face when they left, in the bottom of our hearts we loved it, each of us. They would only take two or three days on those trips, and for those of us remaining it was like a mini vacation from the strict discipline of our mother. We loved her very much with all our hearts for being such a noble and lovely mother to each of us, and especially for me, who at this time was the youngest. As my brothers and sisters would say, they gave me special treatment not only because I was the youngest but also because I was so different in all aspects, in personality and character, from the rest of my brothers and sisters.

But Mima despite all the good things just mentioned, she was very strict in her discipline of us at home. It was perhaps out of an overdeveloped sense of caution and she went overboard, but she even went to the extent of telling us which kids we were supposed to play with. She never allowed us to associate with any new kid that moved into our neighborhood until she had thoroughly investigated the background of the family. She would continually repeat to us, "Tell me who you hang around with and I will tell you who you are." For that reason, her level of discipline made us feel like caged birds. Papi was always away at his businesses, but her favorite threat was to tell us to wait until he got home. When they both were away, it felt like the door to the cage had been opened and left unattended. We all of us tried to enjoy that to the maximum, whatever amount of time of freedom it was.

Because of this, Leo asked me, "Do you want to meet my girlfriend, Kezia?"

I said, "I love it—but I thought maybe we could go watch baseball."

"Oh, no—baseball is boring. You'll have a lot more fun if I take you to the gypsy camp. She's a gypsy, and they live over by the river's edge. At least for now—by tomorrow they could be at the edge of the mountain. That's why I love her: they are free spirits."

"OK, OK—I'll go with you." I was so happy to do things with my big brother and to get out of the house, even though it wasn't baseball. Innocently I asked, "Well, since we'll be by the river, we can take our poles and go fishing."

"Of course! That's the best thing of all we'll be doing. If we're lucky, we'll have lunch and dinner."

"Oh, Majito will tell Mima! You know what she would say if I went to the river."

"Don't worry. If we get Majito to do this, Mima won't even see the bones, since she'll grind them up and give them to the chickens."

"OK. What do I need to do?"

"The only thing is that you can't tell a word to anyone, not even your sisters. They're tattletales, remember."

"OK. I won't say a word to a soul."

"Especially to Mima. She's told me a hundred times not to take you to the river."

"OK," I said uncomfortably. I didn't like to lie to Mima.

"Well, I need your help."

"What do you need me to do?"

"Very simple. Go to the balcony on the patio and keep your eyes on Majito and Camila. If they leave the patio towards the stairs, come tell me immediately. I don't want them to see me sneaking the fishing poles out of the house."

"Very well, no problem." I ran out onto the veranda and poked my head through the spokes of the railing. I watched them putting the laundry up to dry in the sun on lines. It was the weekly washing of all our clothes, the table covers, and everything else that needed to be laundered. I watched them carefully; it usually took them the entire day. Because it was such a lovely day, they rushed to do it so that the entire load was dry before the afternoon or evening rains dampened them again.

My brother knew the exact itinerary and that they would be taking all day doing this. We were supposed to stay in the house and listen to the radios in the house. He used the opportunity to go to my sister Disa, who was completely absorbed in one of those Sunday soap operas. She didn't even pay attention when Leo said, "Tell Majito if she asks that I took Julio Antonio to Agripina. He has a stomachache, so I'm going to get him some relief."

Disa said absently, "OK." She obviously didn't want to be distracted.

When we left Disa's room I asked him, "Are we going to Agripina? I don't have a stomachache."

Leo looked at me and smiled. Without saying a word, he gestured for me to stay quiet. He took me by the hand and said, "Let's go."

After we left the house, he rushed to the garden to grab two fishing poles and a metal tackle box. He also took a glass bottle filled with dirt and worms he had dug up from our patio. Holes had been drilled in the cap to provide air. He handed me the tackle box and the jar of worms. It made me feel important because I was helping him. This was the first time I went to the river to go fishing with my big brother. Mima was so worried about it because she always said that hundreds of boys had died there by drowning. The treacherous currents in the river had swallowed enough kids in that town and she had no intention of losing any of hers in that crazy river. A small knot developed in my stomach as I thought about our disobedience, and my heart beat faster than the wings of the hummingbird that followed us along the road to the river, flitting from one flower to another.

Figure 10 Cuyaguateje Bridge

That feeling in my chest of joy mixed with a little fear of the unknown combined with the uncertain curiosity of the unexpected. If we ever were discovered, if our mother ever found out that we had disobeyed her in that particular area, we would be in huge trouble. She considered gypsies to be drunkards, people without scruples who fought amongst each other with knives, and who were most of the time involved in scams and being continually arrested to cheating on their favorite card games. Knowing we were violating two of her restrictions set my heart to ringing like bells in the church in our little town on a festival day. I realized, even though I could not then understand it, that all those feelings in a very strange combination, maybe chemical, psychological, and physical, came together to be essential of life, the real motive of life. For some, this excitement is the motivation and the reason to continue living.

After we walked for a while, we could hear the music of the accordion in the distance coming from the multicolored carts. When we got there, it was like a mobile bazar, with people buying all kinds of exotic fruits, even animals, locals mingling with the gypsies. The first thing we saw when we arrived in the camp was a man who was playing multiple instruments: accordion, harmonica, tambourines, cymbals, and bongos between his legs. He also had a small monkey tied by the neck with a leather leash and a thin chain to his chair with a very picturesque hat with feathers that decorated it. A chin strap kept it in place on his head. His clothing was multicolored; the monkey looked like it came out of a classic comic book. We also saw a man sword and knife swallowing and another one that spat fire from his mouth. As we walked into the camp Leo bought me a paper cone full of peanuts, still warm from the roaster. They were the best peanuts I had ever eaten in my short life.

When I said this to him, he smiled with pride. "Well, I'm glad I introduced you to something new." He took a couple of coins. "Look at this." He dropped them into the can next to the monkey. It started to dance, jump around, and do all kinds of acrobatic leaps. I burst out laughing in delight at its antics. When the monkey was finished, the man sitting in the chair cut a banana in half and gave it to the monkey, who snatched and began to peel it to eat the fruit. Leo said, "Just remember the old saying here in Cuba: with money, even the monkey will dance. Without money, the monkey won't dance."

I had heard Papi say that many times about politicians. I didn't know until this day what that really meant. Politicians, if you don't give them any money, won't lift a finger for anyone. Leo smiled proudly at the knowledge he had taught me another new thing today. "You're a very smart kid. You see? You got it."

I replied proudly, "Thank you."

Another man came over to us with an eagle on his shoulder to offer us cotton candy, but my brother waved him off. I was a little disappointed and looked at him. He said, "Remember, the last time you ate that? You had a very bad stomachache. When we finish here having a good time, I don't want to have to take you to Agripina."

"OK, I remember." What he said was the truth. Evidently that amount of sugar didn't sit well with me, and so I changed my expression to one of happiness. The cotton candy man had been hanging around in the hopes that I would convince my brother to buy me one. When he saw me shake my head, however, he gave up and walked away.

Coming out of nowhere, a beautiful girl with long, black hair and eyes green as olives, came up behind my brother and covered his eyes with her hands. "Guess who?" I smiled, assuming this was his girlfriend. She was about fifteen but had completely blossomed with an hourglass figure. She had a beautiful smile on her face that showed off her pretty, perfectly white teeth. She shook her head at me to make me keep quiet.

After a few seconds, my brother smiled and, knowing who it was, went along with the game. He tried to remove her hands as she giggled. "Kezia. There's no other woman in the world, discovered or undiscovered, that could have the angelic hands that you have, much less the beautiful fragrance of jasmine on her silky skin. It's the greatest smell of gardenias in her hair. No matter how far away I am, I'm always dying to smell it and see you again."

Kezia laughed contagiously in joy. "Oh, how beautiful, my poet. Leonardo del Marmol, Junior!" She removed her hands.

Leo turned around, grabbed her, and gave her a passionate kiss, ignoring all the other people around in the camp passing by at that moment. I was a little embarrassed and confused by this. I looked around in worry. They were very young and wondered if there were some people that looked at them oddly or in outrage, but that small crowd of people looked at them and smiled at the display of young love, ignoring the rest of the world around them. As Mima had told me many times, every person is a different world and each one should live with respect for the others; and what each one does with his or her behind is that person's business and not that of anyone else. I didn't interfere and turned around and walked back to the man with all the instruments and the monkey.

I left them behind to give them the space they needed to finish their business. They continued to kiss each other, but it wasn't a normal kiss. To my innocent mind, they were kissing like they hadn't been eating for several days and were trying to swallow each other's tongue with such a devout passion for food that they didn't want to allow the smallest crumb of bread to fall on the ground. To give them some time I reached into my pocket, took the leftover peanuts, and asked the man who owned the monkey if it could have them.

The man smiled. "Sure. But I want to warn you—don't expect him to dance."

I shrugged. "I don't mind. No problem." I smiled and poured the peanuts in my right hand, showing them to the monkey. He came over and took them one at a time from my hand and chewed with great satisfaction. Like the owner said, he didn't dance. I had a great deal of fun watching him eat. When he finished, I turned to leave to see if my brother had finished his business. The man held me back and said, "Wait." He handed me a small coin. "Toss that in the cup."

I did as he instructed and dropped the coin into the cup. Automatically, the monkey started to dance around again. I smiled, once more remembering my father's comment about politicians. This time, my eyes were the ones that got covered by Kezia. I heard her sweet voice in my ear, and I wriggled as her breath tickled it. "If you like the monkeys so much, I can give you one. I have two in my home." I gasped and turned around.

"Really? Really?" I looked at her in immense joy and nodded enthusiastically. It was like a high watt light bulb was lit. My brother hadn't heard, and I pointed at the monkey. "She has two at home—two!! And she said she would give one to me."

He shook his head, and his expression and words I didn't like one bit. "I don't think that's a good idea. You know how Papi is, Julio Antonio, with animals. After he gave us that beautiful German shepherd a long time ago that was run over by a car—you probably don't remember because you were so little at the time—our beautiful Kimbo died under the tires of a car and we cried so hard for so many days that he promised that he never, never wanted a pet in the house. Only chickens, ducks, any animal that could be eaten, but no pets. He never wanted to see us cry like that again."

Kezia and I said simultaneously, "But that is a dog—this is a monkey."

Leo smiled. "I don't care. Papi said no pets in the house."

I pouted at that. He tried to distract me. "OK, let's go fish. That's what we came here for. Wipe off that sour expression or I won't bring him here anymore." He turned to Kezia. "Why did you say that to him?"

"Oh, I don't know. I thought every father would be happy with such an adorable thing."

"Not our father. Let's forget about the monkey and see if this is our lucky day, and we catch so many fish."

"OK," I said, my face still long.

Kezia said, "I'm going home to get my fishing pole. I don't' want you guys to have all the fun yourselves. That's not fair." They turned to each other and began to drill for oil in their mouths again. She said something in Leo's ear, but I couldn't hear it. As she left, she said, "I'll meet you at the same place we always meet, by the mango trees by Los Hoyos del Rio, down the river."

"Very well," Leo replied. "Don't take too long. Otherwise, we'll take all the fish and you won't have any."

Montauk: The Lightning Chance

Kezia laughed. "I know you. You'll take all the fish for yourself, but I know a little man who is a gentleman, I won't mention his name, that will save the biggest and most beautiful fish for me. Isn't that right, Julio Antonio?"

I didn't want to get in trouble, so I looked askance at my brother and then nodded with a small, mischievous smile.

Leo tapped the visor of my baseball cap teasingly. "Traitor! For the monkey I lost my little brother's love. He doesn't even want to dance the rhythm of river."

Figure 11 Learning to Walk in Front of My Father's Clothing Store

I looked at him, genuinely upset. "No, no! the monkey has nothing to do with this! Besides, you told Kezia very clearly that we couldn't have it because Papi said we can't have pets in the house."

Leo replied to me, "The monkey is for the money and my brother is for the monkey."

"No, no—I don't care about the stupid monkey!"

"Well—I don't know.... Maybe in this case, in our home, well, you know—everybody knows that you are the eyes in Papi's face. Maybe a little monkey, maybe Papi would accept it. I don't know." I perked up at that for a second, wondering what my brother was trying to say.

"What do you mean?"

"Well," he said moving his head back and forth ambiguously while he cast his line into the water, "I think that maybe, after all, it's worth a try. I think you should try—what do you have to lose?"

I dropped my line in next to his. I looked my questions to him. "Leo, do you think Papi would allow me to bring that little monkey home?"

Leo shrugged. "I don't know. Maybe. We can ask. What would be the worst that could happen? He could say no. You could bring it back to Kezia. I assure you she would understand, but at least you would have given it your best effort. If you really, really wanted to have that little monkey."

Kezia called out from behind us. "Hey, guys!" My face brightened as I saw she held a pole in one hand and the monkey in her other.

I excitedly sprang up from the rock I was sitting on and was about to hug my brother, but at that moment a large fish bit on my line and began leaping about, fighting me as I snatched up my pole to try and land it.

Leo yelled, "Don't let it go! That's the biggest fish I've ever seen in this river! Kezia, did you see the size of that one? Come here, grab my pole!" Nearly breaking his neck, he snatched the pole out of my hand as it started to drag me into the water.

My joy multiplied. She had the monkey, and I saw the size of that fish—the day was turning out to be a perfect one to me. Kezia took his pole, and I breathed rapidly. That enormous fish looked bigger than me. Little by little, with the extreme patience of an experienced fisherman, Leo was able to bring the fish over to the riverbank. Everyone nearby had gathered to see this enormous fish. They measured it, and it came out 5 feet 7 inches!

Standing under the sun, I listened to the euphoric screaming not far away of Leo and Kezia. They danced in joy on the riverbank celebrating that magnificent catch. According to Leo, it was the biggest fish he had ever seen anyone catch in that river. He yelled, "We have to

Montauk: The Lightning Chance

take pictures and send them to the local newspaper. We might be famous not just in Guane but in the whole province!"

I could also hear the screaming and jumping of the little monkey that Kezia had named Tonto. My eyes didn't pay attention to anything else anymore—I couldn't take them off, no matter how hard I tried, of the sad eyes of the large fish as it gasped on the ground. It might have been a product of my imagination, or just water remaining from the river, but I thought it had tears in its eyes. I watched its life slowly escaping as it lay there on the sand. Occasionally, it vainly struggled to return to the water. The gasping grew slower and weaker as it approached its final moments, like one of us being strangled to death.

The sun slowly disappeared behind dark clouds, announcing the approach of a storm. We could see in the distance flashes of lightning and a light sprinkling of rain began to fall onto our faces. One of the lightning flashes struck perhaps one hundred feet from where we stood over a mango grove by the riverbank. The fortunate and healthy mango tree, where the lightning struck, sprayed fruit all over, both green and ripe.

Kezia and Leo gestured to me as they screamed in joy at the new endeavor of collecting mangos. She made a pouch out of her long, flowing skirt and Leo pulled his shirt off to do the same. I took my eyes off the fish for a second and looked at them, but I could not concentrate on what they were telling me. I returned to my sad contemplation of the fish. Their voices sounded to me like a 45-rpm record played at 33 rpm. My sadness grew more acute as I watched it die. It was such a beautiful fish. But something caught my attention. The rain was growing stronger, and it started to revive it as water filled in the trail left in the sand between where it lay and the river's edge from where it had been dragged out. The river began to swell as the rain raised the level of the water.

I put both hands to my face and rubbed it, as if trying to wake up. I shook my head, as if trying to free myself from some of the nightmares I had lived through before. I debated internally whether I should let the fish go, which would make Leo very, very mad and probably ruin forever future opportunities to come fishing with him or leave things as they are. When I pulled my hands away from my face, I could see with surprise and terror entering into my heart when I saw blood all over my hands. I looked at them in disbelief, but they were completely full, like many times whenever I had a nosebleed. I touched my nose, but there was nothing there. I looked down at my feet, and the puddle there was filled with blood. I tried to wash my hands in the falling rain, but that appeared to be the source of the blood! I looked now at the rain, and it was indeed the color of blood. I looked at the river, which was now turning pink as the precipitation mixed with the river water, even as the banks continued to swell. The water level had increased to nearly touch the fish, and its motion seemed almost ecstatic as it grew more vigorous.

I could see how life returned to the fish as each second passed. Leo was paying no attention as he scurried around gathering mangos. I looked at the fish in its eyes. As it opened its mouth once more, I could swear it was smiling. As it opened its mouth, something flew out of it at such a high speed that I couldn't even see what it was. It struck me in my face. I reached up with both hands to pull it away and look at it and saw that I held a large bullfrog. In my frightened surprise I had fallen on my behind as I lost my balance. We stared at each other for a few seconds, and I tossed it away and wiped my hands on my clothes. I was surprised that the frog, instead of jumping towards the river started hopping towards the fish. It stopped by the head of the fish and croaked three times. It looked like it was looking at me, singing to me for help. The river was getting more turbulent, and the churning current turned it finally red.

Like I had received an electrical shock, I ran towards the fish. To my surprise, when I put my hand on the tail of the fish to start pulling it, I felt like a very cold current run through my body up to my head, removing all my fear and confusion. Only then did I understand that I was doing the correct thing. I had no more doubts in my heart. I looked at the distance to the water's edge, which was perhaps no more than six feet. I knew I could do it and began to drag the fish back down towards the river. I was still very little, and it took an extraordinary effort on my part.

I had managed perhaps two feet, but the water's edge was near. Leo finally realized what I was doing, and yelled, "No, no! What are you doing, Julio Antonio? Stop!" He grew very mad. "Don't you dare, or I'm going to toast your rear!"

My heart started to pump harder, and I rushed to get the fish to the river, exerting all my strength, paying no attention to anything he was saying or his threatened warnings. Being closer to the water helped me tremendously. Leo, in frustration, saw my increased determination. He yelled his threats even louder. It looked like both the river and nature tried to help me, as I fell down a few times, but the impact of my falling

Montauk: The Lightning Chance

down deepened the impression in the sand, filling it with more water, and making my efforts easier.

When Leo and Kezia finally got to my side, I had managed to turn the fish so that its head was pointing towards the deeper water. As soon as it saw that, it eagerly struggled towards the edge and I had to just give it a push. Leo jumped to try and grab it by the tail. It jerked its tail violently and slid out of his grasp like a piece of melting butter, and then it disappeared into the deep water.

After my frustrated brother got out of the water, having lost his beautiful fish that was supposed to make him famous, he looked at me in a way I had never seen before, anger mixed with hatred. "I will never bring you to fish with me again, you stupid kid!"

I looked up at the sky, the blood-colored rain running down, covering my body. I pointed towards the sky and smiled without saying a word. He completely lost it at this point. He came over to me and slapped me hard on the back of my head. I drove into the sand headfirst like a baseball bat tossed aside from a batter after hitting the ball, leaving a hole in the loose material. I felt the impact on my neck like a whip and flew through the air. I encountered a hidden rock as I hit the sand which cut me on the right temple. At that precise moment, everything began to spin for me. I could, however, see with clarity something that ever had been happening in that little town of Guane in the past hundred years: fish of various sizes began to rain from the sky. Between the torrential rain, one of the fish hit my brother so hard in the head on the side, and he was sent flying and landed next to me.

We both lay in the sand; my head was still spinning, but our eyes locked. He saw at that moment that I was bleeding. He nervously smiled, looking at the rain of fish in confusion. Panic took control of his senses. He tried to wake me up, but I was unresponsive, even though my eyes were open. He shook me a couple of times and crawled on his knees towards Kezia and yelled like a little boy, praying and asking God, "Oh, my God! I killed my brother! Forgive me, my God! I didn't mean to do it; it was an accident. Now I'm the murderer of my little brother. He is an angel. I will never be forgiven."

I could hear him, but it was still in slow motion. I could still see everything of my surroundings, but in my semi-conscious state, all I could hear was the beautiful choral voices of the Schubert "Ave Maria." I could hear Kezia's voice a little more clearly as she took my pulse.

"Calm down, calm down—he's alive."

But Leo, still in the grips of his panic attack, continued screaming his anguish at having killed me. "Damned gypsies! Verena has been telling me all you guys are like the crows, bad luck, and bring your curse everywhere you go!"

Kezia glared at him and walked over to him and slapped him with each hand on each cheek with such force that Leo began to cry. "You ungrateful crappy boyfriend! You're the one who hit your brother, not me! Why did you have to say such a thing? Take it back right now!" She watched him cry and could not stay mad at him for long. She pulled him to her breast, understanding his emotional state.

"Forgive me," he sobbed.

"Take it easy. I'll go to my house and be back right away. I'll bring antiseptic and some other things from my first aid bag." She added in a stronger voice, "You don't leave him for even a minute. The first thing he should see when he wakes up is you asking for forgiveness! Give him your love. Look at what you did for that stupid fish, and how many fish we now have from Heaven knows where! I don't know from where, but it must be from Heaven, since the Devil wouldn't send us a present like this. You should never, *never* raise a finger to hurt your little brother, especially because he has a good heart and wanted that big fish to live. You didn't even bother to ask him why he did it! You are very selfish, looking only for your glory to show off to your friends and be in the newspapers, getting famous from it. You weren't even the one who caught that fish in the first place—it was your brother! He had every right to let it go. I hope this serves as a lesson to you." She gestured once more to all the fish on the ground. "Put them all together and it will be the size of a whale! There are a hundred and fifty people in our camp, and we could feed all those people for a week with all these fish." She shook her head, still a little angry with him.

Leo put his head down and nodded. "I'm sorry, I'm sorry," he repeated several times. He looked at me in the sand, the line of blood on my temple beginning to coagulate.

Kezia took her kerchief and soaked it in the river. She started to clean the blood from his temple. She unwrapped the chain from Tonto and attached it to Leo's belt and put the monkey on his right shoulder. "Keep Tonto with you. When Julio Antonio wakes up, he'll be happy to see him more than anything else." She patted Leo's shoulder and left, telling him "I will tell my friends and family to bring bags and take some of these fish to the village. Do you mind?"

Montauk: The Lightning Chance

"Sure, sure," Leo said, nodding his head. He took Kezia's kerchief and put it on my forehead.

Even though the rain was running all over my body despite the shelter we were given by the trees, I noticed right before my eyes as if Leo was floating away like a magic act. A huge globe floated in his place, illuminated with blue, red, and orange fire around the border. In the center I could see two ladies in white like they were in a tunnel, pointing at me through that ball of fire. Something at the end of that tunnel was like a large multiscreen television on the horizon. It looked like the immediate future. The past and the present. First came the camp of the gypsies. Then after that a group of midgets on top of a platform performing acrobatic tricks. But I had seen no midgets in the camp, so I didn't know where they had come from. Then in that tunnel I saw the river raging, sweeping and swallowing everything like a tsunami, dragging with its force not only the gypsy camp but all the small boats, wagons, cars, horses, men, women, and children, hundreds of corpses floating through the town's streets.

The sweet voice from one of the ladies in white said, "Go back and warn the others immediately to the palm reader in the gypsy camp, Lavinia. If she doesn't believe you, tell her that this is a direct message from her son, Vano. Her job is to make sure that everyone in that village leaves immediately to the highest hills in town. This is the only way that the whole town won't disappear."

I felt an intense heat through my entire body followed by chills from an intense cold that went into my bones. When I opened my eyes, I was completely naked. By my side was a woman of about forty with long loop earrings hanging from her ears, all connected to each other in each ear. She wore a multicolored turban. She was brushing branches of mint and *albahaca*[10] over my body with 95 proof alcohol. It was probably the odor of the alcohol that woke me up, as it tickled my nose and I sneezed twice. I sat up in my cot. My brother and Kezia must have brought me there. I looked around and saw I was in one of the wagons. Beside me was a bag full of fish. Tonto was on the other side eating a banana.

Leo and Kezia looked at me and smiled, more relaxed at seeing me awake and alert. I said to them, "You should take me to Lavinia, immediately. The palm reader. A lot of people will die right here if I don't speak with her at once."

---

[10] Basil

"Take it easy," they told me, practically at the same time.

Kezia said, "You're in Lavinia's house." She put her arm around my right shoulder. "We brought you here to her because while you were delirious you called for her several times."

I looked to my side and saw the lady with the long earrings again, who was still brushing my body. I suddenly realized I was naked and grabbed a blanket to cover my privates. I was still agitated and worried. I jumped out of the *camastro*[11]. I was slightly irritated. "No, I'm not unconscious, much less delirious. I was transported to another place by the ladies in white, the ladies in my dreams who protect me from my nightmares." I shook my head in confusion. "To be honest, I don't know if that place is the past, the present, or the future—or maybe in combination together. All I can tell you is what I saw with my own eyes and what they told me to communicate with Lavinia."

Lavinia looked at me in an unconvinced manner. I could see in her eyes and read clearly her doubts in her face. I said, "The midget acrobats will be the first ones to die."

She said, touching my head condescendingly, "My son, there are no midgets in this camp. You might be a little confused from the concussion on your head. What precisely was it that you saw in your dream?"

I shook my head in frustration, about to lose my patience. I moved a few feet from them, wrapped myself in the sheet to cover myself, and said to Leo and Kezia, "Where are my clothes? We have to get out of here as soon as possible. I don't know how much time we have, but the river and its currents will devour this camp first. Please, where are my clothes?"

Lavinia understood that I hadn't even replied to her last question. She realized that I had lost my trust in her and want to leave at once. She went over to a folding chair, picked up my clothes, and handed them to me. She looked me in the eyes as I took them, moved forward, and took both my hands in hers. This took me by surprise, and it crossed my mind that this might be the best opportunity to give her a personal view of what I had seen. I didn't hesitate or offer any resistance, and not caring for my nakedness and dropped the sheets. I proceeded to take her hands firmly in mine and squeezed them as hard as I could, maintaining our eye contact. I tried to establish a direct link with her mind, something I believed I could do, since she had her own gift from

---

[11] Cot

the Supreme Architect of the Universe (as Papi called God). A few seconds passed, and Lavinia's face started to convulse, her eyes fluttering open and closed rapidly. At the end of this, her eyes remained open and it looked like she had seen the worst thing she had ever seen, and tears rolled down her cheeks. She shook her head then and screamed, "Lord, please—why?" She let go of my hands abruptly.

I realized that she had seen sufficient and wanted to see no more. She looked at me pleasantly and grateful. "Thank you, my boy. God bless you. Even though you are very little, you have a big heart to be able to endure this great pain that you experienced as well. You were the vessel to communicate and let me see it today. Forgive me for doubting you before."

I shook my head. "There's nothing to forgive you for. I'm not the one who should be forgiving you—that's up to God. We all have our own doubts. My ladies know that, and that is the reason they told me that even though the message came from them to mention your son Vano, who is very happy with them. He knows you love him very much."

This time Lavinia broke into a deep cry and moved forward to hug me. She said to my brother and Kezia, "You take good care of this boy. He is a little angel."

She had not even finished speaking when outside of her wagon we heard a loud noise like tambourines or a roaring. Everyone's head raised, thinking the worst. Lavinia opened the blind to look outside. We could all see what was happening. A muscular man was outside with drums on top of a flatbed truck while seven midgets performed acrobatic tricks. He was announcing the circus with ladies in bikinis wearing floral hats riding two elephants. We looked at each other. The midgets completely corroborated my story, if anyone had any doubts. They were now completely convinced, and with a lot more urgency Lavinia took Kezia by the arm. "Hurry up! Tell everyone—alert your family! Anyone who doesn't want to believe you, tell them what you have seen with your own eyes here. You should take every single person you can convince to the highest hills." She turned to my brother. "I'm going to put together every single person I can, but you, your prime mission is to take your brother far away from here, back to where you came from."

Leo said, "Don't worry about us. We're not too far away, and my father built a house on the highest hill in town. Even so, until I'm far from this camp, I won't know peace."

I got dressed and we said our goodbyes. Lavinia tied the monkey to my waste and said, "Take good care of Tonto. I will see you soon." She kissed me on both my cheeks.

After a final kiss with Kezia, Leo and I left the camp. He was so worried that he would take me by the hand to try and force me to hurry along. We could see the rain was no longer as strong, having died down to sprinkles. The sky farther behind us had turned completely black with all the rain behind us. The lighting continually illuminated the horizon, showing that not too far behind us the rain was increasing like it had the past few hours where we had been. Leo was getting more and more worried. He picked me up and started to walk faster, almost running.

"I can walk," I protested.

"We have to get out of here quickly to higher ground," he said, continually looking behind him as if expecting to see the river's flood behind him at any second. He said, "We're not safe until we're out of the *Hoyos del Rio*[12]. It's the lowest part between the mountains in the valley, that's the reason they call it the Holes of the River."

After we walked for around half an hour, we could hear the roar at our back, something like what we had heard before. This time, what we had assumed then was reality now. The noise in the canyon was much louder. We were almost where the road passed through the deep cuts in the rugged hills. They had been formed by previous flooding of the river over thousands of years. Leo pushed me on top of one of the pinnacles to save me. "Run, run! The water is at our back!"

He put me over his shoulder and lifted me like a feather in the air. He dropped me on top of the dirt wall. As I fell onto the grass, Tonto and I rolled over the wet grass two or three times without getting hurt. I recovered and saw what had happened below me. I could see Leo trying to hold onto the edge of the dirt wall, but the debris carried by the current brushed him off. He tried to grab on, but he was continually swept off. I ran along the edge to see if I could do something for him. As I ran, I came a little too close to the edge, a portion of it crumbled beneath me, and I nearly fell into the water. By a miracle I remained on the edge and avoided falling. I could see a cow, fighting for its life, followed by a horse with a long rope tied to its neck along with a piece of the bush it had been tethered to. It appeared from its lack of struggle that the horse was dead.

---

[12] Holes of the River

Montauk: The Lightning Chance

I could see Leo was dragged by the powerful current. I could see he was losing his battle. Like I had seen in my vision, but here there were no midgets, my brother was going to lose his life in this torment. I yelled in frustration and called for both my ladies in white, "Claudia, Zofia! Where are you? This isn't what you showed me, it's not supposed to be this way! I need your help!!"

Immediately, multiple forks of lightning with an unbearably loud clap of thunder came over the grove of huge trees at the border of the cliff, practically uprooting the trees and tumbling them into the river—right on top of my brother where he struggled to stay afloat and pushing him under the surface. I couldn't believe it.

I spread my arms in exasperation. "Really?! What kind of help is that??" I shook my head, not comprehending what just happened. What was going on that made everything go so wrong? The truth was that I didn't see my brother's body come to the surface. I peered through the pouring rain for a few minutes, hoping to see him somewhere. Two tears ran down my cheeks, lost in the water pouring down from my head. Now with the strong winds that looked like they had been pushed by a hurricane and the river eroding pieces of the cliff on which I stood. I looked up at the sky silently. In resignation and disappointment, I shook my head.

I picked up my little monkey, opened my shirt, and put him inside it. He was very grateful for the shelter from the wind and rain and looked at me like his protector.

"Don't worry, Tonto," I said, patting him. "We will be home very soon."

I walked towards the house. When I got there, I saw Majito and Camila sitting on the veranda beneath the long overhang. They stood up from their rattan rocking chairs when they saw me coming out of the rain, worried sick. I was hours absent from the house. They had tears of happiness and relief in their eyes. They knelt and thanked God for brining me home, safe and sound with only a bandage on my temple. I explained to them that it was from a cut I had suffered when I fell. I didn't want to create any more problems for my brother Leo, especially now that I thought he had drowned to death. I ran through my mind the desperation of Leo as he clung desperately to the edge. Tears of gratitude ran down my cheeks as I thought about how he had saved my life.

A little while later I was in my room, dried out and in clean pajamas with my little monkey by my side, after all the excitement a little calmer, Majito brought me a glass of warm milk. I refused it, for when I raised it to my lips to drink, I became nauseous. Something was wrong. Perhaps it was the rain or all the excitement, but I was very dizzy. Perhaps it was the concussion I had. Majito immediately took my temperature and shook her head as she read the results. She shook the thermometer and took my temperature again. It was true, I had a very high fever.

"Camila, fill the bathtub with ice. Let me know when it's ready and go to Emilio's house. Tell him he must come here. Julio Antonio has a very high fever. I don't even know how he's still conscious and talking." She crossed herself. She said in sorrowful worry, "Oh my God. Leonardo and Verena should be back from the capital tomorrow. That is the last thing I expected to have happen to one of their kids."

That was the last thing I heard. Either I fell asleep or I passed out. Three days later, my brother showed up at the house with scratches all over his body. With tears in my eyes, I thanked God for his safety.

CHAPTER 4: HORROR AT THE BATACLAN

Guane
December 1954
Four Years Later

Leonardo was driving back home after a long, hard day of work at his businesses. It was late afternoon, nearly twilight, when the afternoon dies, and the evening is born. It had been twenty-one years since the collapse of the Machado tyranny. Several Presidents had gone through the magnificent presidential palace in Havana, but the political corruption on that beautiful tropical island continued to be business as usual. As the discontent and frustration of the citizens grew daily, this lack of trust in the political establishment reached such a high level that only a very small minority of people voted in the Presidential elections. Everybody considered it fraudulent and illegitimate. Most of the decent people in their communities said very proudly that they had never voted for anyone before and would never vote for anyone until someone put an end to that corruption and all the filth in the political system.

Verena, known to her children as the lovely Mima, received Leonardo with a hug and kiss on the cheek as he was surrounded by all his children when he entered the house. She made sure the kids stayed out of his office and walked with him to his favorite reclining chair right across from the fireplace. She took one shoe off and then the other, placing both shoes by the side of his chair.

Leonardo breathed a deep sigh. "Ah, home sweet home. Thank you, Verena."

She smiled and replied, "Enjoy—you work hard all day." She handed him a copy of *El Mundo*, his favorite conservative newspaper, and covered his legs with a blanket. "Dinner will be ready in an hour."

Majito knocked and entered the room when Verena bid her in. She carried a silver platter with a small bucket of ice, a glass, a bottle of Bacardi rum, and several small plates holding *galleticas preparadas*[13]. Another plate held green olives with red pimentos, another held fresh oysters, and on yet another were small stalks of mint with small pieces of lime. After she placed the tray on a table to the right of Leonardo's chair, he turned on the extension floor lamp on his left. He began to read the latest news in the country and in the world.

As Majito prepared Leonardo's drink, Verena left the room. "I'm going to keep my eyes on the children while Majito takes care of you."

Leonardo replied, "Thank you."

With rapid expertise, Majito made his drink with ice, rum, lime, a little sugar, and some mint. She shook the combination together and poured it into the glass, garnishing it with the mint stalks. Cubans typically called this drink *chingirito*. She handed the glass to Leonardo, who stopped his reading for a few seconds, folding the newspaper in his lap, and taking a small sip of the drink. He looked at Majito and nodded in satisfied appreciation. "Majito, this is the best *chingirito* you ever prepared for me. Thank you very much."

Majito smiled broadly. "Señor Leonardo, I really appreciate it that you like it, but I don't know how you manage to tell me every single day when I prepare it for you that it's the best *chingirito* I ever made."

Leonardo made a comical expression. "That means, as I told you before, that when you repeat the same thing constantly every day, you become a master at whatever you're doing."

Majito smiled and bobbed her head to the sides. "Yes, I've been performing the same routine every day for you, every afternoon, for quite a few years now. If I'm not a master by now, I'm getting very close, because you keep telling me the latest one is the best!"

Their pleasant conversation was interrupted by the abrupt screaming of Verena nearby in the house. "Oh, my God—oh, my God! Leonardo! Leonardo!" The kids were also screaming, but their voices were more excited than frightened.

---

[13] Soda crackers with ham, cheese, pickles, mayonnaise, and mustard.

Montauk: The Lightning Chance

The door to the office flew open. Leonardo, caught by surprise in his chair with the glass of *chingirito* he was trying to enjoy, asked, "What's happening?"

Verena came in, followed by the children. "Leonardo, the Bataclan is on fire!"

Leonardo stood up, the newspaper and blanket falling to the floor. Majito rushed to pick both up and put them in the chair. Without hesitation, he opened the patio door and went outside onto the terrace balcony. The house was built at the top of a cliff, with a view of the entire surroundings and the river flowing through town. Stairs went down from the terrace to the patio below, and from his vantage point on the terrace he could see, not far away in the gathering darkness, the flames leaping up into the night perhaps a mile or two away. A column of white smoke raised into the sky to be lost in the evening clouds.

He held the glass he still had in his hand to his forehead as if to ease a headache. He said in sadness and frustration, "Why now? We had just remodeled that place, investing a fortune in it. The insurance has just expired."

Verena looked at him in shock. "How did you let that happen?" Leonardo took a long sip of his drink and looked at his wife in stressed frustration silently. "After you guys invested all that money, how in Heaven could you allow that to happen?" Verena shook her head in disbelief.

"Very simple," he replied sadly. "Because we have many partners. It wasn't just my decision. I told Bernavet when he convinced most of our investors that we should look for a less expensive insurance policy, with all the political commotion in the country that they took too long in their search for the right company and taking bids, looking for the cheapest one. In the meantime, the policy we had expired. They informed me a few days ago that we didn't have coverage. I told them, 'Pray to God that nothing bad happens. This is the most irresponsible thing I've ever seen you guys do in the time we've been doing business together. As I say all the time, when you look for cheap stuff, you end up paying twice. In the end, it's a lot more expensive.' I don't know how they're going to look me in the face when I already told them that they had better get in gear and get that insurance in the next twenty-four hours, and it's been longer than that since then. Can you imagine it? They put millions of dollars into that place!" He rushed back into the office to turn on the radio near his desk. He rapidly moved the tuning knob to find the local station, and finally found the familiar voice of the announcer.

"The Bataclan is fully engulfed in flames. The local fire department and the local authorities are asking for volunteers, men and women, to help control the fire before it spreads to the nearby tobacco farms. If that happens, the entire town will be incinerated. This fire has already cost the lives of three human beings."

Leonardo didn't waste a second. He put his drink down, sat in the chair, and began putting his shoes on. Verena pulled a shawl on over her head and tied it. Leonardo looked at her. "What are you doing?"

Verena said with her characteristic determination as she finished tying her shawl replied, "I'm going with you. Majito and Camila can stay here with the kids. I want to help you and see whatever we can save."

Leonardo wasn't happy, but he admired his wife's determination. "OK, let's go quickly."

She wasted no time and grabbed a couple of buckets, put one inside the other, and handed them to Leonardo. Verena gave instructions to Majito for the care of the children, to make sure they ate their dinner and were put to bed afterwards. They disappeared into the garage.

They left in the Ford Station Wagon and drove down the road to the Bataclan. Leonardo stopped several times to pick up some of his employees who, after hearing the news on the radio, had left the comfort of their homes to go help. When they arrived, it seemed the entire town had turned out to put out the massive inferno that threatened the entire community. The dense smoke and ash particles got so thick that Leonardo had to turn on the windshield wipers to be able to see as he pulled up.

He looked with admiration at the long human bucket line that was pouring water from the huge water fountain in front of the club continually. Even teenaged kids were there to help pass buckets. Leonardo looked at the building; the structure's beautiful entry with the valet overhang had already been destroyed. Part of the lobby was collapsed. He shook his head for a few seconds with a sad, depressed expression.

Leonardo and Verena, inspired by the enthusiasm of the others, got into the line with tears in their eyes, to help pass buckets. Almost half of the club was consumed. Finally, after several hours, the continued hard labor finally paid off, and the fire was extinguished, thanks to the aid of every single soul in that small town.

Montauk: The Lightning Chance

On the way back, Leonardo and Verena drove every single employee who didn't have cars back to their homes. After they had dropped the others off and were on their way home, Leonardo put the radio on. The announcer spoke of the bravery of the people in the town but announced the latest news. "It is unfortunate that I have to announce that they have found the body of a seven-year-old boy that had been kidnapped a few days before. Someone had removed his organs. The authorities believe that this is part of the Satanic cult and recommend to the families in town that have children between the age of 5 and 10 to keep their eyes open and be careful. These criminals are still at large. Until the authorities arrest these horrible menaces to society, we advise the town to keep all your doors closed. Do not open your doors to anyone at night unless you know who it is."

Verena shook her head in shock. "Oh, my God—if this happens in this small town, imagine what it would be like in a bigger city! You've been wanting to move us to Pinar del Rio, I know our older children only have a primary school to attend in this town and you've been wanting them to go to high school and college. But what is happening there, I wonder? Can you imagine those people who had this little boy killed and tore his organs out—how can they bear this terrible pain? I don't want to think about it. How can they cope with that tremendous loss? I don't think I could live with it, Leonardo!"

Leonardo reached out and patted her on the shoulder reassuringly. "Remember, honey, whatever happens in life we have no control over. We have to leave that in the hands of the Supreme Architect of the Universe, as I call it, or God, as you call Him, and accept that good and enjoy it while accepting the bad with sorrow and resignation."

They arrived at the house. They could see Majito, Camila, and all the kids except for Julio Antonio on the porch of the house, along with a couple of neighbors. Mima clasped her hands to her chest. "Stop! Stop!" Before Leonardo could drive into the garage, she got out. "What happened, Majito?"

Majito had tears in her eyes. "We don't know, Verena. I put Julio Antonio to sleep in his bed, came back not even ten minutes later with a glass of milk, and the window in his room was broken, and he is gone!"

Verena collapsed into Majito's arms. Leonardo walked out of the garage. Leonardo saw what had happened and went over to Majito and picked Verena up. Followed by Majito and the children, he carried

Verena into their comfortable bed in the master bedroom. Majito immediately told Camila to bring the small bottle of ammonia salts from her room. Camila ran to obey the request. Majito filled an ice bag and wrapped a towel around it. She brushed Verena's beautiful red hair to one side and put the ice bag just above her forehead. Camila returned shortly with a small bottle of ammonia salts and handed it to Majito, who passed the bottle just beneath Verena's nose. Verena started back to consciousness with a grimace as the repugnant odor assaulted her senses.

Verena shook her head and opened her eyes. She asked at once in concern, "Did they find him? Did they find my little boy, Leonardo?"

Leonardo was standing by the right side of the bed, holding one of Verena's hands. He looked into her weeping eyes, tears of agony in his own. He put the most kindness and tenderness in his voice as he tried to reassure her as he stroked her hand. It was clear he was trying to contain his own immense frustration in order to give Verena the strength he didn't feel himself at that moment. "Don't worry, my beautiful Mima. Calm down. I promise you that our young boy will be by your side very soon, even if I have to dig holes in the dirt with my hands and nails like a rabbit." As he spoke, he began to grow angry. "Even if I have to drain the ocean and fight with hungry sharks, if I have to fly down to Hell and grab Satan by his own tail and endure the pestilent smell of his sulfurous breath."

Leonardo stopped as Verena abruptly released his arm and waved both hands negatively before him in a clear gesture of fear and desperation. She shook her head emphatically in agony. "Leonardo, please! Don't ever dare the Enemy. Be humble. I know you're not a religious man, but at this moment we need to pray to our God and ask Him and His Son, Jesus Christ, with humility, not with violence or arrogance. You know better than anyone that violence begets violence. That is the last resort we want to use. If we're going to get our boy back, we need all the help we can to get him returned to us safe and sound."

Leonardo's face was long as he tried to resign to this, not wanting to contradict Verena. What she wanted was not what he had in mind to do. In order to calm her down, however, he reached out and took her hand once more between his. "OK, OK. I will do whatever you want me to do and whatever you say. We'll do things without violence, but for now I want you to tranquilize yourself and relax. Remember what the cardiologist told you. With your cardiovascular problem, you cannot let yourself get stressed, take it easy, and not get hyper at all. Remember

Montauk: The Lightning Chance

we have other sons and daughters. If we lose you, I don't know what I would do myself. Please, calm down."

Verena tried weakly to smile in reassurance. She knew Leonardo very well after all the years they had spent together and realized the tremendous effort he was making in trying to calm her down. Before anyone else, he would have blown his fuse a long time ago. But she also realized that the moment he left the room he was going to put a price on the heads of whoever was behind in any way the abduction without any care for the consequences. He would make certain that the culprits would not get away with it. A little frustrated, she said sadly, "Who, my God, could have such a bad nature within themselves to take a seven-year-old boy from our side?"

Leonardo understood her frustration and squeezed her hand. He looked at her and took care to choose his words this time. "You take it easy and be very alert for the phone. The minute I find him and have him by my side, the first thing I promise you to do is to call. But I need you to stay calm so that I can concentrate on finding who is behind this and locate Julio Antonio without wasting a single minute. That can be vital in these cases. As you asked me, I will try not to use violence and leave that as the absolute last card in my hand. Since you're going to stay here with the kids, Majito, and Camila, you all pray as you suggested just now. We will need all the help we can get."

Leonardo looked at Majito and said, "I just want you to be alert and keep the children away from the phone. That is the only way I can maintain communications with all of you. Keep all the doors and windows in the house closed. I don't want to return with Julio Antonio and tell me that another kid is missing. You understand?"

He spoke assertively because this had happened on her watch. "Yes, Mr. Leonardo," she said humbly. "I'm very sorry. I just left him in the room for a few seconds to get his glass of milk, not even a minute, and when I got back, he was gone."

"Don't feel guilty. This happened because it was destined to happen. I don't know why God did this—maybe to teach us a lesson to be more alert about our safety. But it is in His hands." He leaned over the bed and gave Verena a tender kiss on the cheek. "Remember—stay calm. I promise you I will return with our little angel in my hand."

Verena tried to smile, but a couple of tears rolled down her cheeks. In a more certain voice, and squeezed Leonardo's hand, she nodded and said, "I know. I know you'll find him. God be with you. Go. Go."

Dr. Julio Antonio del Marmol

Leonardo released her hand and bent over to hug his children. He left the room and went towards his office. Once there, he went over to his safe and worked the combination to open it. He took a briefcase that he kept by the safe and stuffed several bundles of large denomination bills in an organized way into it. He closed the briefcase and took the Lugar pistol and its silencer. He screwed the silencer onto the muzzle. He took a brand-new telescopic sight adapted for the pistol out of its box and attached it. He put the Lugar in his waist and took out of the safe a small bundle of leather. He opened it, raised his right pants leg and tied the leather strap to his leg. It was an ankle holster with a small pistol. He tested it to make certain it wouldn't move and then adjusted his pants to cover it. He shook his head. "Mima, Mima, Mima—God says that He helps those who make an extraordinary effort to help themselves. I don't like violence, but unfortunately the fire doesn't surrender just to water. Sometimes it needs a bigger fire to contain it." He continued shaking his head. "I don't know who did this, but whoever is behind it will pay with blood."

He closed the safe and picked up the briefcase. As he was walking toward the door, the phone rang. He hesitated for a second, and then walked back in to answer it, leaving the briefcase by the door. He picked it up.

"Hello?"

The nervous voice of his brother, Emilio, answered. "Leonardo, is this you?"

"Yes. Are you OK, Emilio? What's up?"

Emilio tried to calm his brother's anxiety. "You notice I'm a little stressed, eh?"

"Yes. What's up?"

"I know who is behind the kidnapping of Julio Antonio."

"How do you know?"

"Don't even think of calling the police. Have you?"

"No. You know we can't resolve problems with the police here."

"In this case, with an even more valid reason. I found out that several high officers in the police are involved with the kidnappers. They've been bought."

Leonardo interrupted him and asked angrily, "How in the hell do you know all this?" There was a brief silence on the other end. "Emilio? Emilio? Are you still there? Hello?"

Emilio breathed deeply. "Yes, Leonardo, I'm here. But we must see each other immediately. I don't want to give you too many details over the phone, but I'll give you an advance so that you can put your mind at ease and relax a little bit. These miserable sons of bitches not only have your son, but they also have my daughter, Jackie."

Leonardo was shocked. "What are you telling me? Your daughter Jackie also?"

"Yes, yes. Please, no more talking on the phone. We don't know who is listening. I need you to meet me in the next half hour at the bridge over the Cuyaguateje River. Menelao, Nolberis, and Bernavet are here with me."

Leonardo smiled and shook his head slightly. "We will see each other in half an hour. Don't be late. We have to move very fast, because the lives of our children depend on our discretion and efficiency in managing our next steps forward." He understood the seriousness of the situation and asked no more questions. He just repeated, "Half an hour. Under the bridge. OK?"

"Yes. And don't worry about the children. They won't dare to hurt them so long as we do what they tell us." He added with marked irony, "And of course, we will do step by step as if reading from a script what they demand. We don't want to put the lives of our children, especially my favorite nephew, and certainly not that of my daughter's in jeopardy. You understand, Leonardo?"

Leonardo nodded as though Emilio were there. He replied in a strong voice, "Of course, my brother. Of course. I'll see you in a little while." He took a deep breath and shook his head in agonized frustration. He picked up his briefcase and left his office towards the garage. He took the Ford Roadster and drove to the location agreed on.

He was very worried as he drove. Several things crossed his mind. The political situation in Cuba had never been completely stable. After the collapse of the Machado dictatorship there had been many coups and Presidents in a very short period. He had tried to maintain his distance and keep himself more neutral in most political disputes, precisely to try to protect his family. And now this: nothing less than the kidnapping of the smallest of his sons. Even though he had only been in his life for seven years, they had formed a very special emotional bond. This little one had a much different personality than the rest of his children. The first thing that occurred to him when Julio Antonio had been kidnapped was that somebody had wanted to make money, knowing he was a successful businessman. A simple matter of ransom.

But now, following the conversation with Emilio he perfectly understood that the force behind this kidnapping was more dangerous and much more complicated, much worse than his initial dark doubts. He had known for a long time about the double life his brother led as a master spy, but he wondered why *his* son. He thought, *He is the one who is a spy, not me.* He could find no logical answer after revolving the entire situation in his mind. He smelled the tremendous danger surrounding those children now, and since he knew that his brother already had Menelao and Nolberis with him, Leonardo decide to take extra precautions. He pulled off the road about half a mile before he reached the bridge, taking a small detour. He drove along a small road that ran under the bridge used by fishermen. The road was a lonely stretch that was in use only in the very early hours of the morning not just by fishermen but also by merchants who brought produce from the country to transport to the cities by river for a lower cost than by truck. Slowly he drove along the riverbank. Just before reaching the bridge he turned his headlights off.

He spotted a small dogleg along the bank of *caña bravas*[14] that was perhaps 150 feet deep. He parked the car, got out, and opened the trunk. He took out a small machete and cut several branches. He opened the glove compartment and took out a powerful flashlight, holding it down to test it near the floor to check the batteries, concealing the light beneath the car's dashboard. He took the flashlight and then covered the car to camouflage it. Once he was certain the car was well-concealed, he pulled the Lugar out and scanned the area using the sight. He saw Emilio's car in the distance and started to walk towards them.

Very carefully, he walked along the riverbank. Occasionally he saw a fish jump in the shadowy water, dancing in the currents of the second most important river in the whole island. He could hear tropical insects making music like a symphonic orchestra tuning up. Behind that were the bass notes from the bullfrogs, who were in the middle of their mating season. The finishing touches to decorate that beautiful tropical night were the multiple stars lighting the sky. The scenery that looked like a great virtuoso's masterpiece painting.

Leonardo thought, *I am always so busy and occupied with my businesses, and yet live so close to such beautiful scenery! For too many years I've neglected to bring my beautiful wife and my kids to enjoy a night like this. It's an extraordinary gift from nature, especially to me that am completely devoted and passionate for everything in nature that God or the Supreme Architect of the Universe provides to us at no cost at all. Now, in such a precarious and sad situation, I realize how much*

---

[14] Gynerium, a type of bamboo

Montauk: The Lightning Chance

time I've wasted. Ironically, it's taken the kidnapping of my favorite son to realize this.

He had in his heart the uncertainty of the motives of the kidnappers to do this to him. He smiled slightly and shook his head at the sad irony. He thought perhaps that maybe his revelation was a sad and harsh lesson to him from the Supreme Architect to bring him back to reality and in touch with his roots, to open his eyes, and point out to him what in his life truly has worth or not. It made him see everything surrounding him up until now that was stealing his valuable, precious time had no spiritual importance at all. It was all artificial. This beautiful vision of nature that he was perceiving now was bringing happiness to his rebellious spirit. He thought that when this nightmare was all over, the first thing he would do is to bring his family to camp out one night under this extraordinarily beautiful star-filled sky.

A short distance away, Leonardo could see the dim light of a fire under the bridge at the foot of one of the massive steel columns that supported the majestic bridge. He switched his flashlight on and off a few times in a prearranged signal. It didn't take very long for someone by the fire to reply in the same manner. Leonardo held the telescopic sight on his pistol to his eye and adjusted the sights. He could see that indeed it was Emilio, Menelao, and his Masonic brother Bernavet, as each one came into view. Something caught his attention as he scouted his surroundings. Behind his friends, perhaps twenty or thirty feet, a spark of light in the bushes winked briefly into view. The stars started to disappear. Before it was a beautiful night scene; in a few seconds clouds started to cover the stars, and lightning flickered far off, rapidly becoming more frequent as time passed. A cold wind started to blow.

Leonardo adjusted his hat to prevent it from being blown off. He didn't move from his position. He continued his detailed observation of the bushes behind his friend, trying to catch a repeat of that tiny flash of light. He didn't have to wait long. As the lightning flashed once more, he could see more clearly that the light was reflected from a similar telescopic lens like the one he was using. As it moved it gave away its position. *My instincts haven't failed*, he thought to himself with a satisfied smile on his face.

He put his pistol back inside his coat and began to walk towards the bridge in a more relaxed fashion. When he reached them, he said hello to them all.

Emilio came right to the point and said, "The man in charge of the kidnappers is someone familiar. You're not going to believe it. It's the son of Lieutenant Colonel Menocal, the murderer that killed so many families in this town and was cut to pieces by the surviving family members of his victims during the collapse of Machado's dictatorship."

Leonardo did not take this lightly. He stroked his chin worriedly and shook his head. "What does this man have to do with you and me?"

"Not just you and me. He is probably behind the arson at the Bataclan." Emilio stroked his chin in worry this time. He was clearly disturbed. "The name of this gentleman is Bruno Capote, Junior—as he calls himself now. He is one of the highest-ranked chiefs of the secret police for the government in Havana. He's been in town only three days and look at all the chaos he's caused in the last forty-eight hours."

Leonardo held up his hand. "OK, OK. I'm sorry to interrupt you. I know for a fact that you have your own fount of information that the rest of us don't, knowing what you've been doing almost all your life. But where did you get all this information, and where is this gentleman, Bruno Capote, now, and how in the hell do you know he has your daughter and my son? How do you know he's involved with the kidnappings? Please, make it easy for me to understand."

Emilio replied, "He came to see me at my house."

"Hm!" Leonardo replied, even more puzzled by that answer.

"When he came to visit me, he brought 8"x10" pictures of the head of his father on the pole on top of the guard shack at the entrance to the Regimental headquarters. Remember? The people put it there as an example to any who would want to do the same in the future. He is as cynical as his father, and he went to the extreme of threatening me, and said that he is in charge of the investigation into the death of his father and the injustices committed against him. His authority to pursue this inquiry was given to him by the President of the new liberal government himself. He said that when he finds out who was responsible for such a barbaric, cruel act, he would do exactly the same to them as they did to his father: their heads will be on stakes hung at the entry to the town of Guane."

Leonardo shook his head. "Well, well, well—history repeats itself."

Emilio also shook his head unhappily. "I couldn't hold myself in, my brother. I replied to Bruno, Jr. that an independent tribunal condemned his father in absentia not just for the crimes committed in the town of Guane, which became his Waterloo for his crimes, but all the other crimes he committed during the entire period of Geraldo Machado's dictatorship on this island."

Montauk: The Lightning Chance

Leonardo asked curiously, "What was his reply to that irrefutable truth?"

Emilio shook his head again unhappily. "You wouldn't believe it. He is exactly like his father, or worse, and he told me with the same arrogance that he was extremely proud of his father and would not stop until he wiped his beautiful memory clean with blood, if that's what it takes." Emilio stroked his chin again. "I'm sorry, my brother, but I could not hold myself in, and I had to reply to this conniving being. Damn liberals! They don't care about anyone but themselves. I had to ask him, 'Sir, Bruno Capote, if you are so proud of your father, why did you have to change your last name?' That was like a mule kicked him in his testicles. He looked at me with the same hatred that all these radical liberal communists give you when they cannot hurt you or change your ideological thinking.

"With a diabolical smile, like a thirsty hyena of revenge, he replied, 'Maybe you and your brother, Leonardo, will be the next to want to change your last names after I finish my work in this miserable, shitty little town, the one my family and I were forced many years ago to leave behind out of fear of retaliation against you supposedly-humane anti-communist conservatives. That shoe will probably fit both of you guys very well. But now *I* have the strength of the law by my side and in my hands, and I also have an emotional piece of each of you. If you want to see your children alive again, you will do what I tell you to do.

"'My first demand is for you, Dr. Emilio del Marmol. I want the blueprints and schematics for the plans that you stole in Madrid, Spain for the refugee Nazi engineers putting together a factory for RPGs. I also want $100,000 cash. From your little brother, Leonardo, I want his endorsement to the Masonic lodge to clean all the records exonerating the memory of my father. And, as is reasonable, another $100,000 to cover the legal and illegal expenses. With this money, I will be able to buy some politicians that will testify that every single thing you accused my father of in the past was only an unjust, filthy political maneuver.'"

Leonardo listened to all of this quietly. He could contain himself no longer. It was the last cup of tea he could swallow. "Never! Never—do you understand?" He stood up and paced like a lion in a cage, his face red as a tomato in fury. "Blackmailers, extortionists, thieves, and murderers—that's all these people are. Now add to the list kidnappers. I'm going to teach this man a lesson and put in front of their eyes what they don't even know and learn to digest: decency! Damned liberals! No one is worth the spit of a man with a severe case of tuberculosis."

He massaged his forehead with his fingers, silent for the moment in frustration.

Emilio looked at him and said in a disturbed, resigned voice as he checked his watch. "They will be here in twenty minutes. I have a plan—it's a little dangerous, but I have one. Given the time and circumstances, it's all I could put together." He pointed to the bushes where Leonardo had seen the reflection. "Nolberis is there with a powerful sniper rifle. As soon as I know the kids are secure and give the plans, schematics, and money to them, he will put each of them down. We cannot take any chances with these people."

"OK, sounds good to me. Let me go to my car and get my portion of the money."

"No, that's not necessary. Stay here. If you want to do anything, situate yourself strategically. Since you have a silenced weapon, perhaps you can help Nolberis do the work quickly and efficiently." He turned to the rest of the group. "Everyone have their weapons ready?"

Leonardo drew his pistol without saying a word and held it before his chest. Emilio said, "OK, cross our fingers and pray optimistically to God that everything goes as we planned."

They each looked worried but forced optimistic expressions. They separated with a few feet between each other and took up positions to cover each possible entry to the bridge so that it was covered, no matter which direction their opponents came from.

At the same time, not too far away from there on the other side of the river in a small boat, four men were sitting and discussing their plans. I was held there along with my cousin Jackie, who was older, twelve to my seven years of age. We were bound hand and foot, with our hands tied behind our backs.

A very plump man of about forty with salt-and-pepper hair and a captain's hat with pants held up by suspenders was drinking from a beer stein. He filled his drink, a *guayabita*[15] *del Pinar*. He looked at one of the other men and said, "Bruno, when are we getting our money?"

"Pancho," Bruno replied, "don't worry about the money. Keep your eyes on those snot-nosed brats. Do your job until we get back, and you will get your money."

---

[15] A liquor distilled from the guava plant which grows only on the Occidental side of the island

Pancho replied, "I think I'm getting too little for taking care of these two girls."

I had at this time long hair between a dirty blond and red in color. I was also already very feisty. I said, "Come over and look between my legs. I'll take my little girl in my hand and point it towards your face and leave my initials!"

Pancho exclaimed, "That's not a girl!?"

Bruno and his two accomplices laughed at that. He said, "Be extremely careful with that boy. I've been told he's a ball of fire." He pointed at the other two. "I don't even know how they managed to get him out of the house. They probably got him half asleep and still groggy."

One of the men pointed at his eye, which was blackened. "Look at what the sucker did to me!"

"That's nothing," I said. "Wait until I get out of these ropes!"

Bruno said, "Why don't you put a gag on him? We don't want to take a chance of him screaming into the night and ruining our plans." He said to Pancho, "Are you sure you can handle these two kids?"

Pancho spread his hands in disbelief and pointed at me with his pinky finger. "Oh, please! Handle these two?" I looked at Pancho with narrowed eyes. I was already coming up with a plan to teach him a lesson.

The two men accompanied Bruno into the boat. Bruno said, "Slow down with that drinking, OK? You won't know what's happening around you soon."

"Oh, please. I'm from here. I drink this stuff like its water." He patted the large keg affectionately.

After the men left, Pancho walked over to Jackie, who was just starting to develop a bosom. He touched her there and said with a lascivious smile, "Not much there yet, eh?"

Jackie squealed her protest and I glared at him and yelled, "What are you, some kind of pervert?"

He leaned over and slapped me across the cheek. "Shut up, you snot-nosed brat! Bruno was right—I should gag you, if only to shut your big mouth up." He pulled out a pair of handkerchiefs.

As he gagged me, Jackie yelled, "You filthy pig! You wait until my dad gets his hands on you!"

She might have said more, but he quickly used the other handkerchief to gag her, his hands shaking exaggeratedly to show her he wasn't afraid of her threat. He sat down to drink some more. We were concealed from casual view by stacks of frog traps. After seeing that Pancho wasn't paying any attention to us, I started slowly to shift over towards the cages. Jackie was very pretty with large Spanish eyes and long, beautiful brown hair and very pale, white skin. She looked at me in horror. She tried to caution me to not do what I was doing with her eyes, but I ignored her.

Inch by inch, I tried to get close to an empty plate that had leftovers on it left behind by one of the men on the bottom of the boat. There were the remains of a T-bone steak, a fork, and a very sharp knife. I saw that Pancho kept drinking more and more, which made me happy. I don't know if he never noticed the plate or if he even cared, figuring we were secured, bound as we were. I continued to get closer and closer, and finally was able to reach the plate. I leaned back and picked up the knife. Taking care not to cut myself, I began to work on cutting the rope binding my hands. Without missing a single detail, I could see Pancho getting drowsier and drowsier from all his drinking. After a while, my cousin Jackie was getting more and more tense. You could see her horror at the notion of my getting caught doing what I was doing. She kept looking at Pancho and then looking back at me, her eyes wide as she shook her head in her attempts to persuade me to abandon whatever I had in mind.

The rope finally came free. Pancho was even sleepier by now. I removed my gag and started to work on the cords binding my feet. Jackie continued to look back and forth between the two of us like some clockwork doll. I held a finger to my lips to keep her quiet and calm. She couldn't believe I was now completely free as I finished cutting away the ropes at my feet. I moved over quickly to my cousin and began to free her hands. I was almost finished, but Pancho stood up and staggered over to the riverbank to urinate. I decided to give him time to finish and go back to sleep.

I whispered to Jackie, "I'll be back in a few minutes. Stay quiet." I slowly slid into the water. Jackie must have thought the worst, as she began to shake her head in panic, possibly thinking that I was going to use the knife to cut Pancho's throat.

I swam under the boat in the water, the knife between my teeth. I searched for a soft spot in the seams of the boat's planks and tried to create a hole with the knife. When I ran out of air, I would quietly surface and go back under to continue my work. By the time Pancho finished and had fallen back asleep, I had a decent hole cut through the tar. Water was seeping up. As soon as I was convinced that the boat would eventually sink, I climbed back on board.

Seeing Pancho was asleep, I took the gag off Jackie's mouth and finished cutting her free. Slowly, we went over the side of the boat and slid into the water. We swam to the other side of the river. As soon as we reached it, about half a mile from the bridge, we heard gunshots.

I decided not to take a chance on her panicky state and bring Jackie with me. I found her a hiding place twenty feet from the riverbank. "Sit down here. There's a nice comfortable bed of leaves and branches. Take a nap here. I'll cover you up and go see what those shots are about. If I can find a friendly face that can help us, I'll bring them back here."

Ignoring Jackie's protests, I managed to convince her that the best was for her to wait there. I was smaller and could sneak without being seen. I didn't want them by any circumstance to catch both of us again. Then at least one of us would be free to go get help. Jackie was finally able to appreciate my protective attitude. With a small smile, she realized that I was looking out for her best safety and gave me a small kiss on the cheek.

"OK, Julio Antonio. But please be careful, and don't take too long." Her voice had a little whine to it. "I'm scared of the dark, and on top of that you're going to cover me with branches. It's making my stomach jump like I have frogs in it."

"That's nothing to be ashamed about. The dark does the same thing to me. I'm not really a friend of it. Remember, I'm a boy, and you're a girl." I took her hands. I put them on her stomach. "Hold hard to your stomach and repeat, 'I have no fear of the dark, because I am the light. You, the dark, should be what fears me, because when I appear, *you* disappear!'"

Jackie kept her hands on her stomach and began to repeat what I told her to say. A few seconds later, she smiled. "It worked! It worked! The frog is not there anymore! My stomach has stopped jumping like a frog."

I smiled proudly. "I told you—I've been taught this trick by my two angels, the two ladies that protect me from my nightmares. My nanny Majito told me that these two ladies saved not only her life but mine as well, a long time ago when I had just been born and was very, very little. Now it's different. I not only can defend myself; I can now defend others."

Jackie smiled and replied, "*Claro, chico*! Look at how you defend me and freed me from those evil men. But please, don't take too long, OK? And you be really very, very careful. I don't even know how to get home from here."

"Don't worry about it at all. I know this area very well. My big brother Leo has brought me here many times to fish. I'm going to give to those kidnappers an extremely huge headache if they try to grab me again! The only reason they could get me the first time was because I was half-asleep when they took me by surprise." I had conviction in my face and nodded.

I took some branches from the ground and used the knife to cut some more. I covered Jackie with them. "Take a nap. You're probably pretty tired by now. I won't take too long, but in case I take a little longer, don't be scared. Don't leave here until I come back. If you take a nap, the time will fly, and you won't notice how long I'm gone."

"OK, OK," she said, nodding beneath the branches.

"And remember, if you get scared, put your hand on your stomach and apply pressure on it, and you will control your fear."

Jackie smiled slightly and nodded in approval. I left our hiding place. As soon as I was a few feet away from her, I looked around to make sure that no one passing by would be able to see her. With a satisfied smile on my face, I crawled into the deeper bushes farther from the riverbank. This time, I had a mischievous smile. I stopped by some large bamboo branches. I looked for a thin branch of *caña brava*. I found one that was very thin, a very new branch, perhaps seven feet long. I made sure it had the kind of flexibility I wanted from a thin branch. I looked for something I had seen on one of the trips to the river with my brother: a honeycomb in one of the trees. I finally found it and jammed the branch into the honeycomb, taking it clean off the tree. I turned and ran in the direction of the boat where I had left Pancho. Wading into the river, I whirled the flexible limb over my head and flung it into the boat. The comb's exterior was hard enough to break into pieces, and I could hear clear across the river the angry buzzing of the bees.

Pancho yelled in dismayed pain as he absorbed the whole flavor of the boy he had called a little girl. I dropped the bamboo branch into the river. He yelled, "What the hell! Damned snot-nosed brat! Wait until I get my hands on you!! I will rip your head off and cut you into pieces. I'll use your meat to feed the bullfrogs!"

The hairs on my neck raised at that. I tried to swim as fast as I could to put some distance between myself and the boat. As I swam

Montauk: The Lightning Chance

away, I saw how the boat had started to sink, listing to one side, as the water continued filling it from the hole I had made. I didn't go very far when I heard the large splash that might have been Pancho jumping into the river. It certainly was something large and heavy. There was more screaming behind me.

"Damned bees! They must be killer bees, because they even know how to swim!"

I shook my head and continued to swim with the satisfaction that Pancho was getting a taste of his own medicine from my little warriors. Even after he had jumped into the water, it was clear they were pursuing him. I knew I didn't want to have any chance of coming across him, so I swam in the opposite direction—towards the bridge. The other side of the river was further away, but it was worth it to avoid an unpleasant confrontation with Pancho after this incident.

When I arrived on the far side, I discovered one of the kidnappers, clearly dead, his mouth gaping open and a bullet hole in his forehead. The blood had not yet coagulated and mixed freely with the river water. I decided to return to Jackie's hiding place.

A little later I reached the place and gave her brief description of what happened, trying to bring to her more tranquility by letting her know that at least one of the four kidnappers was out of the fight, and that Pancho wasn't going to have much will to fight anyone after his encounter with my little soldiers. I said, "Until we find out where the other kidnappers are, the most prudent thing to do is for you to stay hidden right here and not move. We don't know how many more of these men are involved in this plot."

Jackie agreed in a more relaxed fashion, now that she knew one was dead and that Pancho wasn't going to bother anyone for a while. She wormed back into her hiding place, and I covered her once more.

I started to cautiously make my way towards the bridge, as I had seen the flickering light of a small fire in that direction. I wanted to know if they were friendly, or yet more members of the kidnappers' ring. I prayed and hoped that they were friends of my father—in that case, they would be able to help us get out of our situation and return us safely home.

I moved cautiously forward a few feet at a time, pausing each time to listen. I heard Pancho's continued swearing and screaming for help from the group of men surrounding the fire on the other side of the river. I was about 150 feet away at this point. The men under the bridge without hesitation moved, two of them going to bring Pancho to where the rest were. They sat him down on a rock, his arms looped over their shoulders. The first sprinkles from the approaching storm began to hit. It became harder for me to see anyone's faces or the details of what they were doing.

The sprinkles started to turn to rain, which then began to pour down heavily. Even though I was under a strong, dense flamboyant tree, the water made its way between the heavy branches, wetting my hair. Soon I was dripping wet from head to toe. The sound of the rain pouring into the branches and on the river made it impossible to hear what was going on. I was undecided whether I should return to where Jackie was hiding or move closer to see what was going on here. I thought that what made them inaudible to me would do likewise to them, and so I moved cautiously forward. I still held the knife in my right hand, ready for anything. Once more, a few feet at a time, perhaps five steps and then pausing, I made my way closer.

Their backs were to me, and I could not see either Pancho's face or what they were doing to his body. I stopped about fifty feet away, now that I could hear their voices. I figured I would have an advantage, since I was in the dark and the fire would blind them to the darkness and light them easily for me.

The first voice I heard was Pancho. He was complaining and moaning as one of the men took the stingers, one at a time, out of his face and naked chest. When Emilio had finished as the others observed, Pancho said in grateful humility, "Thank you very much, gentlemen. I swear that I don't know where the kids you're looking for are. But I promise you if I see them, I will let you know immediately."

At that moment, as if Providence wanted me to hear him clearly, the intense rains stopped, as if by magic. A very strong flash of lightning hit in the center of the river, throwing water about fifty feet into the air. The water swirled like a waterspout and a rainbow erupted in the light. All the men whirled towards that divine effect, fascinated by it. It was one of the most beautiful natural phenomena any of us ever beheld. It looked like a masterpiece from the hands of the Supreme Being. At that moment I could see all their faces. A scream started in the depths of my stomach and through my chest as I yelled, *"LIAR!"*

My scream hit the upper registers in pitch as I held my hands up like a megaphone. The echoes of my shout echoed underneath the bridge. I put my right hand to my mouth to contain the enormous joy I felt at seeing my father, my uncle, and their friends—all helping the bandit Pancho in supreme irony. I felt like God had sent me there at the

Montauk: The Lightning Chance

right moment. Like a tiger I jumped down from the bushes in front of them.

I screamed once more at the top of my lungs, "Liar! Kidnapper! I'm going to castrate you!" I waved the knife I held in my right hand.

Pancho jumped up from the rock and fell into the dirt. He crawled like a snake away from me. Emilio, who had been the one removing the stingers, whirled as Pancho screamed, "Oh, no! You again? Please, help me, please!" He crawled towards Emilio. "This is not a normal boy—he came from another world, an alien from Mars! Help me, please!"

I repeated, "You kidnapper, liar, abuser! And on top of that, he touched my cousin Jackie inappropriately on her boobies!"

Emilio heard that. He had been trying to stop me. Now he gently, politely took the knife from my hand, reversed the knife to stab, and jumped on top of Pancho. My father and the others had to jump in quickly before my uncle could nail the man in the chest. Pancho, like a coward, cried like a baby and asked for forgiveness for his crimes. At the same time, my father and Menelao tried to calm Emilio, took the knife out of his hands, and tossed it at my feet. I scooped it back up.

Bernavet came over to Pancho and began slapping him back and forth across the face. Pancho screamed in pain as each blow aggravated the swelling from the stings. He pulled his pistol out, cocked it, and held it to his head. "You royal piece of crap—I have a girl that's eleven. I'm wondering whether I should blow your brains out now or turn you over to the authorities so they can put you in jail for the rest of your life." He then used the pistol to pistol whip Pancho, who rolled on the ground, sobbing.

My father yelled, "No, no! We don't know who is on our side and who is not in the government anymore. Turning him over to the authorities is like setting him free again. Besides, we don't know where Jackie is."

I smiled. I had been watching closely. "If that's what you're worried about, kill the pervert. Don't worry about it, any of you guys. I have Jackie in a very secure place."

Uncle Emilio looked at me in gratitude and profound relief. I could see tears in his eyes. He asked, "Did you do that? Did you leave her behind to come look for us?"

"Yes. That is what a gentleman does!" I said with pride. "Looking for you or a friendly face." Pancho's eyes opened miserably. His face reflected his terror at my dismissal of his life. "Anyway, I'm alive and fine—just some bruises from the abuse this man did to me, but Jackie is OK and I left her in a safe place. I want to remind you of something Mima tells us all the time that's written in the Bible: that we should never kill anyone. Is that not true, my uncle?"

Emilio nodded his head. "Yes. The Bible also tells us an eye for an eye and a tooth for a tooth." Pancho swallowed hard, his eyes bulging in terror. "It also tells us that kidnappers, liars, thieves, those associated with Satan, cults, diabolic plots, and sexual degenerates, should be exterminated from the face of the Earth." He shot Pancho a dirty look, who was trying to pretend he hadn't heard that, Bernavet's pistol still in his face. A dark stain appeared in his crotch as he urinated in fear. He began to pray.

Emilio turned to Pancho, pointing at several documents spread out on a rock near them. They looked like identity cards, passports, and other personal documents. "Those are the documents that show the three members of your kidnapping criminal enterprise are all members of the Democratic Socialist Coalition Party, formerly known as the Liberal Party, and changing its name for the third time now, Progressive Action Party. They are the same devil disguised with changed names and faces, continually hiding and making us all victims of their crimes."

Bernavet tied Pancho's hands and feet and searched his pockets. He found the same documents that had been found on the other three accomplices they had put down. He showed them to the rest of the group and dropped them down on the rock they were using as a table. He asked, "What are we going to do with this piece of filth?"

Menelao replied, "Well, this is the only survivor of the group they sent after us. We all know their intentions, and it was not to negotiate with us. Like I said before, the moment we told them that we had the money they asked for and all the other stuff they demanded, what did they do? They started to shoot at us!" He touched Nolberis' shoulder gently. "Thanks to the good attributes and magnificent aim of our great friend Nolberis, he put all of them out of commission at the cost of only a flesh wound on Bernavet's shoulder. Thanks to the Lord, we are still alive. This shows clearly that they came with the sole intention of what we already had assumed: rob us, kill us, and Heaven knows what kind of plans they had for the kids." Pancho mumbled something inarticulately. Menelao looked at him with a nasty glance. "What? What? Speak up clearly—what did you say?"

Pancho summoned up his remaining strength. "I know what Bruno had in mind for your children. He told me to be extremely careful with these kids because they were worth a fortune. I have buyers already for both. His clients, German doctors, are waiting already to finish the transaction with those guys and are waiting for their organs."

Everyone looked at each other in shocked silence and ashen faces. Menealo said with strong conviction, "Leonardo, I've been thinking in silence to put Pancho in the coffin you left so many years ago in my garage in San Luis and let him rot in there. You never came back to pick it up. I think it will be of good use for this moment. But now that I hear from his own mouth what they were thinking to do with your child and Emilio's daughter, it would be a criminal waste to use that beautiful coffin on this piece of crap. It would be an even bigger crime to turn him over to the corrupt and questionable authorities in our country and give him the opportunity to walk free again in a short time. It will only give his criminal mind the luxury to conceive something even more sinister against one of you guys or one of the members of our families."

The other men stroked their chins in thought as they digested this silently. They were clearly examining their consciences. One after another they looked at each other. My father was very serious this time when he spoke. "I'm in complete agreement with what you just said. I am in more agreement with what you have in mind. I appreciate that you did not verbalize it in front of my son, who is still much too young to hear this. Thank you, my cousin."

"You're welcome, Leonardo. We all have a hard time dealing with this evil force, and we're walking a thin line to not allow it to invade our minds. But I think that we should discuss this more in private." He pointed to me. "Not at this moment."

My father turned and said, "We will do what we are supposed to do. We will do the right thing." He turned to me. "Julio Antonio, where did you leave Jackie? Is it far from here?"

I shook my head. "Not very far."

"Go and bring her over here. Take your time—don't rush yourself. I don't want you guys to get hurt after going through all this ordeal in the darkness of the night."

I understood perfectly what my father was telling me. Whatever they were going to do to Pancho, they didn't want me there. Emilio said, "I will go with him, if you guys don't mind and don't need me here. I'll make sure that they're both OK and bring them safe and sound back home. Whatever Leonardo decides, he has my vote, if it comes to that."

Pancho looked at all the men. He sobbed, "Please, give me another chance. I made a mistake. I'm not a bad man!" He looked hideous from all the swollen stings on his face.

My father looked at him. "You should have thought of that before you did what you did for money, power, or whatever reason you did it. Even though my son is very young, I call him my old man. He's the only kid I've ever seen at the age of seven that I can have a full conversation with and give me a right answer every time. He proved it to us again today by putting his own safety on the line to protect his cousin despite his youth and by using his common sense. I believe that he doesn't have to be a witness to any more than he's already seen."

Emilio took my hand, and Bernavet held his hand out to me. "Would you please leave your knife here?"

I handed it to him, and my uncle and I walked into the thinning rain, which was rapidly turning into a mist. A very sweet, calm breeze blew across the land. We were about a hundred feet from the bridge when we heard a shrill scream followed by two shots, their reports echoing from under the bridge and along the canyon. I started to turn, but my uncle put his arm across my shoulder and kept my face forward with his hand.

"No—don't turn around. Sometimes we must leave our curiosity in the hands of our imagination. That way, the ugly things that occur in our lives don't have the grip to damage us in the future physically and psychologically. As we say here in Cuba, what the eyes cannot see the heart will not feel."

Even at my young age I immediately understood that my uncle was trying to protect me in the same way I had been protecting my cousin, Jackie from those depraved sexual deviants. We walked for a while and I showed my uncle the hiding place where I had left my cousin. They exchanged a very emotional embrace at being reunited, and I saw the tears in his eyes. He gave Jackie so many kisses that I had to admit privately I was a little jealous. Even though I was a boy and I didn't need a bunch of kisses, if I could choose what to want, it was a little more demonstration of affection from my father. I knew my father wasn't as capable of it as my uncle, because they were different personalities. I didn't understand it at the time, though. My uncle Emilio, on the other hand, showed me more love, gratitude, and emotion than my own father when he saw me. I had to confess that he produced tremendous sadness and perhaps more psychological damage than if he had allowed me to cut Pancho into pieces or at least allowed me to be present when they administered justice to him. After many years, I came to understand that we all don't show emotion in the same way. My father, to me, was the greatest man born, my best friend, my best example, and my greatest pride—and he was an introverted man and a human being, with his own collection of virtues and vices like the rest of us. Unfortunately for him, it was almost impossible for him to manifest his feelings especially in front of a group.

We sat in the hiding place for a while, and my uncle listened in fascination to the story of how I managed, against Jackie's will, to get the knife and release both of us from the houseboat, how I abandoned her in the river and disappeared for a while, and had instead gone under the boat to create a hole to sink it. As she told the story, Emilio interrupted her to give me a huge bear hug. He would repeat then, "You showed these conniving kidnapping delinquents what a real del Marmol is all about. As the marble we get our name from, so should the free man's character be—white, strong, and resistant."

I understood my uncle was in no rush and was using the time to chat a little longer, probably awaiting a signal from my father that it was safe for him to bring us back. I had already seen the body by the riverbank and knew they couldn't leave it behind for the fishermen and merchants to come across in a few more hours. I knew also, even at my young age, why Bernavet asked me for the knife. I had wanted to keep it for myself, but out of respect to my elder I acceded to his request. We came back we heard the whistle that my father and uncle would use to communicate with each other. We found all of them wearing only their underwear and washing themselves in the river. If I wasn't certain what they wanted the knife for, it was really clear to me now. As strange as it sounds, none of those memories really stayed in my mind for very long unless I wanted to summon them, but the freshest and greatest memories that stayed with me and will be etched there until I die is the love, kisses, and tears of happiness of Mima, Majito, and Camila when my father brought me home safely. That feeling of love has stayed with me all my life and will do so to the end of my days.

Dr. Julio Antonio del Marmol

CHAPTER 5: THE POWERS HIDDEN IN OUR MINDS

The Town of Guane
September 1956

    I was screaming in the bedroom in the middle of the night, soaked in sweat. I was around nine years of age. My mother tried to wake me up. I recall seeing her face fading in and out in the midst of this turmoil. They sat me up in my bed, and my father saw deep scratches on my chest and the back of my neck. Mima checked my temperature using her cheek against my forehead. She turned to my father and said, "My God, he's boiling with a fever."

    My lovely black nanny, Majito, came into the room carrying a large container of cold water and some towels. She tried to assist my mother by drying my face and attempting to calm me down. Mima started to cry, asking, "God, why has this happened to my child? This is not the first time." She looked at my father. "What is wrong with him, Leonardo? What is wrong with him?"

    Papi sat with a deeply concerned expression and tried to console her by touching her face. "Don't worry," he said. "I will call my brother Emilio." He stood up and walked out of the room. He soon returned with my uncle, an MD who specialized in pediatrics and obstetrics. He was a balding man with a very aristocratic demeanor, and he was dressed all in white. He examined me with a stethoscope.

    Then he noticed that the deep scratches went far down my back, even to where I could not reach. He shared a look of puzzlement with the others, but otherwise said nothing. My father had been watching and stood up. My uncle was extremely concerned. He filled a syringe with medicine and injected it into my buttocks after Mima and Majito turned me over.

I saw his very disturbed manner as he spoke quietly with my father in the corner of the room, discussing my scratches. My father shook his head repeatedly. I was half-asleep, groggy from what I could only assume was a sedative that he had given me. I looked at Mima, who said, "Go to sleep, my love. You will have no more nightmares. I will be here to protect you."

As I grew groggier, everyone began to leave the room save for Majito, who stayed with me until I passed out. I later learned that my uncle had said to my father, "We have already performed every test we can do. This child is in as perfect health as one can expect. He's as strong as a bull, and you should be happy for that. My colleagues at the university concluded that this is something inexplicable. There is no logical reason for him to have scratches on his body in places that he cannot even reach. Even if he could, you guys have been very, very responsible to keep his nails trimmed and filed so that there is no possible way he could do that to himself. You may not believe what I'm about to tell you, my brother."

"Try me," Papi said. "I have complete trust and confidence in you. If anyone can help him, it's you."

"Scientists call this 'genetic link.' People who believe in the paranormal believe it is a spiritual connection between different generations." Mima and Majito were shocked by that statement, while my father shook his head in disbelief.

"For God's sake, my brother," he said, "don't tell me you believe in that witchcraft garbage. Do you know what you're saying, Emilio? Don't put things in Verena's mind—that's all I need! Please, she will take what you're saying very seriously."

My uncle smiled and shook his head. "Leonardo, my brother, you have to have an open mind. I'm a man of science. I don't believe in 'voodoo crap.' But science has its limitations. We must keep an open mind and look ahead when we don't have answers for what your son is going through. We don't know what is creating those scratches. Normally, in an average child, nightmares and fevers disappear in the first years of their lives. Your son is about to turn nine, and this has been happening for a long time. We have no answers or way to respond to the symptoms. In my professional medical opinion, you should take him to a spiritual doctor to explore what science cannot explain."

Papi shook his head unhappily, but my uncle continued, "You know better than anyone that I am a doctor, and I don't believe in these things. But remember what happened to you and I a few years ago. I don't' have to say to you the names of those two ladies, or do you want me to remind you?" Leonardo waved his hand to show it wasn't necessary. "Keep your mind open, as I have done. To this day I still cannot plausibly explain where those two ladies came from or how they had the knowledge and information they provided to us. But he is my nephew. Every time I see him like this, I must sedate him, because I don't know what else to do for him. My heart breaks every time. Do you understand my frustration? Let these people try; my colleagues agree."

Papi said, "OK. Thank you very much, my brother." They embraced and exchanged kisses on the cheek.

The next morning, I woke up to see Papi, Mima, and Majito looking at me. It was a beautiful day in September. Mima said, "Good morning," as she gave me a hug. "Do you remember what happened last night?"

"No," I replied with a shake of my head. "What happened?"

"Don't worry about it. Go and have breakfast. You have to go somewhere." Mima checked my temperature. "He doesn't have a fever anymore." They all smiled in pleasure at that announcement.

Papi said, "I'm not going. You take him with Majito and see what you can find out."

Mima nodded and said, "OK. Thank you." She turned to Majito. "We will go and see Gojita."

Majito's eyes widened. "My lady, you don't have any fear? Some people say she is a witch."

I jumped out of bed with more energy than ever. "No, Majito, that's not true. My friend told me she cured his father from pain in his neck and headaches that he'd been suffering from for years. Many doctors had tried to cure him and failed. If she cured Alfredo's father, she must be a good person. She cannot be a witch."

Mima smiled and looked at me in admiration for my reasoning. She asked me, "Who do you take after to be so smart?"

I looked at her and said, "I take after my Mima and Papi."

She leaned down and kissed me with a gentle laugh. "OK, let's get ready. I'm going to go get dressed." Majito remained in the room to get my clothes ready.

Montauk: The Lightning Chance

Once everyone left the room, I said to her, "Can I tell you a secret?"

She looked at me. "Of course, my son. You know you can tell me anything, and I will tell no one else."

"Are you sure? Not even Mima and Papi?"

"Of course."

"Well, Mima asked me if I remembered anything about last night. I told her I didn't remember much of anything, but that's not really all true."

"Why is that?"

"I remember some."

Majito sat down on the bed and put her hand on my head. "Sit down with me and tell me."

"I had a vision. I saw my little brother, Nando, playing on his tricycle in the driveway. A salesman that comes all the time to Papi was saying goodbye to everybody and leaving. He didn't see that Nando was behind his car, and so he got into his car and put it in reverse. He ran right over Nando. Nando died, but Mima brought him back by pushing on his chest several times. When everyone was crying, thinking he was dead, he came back to life. I saw him dead, and that is why I screamed and cried."

"Why didn't you tell your parents that?" she asked.

"I didn't want to break my promise to those two ladies dressed in white that appeared in my dream," I replied. They told me that I should keep my mouth shut and not tell anyone about this, but I will be the one who saves my brother from a certain death, and I had to have my eyes open—very open—to not let that happen. That's why I've been so close, watching him every day. I was afraid they were going to think it was me who brought that on him."

After we were dressed, Mima, Majito, and I visited the small *bohío* that belonged to Gojita. The thatched hut built of palm trees was in the middle of nowhere in a very poor, rundown area. Gojita was an old West Indian woman with a lot of wrinkles on her face. She dressed all in white, including a white turban.

Gojita greeted us with a big smile, revealing that she was missing some of her front teeth. After smoking a cigar and lighting some incense before a strange altar, she laid her hands on me. The whole experience was very scary, and my fear must have been evident.

As she touched me, her eyes widened in astonishment. "This boy is very strong, probably stronger even than I am," she said. "He is attached to a spirit—I think that of his great-grandfather."

She was speaking of my father's grandfather, Major General Donato Mármol Tamayo.

"Whenever he is in danger or whenever a major threat faces others," Gojita continued, "he will have these nightmares. The spirit scratches him in order to call his attention to the impending menace. He will never be afraid, so long as he learns how to use this gift."

She pled with my mother repeatedly to bring me back so that she could teach me to channel these good energies, enabling me to help a lot of people. Mima politely declined, explaining, "His father is a Mason. It was hard enough to get his consent to bring him here today. There is no doubt that he would never permit me to bring him back again."

Gojita shook her head in discontented disappointment. "What a pity. That is the only way this child will understand and use this precious gift he carries within him."

Mima assured her that she would at least try to bring my father around. They embraced, said goodbye, and we left. Although we would never again return, that conversation became indelibly imprinted in my memory for the rest of my life.

The next day was beautiful and sunny. I was playing marbles with my friends on the sidewalk outside my house. We had drawn a circle on the cement with a line the person pitching the marble into the ring had to kneel behind. My little brother Nando was running around crazily, riding his tricycle. I was keeping my eyes on him as we played. He swerved off the sidewalk into the gutter to turn around and then pedaled back up the drive. There was perhaps a two-foot drop in elevation from the top of our driveway to the street and he was using it as a small hill to give himself some speed as he went down it.

One of the salesmen to my father's stores would come by weekly to take Papi's orders for his business needs for the coming week. He came unusually late that day and because other cars were parked on the street, he had to pull into the driveway, blocking a small portion of the sidewalk. In the distance we could hear the musical bells of the ice cream truck. Everyone stopped playing and formed a line at the sidewalk. I picked up my marbles and put them in my pants pocket, as did the others. We each of us had bad experiences with other kids stealing our marbles when we were distracted before.

Montauk: The Lightning Chance

Nando was five years old at this time and had plenty of energy for that tricycle. When my turn came, I bought two chocolate popsicles: one with vanilla dipped in chocolate for him and the other my favorite, pineapple dipped in chocolate for myself. He was used to me getting his ice cream for him, and so waited until I had purchased our treats. He abandoned his tricycle and came tearing over to me at breakneck speed to get his ice cream. I handed it to him and paid the attendant for both of them. I saw Nando take his ice cream and sit down behind the car of the salesman to eat it.

It didn't occur to me that there could be any danger there. When the salesman had completed his transaction with my father, he had a large box that would have to placed in the trunk where he would naturally see Nando. I had observed this routine many times. Unfortunately, this time the salesman had changed his M.O. He had the trunk so full that he brought the supplies for my father in the front seat of his car, and so only walked around the front of the car—where he would have no way of seeing Nando.

All of this happened in a matter of seconds, the brief time during which I was receiving my change from the ice cream man. When I turned around to put the change in my pocket, I looked up to see the car apparently swallowing my brother and his tricycle! Nando disappeared beneath the car and the ice cream in his hand went flying.

With a speed I would never have believed, my vivid nightmare flashed before my eyes. I reached into my pocket, grabbed a handful of marbles and tossed them at the back window of the man's car. "Stop!!" I yelled. "My brother is under the car!" The marbles caused the window to shatter into small fragments and made a terrifically loud noise.

The salesman realized something was horribly wrong and slammed on the brakes. That reaction was all I wanted. The car stopped only a few hairs away from running over the body of Nando as he was turning out of the driveway. There was a horrible grinding of metal as the tricycle was mangled beneath the car.

Mima heard the screaming and came running out of the house. Everyone in the house followed her out as did everyone in my father's store next door. After the salesman told them what had happened, I received a great deal of praise for my quick thinking. My heart must have been beating a hundred miles an hour—I was that scared of what might have happened to Nando. I tearfully saw my brother's mangled body being pulled out from under the car of the salesman as my mother started administering CPR to bring him back. I saw my brother move and heard him moan. I crossed myself and silently thanked God for saving the life of my brother.

Interchapter: The Placebo Effect

The next morning, I walked home from Papi's clothing store and stopped in the Catholic church that was around four blocks from my house. I wanted to give the father a contribution my mother had sent along with me, a check for the poor people. The priest gave me a couple of medallions to give to members of the family, some with the Virgin Mary, some with the Caridad del Cobre. When I came into his office, I saw a girl that I had a crush on with long, wavy blond hair walking in the gardens and collecting flowers.

She wore a colorful, flowery headscarf. My nine-year-old mind understood a little better the secret or secrets that even I myself understood were hidden deeply in my mind. As time passed my mind little by little let them go very slowly, day by day, tying to protect me creating unnecessary panic that could bring irreversible serious psychological damage to my mental and physical future ahead. For that reason, that day in 1956, maybe as a small test from my subconscious what I had in my mind was my first attempt to travel into the future or another dimension. Not as a dream or a nightmare; before I had been experimenting. This time, in plain, sunlit day, without any disturbance or drama of any kind involving any member of my family, but instead in the pleasant company of the beautiful girl I liked very much with her blue eyes like the summer sky who had stolen my little tender heart at my young age. We sat down on a long cement bench in the church garden.

Each of us had an ice cream popsicle in our hands. This sweet, beautiful girl was the daughter of one of the biggest cattle ranchers who owned several butcheries in town and around the entire province. Her name was Teca Sayas-Bazan. Even though we were both too young for any romantic relationship, I felt something extremely special for that sweet, lovely girl. She made me feel like I was floating in the clouds whenever I was around her. The merest touch of her beautiful, long fingers of a professional pianist which she was at such an early age already a virtuoso, her angelic voice gave me goosebumps whenever I heard her sing Schubert's "Ave Maria" in church. It always brought tears to my eyes. I asked my mother once why my skin got goosebumps whenever she was around. Mima told me that it was something special we occasionally feel once in life, men or women. She said that many experts called it "love."

Since Mima was much smarter than me, I figured that I was in love with that sweet angel, Teca. At my tender age, I felt she had been sent from Paradise by God to keep me company for the rest of my time on Earth. Little did I know that nothing is forever.

We were talking like adults, very normal things, about what we were learning in school, and it was then that I confessed to her that I had been composing some music at that time and I was going to dedicate it to her. I called it "Love and Its Power."

She asked, "What do you mean, you're dedicating it to me?"

"I wrote that song thinking about you and how I feel about you," I replied.

This motivated her to smile at me beautifully. She moved along the bench towards me and gave me a little kiss on my cheek. I heard the bells of the church ringing joyfully and violins full of emotion in my heart. It was logical for me to want her to feel at least close to what I felt at that moment, so I took her in my arms in order to return the kiss on her cheek. Unfortunately, she moved in a different direction, and our mouths came together. It was my first and sweetest kiss I ever had. Her lips felt like rose hips. I was ready to immediately apologize, but she surprised me with a big smile, stopping me with her right hand and a satisfied expression on her face.

"I know that wasn't your intention, but I loved it," she said with a rather sensual expression. I was a little afraid and confused by this. She noticed that. "Didn't you like it, too?"

"Yes, yes—I liked it very much!" I said rapidly. "Of course, *claro*! I loved it very much. You have very sweet lips."

She grinned at me and held up the popsicle she had been eating. "Of course, they're sweet."

We both laughed, and to this day I regret not reciprocating that beautiful kiss. At that age, though, what else can one expect? Our conversation was beautiful, but something strange and extraordinary happened, like when I had hit my head on the rock years before in the gypsy camp. Teca's voice seemed to go slower, once again like a 45-rpm record played at 33 rpm. Finally, her voice and everything else around me gradually disappeared. It was like I was on a stage and people were removing each set piece, one at a time, like the play was finished and the set crew were removing the scenery.

Dr. Julio Antonio del Marmol

Other images started to form to replace the scenery, little by little. First the figure of Papi, then his cousin Menelao, then my uncle Emilio, and then Papi's best friends, Nolberis and Bernavet. But what surprised me more than anything was the presence there of my cousin Jackie and another girl about her age with large, black eyes, olive skin, long black hair, and a narrow, long face. She looked like a flamenco dancer, and I had seen her before at my birthdays and family gatherings. She was Maitel, Bernavet's daughter, and we had never been close, but she looked like a nice girl. Everyone looked very distracted as they looked at a large table that had what appeared to be a map with the internal arrangement of a building, perhaps a set of blueprints. For a moment I though that all of this was a product of my imagination or another of my vivid dreams, until Maitel smiled at me in acknowledgement of my presence.

Nonchalantly I pinched myself to see if I was dreaming or awake. The place we were in was luxurious, like a suite in a very expensive hotel. I was near a window that was closed. I parted the curtain slightly so I could look out the window and realized that we were not in Guane. The building was very tall, and I could see the cars driving by the Havana Malecon. I didn't know exactly what that building was called at that moment, but we were certainly in Havana. We had been there many times to visit my grandfather and other relatives.

A man with a receding hairline entered the room with several plates of food. His face was familiar to me. He was around 40 years of age, medium height, and I could not place exactly where I knew him from. He said to the others, "Today is Sunday, March 10th." He pulled a few bottles of champagne out of the bag. As he spoke, he served several glasses of the liquor. "The dictator Fulgencio Batista y Zaldivar is celebrating his coup de tat and his regime will be collapsed three days from now, Wednesday, March 13th, 1957." I deduced that today is Sunday, March 10th, 1957. They raised their glasses in toast. "We will celebrate his death and the end of his tyranny, right here in this same hotel, the Havana Riviera."

My uncle Emilio raised his glass. "I don't think it will be proper, much less secure in our line of work, to come back to the same place we planned all this. We should reconvene, hoping everything goes as planned, later in the FOCSA Building. Using a different location just to prevent us regret meeting in the same place should anything go wrong."

Montauk: The Lightning Chance

Figure 12 FOCSA Building

The others agreed with this idea. They raised their glasses toasted the death of the tyrant, and I could not help but have chills all over my body. The frog in my stomach started leaping again. I put my right hand on my stomach and repeated to myself in my mind, *Everything will be OK. If not, what is the purpose for my being here today?* I repeated this a couple of times to convince myself that behind my witnessing this had to be for a good and noble purpose. Every person in that room was fighting for freedom and the common good of everyone, not just in Cuba but around the world.

But something I didn't completely like was in the middle of all of this: the toasting someone's death. I didn't feel that it was a moral or good thing to do. I didn't care how conniving the other person could be; we should do justice and exterminate if necessary, but not with a morbid need to cheer or celebrate the death of anyone. In my opinion it was not dignified or necessary. Unfortunately, I didn't think it said anything good about us. I considered it would bring out the bad villain in anyone and bring us down to the level of those we despise.

In the middle of all that, I noticed that my ladies in white, as I preferred to call my angels, weren't present. I wondered if it was because whatever they were planning was not completely cleared at the divine level or matched the divine light they normally circulated. It might have been just because I had tried to excuse everyone there. I had grown up enough already, and as the mother that slowly lets her babies alone so that they can learn by themselves to succeed and survive without constant attention, I was very harsh with myself and correcting myself that I was only nine years old. I shook my head; of course, at this age neither Mima nor Majito gave me baths anymore. I was now doing that on my own as well as other things like eating, picking out my own clothes to wear, and so on. I smiled and thought I did a good job of convincing myself that after all celebrating the death of the tyrant took my family out of the good and close to the bad. It probably was the only reason that my two ladies weren't present at that time, causing me to travel alone.

Menelao started to explain what the plan they were following would be. "For us, it will be very difficult to know the precise time we will hit the Presidential Palace or if the dictator Batista will be in his offices there at that moment." He looked at the two girls and me. "For that reason, I want you guys to be dressed as Boy Scouts, go into the Palace on March 13th, on a special commission to bring a present that is supposed to be given to the President from the Boy Scouts institution for the celebration a few days ago. Then, if he's there, when you leave, you can give us the green light for the assault. The young, suicidal commandos from the FEU will be waiting for us. As soon as you move out of the Palace, a car will pick you up and we'll come in to end that horrible tyranny that has cost the Cuban people so many lives. We will do this in three days."

I continued to stand by the window with my back against the wall where I had peeked through the curtain occasionally. I noticed the traffic was dying down outside. I shook my head. At that precise moment I started to see what would happen on that day they were discussing as a vision came before me like projected on a giant movie theatre screen. What I was watching was nothing to celebrate at all. That dictator, just after we left the Presidential Palace almost followed us right on our heels, abandoning the Palace without a scratch. He had been advised and protected by the Satanic, evil, demonic group that had a mole inside the FEU. They had already told the dictator everything just discussed now, and that the signal for him to leave would be three Boy Scouts showing up.

I saw in my vision many, many young boys, practically still in their teens, some killed, some taken to different prisons by the police. They would be tortured by pulling eyes and nails out, cutting their testicles, and instituting the highest persecution around the island in revenge for this plot, the worst the dictator had enacted before. It would be a bloodbath. The attempt on the dictator's life would turn out to be an utter fiasco.

I slid slowly down the wall until I sat on the floor, my head on my knees and my hands on my face as I watched the details for this massacre unfold before my eyes. As I shook my head in my hands, my uncle Emilio's eyes watched me. I screamed aloud in agony, "No! No!!"

He was seated at the table around the others. Together with my father, they came over to me, one on each side of me, putting their arms around my shoulders. My father said, "Julio Antonio, what have you seen? Why are you so disturbed?"

I looked up with tears in my eyes. "You should abort this plan. It will cause thousands of young lives, institute the worst retaliation this regime will ever take, and bring only more tears and blood to our people. Not even taking into consideration that almost all of you will wind up dead, savagely tortured by the *esbirros* of the dictator."

My uncle shook his head and looked at my father. "What do you want to do, Leonardo? We both know your son has a gift. The others might not understand what we're talking about."

Menelao spoke before my father could answer. "I will continue with the plan. We have too many people involved, and we cannot stop now. It's too late. What will everyone say? They're waiting, ready to give their lives for what we planned so long. The superstitions of a nine-year-old kid is causing me to abandon a plan I came up with myself. I know you have reasons, and I believe in what your son says. You guys can do whatever you think is safe for you, but I will continue with this plan to the end."

I replied, "Then, uncle, this will be your end. You will be one of the first to die." Tears rolled down my cheeks as I spoke. "Record this in your memory so that when it comes true you will not regret it, since we warned you way, way ahead of time."

He shook his head. "We cannot stop it. It's too late."

As he spoke, I heard a very loud scream. It sounded like Teca's voice. Then a very bright light forced me to close my eyes. When I opened them again, I was in the same place I was before, sitting on the bench next to Teca. This time, my body was completely naked. I could not explain why; I only saw Teca covering her eyes and running away through the garden as if she had seen a ghost. She dropped her headscarf on the ground. A few steps from there where we had been sitting and having a great conversation, I saw the two popsicles starting to melt. Clearly, I had not been gone too long.

The sky turned dark rapidly. Lightning flickered, and thunder rolled from far off. It started to sprinkle. A soft, cold breeze started to blow across my face and body. I got chilled from it in my nakedness. In confusion I looked under the bench for my clothes, but they weren't there. I finally picked up the headscarf dropped by Teca and wrapped it around my waist as best I could to cover my private parts. I made the decision to leave as it was growing quite dark. Trying to remain unseen by anyone, I started to walk through the soft rain, worried about anyone seeing me half-naked as I was. Though the headscarf covered my front, my rear was completely exposed to view.

The church was constructed on a small hill. As I walked into the darkness, there were only occasional light poles. I thanked God for that, since people wouldn't see me clearly in the dark, and thanks to the rain no one was around. They had all sought shelter in their homes.

When I was only a hundred feet from the house, I could see the porch light was still on. I was very happy to see this, since it meant that my father had not yet returned from his businesses, and I would not have to face him as I was. Neither Mima nor Majito turned that light off until Papi had returned home. This also meant that dinner had not yet been served. I picked up my pace to get into the house and get some decent clothes and cover myself from this very embarrassing situation. I could not understand where my clothes had gone; how could I possibly explain it to anyone else?

The only person who might be able to explain that was Teca Sayas-Bazan, my only witness. I could only assume, however, that I had gotten naked in front of her. She might not even understand what had happened and run away in panic, which I could later corroborate when she finally gave me a chance to speak to her again. Distracted in all my thinking, completely confused from my last, very sad experience, and filled with frustration that I could not even completely digest, I walked home.

In the shadow of the night not too far away from me I saw four teenagers bending over by a beautiful, yellow and white Ford Thunderbird 1957 sports car stealing the hubcaps, the plate screws, and air caps, and putting them in a sack. One of them kept watch. He saw me first and I heard him say, "Hey, hey! A little girl is coming from the sidewalk."

Since I had long hair, which was unusual for a boy at that time, I had to cut this kid some slack for his stupid confusion. It usually bothered me enough to lose my cool and administer a lesson for being

Montauk: The Lightning Chance

mistaken for a girl in other situations, this time I could understand it: my lack of clothes, only a headscarf around my waist, a boy my age walking alone in the rain and dark with his rear in the air, it was understandable. So when the muscular one, who appeared to be the leader and most aggressive of the four, a kid with large lips and dark, curly hair of about fifteen years of age with a razor blade in his right hand with a sadistic, sexual smile touched his own privates with his left and pulling the zipper down, said, "Come on, pretty girl. Kneel down and start to lick my banana popsicle." I simply raised the headscarf with a pleasant smile on my face. "Oh!" he said in revulsion. "Look at this—we have a transsexual here. You're too little to play these games, my friend."

I shook my head and tried to remain patient. "I'm not trying to convince of you of why I'm dressed this way or not. I'm not transsexual, I'm not a homosexual, I'm a male with high levels of testosterone. Whatever you can cook up in your head will not be even close to the reality of why I'm wrapped in this girl's headscarf and half naked. I don't think it's any of your business, unless I believe that important matter now for you and you will be more interested in and benefit from is to move away from me and let me pass through for your own safety. I'm going to give you two reasons for that." The kid looked at me incredulously. "The first one is that I can make you so miserable that you will pee in your pants and beg me for forgiveness. Believe me, I'm not bragging. And that is the best that could happen to you. The second one is that I could scream. I only live a few feet from here, and my father will cut you into pieces if you screw around with me, not counting our neighbors, especially the one who owns this beautiful Thunderbird—the one you've been taking a few feathers from. He won't be happy at all." I pointed at the dirty pillowcase on the ground by their side. They had probably been collecting things for hours, using the darkness of the night, the rain, and the fact that people would stick to their homes. I raised my arms, shook my fists, and said with a stern expression, "I will make this clear once more. I don't want any problems with you guys. I want that very clear. Again, I'm not a transsexual or anything like that. Do you understand?" I nodded at them, inviting a response. I began to get a little ticked.

Still with his blade in his hand, he shook his head, his face still showing his aggression. He picked up the pillowcase with his left hand. "I don't give a damn if you're a transsexual, faggot, or whatever you want to be. My problem is that you've seen my face, and I'm not going to give up these things. You're the only witness who can identify me or my friends. We have to close your mouth forever." He gestured, and his accomplices hesitantly surrounded me.

I took a couple of steps back and stared him in the eyes, trying to bring him towards the circle of light beneath the streetlamp. "You don't have to worry about that at all. I don't stick my nose in what isn't my business. But I have to warn you again—if you make a move, you won't leave me any alternative to damage you for the rest of your life." I took a couple of steps back and took a combat stance. "Go ahead—your move."

He raised his left hand, and said undecidedly, "Do you know jujitsu or something like that?"

I could see in his eyes that I had confused him. He hesitated to move forward. It must have disoriented him, coming from such a young kid. Maybe my strange clothing, but I took the opportunity and said, "You have a problem in your life. You have a nocebo effect in your brain. You should look immediately for professional help. Your mind will deteriorate to the point that you will die very young."

He looked at me nervously, while the guy who appeared to be his right arm yelled, "Cut his throat so he stops running his mouth and saying stupid things like that!"

I raised up on my toes to the mulatto kid who spoke. At the same time a loud clap of thunder shook us all. They started. I looked into his eyes. I raised my arms and began to shake as I concentrated intensely on him. He began to tremble visibly, and his feet left the ground as he levitated up a little, perhaps three or four feet, just enough to put a healthy fear in him and the other boys. His eyes fluttered as he shook, and a line of drool escaped his mouth. He remained up for perhaps ten to fifteen seconds, then I let him down. Two of the boys started to run for their lives, one of them dropping his knife on the ground.

The leader was still aggressive, but I could see the fear in his eyes. "I'm not afraid of you!" He pointed at the two running off. "I'm not like those cowards."

I took two steps forward, this time locking my eyes into his like daggers. When I got close to him, he looked at me in terror, and his blade slid limply out of his hand. I used that opportunity to take him by both hands and squeezed them hard. His pants grew wet, and urine ran down one pantleg to mix in with the rainwater on the sidewalk. Then and only then is when I put into his mind all I had seen in the Havana Riviera, all the torture, the kids being killed, the people in prison with their eyes and nails being torn out, the castrations, and finally the attempt to kill the dictator.

The young delinquent screamed, "I'm sorry! I'm sorry! Please stop it—I don't want to see anymore!"

I decided he had enough and let go of his hands. He ran off, leaving behind his razor blade and the pillowcase of loot. The mulatto remained, petrified as he watched everything I did to his friend. He said, "Forgive me, please—don't hurt me!" He ran off behind his friend.

As I watched them leave, I crossed myself and gave thanks to God for the mental strength that He provided me to get out of that complicated problem. I walked to the house and snuck onto the patio to avoid questions from Mima for my attire. I had no answer to give her for any of her queries.

After I entered the house by the patio door, I went over to the laundry hamper, and picked up the clothes I had worn the day before. At that moment I heard the garage door open. My father was home and entered the house. I made myself noticeable. When Mima asked me where I had been, I replied, "With my father at his business. Then I went to do what you told me to do at the church, and then I spoke with my friend Teca." She smiled, as Teca was part of the list of approved families for us to talk to.

I took a long, hot shower to try and dissipate that bad experience in my mind. I tried to maintain my mind in a placebo effect, by going back before all of this happened and thus avoiding the nocebo effect of a not very pleasant day, full of agony and sadness concentrated in such a short time.

CHAPTER 6: FROM DIRT TO KING

Town of Banes
Oriente Province, Cuba
1910

Figure 13 Sugar Cane Wagon

    Ruben Zaldivar, a little 10-year-old mulatto boy with thick lips, black hair, and large eyes, ran with a group of other kids slightly younger than himself. They ran along the dusty roads without any shoes behind a sugar cane wagon pulled by bulls. Ruben was the largest of the group, so he attempted to grab a stalk of cane that hung out further than the others. They tried not to make a great deal of noise. In soft voices, they encouraged Ruben in his efforts, "Get it! You almost did it last time, try a little harder! It's almost out!"

Montauk: The Lightning Chance

The drover continued yelling the name of his bulls to encourage them to keep moving as he poked them with his *garrocha*[16]. Between his own comments and the groaning of the wheels he couldn't hear the kids at all.

With a little frustration, the little boy after several failed attempts at grabbing the cane decided to get his *sevillana*[17] out of his pocket, pushed the button to spring the blade out, and began to cut away at the restraining ropes across the back of the wagon. He was goaded by the gestures of disappointment by the kids. Suddenly, half the load came free and fell out on top of the kids, who began to scream in terror.

The wagoner heard the screams and turned. Seeing half his load lying in the dusty road, he shook his head in irritation. It would take at least a half day to reload his wagon, if not the full day. Kids were struggling to free themselves from beneath the avalanche of cane. As the man came over, he became even more upset. He put his hands on top of his head at the disaster these kids had made of his load.

He yelled, "You little bandits!" He began to flail at them with the whip and slapping them in the rear ends with his *garrocha* to encourage them to extricate themselves. "Damned snot-nosed brats!" He tried to catch one of them, but because his hands were already full, they slipped away. He dropped both instruments into the dirt and grabbed Ruben by the legs, recognizing him as the oldest of the kids and likely the responsible one. The other kids ran off in different directions. Holding Ruben by one leg, who was struggling to get up and run off, he said, "Oh, no—you're not going anywhere. You're going to help me put all of this load back into the wagon."

The man was perhaps 30 years of age, tall and muscular from his work, with a thick moustache. He was dressed in an old, ragged guayabera[18] with short sleeves. When he saw the face of Ruben, he yelled in surprise, "You're the bastard son of Belisario Batista Palermo and Carmila Zaldivar! Look at what you did, you arrogant piece of crap! You've been good for nothing since the day you were born."

Ruben, angry with outrage as he heard the aspersions against his character thrown his way. Being called a "bastard" was the worst offense

---

[16] A long pole with a nail or small spike attached at the end used in bullfighting. Drovers would use them to goad bulls into motion when the persuasion of a whip failed.

[17] A very large switchblade used by Cuban gangsters

[18] A style of Cuban men's shirt

anyone could be called at that time, especially when it happened to be reality. The whole town knew about it. His father, Belisario, had never wanted to recognize him at the time of his birth. He yelled back, "Liar! I'm not a bastard!" He struggled to get free from the drover's grasp, kicking the tall man in the groin hard, which nearly drove the man to the ground in pain. Rage still in his face, the grasp did not slacken. "Let me go!!"

The drover was more indignant than furious. Once the pain had dissipated, he stood up, grabbed Ruben by the back of his shirt, and rubbed his face in the dusty road. Not satisfied, he rolled Ruben over, and with one hand, picked up a handful of dirt. With the other he forced Ruben's mouth open, making him eat the dirt. He yelled, "You should learn to respect adults, you little piece of shit!" He slammed the boy onto his back, grasping him by the throat with one hand and kneeling on his chest. "Damned bastard! This is what you are, and this is what you should eat like the worm you are: dirt!"

Not far away another wagon loaded down with sugar cane approached. The drover heard the yells of the other drover, "Casi-MI-ro! Viji-LAN-te!" he almost sang.

The drover turned to see what was happening behind him. This distraction enabled Ruben to pull his *sevillana* out of his pocket and stab the drover holding him down in the belly. He felt the pain and looked down, staring at the blood pouring from his abdomen in disbelief. He let go of Ruben and put his hands over the wound to stop the bleeding. He could not comprehend that this little boy, now turned into a criminal, had been capable of such a horrible act at that young age. Ruben slipped away from beneath the drover's knees as the man stood up and began to walk towards the other wagon, waving his right arm to signal his need for help. Knife still in his right hand, Ruben stood on the road rather than running away. He advanced towards the wounded man, his eyes filled with hatred and his face distorted in murderous intent.

With the drover turned, he stabbed the man in the chest. He yelled at the stricken man, "You are the one going to eat dirt, *cabron*[19]! I will never eat dirt again, even if I have to associate with Satan!" Taking advantage of the drover's weakness from loss of blood, he stabbed him twice more in the chest on the left side, clearly seeking the man's heart. This time, however, two shots from the other wagon rang out.

---

[19] Asshole

The other wagon was quite close now, and the other drover saw the criminal act being perpetrated against his coworker. He had taken a rifle out and fired off two warning shots, but it was now pointed right at Ruben. "The next shot goes into your head, bastard!"

Even though Ruben looked at him, ready to kill him as well, he saw the man was perhaps two hundred feet away. He decided to call his attack off, turned, and ran away from that place. Rifle in hand, the drover yelled after him, "Little delinquent bastard—I know who you are! I will send behind you the *guardia rural*[20]!"

Ruben, without stopping, yelled over his shoulder, "Go to hell, you *cabron*, and everyone else in this goddamned town that's called me 'bastard' since the day I was born!"

The drover helped his wounded friend, who had collapsed. Ruben continued to run off into the fields of sugar cane. He tried to wipe the blood off the blade on his shirt. After a while he arrived in town. He entered a *cuarterias*[21] and yelled, "Go to hell, all of you in this goddamned town! I'll return and punish everyone without exception, all you who call me a bastard!"

He ran through the area to his house. His mother saw the blood on his shirt immediately and asked him harshly what had happened. He paid no attention to her and went to his things. He took his piggy bank, broke it open, and gathered the coins. He put it in one of his socks, tied it in a pillowcase he took from his bed. His mother followed behind him, the questions continuing uninterrupted as he packed clothes and a few belongings in the pillowcase. She came up and shook him by the collar of his shirt. "Answer me, *carajo*[22]! I'm your mother!"

He turned and looked at her in hatred. He ripped his shirt off, balled it up, and threw it at her feet. He yelled, "It's all your fault! You'd have been better off not having me than having me called a bastard! It's all your fault, you goddamned puta!"

She slapped him across the face, knocking him down. He rolled across the floor and jumped up like a spring. He pulled the knife out of his pocket, snapped the blade out, and advanced on his mother with the same thought of murder he had before. He raised his hand, the knife

---

[20] Rural police

[21] Communal living quarters with a single bath facility; in the country, frequently resembling ranch bunkhouses. Only the very poor live in such places; in the cities, they were tenement buildings.

[22] Damn it

ready to stab her in the chest, but an old lady appeared in the doorway and yelled, "Stop, Ruben Batista y Zaldivar, stop! What are you doing, for the love of God?"

It was his grandmother, who he did have respect for. He stopped and, still glaring daggers at his mother, he yelled, "You are a puta, and this is what you deserve for bringing me into this world filled with humiliation and shame! I will never return to this shitty town again!"

His mother was enraged and yelled back, 'Ungrateful piece of shit! I should have listened to your father a long time ago and aborted you and dropped you in the dirt to serve as fertilizer! He's always right and look at you—you're not even good for taking the dogs out to pee!" In her fury of emotion, she ripped open her blouse, exposing her firm, still beautiful breasts. "But like an idiot I gave you my teats to give you life. From these you survived, and I have suffered worse humiliation than you could ever dream; but I kept you alive, you miserable, ungrateful piece of shit! Why don't you drive that knife into my chest and kill your mother, *malparido*[23]! You have no pride, you're a lazy bum. You've been slowly killing me for a long, long time with your filthy eyes, accusing me and recriminating me for sacrificing and going through all the pain of having you, for even bothering to have you instead of aborting you and killing you when you were an infant!" She screamed at him, filled with rage, moving closer and closer to him, as if trying to provoke him. "Come on, bastard! Kill your mother! Come on, I don't fear you! That way, you'll go directly to Hell, by Satan's side, where you'll be happy!"

He actually raised the knife, determined to stab her. Before he could, though, his grandmother yelled again, "No, Rubencito! That's the most horrible crime you could ever commit—killing your own mother. Even if you don't love her, don't do this to me! You know I love you and have since the day you were born!" She pled with him, tears in her eyes, and her voice cracking. Her efforts worked, and he stopped.

Ruben yelled, "I will no longer be Ruben, like it, or anyone like it, until my father goes to Hell, too! My name will be from now on Fulgencio, and my last name is Batista! To you, Carmila, as my father, you should both go back to Hell from where you probably came! You've done so much damage to so many innocent people like me that you're not normal human beings!"

---

[23] Bastard

Montauk: The Lightning Chance

Figure 14 Fulgencio Batista

Fulgencio, as he wanted to be known as from this point onward, picked up his pillowcase from the bed, tied a piece of shoelace from an old shoe to close it shut, and threw it over his shoulder. He went over to his grandmother and kissed the poor old sobbing lady's cheek. She hugged him and said, "God go with you, my son." She pulled some pesos out of her blouse and handed them to him.

He smiled diabolically and replied to her, "Better the Devil, Grandmom. God has never been generous with me. I don't think He wants anything to do with me; He abandoned me a long time ago."

She clapped her hand to her forehead. "Oh, dear God! Forgive him!"

Dogs were barking outside. A woman outside yelled, "Anyone who has something to hide, run! The *guardia rural* is here!"

Figure 15 **Guardia Rural**

Fulgencio went to the back room and jumped out of one of the windows. He left that place without a second glance. He ran until he reached the train tracks. He jumped on the back of one of the boxcars for the United Fruit Company that was bringing bananas and other fruit to the capital, and slipped between the crates of fruit, eating whatever he wanted. He arrived in Havana and disappeared for many years as a fugitive without any documentation proving his new identity.

Many years later, this small delinquent grew into an adult and enlisted in the army. From soldier he was promoted to Sergeant and became a telegraph operator. Eventually, he rose to the rank of Colonel, then General, finally getting elected President of Cuba. His inauguration day had to be postponed when they discovered, while checking into his past, that the name Fulgencio Batista did not exist in any birth records or provincial records. He had to pay a large sum of money to a judge to finally clear the old bastard's criminal record by expunging the matter of the drover's murder in Oriente. This completed his transformation from dirt into the reputable "king" of Cuba, the President.

Havana
March 10, 1957

Typical of tropical weather, it was raining heavily that night. Eighteen people sat comfortably around a circular wooden table with a globe of the world at the center. Everyone was dressed in black hooded robes, like those worn by monks, but with the logo of their diabolic cult on the left breast. The leader's robe, however, was blood red instead of black. The table had an indentation at one side, raised higher like a throne for a medieval king. Each robe bore a number on the right breast, 1-18, with the red-robed leader bearing the digit 1. He sat in that throne.

The leader stood up and said, "No more rebel students! No more political parties! No one ever will force us to eat dirt ever again, because we are the future of not only this country but of the world. We will take control. Even though we have suffered several small setbacks that forced our organization to go underground and have lost several leaders along the way, our magnificent, supreme teacher has promised that we will have a new dark priest coming to us very soon. He will guide us to the final triumph, the conquest of all of humanity, placing the population of the world absolutely under our control, physically and spiritually. When our teacher finally comes to us, we will follow him right here on Earth for the centuries throughout Eternity. Loyalty always and forever to our supreme teacher!"

Everyone rose to their feet as well. He pulled a dagger out. Symbols of serpents decorated the hilt, with strange diabolic representations of bats and dragons on the pommel. The blade was double-edged and engraved with multicolored lines. He stabbed the dagger silently into the globe. Each member took a turn rotating the globe and stabbing a similar dagger into it, each claiming a part of the world. They all cheered three times. They held their arms out in symbolic unity over the table silently three times. They all took a small sip from the mugs which sat on the table before them.

Up until now the room had been nearly in the dark with only a few candles in candelabras providing feeble light. Everyone had been waiting for this moment. A man in a tuxedo and top hat entered the now completely silent room. He proceeded to light the unlit candles, providing greater illumination to the room. One of the members of that strange cult casually fixed his hood. The caduceus on the surface of a medical school graduation ring shone for a few seconds as he did so. The expression on his face was preoccupied and discontented, unlike the stern, grim expressions on the others.

The tuxedoed man brought clean placemats, removing the old ones, placing a shot glass on the new mat. He refilled all the mugs with what appeared to be red wine from a large jar. No one touched the newly poured wine in solemn respect until the man finished his round. He left for a few minutes and then returned with two buckets and a butcher's block on top of a rolling cart. One bucket was covered, the other one was open and empty. A very sharp meat cleaver lay on top of the butcher's block.

He took a thick insulated elbow-length glove and put it on. Very carefully, he opened the covered bucket after placing the open bucket below the block. The sound of several rattlesnakes shaking their tails was heard. He stuck his gloved hand inside quickly and with the efficiency of a master chef pulled out a single snake, letting the cover fall shut on the bucket. He held the snake down on the butcher's block and deftly cut the rattle of the tail off. Still holding the snake firmly by the head and went around and filled some of the shot glasses with its blood. As soon as he was done, he chopped the snake's body up with the cleaver and swept the pieces into the bucket. Then he opened the closed bucket and repeated the process until all the shot glasses were filled.

Once he was done, the tuxedoed man gathered his equipment together, bowed ceremonially to the cult members, and silently left the room, closing the door behind him. The leader took the shot glass of blood and poured it into his glass of wine. The other members followed suit. Then they took what appeared to be fancy chopsticks, decorated with Egyptian symbols in red, yellow, blue and black that had been left on red linen napkins embroidered with the cult's emblem by the glasses. They used these to stir the blood into their wine. Like a ritual, everyone stirred their drink at the same time.

The leader stood up with the mat in his left hand. "Today I want to give you a small lesson. It has a name: the secret to learn how to be silent and get full attention. When we're talking all the time it is very rare that we learn anything. When we listen with patience to others, our minds become fountains of knowledge. With silent attention, always, we will conquer the respect of others and the right to be listened to with attention and respect when our time to talk has come." He paused for a moment. Silence spread over the room. The others stood up and applauded his lesson.

The man with the caduceus ring stood up and clapped like the others, but not with the same energy that the others demonstrated. The leader gestured with his right arm to stop the applause. Everyone sat back down.

He continued, "Soon, very soon, I can guarantee to everyone here that there will be no more protests in the streets. The opposition will be buried forever. The most beautiful thing about this is that our enemies will give us the opportunity and justification that will be validating us to conduct ourselves that way." The other members glanced at each other curiously. "In the blink of an eye we will destroy them because I have eyes on my back." He added that last with assured emphasis. "They believe they will soon destroy us, but I have a grand surprise for them. They will never be able to forget it. The only revolution that we will be allowing in this country that will spread all over the world is the revolution of our power, the absolute physical and psychological control and the irrevocable control of everyone's mind, men, women, and children, all over this planet. Like I said at the beginning, very soon, in only three days precisely, on March 13th, 1957. This is why we meet today to celebrate the anniversary of our grand triumph and conquest of power, our beautiful March 10th, 1952."

The man with the caduceus ring, my uncle Emilio, shifted restlessly in his chair. He thought, *How can this be possible? How could my nephew have known all the things that are going to happen? How can THEY know what is going to happen to use it for their own benefit?* He could not wait to get out of there and go to his allies to immediately abort what was planned for the 13th. His impatient movement stopped abruptly as he realized he might draw attention to himself. In an unwanted gesture of worry his hand rubbed his forehead, and the ring shone once more in the flickering candlelight.

Not noticing, the leader continued, "We have allies everywhere, ears and eyes at our service and the service to our master teacher. We have people even in the guts of our enemies. That is why we will prevail at the end and have the final, universal triumph. We will be the only winners in the end and fulfill our dreams." He raised his mug filled with blood mixed with wine and yelled with emphasis, "Death and destruction to every one of our enemies! Cheers for our triumph!"

The others raised their mugs and began to drink the strange beverage to the last drop as a ritual to death and glorification of force and power of Satan. He said, "To our master, Satan, for our power and control over the rest of humanity! Hoorah! Hoorah! Hoorah!!"

Dr. Julio Antonio del Marmol

CHAPTER 7: THE DEVIL'S EMISSARIES

City of Bogota
Capital of Colombia
1954
Sunday

Figure 16 Bogota, Colombia

In a night of torrential rainfall during the tyranny of General Gustavo Rojas Pinilla, gunshots rang out in the distance as a man ran in the shadows of the night through the streets of an extremely poor neighborhood, his pistol in hand. He looked continually over his shoulder to make sure that he had eluded his pursuers. He stopped for

Montauk: The Lightning Chance

a few seconds, panting heavily after he turned a corner and leaned against the brick wall of a building. Seeing that no one was immediately coming, he leaned, cheek against the wall, to peer around the corner, his hat in one hand and pistol in the other. Rainwater ran freely through his hair as he looked down the empty, darkened street lit by a solitary streetlamp. He looked again, reassured that he had successfully thrown off those chasing him.

Convinced that he was now safe, he slowly came out of his hiding place and put the pistol away in his waistband. He walked at a normal pace towards a small bridge ahead of him. A car sped around the corner, unable to see him in the rain until the last moment. The driver leaned on the horn angrily as the man was nearly run over. The man realized that he was in the street and not the sidewalk. He made an apologetic gesture towards the driver with the left hand which still held his hat.

"Idiot!" the driver yelled. "Get on the sidewalk!"

He jumped onto the narrow sidewalk and continued walking towards the other side of the bridge. As he crossed the bridge, he saw the lit signs of various businesses, providing greater illumination than where he had come from, certainly a more prosperous neighborhood. He noticed a large, arched sign marking a cabaret named The New Buenos Aires in bright red and blue neon lights. It did not look particularly fancy. The neighborhood was still evidently poor, but it was a better one than where he had just come from.

He went inside the cabaret and looked for a table in a shadowy corner far from the door. He wanted to make sure he had a clear view of the front door. A beautiful young lady was playing the piano and singing an old tango, "Mi Buenos Aires Querido." A man with a long beard was playing the accordion, a black man played the bass, and a younger man with hair glistening in the lights by the Vaseline in it was on the drums. Even though the outside didn't look all that great, the inside was very tastefully decorated, certainly better than the area led one to expect.

A waitress came over to him, a young girl with black short hair with extremely thick, exaggerated makeup on her face. She held a notebook and pen and asked, "What is your pleasure to drink, sir?"

He had not yet sat down. He was shaking his raincoat out and laying it over a chair next to him. He turned around and replied, "A burgundy wine, please, just a glass. Is the kitchen still open?"

"Yes, sir," she answered with a nod as she smacked the gum she was chewing loudly. "What would you like to eat, handsome?" She smiled flirtatiously as she shook her breasts suggestively while he sat down.

The man smiled and obliged her by looking at her breasts. He held out his right hand. "I am Adolf."

The young woman smiled once more and nonchalantly took his hand. "Bogota."

Adolf looked at her incredulously. "Really?"

"Yes, that is my name, really. My father is Argentinian—as a matter of fact, the owner of this place. But he always loved this beautiful city and came to visit here when he was very young. When I was born, they told me that it is the reason he named me Bogota. My mother preferred Argentina, but according to them, they fought about it for many days, but in the end, like the football teams, Bogota prevailed, and Argentina lost. That is the origin of my name."

Adolf smiled. She asked again, "Well, what would you like to eat?"

He replied, "If you guys have a Spanish chorizo…" She nodded. "I want a big omelet with a lot of chorizo, bell peppers, onions, and anchovies."

Bogota grimaced in revulsion. "Very well," she said with a mischievous smile, "I love chorizo, too. But not with anchovies. All right, a glass of burgundy wine, an omelet with a lot of chorizo, onions, and anchovies."

Adolf said, "Thank you very much."

Bogota turned and left, letting her hips sway suggestively, her firm buttocks wiggling noticeably. Adolf watched her as she walked away. Bogota, as she was by the door to the kitchen, turned slightly to look back towards him to make certain he was still watching. When she saw that she had his full attention, she smiled in satisfaction that this elegant, well-dressed man had indeed been watching her. It was a boost to her ego that, though she was no longer young, she still had the power of sexual attraction.

After she went inside the kitchen, Adolf stood up, picked up his raincoat, and started to walk towards a small hallway with a sign indicating where the restrooms were in red lettering on a white background. He went inside the men's room, closing the door and double locking it. The small restroom had a single seat, a urinal, and a single stall with a toilet inside, of an old-fashioned design with the tank up top and a chain hanging down to flush.

Montauk: The Lightning Chance

He put the raincoat on top of the stall wall. Then he removed his suitcoat and put it with his outer wear. He could see a bloodstain on his expensive white linen shirt on the left sleeve. He took his tie off and put it with the rest of his other garments and proceeded to unbutton his shirt. Once it was off, he carefully put it with his other clothes, carefully making certain the bloodstain remained on top so nothing would get on the rest. He began to examine his wound. There was a small hole from a small caliber pistol. It looked like the bullet was still in the wound. He turned on the hot water faucet, letting it run for a while. He took a handful of paper towels and lined the edge of the sink with them.

Adolf pulled a switchblade knife out of his pants pocket. He pressed the button and the blade snapped out. He held the blade beneath the hot water, turning it over to make certain both sides were sterilized. Steam was visible coming off the water, and the mirror over the sink began to fog up. Once he felt he had done it long enough, he started to dig carefully into the bullet hole, attempting to extract the piece of lead from the wound. He grimaced in extreme pain for a few moments, and then took some paper towels to clear the fog off the mirror to enable him to see more clearly what he was doing.

A few minutes later of digging, the bullet finally popped out and fell into the sink, rattling around as it was caught by the drain grill. He breathed a deep sigh of relief as the water washed the bullet clean. He cleaned his wound with napkins and hot water and washed the blood out. He took a small travel bottle of Jim Beam bourbon whiskey and opened it up to pour it into his wound, groaning in pain as he did so and grimacing. He took one of his white handkerchiefs out of his back pocket and held it over his wound. He pulled a burgundy pocket kerchief out of the breast pocket of his jacket, made a triangle with it, and then wound the edges into a narrow band so that he could improvise a bandage.

When he was done, he pulled a Lugar pistol from his waistband. He checked it to make certain the magazine was full, reloaded it, and replaced it in his waistband. He took the shirt with the bloodstain on the sleeve and held it under the water to clean it as best he could with the hand soap he had. It wasn't the greatest result, but it was better than it had been. He wrung the excess water out of the shirt into the sink, dried it as best he could, and put it back on. He had almost finished dressing, and he was tying his necktie when the door handle rattled. He quickly spun out of the line of possible fire through immediate entryway of the door, pulling his pistol as he did so. Somebody knocked, but he remained silent. He heard Bogota's voice.

"Adolf? Are you OK? Are you still there? They told me you came this way towards the restrooms."

Adolf breathed a sigh of relief at that. Only then did he reply. "Yes, thank you. I'm almost finished. In fact, I'm opening the door now."

He opened the door with his raincoat draped over his arm. Bogota said with a smile, "I thought I might have scared you off, and you had escaped me through the window of the bathroom."

He smiled. "You're a very funny woman. How could it be possible for a man to run away from a woman as beautiful as you are and with such an original and distinctive name? No man could fear you—to the contrary, they should run after you."

She smiled broadly and slapped him on the arm—right on his wound. He could not control an involuntary grunt of pain and wince. As they walked together back to his table, she realized what had happened and asked, "Are you all right? Did I hurt you?"

Adolf forced a smile, but his pain still showed through it. "I fell and hurt my arm today. It's nothing serious or anything we have to worry about."

"Oh, I feel better now—I'm sorry. I didn't know you had that injury."

"Don't worry about it. You didn't know."

"Well, I served your omelet a little while ago. I hope it's still warm. If it isn't, please let me know and I can reheat it for you."

She remained by his side until he took a piece and nodded that it was all right. She smiled and went to attend her other customers. The music continued in the place, and a new pair of entertainers performed for the little crowd in the cabaret, flamenco dancers with castanets in folk attire. As he enjoyed his food and watched the stage, he realized that two policemen had entered the place. They had a picture that they referred to as they looked around at the customers. They began a table to table search, clearly looking for someone.

Adolf had nearly finished his omelet when Bogota approached him. She started to take his plate as he drank the last sip of his wine. "Do you want another glass?"

He thought about it and said, "No, I'm good." He reached into his inside jacket pocket with his right hand and pulled out a heavy gold coin with an imperial eagle on one side and a Nazi SS skull on the other. He handed it to Bogota without a word. Her eyes widened in shock.

At the same time, two men dressed in fedora hats and trench coats ran in the front door. Both had pistols drawn but pointed towards the floor. The spotlights that illuminated the main entry were directed here so that the bartender, who kept an eye on the entire area, should he see anything wrong could hit the silent alarm to alert the police. One of the men had a nasty scar running down the right side of his face. They came into the bar and hesitated, not expecting to see two uniformed police officers there. Both policemen looked up, noticed the men, and started to pull their own weapons. Without hesitating, the two newcomers gunned the policemen down.

In the few seconds while the bullets were flying, Bogota jumped onto the chair with Adolf, pressed a button under the table, which rotated around on a turntable. Bullets tore into the bottles of liquor, shattering them and spraying the bar with alcohol. The black man playing the bass fell over backwards, a bullet hole in his forehead. An empty table reappeared from the pivot point, and Bogota and Adolf found themselves in the wine cellar of the establishment. Aside from the turntable, the wall was solid brick, giving them full protection. Across the room was a window looking into an office.

Bogota said, "Wait here." She opened the door to the cellar and ran into the office to a man sitting in there. He was a short man, half bald, very well-dressed, with an aristocratic air and thick glasses, heavyset. He was in his late 50's or early 60's with a thick, neatly trimmed beard that was completely white. He was seated in a reclining chair. She went up to him and handed the coin to him. He took his glasses off, put a jeweler's loupe over his left eye to examine the coin. He stood up and walked into the wine cellar with Bogota.

He walked over to Adolf and put his right arm on the man's should. "Comrade, welcome to Colombia. You have nothing to worry about—you are in good hands. First things first. Right now, we have to get you out of here immediately. I have to take you to a secure house, and later we will ship you first class to Argentina, where we will not only be more secure but you will also have surgery on your fingerprints and a completely new identity. I can guarantee you that the damned Israelis will never find you."

Adolf smiled in gratitude. He stepped forward and extended his hand. "My name is Adolf Schüttelmayer. Thank you very much and the pleasure is all mine."

Bogota's father raised his right arm and went to shake Adolf's hand. "My name is Juan Alberto Shaniya."

They embraced affectionately. Adolf kissed Bogota on the cheek. Both men left the place through the back door into the dark alley, where there was a beautiful silver metallic 1954 Mercedes-Benz Gullwing Roadster guarded by two black men. They said good night to the men, opened the doors, and got inside while the men opened the barricades so the car could leave.

He looked at the brand-new car with a big smile. "It pleases me to see that your business is so prosperous in this country."

The Mercedes was more than a car. It was simply a symbol of intelligence and success. Alberto replied, "Thank you. Business has been great."

Several police cars were arriving as they pulled out into traffic. Adolf commented, "The Mercedes-Benz is the most impressive proof and testimony of the genetic superiority of the brains of the Aryan race". Adolf looked through the window out at the city as they drove off. As they put some distance between themselves and the poor area where the business had been established, now they entered the better, wealthier sections of Bogota.

Alberto smiled and nodded. "It is indeed, comrade."

Adolf smiled. "Now I realize why you named your daughter after this city. It's very beautiful." The difference between the place where they were before with this section was a very dark night and a sunny day. It was like another world. "Evidently the rich people in this country don't have much appetite for alcohol, eh?"

Alberto replied with a cynical smile, "Most of the people who drink alcohol do so because they want to forget their problems and misery. Rich people resolve their problems with money. They only drink in celebration and on festive days, not enough to maintain a prosperous and lucrative business in this town."

Adolf smiled, nodding in agreement. They drove silently for a while as they traveled across the picturesque and generally colonial city of Bogota. As they passed the commercial centers with their brilliant clothing displays, Adolf said, "If it's not too much trouble for you, I want to stop in one of these stores to buy one or two dress shirts. Unfortunately, in my rush to leave the place where I had been hiding, I hadn't even been able to pack the few clothes I was carrying with me." He opened his raincoat and jacket to show the bloodstain on his shirt.

Montauk: The Lightning Chance

Alberto replied, "No problem, absolutely." He stepped on the brakes, waited to make a U turn, and then drove back to a gentleman's clothes store they had just passed. "I didn't know you were wounded. I will bring a doctor who is completely trustworthy to check you out."

"No, no—that's not necessary. I already got the bullet out."

"This is in the package. It won't add any more cost to you."

"That's not the point. I don't want people to notice I have a gunshot wound."

"You don't have to worry about it," Alberto reassured him. "Remember, you are our responsibility now, and that wound could get infected. We have to take every precaution, especially when it comes to your health."

Adolf nodded. "Yes, I know. But please make sure the doctor is absolutely trustworthy. As I said, it's very obviously a bullet hole."

Alberto smiled. "Take it easy. We've been doing this for twelve years. We have never, ever lost one of our packages. Not even one. Relax. All our people are bulletproof. We can trust them 100%."

Adolf nodded. "Yes. You guys were highly recommended for the excellence of your service, the best in the business with discretion and loyalty to our cause."

Alberto parked the car, and they got out to go inside the men's store. "Thank you. Let's hope that we will continue to maintain that reputation for many years ahead and that we can regroup when the time comes for our final triumph."

Both men smiled and nodded in complete agreement. A little while later, they came out to the Mercedes with a couple of clean white shirts and continued their journey through the city.

Alberto said, "Our contact that will take you from Colombia to Argentina will be here in two days. Use this couple of days to relax and rest. His name is Adolfo Mena Gonzalez. Even though he received a large amount of money for what he's going to do, he's one of us. That means he's one of the loyal followers of the Führer, prepared to lose his life in order to protect yours. That's something we cannot find these days with all the money in the world." They both shook their heads.

"When he takes you to your final destination, then and only then will you be giving him the same coin you gave to me." He reached into his jacket pocket and held up the coin he had been given. "That is how he will collect his fee later on. You don't have to pay a dime for anything. We cover all the expenses. This is part of the agreement and our job so you don't have to carry anything with you that could compromise you like large amounts of money. It's all part of the package." He shook his head with a smile. "The irony of all this is, I believe, is that you guys should stop using pseudonyms based on the Führer's. The moment could come that we'll have to relocate *him*, because he might not be dead, like we've been led to believe, and that could be a huge tragedy."

Adolf smiled, this time mischievously as if he had secret information. He said, "Why a tragedy? Remember, there doesn't exist a better hiding place these days than to hide in plain sight." Alberto glanced at him a little incredulously, and then both of them laughed and nodded.

A few minutes later they arrived at a tall, elegant skyscraper in one of the most luxurious neighborhoods in the city. Alberto entered a code for the gate leading into an underground parking garage, and they drove down. They parked and went into an elevator marked "Penthouse Only." Alberto pulled a special key out of his pocket, similar in design to a safety deposit box key. He entered it to the keyhole outside the elevator door. They entered and went straight up to the penthouse on the 19th floor.

The doors opened into the middle of the living room. It was a beautiful space with a white baby grand piano with a polar bear run, head still attached, beneath the piano. Alberto smiled in satisfaction at seeing Adolf's admiration as the other man looked around at the beautiful statues, Picasso artwork, and all the other tasteful décor. He showed Adolf the magnificent double freezer with attached refrigerator and what looked like a commercial bar, he indicated the vast quantity of food laid in: ham, cheese, veal, all wrapped in an organized fashion in the freezer. The central bar was full of bowls with different fruits and a wine rack in the kitchen filled with bottles of the most expensive wine and champagne. After he showed the whole place and explained how to use the key and intercom, Alberto handed Adolf the elevator key. "The only way in and out of this place is that elevator. Remember the code: the new Buenos Aires of gold."

Alberto showed Adolf the intercom button that would allow him to buzz anyone in from that panel. "We probably will not see each other for some time." He opened his arms. "You have a great trip and I hope we see each other again when our day comes, and we can be on top of the world once more." They embraced. "Remember, your contact will be here in two days. I will call you one hour before he arrives so that you'll be ready to leave."

"Thank you." Adolf replied.

Montauk: The Lightning Chance

The next day, Adolf got up and prepared a good breakfast to eat with champagne. He had finished when the buzzer on the elevator sounded. He was watching the local news on the television. He jumped out of his chair in surprise since he wasn't expecting anyone. He walked over to the table, picked up his pistol, and checked his watch. It was only 8:30 in the morning. He didn't know who would be buzzing the door at that hour. He put the pistol in his waist and walked over to the intercom. "Yes, who is it?"

A man's voice replied, "Good morning, Mr. Adolf. I was sent by the New Buenos Aires of gold. My name is Dr. Emilio del Marmol. I believe you and I have a scheduled visit today. If it's too early for you, that's not a problem. I can come back a little later."

Adolf replied, "No, not at all. Come in, please. Step into the elevator. I'll buzz you up." As he spoke, he pressed the buzzer, and down below Emilio saw the elevator doors open.

"Thank you. I will be with you in a few seconds."

"All right. I'm here waiting for you."

Emilio stepped into the elevator. Adolf began to clean the table where he had just eaten his breakfast so his guest wouldn't see a mess. After he took the dirty dishes and placed them in the kitchen sink, he returned and sat down in the same chair he had been using in front of the television, where he had been reclining in comfort in the La-Z-Boy.

After a few minutes, the bell on the elevator pinged and the elevator doors opened, announcing the arrival of someone in the penthouse. Adolf didn't even stand up. He just signaled with his right arm, waving the doctor over. "Doctor, come in."

Emilio walked over to Adolf, his medical bag with his name embossed on it in hand, typical in design for the time, a leather back with handles of the same material forming a loop on each side of the bag for handholds. Metal hinges provided both a structure for the opening of the bag as well as a locking mechanism to hold it open without fuss. After formal introductions, Emilio set his bag down on the dinette table and opened it. He said, "Well, if you don't mind, please, could you remove your shirt and undershirt? I have been informed that you have a bullet wound in your left arm." Adolf removed his shirt and undershirt as requested; as he did so, Emilio turned on the hot water in the wet bar's sink, removed several instruments and placed them in the sink under the water. He pulled out and carefully folded a sterilized towel to lay the instruments on once they were themselves sterilized. He hung a stethoscope around his neck, pulled one of the chairs at the table out, and said, "Please, sit here if you don't mind. If you need some pillows to make your back comfortable, do so, since we'll be here several minutes while I check the condition of your wound and the extent of the injury."

Emilio took his pulse, measured his blood pressure, and listened to the strength of Adolf's heartbeat with the stethoscope. He put a thermometer in Adolf's mouth to record his temperature. Several minutes later, after he had finished his preliminary checks, Emilio said, "You have no fever, your pulse is normal and in order, your blood pressure, too. This is in general a good sign that you so far are in good shape."

Adolf smiled proudly and nodded. "I told Juan Alberto that this wound is nothing to worry about, something of no importance. Just superficial, not even a reason to bother you, doctor, but he was the one worried, not me. I've been in more difficult situations, even on the border of death, and my body came back into shape without any difficulties."

Emilio smiled. "Remember, nevertheless, always it is prudent to get a professional opinion. Let me explore your wound. That will determine my final diagnosis. Without seeing it, you could be in great shape today and die tomorrow." He smirked slightly at Adolf's worried reaction. As he opened the bandages, he asked, "Who cleaned the wound?"

"Oh, a doctor friend of mine, but he did it in a rush," Adolf lied.

Emilio put rubber gloves on and applied a little pressure on the skin around the wound gently. Immediately a slightly yellow, pus-filled liquid began to spurt out of the wound. Emilio shook his head discouragingly. "Whoever pulled that bullet out of your arm should not practice medicine anymore. You don't bandage such a deep puncture without putting in a drainage bandage so that the infected pus can drain out of this wound."

Adolf grimaced unpleasantly. It was clear he was not completely certain what Emilio was talking about, so Emilio went on to explain, "This wound needs to be disinfected at once. We'll probably have to remove some of the tissue around the border and probably open the wound at the surface so we can thoroughly clean the tissue that has died in the past forty-eight hours. After I finish, I'll probably have to put some stitches on it."

Adolf looked puzzled. "Such a small wound, like this one? I cannot explain that."

Montauk: The Lightning Chance

Emilio patiently replied, "Yes, sir—granted, it is a very small wound in diameter. But it's very deep. Whoever pulled that bullet out forgot to remove the small fragments carried into the wound with it. This bullet was the type that had a small explosive charge to create small shrapnel in the wound. It's not a commonly used type; this projectile is especially designed not to wound the victim but to kill him. As I said, on impact it releases smaller bullets—they frequently cause additional internal damage. They are difficult to locate and produce as a secondary effect a massive infection. A small bullet like this does not commonly kill the victim. Most doctors don't have enough experience to look for the smaller fragments and leave them behind in the person's body." He removed his gloves and dropped them in the trash container near the wall of the dining room. He rubbed his forehead in obvious concern.

Adolf said, "What do you need to do? I'll do whatever you feel is necessary."

Emilio said, "I have everything necessary in my bag to successfully perform this surgery without having to go to a hospital. I have local anesthetic so that you won't have to suffer. I might administer another kind intravenously which might make you drowsy, but you won't fully go to sleep: it's not a full general. When Juan Alberto told me that you have a small bullet wound in your arm, I prepared myself for the worst." He took a deep breath. "This is not the first time I've had the opportunity to confront this kind of projectile. This is common and very much used by the Israeli intelligence. I can assure you 100% that whoever shot you had the premediated motive that you would not survive this. Ninety percent of the time, as I said before, those small bullets get left behind in the body. By the time they get discovered, it's too late in most cases. The patient dies, like you said, from a simple, tiny, little bullet that didn't even damage any internal organs. They cannot explain to themselves how this is possible."

Adolf had sweat on his forehead as he listened. He nodded. "Very well, doctor, let's do this. What do you need from me?"

"Like I told you before, put your arm on top of the table, relax, and lie back in your chair. I'll inject you with the one anesthetic that will make you groggy. I've been sterilizing my instruments in hot water, so now I'll dry and organize them while we wait for it to take full effect. I will also inject it around your wound so that the wound itself will be thoroughly numbed while I look for those fragments."

Adolf was very nervous now, and asked in a worried tone, "Will this take much time, doctor?"

Dr. Julio Antonio del Marmol

"It all depends on how difficult the fragments are to find. We don't have X-ray equipment here, so we'll have to do it the old way: explore and probe until everything is clean. That's why I need to open the wound more, so that I can ensure that I leave nothing behind. The most appropriate way to do this is to take you to a hospital for an X-ray of your arm, but I know in your case this is not an option. We'll do what we have to do due to the circumstances." As he spoke, he put on a fresh pair of gloves. Not wanting to see what was being done, Adolf turned his face away to watch the TV while Emilio worked. Emilio tied a rubber band around Adolf's arm before inserting the needle into the arm. After shooting the anesthetic into the vein and noting that Adolf wasn't watching, Emilio carefully unscrewed the syringe and replaced it with an empty vial, carefully drawing some blood into it. After he had filled the vial, he unscrewed it and plugged it with a towel while he replaced it with another ampule of anesthetic, which he then shot into the arm. He wrapped his handkerchief around the vial and carefully concealed in inside the breast pocket of his jacket.

Emilio pulled forceps out of his bag. One at a time, he placed the instruments that had been lying in boiling water onto the towel with them. Once he had cleaned his instruments carefully, he looked at Adolf and saw it was time to go to work. He sat down and started to open the wound in an X pattern with a scalpel.

One after another, he eventually probed around and removed six fragments from Adolf's arm. The entire procedure took nearly two hours. The entire time Adolf kept his eyes fixed on the television so that he couldn't see what was going on. To his credit, he made not one sound or uttered a complaint, even when Emilio was digging deep into the wound in his search for fragments.

When Emilio had finished suturing the wound and cleaned the area with alcohol, he showed Adolf a container with the six small metal fragments. "Six! I was only expecting two or three."

"You didn't have to tell me," Adolf replied. "I was counting the clink each time you dropped one into that metal bowl." He looked at Emilio gratefully. "Every single day of our lives, if we're smart enough, we learn something. Thank you very much, Dr. del Marmol."

Emilio gave him a small smile in reply. "No need to. I was just doing my duty as a practitioner and for honor to do a good job."

Adolf reached into his pants with his right hand and pulled out another of the gold coins like he had given Bogota. "This is not a payment. It is a token of gratitude."

Montauk: The Lightning Chance

"No, no—under no circumstance can I accept that. It's too much. Besides, Juan Alberto already paid me in advance, and the payment was very generous, so that I would also maintain absolute silence and confidentiality for what I did here today. It's not necessary for you to reward me again. I believe he also told you that this is part of the package and should not cost you a single penny more."

Adolf insisted and pushed the coin into Emilio's hand. "This is a personal gratuity from me to you, not only because you saved my life but also because you taught me something that I didn't know until today. That alone is worth this payment and more—it might enable me to save the life of somebody else. I didn't know about this new technology, bullets of very low caliber that our enemies are using in order to be certain that their targets don't survive their attacks. You do what you want to do with this coin when you get out of this building but keep it now so that I feel like I did the right thing." Adolf dropped it into Emilio's breast pocket of the white sport coat.

Realizing he had no other choice but to accept it, he said, "Thank you very much."

Both men walked to the elevator, and after Emilio thanked Adolf once more for his generosity, Adolf replied, "It's not enough. You deserve a lot more, like I said before."

The door to the elevator closed. Emilio put his medical bag on the floor and carefully checked the walls with both hands for hidden cameras. Only then did he pull the vial of blood out of his coat and open his bag. He pulled out a wooden box for samples, opened it, and inserted the vial. After closing the box, he carefully replaced it into his bag, closed it, and waited for the doors to open. The small light counted down until the G for "garage" lit up and the doors opened. He got out and walked towards his car, a white 1927 Mercedes-Benz convertible SSK with a red interior.

He opened the passenger door and carefully put his bag in the front passenger's seat. He walked around behind his car to the driver's side. He opened the door and sat down behind the wheel. He closed the door and leaned over to the right. Very carefully, he opened the bag and removed the vial with the blood sample. He mixed the entire vial in with a sodium fluoride solution in a test tube, which would preserve the blood and act as an anticoagulant.

This was the key evidence in identifying if that man was really Adolf Hitler in disguise or one of his doubles. Another container in his box of samples had a test tube with something that looked like semen floating in the solution.

After he closed the box of samples, he carefully put in a secure place in the bottom of his bag. He started his car and drove out of the underground garage into the city. He checked his Pate Phillip wristwatch since he had another important appointment to make. As he drove through the city traffic, he noticed a car that changed lanes when he did and otherwise duplicated his maneuvers. He got the strange feeling that he was being followed. To make sure he wasn't overreacting and being paranoid, he changed lanes several times and took a very sharp turn to force the car behind him to be obvious. It was a black 1954 Ford Thunderbird, and it certainly was following him.

He saw an alley to his right, a truck entry for a loading dock further in. Before the car turned the corner, he shot into that access alley. It looked like a flea market or a street bazaar on the other end. He drove through the market slowly for a few minutes to the other end of the ramp for the loading bay of the warehouse which formed one of the buildings bordering this market square. He stopped halfway up the ramp without turning off his engine, keeping an eye in the rearview mirror to see if the Thunderbird had followed him.

He took the opportunity of having that empty alley to try and hide himself to shake off his pursuers. His luck was so great that a truck full of chicken cages pulled in behind him and began to unload its cargo. He was camouflaged from immediate view but could still see the traffic crossing in the street behind through the wire of the chicken cages and saw the Thunderbird pass by. He sat there patiently, waiting for the truck driver to finish his job and leave.

As they removed the chicken cages, however, his camouflage gradually disappeared. It didn't take much time evidently for the black Thunderbird to go around the block, and then spot his car in front of the truck. They pulled over, and he saw in the rear mirror a man and a woman, both with pistols in their hand, get out of the car and start walking toward him.

This proved beyond any doubt to him what the intentions of these two individuals were. Unfortunately, he realized now that he was the one in a trap. He could not back up because of the truck, and he could only go into the warehouse by driving forward. As they approached, the man yelled, "Get out of the car right now!"

He saw no other alternative as he watched the two approaching him: he drove his car into the warehouse to do what he had been trained for as a master spy. He floored the accelerator so that he shot up the ramp. People carrying boxes jumped out of the way as he blew his air horn and ran for their lives, leaving behind boxes of vegetables and produce to get out of his way. When he reached the entrance to the warehouse itself, he went airborne, smashing through bottles of water and soda, avoiding whatever he could and outright hitting whatever he couldn't.

The pair ran after him, shooting at his car. Two bullets went into the trunk, sparks flying as the bullets struck the steel body. Between the hail of bullets and panicked people running, the two went to their knees like professional marksmen and took more careful aim before firing. Like professional assassins, they shot with precision, but Emilio was zigzagging through the warehouse, making it difficult for them to aim. Between the car and the bullets, bottles of various liquids were shattered and splattering everywhere.

He finally came up to what appeared to be a wall. He slammed on his brakes, and his tires squealed in protest. The man yelled again, "There's no way out of this place! You'd better give up, or you'll die here today."

Emilio kept revving his engine as he spotted an opening set of rolling bay doors. He didn't wait, he turned the wheel hard to the left and accelerated towards the doors. Just outside the door was another ramp for the loading of merchandise, but there was no way out there, as there was already a truck on the ramp. There was also a raised platform ninety degrees from the loading ramp that semi-trucks would back up to so that merchandise could be unloaded directly from the cargo module. A semi was in the process of making the turn to back up to that ramp, and Emilio slammed his hand onto the horn. The driver of the semi slammed on his brakes, wondering what was wrong, and Emilio's car flew into the air over the platform, metal screeching in protest as he scraped both the warehouse wall on one side and the rear of the semi's cargo module on the other side, barely fitting in the gap. It was enough, and so he shot through it. He slammed down hard onto the pavement, more sparks flying up beneath him. He turned into the traffic in the street, as it turned out on the opposite side of the warehouse. He drove several blocks to put plenty of distance between himself and his pursuers. He pulled into a service station that had multicolored banners advertising an assortment of cars for sale. They were even offering a special that month for body work. He only wanted to assess the damage to his car and refill his gas tank.

The attendant was a man of middling height, completely white hair with a matching moustache and thick-lensed glasses. As he pumped the gas, he cleaned the car's windshield. He clucked his tongue as he looked at the damage. "What a pity to see the paint damage to your beautiful car."

"It just happened not even fifteen minutes ago," Emilio replied. "I scraped it against a couple of big semis."

The attendant saw the medical bag in the front seat with Emilio's name on it. "Is that your bag, doctor?"

"Yes, my friend." His tone was friendly but, being a spy, he was cautious. It was a little suspicious for this guy to be curious about the bag.

The man held out his hand in a friendly fashion. "My name is Israel."

Emilio smiled at the irony, assuming that it was Israeli intelligence that was after him. Maintaining his calm, he took the offered hand and said, "How much do I owe you, Israel?"

Israel smiled but did not answer. Instead, he said, "I'm one of the owners of this establishment. We specialize in work like this." He patted the damaged body. "We have a monthly special going right now, exceptionally low prices. In the time we repair your car, you can choose whichever car we have here on the lot and use it for however long it takes for the work to be done, without a single penny added to the cost."

Emilio was a little more relaxed at the sales pitch. He looked Israel in the eyes, keeping his antennae up as he tried to assess what the man's actual thoughts were. As he thought about the offer that was just made, he used the opportunity to think how good it could be to immediately change the car right there. Israel, like a good salesman, saw that Emilio was thinking about it. He tried to close the deal right there. "You are a very elegant, educated, and refined man. You should not be driving around this city in a car in this condition." He added with a small smile, "The car we drive is the best business card for our customers. For you, it could be the worst image for your patients."

This time, Emilio smiled, knowing and accepting the indisputable talent for sales that Israel possessed, from attendant to a gas station to rapidly move ahead to first class salesman. He scratched the back of his neck and started to walk towards the cars parked in the lot, a large smile on his face. He thought that this man must have been put there by God to save him from his situation.

Montauk: The Lightning Chance

Emilio said, "How long do you think it will take to fix my car, and what is your best price?"

Israel grinned from ear to ear at having a sale to close. "For you, today, only 80 pesos. No more than two days in order to make it a particularly good job, immaculate. It will be like brand new when you come back to pick it up."

Emilio took his time looking at a Series 80L Chrysler Imperial convertible roadster. It was a red car with a beige interior and white-walled tires. He asked, "Can I take this one?"

Israel replied, "Remember what I said—whatever car you like best you can use for the few days it takes for me to repair your car."

He put his right hand on the Chrysler and said, "OK, you have a deal. I'll take this one."

Israel immediately picked up the medical bag and brought it over to the Chrysler. "Careful!" Emilio cautioned.

"I know—you have delicate medical instruments in here."

"Not just that—I have some blood samples in there, too." Israel finished carefully putting the bag in the car. Emilio took his personal things and a few bottles of juice and water while Israel finished up and wrote out a receipt. "How much do I owe you for the gas?"

"Don't worry about it, a couple of pesos. I'll add it to your bill when you come back. The car you are taking is completely full of gas, and that's also on the house. You don't have to bring it back the same way."

Emilio was impressed with how good a deal this was. It seemed like the best thing that happened to him that day was to stop at this service station, perhaps as recompense for the bad time he had just endured. Whoever was looking for him would now be completely thrown off with him driving a different car. He checked his watch once more to be certain of the time. He was running late for his previous arrangement. It was around 12:30, right after noon. There was a beautiful tropical sun shining on the prosperous city of Bogota.

As Emilio drove out of the station, he kept his eyes in the rearview mirror. He knew in his heart the possibilities of being recognized or found by his enemies would be extremely remote now, especially with so many people and driving a different car. But his spy instincts many times clashed with his own logic as well as those of other normal people. These instincts had saved his life many times before, and he was not about to abandon them now. He was like an old dog, with a lot of experience and a master of different tricks as to how and where he could defend his bones from other dogs that wanted to take them.

His instincts took him safely to the end of every mission he had been running around the world. He didn't want to start down a different track than what he had been doing all his life. He saw a building in the middle of the city and identified it. He drove into the underground parking lot in a commercial zone. Once he found a spot and parked his new acquisition, he looked at it admiringly before walking off with his medical bag in hand. He walked towards the elevators.

A group of young students were waiting for the elevator as he approached. They stepped back when the door opened to allow people out of the compartment, and then rushed in. He followed them, noticing that one of the students had already punched his number, 2, which was a terrace with restaurants surrounding the open-air plaza. All of them got out of the elevator then, Emilio following last.

People ate around the plaza in peace on that sunny day. At one table, with a glass pitcher full of iced tea and two glasses set before him, his old friend and confident, Mr. Xiang, waited. Also present was a valuable new contact within the organization that tried to protect the high-level Nazi criminals and relocate them around Central and South America or the Caribbean Islands. They did not know that Bogota and her father were Emilio's contacts or that the New Buenos Aires was where Emilio and his counter espionage network operated, taking the exact location of where those people were to be relocated.

Emilio looked at his watch and saw that he was nearly half an hour late for his meeting. He put his medical bag on one of the chairs and said with a sad face, "I have to apologize to you guys before anything for being so late. It was beyond my control."

Both Xiang and Bogota, with small smiles on their faces, waved it away. Bogota said, "Don't worry about it, Dr. del Marmol. We know how difficult it is to move in this city, especially at this hour when everyone is coming out for lunch."

Xiang, with his glass of tea in his left hand smiled and waved the apology off.

Emilio looked around, scanning the crowd slowly as if he were taking pictures of the entire area. Xiang, after knowing him for so many years, put his glass of tea on the table and held his hand before his mouth so that anyone who might be watching would not be able to read his lips. He looked at Emilio intensely and asked, "What happened?"

Montauk: The Lightning Chance

Emilio returned the look and held his hand to his mouth for the same reason and answered, "Somebody attempted to take my life not too long ago. Something unexpected. That's the real reason I got here late."

Xiang asked, "Problems with the wounded Nazi?"

Emilio shook his head but could not answer because a young waiter came over to take their order, interrupting the conversation. Emilio ordered the same jasmine tea they had as well as a plate of almond biscuits.

Once the waiter had left, Bogota couldn't wait any longer and asked, "This attempt was before or after you attended to the wound of Adolf?"

"After," Emilio replied. "On my way to come here to see you guys."

Bogota put her hand on her forehead and squeezed it in confusion. After a few seconds, she muttered to herself in a near whisper, "Hm, hm, hm. Very strange. Very strange."

Mr. Xiang asked, "What are you saying?"

She repeated it and added, "I was talking to myself. This is very weird. The only two people that had knowledge that Dr. del Marmol was going to see Adolf were my father and me. Nobody else, absolutely, knew about this. That leaves only the possibility that whoever took that shot at you was probably sent by Adolf's own security, to put you down, probably without leaving any witnesses. If this man is who we really think he is, whether he's a double or a clone of the Führer, it's possible. Even if he's had cosmetic surgery, the resemblance is very close. If that is the case, they won't want to leave any traces. His protectors, in order to keep his identity completely sealed, will go to any extreme."

Emilio held his chin in thought and nodded. "Yes. It's a good theory. If nobody except you and your father had any knowledge of my visit to that place this morning, the only reasonable, logical explanation for this attempt could only be attributed to what you just said. Unfortunately, logic sometimes is not applicable or even close in our crazy work of espionage." The waiter returned with an empty glass for Emilio and a plate of biscuits. He refilled the pitcher with more iced tea.

After the waiter left, Emilio leaned on the table with his left arm and rubbed his forehead with the fingers of that hand. His face was sad. "Unless whatever is not logical in my imagination becomes an irrefutable reality...." He didn't finish his sentence as a terrible thought struck him. Very slowly, he reached out with his right arm to grab Bogota's arm, who looked at him nervously because of the strange way he was staring at her, "Did your father know that you came to meet with us today?"

"Of course. He even told me to give you his greetings."

Emilio, still with his hand on her arm, his left hand still rubbing his forehead, let go of her and put it back over his mouth. "Please maintain your calm. If I'm not seeing illusions, I see a little glint of light from the sun in one of the windows about half a block away in that tall building. If my instincts haven't failed, I think we're all in very imminent danger."

Mr. Xiang and Bogota looked at him in concern. Without showing any expression on their faces but with their eyes. Mr. Xiang, who had worked by Emilio's side for so long, knew that such a statement would never be made unless he was convinced that what he said was true.

Bogota asked as she covered her mouth, "What do you want us to do, Doctor? Please, let us know."

Emilio nonchalantly filled his glass from the pitcher of iced tea. He picked a biscuit up from the plate. "When I count to three, we all stand up at the same time. We will run in different directions. In case they want to shoot, it will be very difficult for them to decide which to shoot first and increase the chances of the others getting out of here alive. Do you understand?" They nodded. "Then we will meet at 10 tomorrow morning at Location number 10." He looked directly at Bogota. "I don't want you to tell anyone—*anyone*—that we are meeting tomorrow or where or when."

Both Bogota and Mr. Xiang nodded. "The most important thing is that we put the samples I have in the test tubes in a safe place. Not only the blood sample I just took from Adolf, but also the semen sample that our people took from the vagina of a prostitute in Spain that he slept with. They need to go to the lab immediately. Let's hope they're a match to our target. I have both in my medical bag. When we get up from the table, I will take the bag. Mr. Xiang, I want you to run, but double back to meet me in the back by the elevators after we get under cover inside the building. Bogota, I want you to run in a third direction, but meet us as well by the elevators. Mr. Xiang will take the samples directly to the lab without stopping anywhere for anything or anyone. This is a basic plan. Let's hope that nothing happens. If something does, we'll change plans. But if that individual that I saw in the window with the tinted glass to my left doesn't make his move, then we'll know that my instincts aren't accurate. This glint could be sunlight reflecting off the lens of a

Montauk: The Lightning Chance

pair of binoculars or it could be off the telescopic sight of a sniper rifle. That's why I don't want to take a chance and stay here a single moment longer like sitting ducks. The worst scenario is if that man behind the window is not intending to assassinate us at this exact moment, there's a possibility that he's observing us to do it later. Nevertheless, where did he get his information about our meeting, at this precise time and place? We have to take that into consideration as well as the attempt that was made on my life earlier today. How did they know the route I would take after leaving Adolf to come to you? When we mix all these ingredients together, we unfortunately come up with a fish sandwich with a lot of bones." He shook his head, clearly disturbed. "Unfortunately, all of this craziness has become an integral part of our lives in espionage."

When he was finished speaking, he picked up his napkin and shook it like he was shaking crumbs off, wiped his mouth, and put it down on the table, one corner hanging off the edge. "OK, are you guys ready?" They both nodded slightly. Emilio took out the gold coin Adolf had given him and handed it to Bogota as a distraction for their watcher. He said in a very soft voice, "Tell your father that this coin was given to me by Adolf as a gratuity for my good work. But because your father paid me in advance, I don't think it's appropriate that I keep it."

Bogota looked at him, admiring his honesty. With a small smile, she said, also in a low voice, "Honesty is a great virtue possessed only by beings of great truthful spiritual values."

Emilio returned the smile. "Thank you, but that is the proper thing to do. I don't think it's anything to be proud of." He leaned back slightly in his chair, reaching out for his medical bag. "OK, ready? One. Two. Three!"

They all stood up and just before they started to run, three shots rang out in succession. The first one shattered the pitcher of iced tea, spraying the substance all over them while more tea ran across the table to pour down the sides. To the terrified eyes of everyone around, the second shot went right across Mr. Xiang's white coat, not hitting him but burning a black line in the material to show its passage. The shot continued and went instead into the face of a young female Asian student that was sitting right behind them. The third shot, unfortunately, went right into the left arm of Bogota as she reached out to accept the coin from Emilio.

She made no sound save for a grunt of pain and grimaced. Instead of running as they had planned, all three dove behind one of the tables which had been overturned by people scattering in panic. Emilio, as fast as the bullets raining down on them, yanked down the napkin he had left on the table. He folded it several times and handed it to Bogota, instructing her, "Put this over that wound and apply strong pressure to it, all the pressure you can, so we can prevent you from losing too much blood." He turned to Xiang. "Are you wounded?"

Xiang shook his head. "No, no—the bullet just crossed in front of me quite close." He showed the singe mark. "The bullet meant for me killed that poor girl at the next table." He pointed at the unfortunate student. They saw that the hole in her cheek was quite small.

Emilio said, "Yes, it looks like, thanks to God, that we moved just in time at the exact moment that sniper started to fire. The bullet for me is what hit the iced tea pitcher. When we changed position, fortunately for us, we took him by surprise. I think that one hit that other girl." They looked toward where Emilio had pointed, and there was another female student who was sitting under the table next to her dead friend, crying. It looked like she had an injury in her arm, blood pouring from the wound. She looked around in absolute terror.

"They wanted to kill all three of us simultaneously," Emilio continued. "It looks like my instincts were true." He opened his medical bag. He removed the small container with the test tubes containing the blood and semen samples. He said to Xiang. "I believe it's time to change our plan. We must throw off this sniper. You will take the samples directly to the lab. That is evidently what they are after." He turned to Bogota. "You will be running in a zigzag pattern in the opposite direction, but you will double back and meet me by the elevators. I want you to come with me to my safe house. That way I can attend to the wound in your arm. It may look like nothing serious, but it has the signature of the same people who tried to kill Adolf. Maybe even the ones who tried to kill me today."

Bogota and Mr. Xiang nodded in agreement. The firing had stopped for the moment. Emilio held up his arm to gesture for them to wait for a moment and not get into the open. They all knew the sniper might be waiting for the opportunity to make a killing shot. They waited behind the tables while everyone else ran around in panic.

"We have to be patient," Emilio repeated. "The sniper knows he'll have to leave his position very soon for his own security, but he'll try to stretch it the most he can to take advantage of our own instinct of self-preservation. He's expecting us to run from the danger like normal people. That is why he's waiting until the last second; that's the only way he can complete his job and collect for his work. Whoever is behind this and sent him to do this job won't be content with these results: only one of us wounded and that only a flesh wound. That's why we cannot move and must be very patient. He is behind a window and waiting until the last possible second he can for his final opportunity to put us down with his next three shots."

On the terrace people were screaming and running from one end to the other. In the distance sirens of police cars could be heard, and they grew nearer. Emilio smiled at the sound as he imagined what was going through the sniper's mind at that moment. The sirens were the first signal to the sniper that his time had come to an end. Using his own instinct of self-preservation, he would have to withdraw from his position. This was now a crime scene and it was the last place he wanted to be when the authorities arrived. Out of nowhere more shots rang out, peppering the tables, moving some chairs around and splinters flying up from the wooden tables. Emilio smiled again at this display of nervousness and anxiety from the sniper. "He's trying to flush us out. He only has seconds left." He kept his hand up to hold his friends.

The sirens sounded like they were entering the underground garage. Emilio opened his medical bag. He moved a few things aside until he found a long object wrapped in navy blue velvet. His expression was happy; clearly, he had found what he was looking for. He unwrapped it and revealed a silencer. He closed the bag and handed it back to Bogota. He pulled a Browning high-powered semi-automatic 9mm pistol from his waistband. He screwed the silencer onto his pistol and started to count with his left hand. "One, two, three—go! Now!!" He took the medical bag from Bogota's hands, put it on top of one of the tables, and braced his right arm over it, keeping himself covered as best he could. He closed his right eye and took aim over towards the window he had previously seen the glint. He began a nonstop barrage of pistol fire towards that window. Only two shots were returned from the sniper, poorly aimed as the shots hit the concrete by Mr. Xiang's feet as he ran. Emilio's fire confused the sniper. All the bullets fired by Emilio struck the window of the building, breaking the thick glass. Even from a half block away one could see the reflected sunlight off the shower of small pieces of broken tempered glass raining down.

Curtains blew in the wind out of the shattered window. Now that there was no glass in that window, he could clearly see the silhouette of a man with a rifle in hand that was trying to look for cover as Emilio continued firing until his magazine was spent. More secure, Emilio stood up behind the table. He braced his pistol over his left arm as he tried to shoot the form directly. The sniper tried to run for his life. Without the window shielding the sniper from immediate view, he was exposed to fire himself. Once the last bullet was fired, Emilio removed the empty magazine, put it in his pocket, and slapped a fresh one in its place. However, he didn't see any more movement; he ceased fire.

All he could see in those windows were the curtains billowing out in the breeze. As soon as he saw the danger was over, he took a napkin from the table left by Mr. Xiang, folded it several times, and went over to the injured student. He gave it to her and instructed her to put it on the wound and apply the most pressure she could after he examined it. "The ambulance will be here shortly." The poor girl looked at him in panic as she noticed his gun. "It's only a superficial wound, you'll be OK." She continued to look at him with an expression of gratitude mixed with terror.

She said in a shaking voice, "God bless you, thank you very much. You can go without any worries. I didn't see or hear anything." Her lips trembled with fear as she tried to reassure Emilio that he had nothing to worry about with her.

Emilio smiled without believing a single word of her protestations. He didn't care whether she said anything; he had nothing to worry about himself. His only concern was to get out of there and regroup with Bogota and Mr. Xiang. He also urgently wanted Xiang to manage to make his delivery to the lab in one piece. He picked up his medical bag and scoured his surroundings. He double-checked the window in that building. Apparently, the sniper had either been wounded or already vacated that building.

Walking at a normal pace, concealing his pistol under his jacket, he walked towards the elevators where he was to meet with Bogota. When he got there, he wordlessly gestured to Bogota to follow him. Instead of taking the elevators, they went down the stairs, just in case.

When they reached the floor where he had parked, he went to the passenger's side of the Chrysler and opened the door for her. Bogota sat down, and he asked, "How are you doing? How do you feel?"

"A little nervous, but I'm not in any pain." Given the circumstance, she added, "This is the first time I've been shot. I don't feel any pain at all, just the occasional throb."

Emilio opened his bag and pulled out two bottles of pills. He shook two pills out of each bottle into his hand. He opened the glove compartment and removed a small bottle of mango juice. He handed her the pills and bottle. "Drink this. It's an anti-hemorrhagic medication so that your blood will quickly coagulate and prevent you from losing too much blood. The other is a pain killer, just in case. If you don't have any right now, you will definitely be in pain later."

Bogota nodded. "Thank you." She took the pills and noticed Emilio pulling the gun from his waist, checking it and removing the empty magazine from his pocket. He replaced it with two new ones. "What are you going to do?" She asked.

"I will try to intercept the sniper. At the very least I want to get close enough to him to see his face. I want to know next time who it is that's trying to put us down so that he can't catch us by surprise anymore. Then we can leave here. You're secure with me. Nobody knows about this car. It will be impossible for anyone to find you here. You're sure you'll be OK if I leave you here for a few hours?"

"Don't worry about it. Go and find that man and see if you can kill him." She lifted her skirt, revealing a pistol strapped to the thigh of one of her legs.

"Thank you. This is for your own security. We have to try and get this guy, so please don't move from here. This car is completely secure as a safehouse. Nobody can connect this car or any of us."

She nodded. "OK, OK. Go. Take it easy. I'll be OK. I won't move from here until you come back with the head of that wannabe assassin."

They both smiled. Emilio closed his medical bag and put it in the trunk of the car. He returned with the keys and put them in the ignition switch. "If I'm not back in two hours, you go to the safehouse. The name of the place is Culper XX. You know what I'm talking about."

"Yes."

"I'll see you there a little later. This is just in case if this takes me longer than I had told you."

"Very well."

Emilio left the parking lot and walked directly to the elevators. He entered the first car that presented itself and went back up to Level 2. When the doors opened again onto the scene of the crime, he observed the building and terrace from his position, studying the situation to avoid going into the crime scene but at the same time going towards the building. He pointed towards it and counted each floor down. Eight floors. He turned and watched the police and people milling around. He disappeared into the crowd and went into the elevator, punching the button to take him to the lobby.

When the doors opened, he left it and walked across the lobby rapidly, but not too fast, and exited the structure. Outside, he picked up the pace, walking towards the structure with the tinted glass. He pulled his handkerchief out of one of the back pockets in his pants and wiped the perspiration from his forehead. He passed through the crowd of people in the street, crossing to the other side of the road. When he got close to the building, his shoes began to crunch on the pieces of glass. He looked up, double checking that he was in the right place. He could see the curtains above his head still doing their dance in the breeze.

The building turned out to be a luxury hotel. A uniformed doorman greeted him. He was powerfully built with a thin beard. "Do you need any help with your luggage, sir?" noting Emilio's light gray pants, shoes that matched in color, white linen dress shirt, gray tie with white stripes, and a white sports jacket. He wore a white panama hat with a gray bandana. His attire was perfect for that place.

"No, thank you. My assistant will probably need it. She's coming behind me, and you can help her."

"Very good, sir." He opened the door for Emilio. "Whatever you need, sir, I'm at your service here."

He looked at the doorman's name tag: Carlos Martinez Gallardo. "Thank you, Carlos."

Carlos gave him a little polite bow and closed the door behind Emilio. Emilio walked over to the registration desk. He casually changed direction to mix in with the rest of the guests and then headed towards the hotel elevators.

The doors opened and Emilio walked in. He pressed the button for the Eighth Floor. Some men came in behind him, speaking in Ukrainian amongst themselves. He understood enough to know they were talking about the danger behind the possibility that Hitler was still alive, and the Nazis might try to regroup in South and Central America, which would be a tragedy for the world to see him ever in power again. Peace would never settle in the world until everyone knew for sure that Hitler was in fact dead.

Emilio tipped his hat to them to indicate his agreement with them, and he watched them as they got out on the fifth floor. An ancient lady entered after them with a small Yorkie. "Eighth Floor, please," she started to say, and then noticing that it was already punched, she smiled and picked the Yorkie up in her arms. The elevator doors closed and continued its ascent.

Montauk: The Lightning Chance

When they reached the eighth floor, Emilio waited patiently until the lady had exited and then walked in the opposite direction from which she had gone. He carefully scanned the carpet, looking for any evidence on it to assist him tracking the sniper in that dark gray carpet. He looked at the walls, checking each door on each suite as he walked along, looking for any trace or clue that would serve as evidence to help him locate the assassin.

At the end of the corridor, he finally found what he was looking for: a couple of bloody fingerprints on the door frame. He smiled, knowing that meant that he had managed to wound the sniper. He touched the blood, noticing it was still fresh. He took his handkerchief from his back pocket and placed the tiny corner of it on top of one of the fingerprints there and pulled it back to examine the blood on it closely. It was not only fresh—it was also was very recently put there. There was no sign of coagulation in the print.

Without hesitating in the slightest, he drew the Browning with his right hand. He pushed the button on the door with his left hand, but there was no reply. He buzzed several more times without any sign of occupancy, he reached into his pocket and took out a set of master keys on a ring. He tried one after another to see which would work, and the third one did the trick.

He carefully entered the suite. "Is anyone here?" he asked. He repeated the question three times as he walked towards the window.

As he drew near the window, he felt glass crunching beneath his shoes once more, cracking as he trod on the tiny pieces of confetti. He could see a tarp on the floor before the window and a large spot that initially looked like paint. He quickly realized it was blood. To be sure, he knelt and touched it with his fingers. It was still fresh but was just beginning to coagulate—no more than half an hour old.

He saw a bunch of paint cans and brushes around the room. Evidently the suite was empty, and they had been either repainting the walls or doing remodeling work. He searched the entire suite and found nothing. It was time to leave, and he started to follow the almost imperceptible drops of blood down the hall, wherever it took him.

They led to the stairs. With extreme caution, he opened the door to the stairs. Still following the trail, he walked down to the seventh floor. He could see more obvious blood smears on the rails. The rails here were light gray, clearly showing the red. He continued down the stairs, making as little noise as possible.

On the sixth level, he saw a narrow canvas bag lying behind the trash can, which caught his attention. It was placed to be as imperceptible as possible, like someone had tried to hide it. Emilio pulled it out from behind the can and opened it. He immediately noticed it was soaked in blood. The sniper rifle was inside the bag. Apparently, the sniper in his rush didn't want to carry that heavy load and decided to leave it behind in case he was caught before leaving the building. He wanted no evidence to connect him with the shooting that day onto the terrace of the building opposite. He must not just be wounded; he must be gravely wounded. He put the rifle back inside the bag and replaced it where he had found it.

Emilio continued his careful descent down the long stairs. Out of nowhere he heard two shots. They could have come from the level immediately below him. He stepped back, his head against the wall, pistol held high. He heard two more shots. They sounded like different weapons, and the echo thundered up the stairwell.

The stairwell was silent as a tomb for a few seconds. He heard a pained cough of someone down below and the shuffling sound of someone crawling along the stairs. There was also the sound of some heavy object against the metal of the stairs. Emilio, pistol in hand, cautiously leaned over the rail and looked down the stairwell to see if he could discern what was happening below him.

The first thing he saw was the figure of a woman leaning against the rail, seated on the stairs. Her chin rested on her chest—it looked like she was either unconscious or dead. Emilio remained still for a few more seconds to see if the woman moved. He realized that she was no threat. Carefully, he descended the stairwell one step at a time, taking pains to make as little noise as possible.

When he reached the next landing, he also saw a man with a livid scar on his face, resting like the woman against the wall of the stairwell. Next to his hand on the floor lay a Lugar pistol. It appeared that he was the one who fell down last in the duel between the young woman and himself. He could see now that the woman was quite beautiful. Emilio kicked the pistol several feet away with his right foot, just in case the man was still alive.

Emilio lifted the woman's head. To his surprise he saw that it was the young tango singer from the New Buenos Aires. He took her pulse and confirmed that she was indeed dead. He took another Lugar pistol out of her hand and stuck it in his waistband. He searched her but found nothing else of great importance, aside from a small pistol tied to

Montauk: The Lightning Chance

one of her legs and in the same style of leather strap an extra magazine for the Lugar. He went through her clutch bag but found nothing inside it. As he moved her, something caught his attention—something shiny in the cleavage of her bra. He opened her bra up in the front, and six Nazi coins with the eagle on one side and the SS skull on the other, rolled out. Emilio shook his head in puzzlement. That proved that she was a Nazi agent, or at the very least a corroborator. Just one coin was extremely valuable, not just for the intrinsic value of the gold but also the tremendous value that the Nazi organization attached to it as an identifying token. Evidently, she had been paid by the same masters that tried to reorganize the Nazi organization on the American continents.

Emilio heard a movement behind him. He spun around, pointing his silenced gun at the man with the scar. He stirred as he regained consciousness. He certainly had lost a great deal of blood. His eyes locked with those of the man, and he saw fear and terror in the man's face. He looked for his pistol but realized that it was far out of reach. He froze.

Emilio said, "Don't even try it unless you want to die quickly."

The man tried to lean over to his right, but all of the bullet wounds in his body prevented him from being able to do that comfortably. Emilio could see the difference between the wounds from the Lugar of the woman and his own Browning. He knew he had found his enemy. The man, exhausted by even that effort, collapsed limply in a heap.

Realizing the man was too far wounded to be a threat, Emilio thrust his Browning into his waistband opposite the woman's Lugar. Emilio stood up and helped the man into a position more comfortable to sit in against the wall.

He leaned in close to the man. "I don't know who you are. I've never seen you before in my life, and I have no clue who sent you to assassinate us, but what I can almost assure you is that you have enough gunshot wounds in your body to kill an elephant. You know I'm a doctor, and evidently none of those bullets —either mine or hers—hit any of your vital organs. As a medical surgeon, I'll give you a 50/50 chance, unless you're bleeding internally, of survival. And if I take you immediately to a hospital, that is. The only thing that can kill you right now is your current loss of blood. Unfortunately for you, I don't even have my medical bag with me where at least I could give you an anticoagulant to improve your chances of living, at least until you get the necessary medical attention. Instead, your life is literally bleeding out of you and it all depends now on your physical strength as to how much longer you can endure this stress."

Emilio saw the opportunity to exert strong psychological pressure and perhaps induce him to talk. He continued in the most clinical tone of voice he could as he took the man's pulse and checked his temperature with his hand, "Your pulse is very weak. If you keep losing blood like this, I don't think you have much chance even to get to a hospital alive." The man's eyes opened, and he looked up at Emilio in fear. Emilio opened the sniper's shirt, untied his necktie, and began to examine the wounds. He shook his head in discouragement. "It's a miracle you're still alive." As he continued his examination, the sniper looked at him distrustfully.

He summoned the strength to speak. "What is it to you if I live or die? I tried to kill you and your friends."

Emilio looked him dead in the eyes and pulled his handkerchief out of his pocket, folded it several times, and put it on the wound that was bleeding the most. "Put pressure on this wound. This is the primary source of blood loss." He took the sniper's right arm and put the hand on the handkerchief. The sniper's look blended confusion with wonder.

Emilio stood up, understanding the man's confusion. At the same time, he was evaluating the sniper's intellectual level. He didn't immediately answer the man's question, allowing a few seconds to pass to see if the sniper would understand. He walked over to the pistol on the floor and stuck it into his waistband in the back. Then with a sarcastic smile, he answered the man's question. "If I continue collecting weapons today, I'll be able to open my own business in weapons." He came over and sat down in front of the man, next to the dead woman. "You know because I was your mark that my profession is to save lives. I'm a doctor first. My business is not the ending of life. My destiny or whatever you want to call it took me to this life of espionage, but that doesn't mean I have to convert myself into an unscrupulous killer without any feeling for human life. Our job in intelligence is a very macabre game because we play with our lives every day. Today, the pendulum has swung over to you, tomorrow, for all we know, it could swing back over to me. I could end up riddled with bullets like you some day." He pointed at the woman. "Or her."

As he always did when he thought, he rubbed his forehead with the fingers of his left hand. The sniper began to talk. "I have three children: one 3, one 6, and a 10-year-old. What do you want? Not to the hospital, I can't go there. Why do you want to take me to someplace safe and patch me up?"

"I have a car nearby and in it I have what I need to give you a very good chance to survive, all the necessary instruments and medication to do the job."

The sniper repeated his question. "What exactly do you want in exchange to save my life?" This time he said it with greater urgency.

"Very little. All I ask from you is that you tell me all the truth. You know what I mean: *all* the truth. Who contracted you to kill us?"

The sniper hesitated and took a deep breath. He sighed in defeat. He looked Emilio in the eyes, this time with conviction. "As one man to another, please keep this between us, whether I live or die."

Dr. Julio Antonio del Marmol

CHAPTER 8: TRIPLE AGENT OR MERCENARY?

Emilio looked at him. "I don't think you should worry about that. The people who sent you to kill us won't be able to retaliate. I can promise you they will be killed."

"That's beside the point. Just keep this between us. You can do whatever you want with them, but please don't mention my name."

"I cannot promise anything, but I will try my best. I can give you that much."

"The man who sent me to kill you is Juan Alberto, the owner of the New Buenos Aires."

Emilio had not stopped rubbing his forehead, but he did this time, very abruptly. He was shocked. "How is it possible that Juan Alberto would send you to kill his own daughter?" He shook his head. "No, no—unless this man is a very sadistic and unscrupulous criminal with no decency at all."

The sniper compressed his lips in regret and shook his head. "No, no—Bogota was only supposed to be wounded. You and your friend were the targets that were to die today. Juan Alberto made it very clear to me that the first bullet should be for Bogota, but only in her arm. Whatever else happened, that bullet should be the first for her because this would be the one that would exonerate him even if one of you guys survived the attack. Speaking of sadistic and unscrupulous," he pointed at the dead woman, "first he sent me to kill you guys and wound his own daughter. Then he sent this rabid dog behind me to kill *me* so that there would be no witnesses as to what happened today. You tell me what that says about him."

Emilio was silent for a few moments. He started to rub his forehead once more, this time with the fingers of his right hand. He shook his head and clucked his tongue. "Juan Alberto, Juan Alberto." He looked at the sniper again. "What's your name?"

The man looked at him in confusion. "My name is Ramon Valenzula Valdivia."

Emilio held his hand out. "You know my name already, probably memorized it, since you had me as a mark. You've probably studied me minutely."

Ramon tried to smile but it turned into a grimace. He pointed to his wounds and shook his head. "Evidently not enough. If I manage to survive this catastrophe I got involved in today, maybe I can learn a few things from you, Dr. Emilio del Marmol."

Emilio smiled. "Only if you tell me *all* the truth. Remember, I'm a man of my word. If I weren't you would never leave the operating table. I'll tell you this now so that you have time enough to recuperate if you tell me *all* the truth. You know what 'all' means, don't you? That is what I asked for in exchange, which I think is very little. But you probably wouldn't like me to offer you half a surgery when I said I would patch you up. When I'm in the middle of surgery and have your guts on the table, I can't say I'll give you the other half later." He spread his arms. "Really? Will you agree with me on this?"

Ramon nodded. His face had gotten very pale from all his blood loss. With his remaining energy he said, "I promise you today that I have told you the entire truth of what you asked me. If there's anything you want to know later about anything else, after you patch me up, I will answer every single question truthfully. From this day onward, you will have my absolute loyalty because it takes a man with qualities superior to mine to try and save the life of the man who had tried to kill him. Whether or not I survive this ordeal, you have given me a great lesson today, Doctor, that I will never forget as long as I live. You have earned my absolute respect."

"Thank you very much. Your words give me great satisfaction. Since you gave me the right answer and the truth to the question I asked, I have several more questions to ask you later on. Don't talk anymore—you need to conserve your strength, or you won't be able to answer those questions. Where did you leave your car?"

"It's not a car. It's a black panel van. It's parked behind this building, not in the underground garage."

Figure 17 Underground Parking Structure

"Of course," Emilio said. "You are all professionals. Parking underground would delay your exit." Ramon, with great effort, pulled the van keys out of his pocket and gave them to Emilio. Emilio accepted them and said, "I'll return in a few minutes."

Ramon tried to smile again but couldn't manage it. "The only rush I have right now is my race against Death."

"If you hang in there, I will help you get to the end of that race and win it. I want you, if you've been honest with me, to help me with some other things and information I need. I want you to live and enjoy life for a little while longer. Hang in there and keep your sense of humor."

Emilio got up and saw that they were on the Fifth-Floor landing. He walked into the corridor and over to the elevators. He entered the car and pushed the button. He saw the elderly woman with the Yorkie was inside. He noticed that there was a roll of money bound with a pink rubber band on the floor next to his foot. He bent down and picked it up. "I believe this is yours."

The old woman looked at him in surprise and clutched at her breast. "Oh, my goodness! I was going to pay for the entire week here at the hotel with that! How did if fall out of my bra like that?"

Emilio handed her the roll of bills. She looked at him in gratitude. "You are a great gentleman. Thank you very much! I cannot understand it. This has never happened to me before. Maybe when I picked my dog up it fell out. He's afraid of the elevator, and I might have been distracted when I did so."

Emilio petted the dog. "He's very cute." The dog wagged his tail enthusiastically. "Don't worry about it. We all get distracted sometimes and when we least expect it, while we're unaware of our surroundings, that's when bad things happen. Sometimes thieves take that opportunity to pick our pockets."

"Thank you. You are a genuinely nice gentleman. If the thieves in Bogota continue crowing like roosters, the city will become a huge cock fight."

At that moment the elevator arrived at the lobby and the doors opened. Emilio said, "Remember, just like a pharmacy you might find everything all the time in Bogota." He tipped his hat and bowed slightly to her. "Madam, you have a beautiful and pleasant day."

He walked to the lobby towards the concierge and asked for a wheelchair. "My friend has been drinking a little too much, and I want to bring him outside for some fresh air. He doesn't want to make a scene."

The concierge asked, "Do you need any help?"

"No, thank you. He just doesn't want to make a fool of himself by falling down. Please, keep this to yourself." He handed the man a generous tip.

Emilio wheeled the chair back to the elevators, got in the available car, and hit the button for the Fifth Floor. He saw the woman with the Yorkie coming back, and quickly jabbed the button to close the doors. They started to close, but the little dog jumped out of the woman's arms and ran into the elevator. Emilio had no choice but to hold his arm out to stop the doors. He shook his head at how extraordinary things always seemed to happen.

The old lady recognized Emilio once more with her thick lensed glasses. "Oh, thank you very much to hold the elevator for us. I cannot believe it, but apparently Poochie loves you so much that he conquered his fear of the elevator after so many years, jumped out of my arms, and ran over to you!" Emilio couldn't help but reach down to pick up the small dog and pet him. "You are definitely an angel—first you find my money, and now my dog loves you. You wouldn't believe it, but he was run over by a car a long time ago. Ever since then, he's been afraid of everything. I have to pick him up even to bring him into the elevator—I guess the noise of the machinery reminds him too much of the car."

Emilio smiled. "That is love. Sometimes it causes miracles to happen. All I did was give him a little pat. Evidently he is grateful to me." Emilio reached up to press the button for the Eighth Floor for her.

As the elevator started its ascent, the old woman held out her hand. "My name is Conchita. Nice to meet you."

Emilio took her hand. "I am Dr. Emilio del Marmol."

She put her hand on her chest. "Oh, my! A doctor!" She laughed a little nervously as she blushed like an adolescent girl. To cover her embarrassment, she noticed that the button for Fifth Floor was lit, with only two of them in the car. Innocently she asked, "It's strange. I didn't push number 5. Did you?"

"No." He was keeping his eyes on her. "It's possible someone on the Fifth Floor is calling the elevator."

"Oh, that's true, it's possible."

The bell chimed and the doors opened onto the Fifth Floor. The familiar faces of the Ukrainians stood outside. They were still talking about Hitler, but this time they were speaking about the connection between Hitler, the jihad, and Amin al-Husseini, the Palestinian Armed Nationalist, who was the leader and grand mufti of Jerusalem from 1921 to 1948. They spoke of the violence and terrorism indoctrinated by the Nazis, using Islam's religion to cover the oppression of the ones not conforming with their political ideas.

The elevator finally arrived on the Eighth Floor. Conchita got out with her little Poochie. Emilio allowed them to go first before he stepped out. The lady curiously looked back to see if she could see which suite was his, even though they were going in opposite directions. Emilio began to get a little paranoid and slowed his pace to give her time to get to her suite before he reached the turn in the hallway ahead. He even stopped a couple of times to pretend fixing the wheel on the wheelchair. Finally, Conchita arrived at her suite and entered it.

As soon as he saw that she had gone inside and closed the door, he folded the wheelchair up and picked it up. He went to the door to the stairs, opened it, and put the wheelchair against the wall behind it. He closed the door and rushed to the suite where the sniper had been before. Using his master keys, he walked inside, walked over to the curtains, and pulled one down. He removed the clips, discarded them on the floor, and folded the curtain up. He rolled it into a more manageable bundle, tucked it under one arm, and closed the suite. He went back to the stairwell and got the wheelchair as well. Carrying both curtain and wheelchair, he went down the stairs.

When he arrived on the Fifth Floor, he discovered that Ramon had fallen unconscious. He checked Ramon's pulse and temperature again and saw that the man was still breathing and alive. He opened the wheelchair, put Ramon in it, and then used the curtain to cover Ramon like a blanket, covering all the blood at the same time. The only different between a blanket and this fancy curtain were the tassels along the bottom, so he tucked those underneath Ramon.

He looked around to make certain nothing looked suspicious. He removed his hat and put it on Ramon's head to make it look more natural. He picked up the woman's body dragged it behind the trashcan on the landing, camouflaging it there. Unless someone looked at it directly, they would never notice it.

He pushed the wheelchair into the hallway and took the elevator down to the lobby, breathing a sigh of relief as it started to descend. The doors opened onto the lobby, and the first thing he saw was a group of police officers waiting for the elevator. Other police and medical personnel with stretchers and first aid bags were rushing up the stairs. They allowed him to pass with the wheelchair. He nodded his head and thanked them, passing right beneath their noses with the wounded man in the chair.

Another group of police were interviewing the man staffing the registration desk. A uniformed officer that looked like perhaps the chief of police with a couple of plainclothes detectives held the door open for him. They looked at him curiously, but Carlos greeted Emilio cordially in front of the officials.

Carlos said, "Your lady assistant told me that your luggage will be coming later."

Emilio concealed his puzzled surprise. "Thank you. I'll compensate you later, OK?"

The curious look in the detectives dissipated with this exchange, and Emilio breathed a mental sigh of relief. He rolled the wheelchair out onto the sidewalk and walked at a brisk pace.

Ramon stirred. "Are we there yet?"

"Shh, OK. Stay quiet, please. We're almost there," Emilio said.

Emilio looked around for the black van. As soon as he saw it parked in the street, he rushed over to it and opened the back door. He jumped inside and physically hauled the wheelchair with Ramon in it into the back of the van. Emilio undid his belt and used it to secure the wheelchair from rolling freely around as the van drove. He saw a black travel bag on the floor. He opened it and saw several sticks of dynamite, hand grenades, and what appeared to be a long string of firecrackers. It looked like the complete paraphernalia a professional hit man would use in his line of work. He put the bag behind the wheelchair to chock the wheels and further stabilize the chair. He got behind the driver's wheel and casually drove it to the underground parking garage. He checked his watch and saw that only 45 minutes had passed.

Ramon woke up and asked again, "Doctor, Doctor?"

"Yes, Ramon—what's up?"

"Did we get out of the hotel without any problems?"

"Barely. But don't talk now. Save your energy. With the help of God, I will manage to patch you and Bogota up. She is also wounded, remember?"

"Oh, my God—yes! And I'm the one who wounded her! We'll definitely need the help of God with both of us under the same roof. When you tell her what I did, all Hell will break loose"

"What goes around comes around, as the North Americans say. Don't worry about it—I'll act like a referee between the two of you. I'll work at convincing her that you're not such a bad guy after all."

"Ha! I'd like to see how you convince her of that."

"She's a very intelligent woman. She'll understand."

They had arrived and gone underground. Emilio parked the van on the opposite side of the garage away from his car. He said, "I'll return immediately."

Ramon kept his sense of humor. "If it's not too much of a bother, will you please bring me a shake of blood? That should hold me for a few more hours."

Emilio shook his head with a small smile. "You should keep your mouth shut until I patch you up and you get better, if you want to keep enjoying the world of the living." He carefully closed the van door and cautiously walked towards the Chrysler.

As soon as he saw that his surroundings were clear, he continued forward. He saw that Bogota was sound asleep in the car, which made him feel better. He opened the trunk and got his bag. Deciding to let her sleep some more, he closed it and went back to the van. He opened the rear door and found Ramon unconscious again. He pulled out the instruments that he had sterilized back in the condo for Adolf but had gone unused. He pulled out a syringe and some test tubes. He mixed some anti-coagulants in the test tube and poured the mixture into the syringe. He injected it and took Ramon's pulse. Seeing that the man was breathing properly, he closed the door and went back to the Chrysler.

He opened the trunk and put his bag back inside. He opened the passenger door and put his hand on Bogota's shoulder. She started as she woke, reaching for the gun strapped to her leg. "Hey, it's me, Bogota. Take it easy. It's me. I'm back."

Montauk: The Lightning Chance

"Oh, I'm sorry." She looked at her watch. "I wasn't expecting you so soon."

Emilio smiled and took her temperature with his hand on her forehead. "I wasn't, either. Everything worked just fine, and I have information that you won't believe. Before that, though, you have no fever and your pulse is normal. I have to tell you something very serious now. I cannot make the story too long, however, at least not for now, because I have no time to lose. I have the sniper in the van in this parking lot, but he's very seriously injured. He's been shot several times. I need to patch him up for several reasons. I want to save his life." Bogota looked at him in astonishment.

She drew her pistol. She said, "We cannot let this criminal live! He nearly killed all of us! You've got to be kidding me!"

Emilio looked straight in her eyes. "I want you to understand what I'm going to tell you now and open your mind fully. Remember what you've been taught in the very intensive training that we've all had to go through to be able to hold the high clearance in order to work together. The first thing you must do is forget your personal emotions, completely. What I'm going to reveal to you right now is extremely delicate. It might touch the deepest emotions that even you might not recognize you have because they are deeply buried in your mind. This must be exceedingly difficult for you to digest, especially as it involves our loved ones and very close members of our families. What I'm about to say to you will tell me if you can continue forward in these missions. I want you to tell me if you can or are not prepared enough to handle all of this. I need your complete honesty and I need you to tell me now. My life and the life of Mr. Xiang and many others that are playing with us in our circle depend on that. Do you understand me?" He spoke firmly and with authority, a tone he had never used before with Bogota.

She looked at him, surprised by this new tone. She realized the gravity of the conversation and put her head down as a sign of respect, understanding that what Emilio had in his mind to tell her was something far bigger and more important than the life of the sniper. She was a little embarrassed by her initial reaction and extended her arm to take Emilio by the wrist. "I'm sorry," she apologized, "it was not my intention under any circumstance to disrespect you."

Emilio nodded. "I know. All I want is for you to remember that in this business we're all in, nothing is ever personal. When we forget that we lose our perspective and lose our grip on what we really are doing. Many times, we put at risk not only our lives but also the lives of those working close to us. To get straight to the point, we have a major problem, one we weren't prepared for, unfortunately. There is a very high percentage of probability that your father, Juan Alberto, is the one who is behind not only the attempt on my life but also the one all of us just survived." Bogota's head shot up and she looked at him in surprised disbelief.

"Most of the evidence is accusing him of being not just a double agent, but a triple agent. He's turned out to be a simple mercenary; and like a mercenary, he serves whoever pays the most." Emilio paused and looked at her closely. Bogota was clearly disturbed and shook her head in abject disbelief. A couple of tears ran down her cheeks. She bit her bottom lip in genuine frustration.

Her right hand rubbed her belly in silence as she looked down at it. She said in a broken voice, "Your grandfather is a traitorous dog." Emilio kept his silence. She looked him in the eyes. "To be honest with you, even though this is the hardest moment I have ever experienced in my life and it's difficult for me to say, I already had my suspicions. After the attempt on your life today, my suspicions rose to an even greater magnitude." She paused briefly. "What probability do you estimate that you could be wrong?"

Emilio looked at her sadly with a long face. His eyes were slightly teary. He turned his head and wiped them on his sleeve. "With a broken heart I must tell you from 0 to 1%. That is precisely why I need to keep this sniper alive." He said that last emphatically. "Based on his testimony and what I could see with my own eyes, your father sent the Spanish pianist, Sarita, behind him to kill him so that there were no witnesses and clear himself of any involvement." Emilio stroked his forehead once more with his fingers, like he did whenever he was stressed. "Maybe this will be some consolation to you, but according to the sniper, Ramon, your father's first requirement was to send to you as a courtesy the first bullet fired against us, but he was to be absolutely certain that that shot was not fatal to you. You were only to be wounded. This was to serve as his alibi that he had nothing to do with the murders of Mr. Xiang and myself. Of course, you can take it both ways: he did it out of for love for you or for his own convenience, so that you could be a witness for him."

She tried to smile but only managed a grimace. She shook her head. "Knowing him—it was for his own protection. What kind of consolation is that? Thank you, but no thanks."

Montauk: The Lightning Chance

"Of course, I have more evidence that I can't discuss with you right now. We're on a tight schedule if we want to save the life of the only witness who can tell everyone, not just us, the truth about your father. You know the protocol that we have to follow. Unless in the next 48 hours a miracle occurs and your father gets exonerated, he will not continue living. Every single minute that your father lives right now represents an imminent danger to all of us." He finished with an ambiguous tone, stopped, and remained silent for several seconds.

Bogota looked at him sadly and held his arm affectionately. "I'm sorry. I know this is very difficult for me, but I think I know that it's the same or worse for you, because you deposited all your trust in him. For me, don't worry about it. I only ask you something: before you give the order to terminate him, make sure that you have no doubts in your mind at all that you're right. Another thing I would like to ask you: please don't be the one to execute him." She stroked her baby once more and looked at Emilio in frustration. "I would love to confront him but being his daughter, I know that he will deny everything, even when the proof is undeniable. I know his personality and he will never admit anything to me. He'll give me some illogical excuse even though he knows it makes no sense at all."

Emilio took her hand between his. "One thing I can assure you of absolutely: that is, for the time being, if I have the smallest doubt in my mind, he will continue to live. But something I must warn you about—please, under no circumstance should you make the mistake of confronting your father, especially if you're by yourself. I know him very well, and the type of personality he has; if he feels that he's been trapped or intimidated by anyone, especially you, he is capable of even killing you, even though he would regret it later on. And that will be a tragedy." He touched her belly tenderly. "I could not continue to live if I lose both of you guys at the same time."

Bogota began to weep silently. "No, no—don't worry. That is a mistake that I don't have the luxury of allowing myself to make. It's not just my life, it's also the life of my child. No matter how much my emotions and rage are telling me that I want to see the lie reflected in his face, I know that he's converted himself into a disgrace, all for money. He's nothing less than a filthy, traitorous pig." Tears rolled down her cheeks freely as she spoke.

"OK, OK," Emilio said to try and calm her down, "we need to get out of here soon if we want to save the life of our witness. How do you feel? Do you think you can drive?"

"Of course I can drive." She moved her left arm a little. "I have no pain at all."

"Of course. With the amount of painkillers I gave you when I left, you won't feel any for four, perhaps six hours. Believe me, though, after that you will feel pain unless you get another shot. OK, since you can drive, follow me in the Chrysler, and I will drive the van with him. We'll go to the safehouse in the Rosales de Bogota, 7th Avenue. There I have all the necessary equipment to attend to not only Ramon's injury but also your arm. We have to get that bullet out of it before it causes an infection. I need to give you some other details about your father that are extremely important, and when I started to suspect that he was working with the Israelis, the Russians, and us, all at the same time, but later."

They left the underground garage, Emilio driving the panel van followed closely by Bogota in the Chrysler. After a while they entered the very wealthy neighborhood where they had a safe house. Emilio had a complete surgical room with equipment ranging from anesthetics to the most advanced medical technologies. After they arrived at the building, Emilio entered a code in a keypad and the security gate opened to admit them to drive into another underground garage. The design was similar to where they had come from, but this just was for a residential area rather than a commercial one. They parked and Emilio, assisted by Bogota, took the sniper in his wheelchair, and rolled it over to the closest elevator. Once in, Emilio pressed the button for the Tenth Floor. As they ascended, Emilio took Ramon's pulse.

He looked up with a worried face. "I hope we got him here in time and he has enough strength to endure the surgery. Do you mind if I take care of him first? I don't think he has much time left."

"Of course not. My wound is superficial, just a flesh wound. It's of no importance."

"Of course it is. Every wound is of importance, and you are a priority. But his condition is worse, and you're not feeling any pain right now. If you start to feel any discomfort, though, let me know and I'll give you another dose. But his condition is not stable at all. He's having difficulty breathing."

"Don't worry about me," she reassured him.

Emilio crossed his fingers. "Let's hope for the best."

The elevator pinged as it reached the Tenth Floor. The doors opened and Emilio with his keys in his right hand rushed to open the door. They entered the magnificently decorated modern suite. The pictures on the walls were impressionistic and modern, van Gogh and Picassos. Emilio rolled the chair into the living room where the walls were solid Venetian multicolored glass. No one could see inside the room. He opened double sliding doors with thick glass panes, pushed a button on the wall, and a powerful surgical lamp illuminated the entire room, revealing what could pass as an operating room in the most sophisticated hospital. Good quality stainless steel beds were covered with sheets, rolling trays with instruments laid out on them, oxygen tanks, and other modern surgical equipment—it would be the envy of any hospital in Bogota. It was an emergency medical facility set up by the intelligence community so that any doctor could treat patients with optimal conditions. Numbered drawers held surgical instruments.

Acting like an experienced team, Bogota and Emilio put Ramon's body on the table. With precision they cut his clothes off rapidly using surgical scissors with the exactitude of an experienced team that had done this multiple times. Using only her right hand, Bogota started to wash Ramon's wounds with antiseptic with a sponge while Emilio prepared himself for his surgery. Bogota laid out the surgical tray that Emilio would need into the sterilizer; as she did so, Emilio added two clamps to the tray. She pressed the button as Emilio washed his hands up to the elbows. With her assistance, Emilio slipped into a mint green surgical gown, helped him into his surgical gloves and don his mask, and then he assisted her into one of her own so that she could aid him.

He spun a circular stool up to a comfortable height to be able to work while Bogota set up the blood bag and IV with antiseptic and sedative and inserted the needle into Ramon's arm. Emilio sat down and started to work, removing the bullets, and cutting away the dead tissue inside the wound. All told, the procedure took six hours to fully clean him up and suture his wounds closed. Bogota brought over a metal gurney on wheels. She took one side while Emilio took the other, and by pulling the linen sheet beneath Ramon transferred him onto the gurney.

They rolled him out of the operating room and wheeled him into a recovery room for him to recuperate. They put him into a bed and hooked up his IVs. Then the two of them went back into the operating room so that Emilio could start to work on Bogota's injury. He sat down on the stool while Bogota took a position on the surgical table. After he removed the bullet and cleaned her arm, he could see that it was the same type of ammunition that he had removed from Ramon. It proved to

Emilio that Juan Alberto had calculated every variable. If he had been successful, when Ramon's body had been autopsied, the authorities would conclude that the same person that killed him was the same one that had killed Emilio and Mr. Xiang while wounding Bogota. Ramon would be considered an accomplice to the sniper who had been eliminated by the sniper.

Juan Alberto had miscalculated because all criminals tend to repeat their crimes. He had not taken into consideration that the other crimes committed previously would leave behind traces for the police to track them down later. Evidently, he hadn't paid too much attention to those little details, not realizing the kind of people he was dealing with. Suspicion would inevitably fall on him, and his own actions would blow his cover. He would expose himself without knowing it as a triple agent, a simple mercenary. That was the more accurate definition for what he had clearly been doing all this time. Now his cover was completely blown—apparently, something extremely important had come to his awareness, and that something would be the Führer. This package was simply too valuable, and in his greed, he had not taken the normal precautions he usually followed. He wanted to protect the package that Emilio had operated on in order to secure his safe arrival in Argentina, when he would receive an even larger amount of money. But he also didn't want anyone else to know about the package, and so this sloppy attempt at covering his trail.

Emilio finished suturing Bogota's arm and bandaged the wound. He started to remove his gloves. He looked at Bogota with a pained look. He knew what she was going through, and he felt a little guilty because he needed her help and had left her for the last. Not only the pain she was going through with the wound in her arm, but the emotional pain she still had at the realization that her father had been a traitor to them. He came over to her and kissed her tenderly on her cheek and then her lips. "I'm sorry that you had to wait so long before I could take care of your wound."

"I know. Our work, not emotions and duty before anything else." She returned his kiss with tears in her eyes and with a thirst for love, the love that they had for each other. Most of the time they could not express it before the others for fear of exposure or looking weak. Now, by themselves, even though they were exhausted from the psychological and physical tension they had endured all day, they finally found a small moment in which they could express their love for each other. They continued kissing with greater passion, forgetting all about the adrenaline rush of the past day. That love exploded like a volcanic eruption that no human power could stop. They began to gently remove their clothes and walk out of the operating room, kissing like a pair of adolescents, touching each other as they walked, leaving a trail of clothes behind them. They finally reached the enormous, beautiful, and elegant master bedroom. As they opened the door, the fragrance of jasmine from the air fresheners alone the walls embraced their noses like a refreshing breeze outdoors.

Almost naked, gently to avoid aggravating the wound, Emilio gently laid Bogota down on the circular bed and they began to make love for a long time, fusing their bodies as one. After several hours, both fell asleep, exhausted and satisfied.

Emilio woke up after Bogota, surprised at not finding her by his side in the bed. He looked at the nightstand and found his pistol and the sniper's pistol lying there. The essence in the air, however, had changed from jasmine to roasted chicken. He put on a bathrobe and picked up one of his pistols. He put it inside his bathrobe and went in search of Bogota. He found her in a similar robe with Japanese symbols in the kitchen of the suite.

Bogota heard him open the swinging doors to the kitchen and turned towards him with a small smile on her lips. "I made dinner for both of us. We haven't done this for a long time, and I think now would be appropriate to enjoy ourselves a little for all the work we did today."

"What are you doing?"

"Chicken a la Marengo, steamed asparagus, shrimp in bearnaise sauce," and Bogota opened the oven door with mitts, and pulled out a tray of golden croissants, "almond croissants for dessert with French vanilla ice cream. Your favorite."

Emilio rubbed his belly in anticipation, smiled, and said, *"Tres bien, Mademoiselle.* If everything tastes like it smells, you've earned five stars as an item on your resume as a chef of high cuisine."

She smiled. "We're always so busy that this is my first opportunity to show you my culinary secrets." She looked at him in satisfaction and added, "I hope that this will add a little more to your recent pleasure. I only ask you one thing, since this is the first time I've cooked for you: be sincere, like you always are. Tell me the truth, even if it hurts. You know I always prefer the truth."

"Yes, I know. That's why I always tell you the raw truth."

"Very well. If you don't like anything at all that I've cooked, please let me know so you only suffer once."

Emilio came over and embraced her around the waist, pulling her close to him. He kissed her tenderly on the lips, and then a little more passionately. Bogota reached out and turned the flame off and covered the pots. She looked at him with a mischievous smile and raise both hands to him. "Well, the food is ready." She pointed to the pots and croissants. "But I've already filled the jacuzzi and it's been bubbling for hours, waiting for you. If you prefer, before dinner, we can repeat our previous experience and add a little more spice in our lives."

Emilio joked with her as he said, "Don't you already have enough spice in your food, honey?"

"Really?"

"Just joking. We can have dinner a little later. I would love to repeat our sexual experience we had before." With even great passion, he kissed her again. "I love the idea of the jacuzzi."

They both smiled and left the kitchen. She said, "Why do you think I prepared the jacuzzi by the time I calculated you would be up, and the dinner was ready, so we would have fun in there?"

They ran like a pair of kids into the master bedroom, only letting go of their hands to allow their bathrobes to drop onto the floor. They jumped into the jacuzzi. As they kissed, they started to make bodily contact in the hot water. She sat on top of Emilio with her hand in the water, seeking her comfort as she leaned back. She slowly sat on top of his legs, taking his face between her hands. They started to kiss passionately, and her eyes closed as they embraced in body and soul, trying to forget all the strange things that had happened that day and enjoying those precious moments they could appreciate as they didn't have them very frequently. They manifested the ecstasies of happiness that they shared each other at that moment as if they were going to be the last ones they ever had in their lives.

After perhaps an hour both were completely satisfied and a little exhausted. They left the jacuzzi and put on their bathrobes once more. They walked into the kitchen, and Bogota served dinner at the small dinette table in the kitchen. As she served, Emilio opened a bottle of champagne and one of orange juice and began to make mimosas. They started to enjoy one of the greatest pleasures life can offer. After toasting each other with their glasses, she decided to make a toast to the baby that was growing in her womb, not very noticeable yet because she was only two months along in her pregnancy. This pregnancy had changed both of their lives, giving them both joy and happiness. Neither of them had planned it, but as Bogota had said, in the middle of all the craziness they had endured during the Second World War, the Nazis, and the Holocaust around the world, that little creature could be a great blessing and the new world of peace and harmony that they had both tried to construct after so much death and misery they had gone through for so many years.

After they finished eating, Emilio told her how great and wonderful it was and compared it to the greatest and wondrous ecstasy of the sex they had had before. They sat down and like two college kids, they began to talk, staring into each other's eyes. Emilio gave her all the details of what had happened that day in the hunt for the sniper and also the details of his suspicions that now had come in a complete circle to prove her father guilty of all counts and the logical reasons for the vital mistakes Juan Alberto had made that not only called Emilio's attention but also the highest levels of the intelligence community.

When he had finished her debriefing, Bogota shook her head sadly. Agony and anger mixed within her and she said, "After all you've told me, I think I have enough anger in me that I could kill him myself." Two tears rolled down her cheeks.

"No, I don't think that will be necessary." They started to clear the table and bring the dishes to the sink. Emilio helped her clean and dry the plates and glasses as they continued to sip mimosas from the glasses in their hands.

The phone rang with the normal code of the safe house: one ring, hang up. Two rings, hang up. Three rings were meant to be answered. Emilio picked up. "Yes, who is this?"

"It's me, Mr. Xiang. Are you OK?"

"Yes. Everything is OK. How is everything in your part of town?"

"The package is secure in the hands of the scientists."

"Emilio replied, "Thank you, Mr. Xiang."

"You are welcome. It is immanent and necessary for us to get together immediately."

"Does it have to be now?"

"Yes," Mr. Xiang replied with certainty. "The information is related to the wounded Nazi." Emilio stroked his forehead with his left hand. He stayed silent for a few seconds. Mr. Xiang, worried by the long silence, said, "Hello? Hello? Are you there, Emilio?"

"Yes, yes. Where do you want meet?"

"In the bar *El Gato Tuerto*[24]. You must be sure where it is. Do you know?"

"No. I've never been there."

"It's a couple of blocks from the New Buenos Aires, but on the opposite side of the street."

Emilio wondered why Mr. Xiang wanted to meet in a place that wasn't safe. It broke their usual protocol, but it must be of critical importance. "OK, I'll be there in half an hour." He checked his wristwatch. "I'm not too far away. I also have especially important information to impart to you. I'll be there for sure in El Gato Tuerto in thirty minutes."

"Very well."

Emilio hung up. Bogota had been sitting by him and heard Emilio's part of the conversation. She asked, "You don't think it's very dangerous for you to be close, especially now, to the New Buenos Aires?" She was clearly worried at what she had heard.

Emilio asked doubtfully, "How do you know that I will be close to your father's business?"

Her expression was mildly sarcastic. "Have you never been in the bar El Gato Tuerto?"

"No. Why? What does that have to do with my question to you?"

She smiled, realizing that Emilio was doubting her. "Emilio—El Gato Tuerto is almost right in front of the New Buenos Aires. It's the primary competition to my father's business." She was mildly irritated at the doubt.

Emilio was silent for a few seconds, thinking about it. He began to stroke his forehead with his fingers again and looked Bogota straight in the eyes. "I believe and don't doubt you because of the way you so spontaneously and naïvely answered my question. But if what you just told me is true, what is the reason for Mr. Xiang to say that El Gato Tuerto is about two blocks from the New Buenos Aires? Just on the opposite side of the street." Emilio thought deeply some more. "I believe that Mr. Xiang is trying to warn me about something. This doesn't make any sense. I have never been in the El Gato Tuerto, and I only met once in the New Buenos Aires. All the business I've conducted with your father have been in different places for obvious reasons, and *never* at his place of business."

---

[24] The Cat with One Eye

Montauk: The Lightning Chance

Bogota stroked her mouth with her right arm. After a few seconds, she shook her head. "Oh, my God—this does not smell good at all. I know that Mr. Xiang has been in my father's club many times. I've seen him there whenever I've gone to the restaurant to help my father when an employee was sick. Why would he tell you it's a couple of blocks from that place? He must have seen it!" She made an expression of frustration. "Oh, no—if my instincts don't betray me, my father's men have already grabbed Mr. Xiang and they want to kill you. It's possible they found out that Ramon has disappeared. He never returned to debrief them after the mission. He's many hours overdue for that. The fate of the pianist Sarita is probably in every newspaper in the city, if as you say you left the body there."

Emilio started to think about it. "It makes sense, what you just said."

"Of course it makes sense. You should not go anywhere near that place."

Emilio smirked. "What do you suggest? Abandon Mr. Xiang to his luck?"

"No, not at all! But you should call for help. Our guys can take care of that for you. We're not killers. We should call the Cleaners. They are professionals and know how to handle this."

"That will take hours. By that time, Mr. Xiang will be dead. I have a plan. We need to close up the room where we have Ramon. These rooms are soundproofed, and all the rooms are self-contained cells with metal walls beneath the façade. We have to lock Ramon in his room. I will increase the dosage of sedative in his IV so that he sleeps until tomorrow or the next day, and then the next step is to discover if your instinct is on track. The first thing we'll do when we get out of here is to buy every single newspaper printed in this town at a stand. I'll explain the rest of the plan to you as we drive. We only have half an hour to get there, and we still need to get dressed. Go dress yourself and grab the weapons. I'll take care of Ramon myself. I want to make sure that after working so hard on him for so many hours of surgery that the bird doesn't fly out of the cage."

"Very well." She left the kitchen, heading directly to the master bedroom.

Emilio went into Ramon's room and added the sedative and checked his vitals. He left the room and double locked the door with a security lock, then went to the master bedroom. Bogota was already dressed, sitting on the edge of the bed and adjusting the pistol in her thigh strap. Emilio got dressed and handed her one of the Lugars. "You're going to need more than that little pistol if we have to come to Mr. Xiang's rescue. Maybe we won't need these weapons with my plan, but it's better to have them and not need them than the other way around. Make sure it's loaded."

Bogota tried to smile, but it was stillborn as a sad, worried expression replaced it. After Emilio put the extra Lugar and his Browning in his waistband, he kissed her on the cheek. "Don't worry. You're not going to need to shoot your father. As you have your instincts, I have mine as well. I can assure you that your father is on a plane far away from Bogota by now, if your instinct about Sarita being in the papers is correct. It is logical because when you told me that it made perfect sense. That's the first thing they're going to do and I can guarantee you one thing. Your father can be many things, but of being stupid he doesn't have a single hair. He must have put together a lot of money in his career as a mercenary, enough to live the rest of his life without having to lift his finger for anything. Enough to have a good plastic surgeon to reconstruct his face like Hitler did so that no one could identify him. But let's stop assuming and go to the jungle of asphalt and concrete and corroborate if our instincts and theories are correct."

They left the master bedroom and walked into the corridor. They went out the door into the hallway. It was around 1 am, and no one was about. They went down to the garage in the elevator.

Emilio said, "I think we'll be safer if we use Ramon's black van. At night it will be less visible and call less attention."

"I agree. Let's use the van."

They got into the van, Emilio driving, and left the underground parking to drive to the supposed location where they were to meet Mr. Xiang. They stopped at a newspaper stand where a truck was unloading the new day's papers. Emilio parked and paid the attendant for four newspapers with different headlines. Every single one had pictures of Sarita the pianist as well as pictures of the New Buenos Aires. According to the news reports, the musician-assassin had mixed with the underworld criminal organizations in Colombia.

Emilio and Bogota looked at each other and smiled in satisfaction. So far, their instincts were good. Emilio gave the papers to her and walked to a public phone nearby. He put some coins in and dialed a number. A voice picked up. "*Policia municipal?*[25]"

---

[25] City Police

Montauk: The Lightning Chance

Emilio replied, "The murderers of Sarita the musician are holding a man of Asian descent they kidnapped in the bar El Gato Tuerto." He hung up the phone. He dialed another number.

"Interpol *internacional*."

Emilio replied, "A high profile criminal will be interchanged tonight in the New Buenos Aires. He has a prominent businessman of Asian origin held captive, kidnapped for an exchange." He hung up and dialed a third number.

"American embassy."

"They have a North American citizen of Asian origin in the bar El Gato Tuerto. He will be killed within the early morning hours today." Emilio smiled and hung up the phone. He walked to the van and continued his route to the El Gato Tuerto to meet Mr. Xiang.

He prudently parked a distance away when they arrived. Bogota pointed. "You see? Like I told you before, it's not even a hundred feet from the New Buenos Aires."

Emilio nodded as he observed the illuminated sign in front of the bar. It had a cartoonish skinny cat, black with a white blaze, dressed like a pirate with a wooden leg, a sword in its right hand, and the scabbard on its left hip. A red patch covered its left eye with a red band tying it to its head. The black hat had a long peacock feather from it and a cigar was in the cat's mouth. Large loop earrings were in its ears. The bulbs around the border of the sign lit up in a sequence, starting at the top of the cat, circling around it, finishing with a red light within the eyepatch that lit up for a few seconds, and then the cycle repeated.

After he watched from the van, casing the place for a few minutes, he checked both pistols. He said to Bogota, "Be very careful. You will come in like any regular customer from the front door. Go to the bar and ask for a drink, but don't sit down. Keep your pistol ready, just in case. I don't think you'll need it but be ready. Observe everything in the bar. Pretend to drink but don't actually drink anything so that you remain alert and clear. I will go in by the back door and try to find Mr. Xiang to get him out safely that same way. As soon as you see me inside, come back immediately to the van. If you don't see me, give me an hour. If I don't accomplish anything in that time, leave. I don't want you harmed. Don't worry about me, I'll manage, and I'll see you back at the safe house in Rosales." He looked her in the eyes. "I'm sorry for my doubts a little while ago."

She smiled. "That's part of the job, unfortunately." She leaned back a little in her seat, put her arms about his neck, and kissed him on the lips. "I only hope that one day you will be able to trust me completely like I trust you."

Emilio smiled. "Why not even more?"

She smiled again. "I will be happy with what I asked for before." She kissed him on the cheek and said, "Be careful, OK?"

Sirens of police cars could be heard in the distance. Emilio said, "OK. This is the moment. Let's give these criminals a pleasant surprise."

They both got out of the van. Bogota walked towards the front entry of the El Gato Tuerto, while Emilio went around to the rear of the van. He opened the door and retrieved the bag from the back. He then walked towards the alley which led to the rear entrance of the bar.

As he got close to it, he saw a large, muscular man sitting on a bench as he guarded the back entrance. Nearby he saw a small private parking lot with several luxury cars. There was also an exceptionally beautiful beige and dark green 1954 Rolls Royce separate from the other cars beneath a canvas car tent. It was cordoned off with red velvet ropes. He surmised that car must belong to the owner.

Emilio was dressed in his usual elegant manner. He approached the man, taking two Habana Monte Cristo cigars from the inside pocket of his jacket. "Good evening, sir. If you could give me some matches, I'll give you one of these so you can share the same pleasure I enjoy." The cigar he held out to the man was clearly expensive and of excellent quality.

Figure 18 Monte Cristo cigars

Montauk: The Lightning Chance

The man hesitated and looked at Emilio a little suspiciously. It was strange for someone to just walk up to him and offer him such a choice cigar, especially as there were matches to be obtained for free inside the bar as promotional tools. But he could not resist the offer, so he pulled out a box of matches advertising El Gato Tuerto and handed them to Emilio. "Sure—who could refuse such a trade?" He smiled broadly at Emilio, relaxing a little bit.

Emilio handed him the Monte Cristo. He bit off the end of his own cigar and lit his cigar. He took a luxurious inhalation from it. Cigar in his mouth, he leaned in and offered the lit match, cupping the flame against the wind with his left hand. The man bit off the end of his cigar and leaned in towards the extended match. As he did so, he exposed the skin on his neck, exactly as Emilio intended. As he started to puff on the flame, Emilio dropped the match and pulled out a small syringe of his pocket and rapidly injected the contents into the man's neck. It happened so fast that the man had no time to react or attempt to avoid the needle.

Emilio took two steps back and pulled the silenced Browning. He trained it on the man. As the man looked at this powerful weapon and saw the silencer attached, his eyes widened. He didn't even reach for his own weapon—he knew what his fate was about to be. Panic reflected in his eyes, and he only said, "I didn't have anything to do with the kidnapping of the Chinese man. Please don't kill meeeee....." His voice trailed off as the sedative took effect, and he fell down at Emilio's feet like a sack of potatoes.

Emilio rapidly disarmed the man, sticking the weapon inside his jacket. Using his feet and hands, he rolled the man under one of the cars to hide his body. He double-checked to make sure it was fully concealed and put the travel bag down on the ground. He took out one of the hand grenades and a roll of string. He opened the door to the Rolls Royce, tied the grenade to the column of the steering wheel, measured the distance from the steering wheel to the car door's interior handle, and cut a length of twine. He tied one end to the pin of the grenade and then carefully looped one end around the interior handle. Without tightening it, he closed the door, and then pulled the twine tight through the car's window. Then he knotted it off so that it would remain taught and then left the booby-trapped car.

He looked around the parking lot and picked the two most expensive cars, figuring they belonged to the gangsters inside. He took two more grenades. He pulled the pin on each grenade and tossed them into the back seat of each car. He rushed inside the metal security door which had been wedged open by the bench the man had been sitting on.

Four seconds later, two explosions shook the place with sufficient force that he had to steady himself against the wall. He put the travel bag on the floor and removed the string of firecrackers. Using another match, he lit off the string, placing it on the floor outside the door leading into the bar and then slipped inside. As he did, his eyes met those of Bogota, who was by now standing to the right of the bar. As instructed, she was pretending to sip a drink. He also met the eyes of Mr. Xiang, who was seated at the opposite end of the bar from Bogota, surrounded by four men. He moved away from the door to the back, casually so as not to call any attention to himself.

The firecrackers started to rapidly explode. Two men walked off to investigate the commotion. The music in the bar was tropical, played from a jukebox. Even though the music was loud, the firecrackers were heard and sounded like firearms discharge. The place was packed, but some people started to leave in concern as they heard the explosions. Some couples stood up at their tables to summon the wait staff to pay their bills before leaving. The calmness of reactions proved to Emilio that this was not an uncommon occurrence here. It was clearly not a high-class night club.

Mr. Xiang had not taken his eyes off Emilio, looking for an opportunity. When the two men stood up and left, he reached forward like he was going to get his drink. Instead, he grabbed the narrow glass vase of flowers and swung it full into the face of the man sitting next to him.

The other man sitting opposite him immediately reached for his pistol. Instead, he pitched face first onto the table, a bullet hole in his jaw. Bogota stood behind him, smoke issuing from the barrel of her pistol. Mr. Xiang, using the confusion of the man he had just struck, performed a sudden Kung Fu dragon punch right to the throat. He stood up. He had hit the man so hard in the throat that the man was gasping for breath from his ruptured his trachea. He pulled both men's pistols out. A shot hit awfully close to him, throwing up splinters from the table as it missed. That shot had come from the bartender, who collapsed forward, a bullet wound in his head courtesy of Emilio. In his death reaction, he had squeezed the trigger as he fell, dropping his long-barreled revolver as he did, which was why the shot had gone astray.

Police sirens could be heard in the distance. Many men started to pour out of what appeared to be an office over the bar on the second story. The first one who came out started to shoot at Mr. Xiang, but Bogota shot him twice in the chest. More came, and Emilio pulled a couple of grenades out of the bag and, pulling the pin with his teeth, threw them both upstairs. He yelled, "Take cover! Grenades!"

Mr. Xiang and Bogota, trained for this, dove to the floor, and hid beneath tables. At the same time, people started to scream in panic and ran. The place erupted in madness as the grenades exploded. The entire upper floor collapsed on top of the bar, shattering glass and mirrors and smashing the bar counter.

Emilio yelled the signal to retreat: "To the place of origin!"

Bogota and Mr. Xiang heard him and started to make their way out by the front door, heading towards the van. Emilio, the silenced pistol in one hand and the travel bag in the other, made his way back out the rear. That bag had become unbelievably handy in the rescue of his best friend. It was like he had been rewarded for being a good friend to the sniper.

He hid in the hallway towards the back door. He put his pistol away in his waistband, and casually left through the rear. As he walked around front, he mixed with the panicked crowd outside, running like the rest of them. As he ran towards the van, he saw the first police cars arriving at the place. Several men, who looked like gangsters, were coming from behind him out the rear, far behind him. Some were wounded, but others were uninjured. They headed towards the Rolls Royce, pistols in hand. Emilio started to count. "1...2...3...4...5..." He hunched over and winced as the explosion tore the night. "Adios, Gato Tuerto," he said.

Perhaps that final explosion was too much stress for the sign outside the bar; it teetered and finally fell over. He arrived at the van and went over to his friends. "Are you OK? Anyone hit?" They both answered in the negative. "Let's get out of here as soon as possible. I'm very satisfied that you're in one piece, Mr. Xiang, but let's put some distance between us and this place. I don't want to have to answer any questions from the local police, Interpol, or our people in the American embassy." He winked at them slyly.

He went in through the back door to stow the travel bag. He checked his wristwatch. "It's already 4 am. I think we should return to our safehouse in Los Rosales. Once we're safely there, Mr. Xiang, you can debrief us in detail how you always manage to get into messes like this."

Mr. Xiang smiled. "Long story, long story."

As they drove off, Bogota asked Emilio, "Are we going to pass by Location #9?"

"Yes. Why? Do you need anything?"

"Yes. I would like to pick up my Mercedes there. It's still sitting in that underground parking lot. Why don't you drop me there so I can pick up my car? I want to go back to the cabaret to corroborate whether your theory goes along with my instincts. I'll meet you guys in the Los Rosales safehouse in two hours. If you like, I can prepare for you guys an excellent breakfast. I think we all of us deserve that before we go to bed for a few hours and recuperate from the loss of sleep this monotonous, routine night for our line of work has given us."

They all smiled and chuckled. Emilio pulled into the underground garage when they got there. They said goodbye to Bogota, and he waited patiently until she got into her beautiful silver 300 SL Gullwing Mercedes.

Figure 19 300 SL Gullwing Mercedes

Emilio took extreme precautions; given all that had happened, he didn't move until he saw her driving away from the garage without any problems or tails. Then he started to follow her like an escort until they left the garage and pulled onto the road. They parted and drove in different directions in the midst of the growing traffic as the city began to wake up to a new day.

Mr. Xiang said, "Since we're driving now, let me give you a little bit of a debrief into what happened last night. After I took the samples to the lab, my contact inside the Nazi group called me. He said that the courier that was supposed to take our package to Argentina and its final destination was already in Bogota. Since he had recently arrived in the city, they had him in their custody. Juan Alberto didn't want to meet the contact face to face. They suggested that I should go and impersonate the contact, because the original one had been kidnapped and was refusing utterly to cooperate with them, despite the psychological pressure they were applying through enhanced interrogation techniques. When they brought him down to another level to continue to exert pressure, he jumped at the first opportunity he had from the sixth-floor window."

Emilio interrupted, "After what happened yesterday, you should not have gone by yourself to meet with that man. Especially since you didn't even let me know about it. I've told you many times when something happens at that level of risk, you have to have a backup."

Mr. Xiang looked sad and ashamed and nodded his head. "You are 100% right, and you have all the reason to tell me whatever you want. This mistake nearly cost me my life. The intervention of you and Bogota was very opportune. That is the reason I'm now safe and alive thanks to you guys."

"We did nothing that you haven't done yourself many times for many of us."

Mr. Xiang felt a little better and smiled. "I interviewed the courier, who identified himself as Adolfo Mena Gonzalez, and we all know that's a fictitious name." Mr. Xiang shook his head with a sour face. "This individual is the same height as Hitler, dark hair, his face is acceptable but not good-looking. He told me something that took me by surprise."

"Really? What is that?"

"He told me that he is not only the courier, but that he is the one who will replace the old leader as the new one. The man he was to transport should re-establish several contacts with him in Buenos Aires, Argentina, but he was to pass the baton of national socialist power to Mr. Gonzales. But he had to do that himself, in person, so that everyone would accept it." Mr. Xiang and Emilio exchanged skeptical looks. Mr. Xiang continued, "We both know the level of egotism all the Nazis have."

Emilio nodded in agreement. "Yes. What I cannot understand, though, is why he decided to share this information with you, unless you really impressed him or intimidated him with your conversation. Maybe he tried to use reverse psychology on you, trying to show you his superior position, imagining that you would bow to him. Whatever his motivation was to share this with you, we must keep our eyes on this guy, no matter what name he's using. He could be a wannabe, or he might be the next anti-Christ."

Mr. Xiang nodded. He looked a little worried. "If I can give you my best assessment of this man's personality, I take the second category."

Emilio's eyes grew wide in surprise. He exclaimed, "Really, Mr. Xiang?"

Xiang nodded sadly. "Really."

Emilio shook his head regretfully. "That really worries me deeply. You very rarely make mistakes in evaluating the character of any of our enemies, not just because you have a PhD in Psychology, but also because your natural talents make me sometimes think those powers are extra-terrestrial or supernatural."

Mr. Xiang bowed his head at the compliment. "I don't know if what you say is possible or not, but there are some things in my personality, it could be an energy beyond what I myself can imagine. But when I looked into this gentleman's eyes, I feel like he's coming from the same place I come from. The big difference is that he comes from the darker, evil side of that place."

Emilio looked concerned. He kept his left hand on the wheel and pointed at Mr. Xiang. "You're starting to worry me a lot about this guy."

"Join the club. This man told me that he has a doctoral degree in human medicine from his country, and he is planning to go on a trip around South and Central America with one of his friends to study the inhuman conditions the imperialistic American capitalists make the poor class live in. This is what he's looking for: to plant that seed for the national socialism throughout the American continent. Does that sound familiar to you?"

Emilio nodded. "Something very familiar to you and I both. How old do you think this individual is? In your estimation?"

"I don't know exactly, but he's very young, probably in his middle 20's."

Emilio shook his head, more worried than before as he shared Mr. Xiang's concern. "We're coming into a new year, 1955. Tomorrow is Sunday, the day of joy and peace for everyone all over the world. It's a perfect day for anyone who goes by imperceptibly."

Montauk: The Lightning Chance

Mr. Xiang looked at Emilio in confusion. "What are you saying?" Mr. Xiang was accustomed to this kind of psychological analysis, that could seem a little extra-terrestrial from Emilio.

"What about his physical appearance did he reflect to you?"

Mr. Xiang stroked his chin with his right hand. "A young man, apparently healthy."

"Did you notice anything odd about him?" Emilio interrupted.

"The only thing odd I noticed is that he has some kind of foul odor. I don't know if it's in his clothes or what, but he told me he came in a merchant ship. I assumed that the smell was of fish, chemicals, or other cargo that ship might have been transporting, that it was because he was sleeping on the ship."

Emilio interrupted again as he saw that Mr. Xiang could not locate the odor precisely. "Could it be sulfur?"

"Yes!" Mr. Xiang said excitedly. "That's exactly it. I kept thinking between the boat and the fish and could not relate it precisely. Sulfur! That damned pig smelled like sulfur, like a rotten egg or a rotten cabbage."

Emilio was pulling into the underground garage of the safehouse by this point. He pulled into a parking space and scanned the area. They were just a little distance from the Chrysler. He turned the engine off. "God help us, because to stop this man we will need Him more than ever. According to my calculation, this young man, the one you interviewed last night, could be from my point of view the replacement or reincarnation to the package. I have no doubts in my mind now, even though scientifically we don't have any proof, that this man is what we think he is. I felt that strongly every single minute, every single second I performed the surgery on his arm that I caught that same smell. I started to think it was because the wound was rotten. Now, however, I realize and can assure you, that that man is the old Hitler, and the young man that you just met, that young Doctor Aldofo Mena Gonzalez or whatever name he's assuming, is his replacement."

Mr. Xiang put both hands to his temples and leaned back in his seat. "Of course! Of course! Now it all makes perfect sense. We think we're penetrating them, and in reality, he is the one who has been penetrating us. That's the reason his contact didn't go along with any pressure, even under torture, and resisted cooperating with our people and jumped from the sixth floor at the first opportunity and die rather than betray his masters. What a coincidence, eh, that he jumped from the sixth floor."

"I don't believe in coincidence."

"Well, since you don't believe in coincidences, how about another one? The man who intercepted me did so only a few blocks from the New Buenos Aires after I had a call with Juan Alberto to tell him that the courier had arrived from Argentina. During that conversation he said that we had to call the package two hours before to provide him the passcode of the New Buenos Aires del Oro."

"As I told you before, not only do we have strong suspicions that Juan Alberto is a double agent, I believe he's a triple spy. Or more accurately, a mercenary. Knowing part of Hitler's plans and this newcomer that could be the anti-Christ, he might have gone into complete panic. You know how these guys work. They kill their own followers when they don't need them anymore in order to leave no witnesses behind. That is why Juan Alberto decided to pass the code to you, because he didn't want to get anywhere near this guy or even talk to him over the phone. If he's terrified, he realizes that this new leader, this young national socialist, the future Fürher, might kill him in order to leave no traces."

Mr. Xiang nodded slightly in thought. "As they say in Cuba, whoever doesn't want soup gets three cups. I'm going to give you another coincidence: what do you think was the first thing that the kidnappers asked me?"

"I don't know."

"The first thing they wanted to know was the code to pick up the package. The second thing they asked me was to talk to you personally. Of course, the first one I gave to them. I knew they already had it; they were just using that to see and test me to see if I would cooperate with them to avoid torture—as you taught me, Dr. del Marmol. That earned his trust. I knew they were working with Juan Alberto. They allowed me to make the phone call because I was cooperating with them to set up the opportunity to assassinate both of us at once. They didn't count on the fact that we have internal signals we use to communicate with each other when we're in danger. I sent that signal to you as an intellectual silencer that couldn't even reach their ignorant ears." Mr. Xiang smiled in satisfaction.

They got out of the van and walked towards the elevators. Emilio said, "All right, we'll continue talking more inside. First, let's check on our patient. I have to debrief you on several topics that will clarify everything we've been discussing. Then we can wait for Bogota to cook that wonderful breakfast. We'll also need her information and fresh intelligence in order to proceed with our plans or adjust or change them."

They entered the elevator and went up to the Tenth Floor. When the bell pinged for the floor, they silently left the elevator and checked their surroundings. No one was around, and they started to walk towards their suite. They were near the door when they both heard the elevator bell once more. They spun around to look behind them, instinctively reaching inside their jackets.

A very tall man with a thick beard, elegantly dressed in a black raincoat and a black hat with white bandana, got out of the elevator. He held a pistol in his hand with a silencer attached. He pointed it at them and fired twice, once at Emilio and once at Mr. Xiang. In response to their excellent training, they both leaped and rolled on the carpet on opposite sides of the wide hallway. The man's aim was completely thrown as he fired once more. The shots tore into the carpet rather than either of his targets. As he rolled, Mr. Xiang managed to pull something that looked like a small flute that had been tied to one of his legs. He raised it to his mouth and blew three times. One of the darts that came out of the tube went straight into the right eye of their attacker. One other went into his cheek, and the third into his neck just below the jaw.

The man stumbled and dropped his pistol. He could not control his movements and fell to his knees. Both Emilio and Mr. Xiang stood up, pistols ready to shoot. They looked at the man who offered no further threat. He looked like he was drunk or drugged and was mumbling, "You guys got me good. Goooood." His head fell forward as he fell either asleep or died.

Emilio and Mr. Xiang went over to him and picked up his gun—another Lugar. Emilio smiled. "Another for my collection." They made sure there was no longer any danger, and Emilio went into their suite to bring out the wheelchair. With Mr. Xiang's aid, they got the would-be assassin into the chair. They wheeled him inside. Emilio looked at the man's eye. "What were you trying to do? Were you trying to take this man down or blind him?"

Mr. Xiang replied, "I did what I could under the circumstances."

"I'm just joking with you, man—you did great. I saved your life today, and you didn't even wait twenty-four hours to pay me back." He jabbed Mr. Xiang playfully with one finger. "You're something else."

They took the man to the surgery room, where Emilio, with Mr. Xiang's aid, removed the bearded man's clothes. His body was covered in tattoos. They covered half his body with sheets, and Emilio put some instruments in the sterilizer. He washed his hands, gloved, and then removed the instruments to start working on the man's eyes. Mr. Xiang acted as a very efficient assistant.

Emilio said, "This man will be one-eyed for the rest of his life. I bet my life if you tried that again that you would never hit someone in the eye in a million years. What were your real intentions? Was it just a coincidence, or did you want to blind him on purpose so he couldn't keep shooting at us?"

Mr. Xiang smiled slightly. "You always love to bug me. That dart is the one that made him drop the gun. If I hit him anywhere else, the sedative might not be strong enough, and he could still have fired off some shots. We should thank God that he was hit in the eye first, because it was divine intervention! If I were that good, my second dart would have gone into his other eye—that way, it would be a double whammy and serve the purpose to make this man abandon the nasty profession of being a hit man, killing innocent people like us."

Emilio smiled again. "Whatever the case is, you did the humane thing any decent person would do. You left him with one eye. I assure you that he will never forget how he lost that eye. That maybe will be a good reason for him to retire. Or maybe it will be his ticket to let him collect on a good health insurance. Maybe you'll make him too incapacitated for the line of work he's been in, which was not precisely selling ice cream in the park."

As he spoke, Emilio finished bandaging the hit man's eyes and took his pulse. He injected into the man the contents of a couple of syringes. "One thing I have to grant you, Mr. Xiang—you gave this man enough sedative to tranquilize an elephant."

"Did you see the size of the animal? I didn't want to take any chances! Besides, I didn't want to shed any blood in the hallway leading to our emergency safehouse."

Emilio grew serious at that one. "I know your intentions are always the best. In reality, the results could not be better, in fact excellent." He turned jocular again. "Literally, an eye for an eye. Besides, if he had forced us to shoot him, we would be forced ourselves to call the Cleaners. That would force us to leave this place immediately because of all the commotion that would create. We managed to neutralize him without shedding blood, and so have given ourselves a window of time. We won't be able to use this place much longer after this incident, but at least we now have the time to interrogate him and assess how bad the situation is. If he came here using his own instincts or followed us without our realizing it, or the people behind this assassination attempt are the ones who provided him with this location, any of those things can change tremendously our priority in leaving this place or not within the next twenty-four hours. Either way, just in case, get on the phone right now and report this incident to Bogota so that she can take extreme precautions when she returns here. What I need from you now is to help me transport this beast from the operating table onto the gurney. I'll be able to handle the rest."

"Very well." After he helped Emilio transfer the heavy man onto the gurney, he left the operating room and entered the dining room. He picked up the phone on the wall there while Emilio rolled the gurney to one of the secure cells next to Ramon.

Emilio prepared a mixture in a couple of bottles and injected the serum into the IV hanging next to the gurney. He made sure the man's limbs were tied down by the restraint straps on the gurney. He left the room, double-locked the door, and glanced through the window in the door before leaving. The hit man lay there without moving, a small smile on his lips. He saluted the man mockingly. "Sweet dreams. We'll see what you have to tell us when you wake up."

Dr. Julio Antonio del Marmol

CHAPTER 9: THE DEVIL'S DOCTOR

Figure 20 Rosario, Argentina

  Emilio walked back to the operating room, removed his gloves, and washed his hands. He tried to put everything back in order as best he could; then he rejoined Mr. Xiang, who was having some green tea in the dining room; the pot sat beside him. They examined the documents they had taken from the bearded man. Mr. Xiang poured a cup of tea and pushed it over to Emilio. "The tea pot is full; I prepared enough for all of us, including Bogota. I put the honey, sugar, and lemon out on the counter. All you have to do is pour, serve, and drink."
  Emilio smiled in gratitude and raised his right hand. "Thank you very much. You know I'm accustomed to only drinking hot water in the morning to detoxify my body and help accelerate the process of bowel movement."

"I know. I've been around you for so long that I know your habits." He smiled. "But my offer is a pure and genuine courtesy."

"The gesture is appreciated. I will take you up on a cup, though." He took a cup and rinsed it out in the sink and then filled it with hot water. He returned and sat down next to Mr. Xiang. "Again, thank you very much for your genuine courtesy."

Mr. Xiang bobbed his head in response. He held up a small promotional card for a Protestant church in Rosario, Argentina. There were some occult symbols on the back with a date printed on it: January 26th, 1955, along with a meeting time of twelve midnight, when, according to the card, "the integration of the bodies will take place." The card was signed by Adolfo Mena Gonzalez. The name it was addressed to was Rafael Sarmiento Diaz. It appeared to be a courtesy invitation to the holder, perhaps something to identify the bearer at the door to the event. Either way, it looked important enough for them to have gone through the trouble of printing the small cards.

They looked at each other, thinking the same thing. Mr. Xiang was the first to speak. "If this man with the beard happens to be Rafael Sarmiento Diaz, he is part of the team of assassins from Adolfo Mena Gonzales."

Emilio furrowed his brow and stroked it with the fingers of his left hand. "Yes, there's no doubt at all that the courier sent this assassin. His first and last name are from the father, and Sarmiento is of Italian origin; but Diaz is of Jewish origin. I have to ask myself how it is possible that this individual with these roots this tree could have degenerated so much to become not only an assassin, but one in the service of the Nazis?" He paused and shook his head, taking the passport of the man from the table. "Before anything else, we have to be sure that this individual is not an imposter working under whatever name this passport holds. The only way we will be completely sure is through an intense interrogation of him as soon as we think he'll be healthy enough."

Mr. Xiang nodded. He rubbed his hands together. "I cannot wait. I think we have a great opportunity in our hands, having not just one, but both assassins as prisoners right here with us. There's no doubt in my mind that this is divine intervention. Only God knows what sort of fountain of information that we can obtain from them."

Emilio nodded his head. "Literally and precisely we can kill two birds with one shot."

Mr. Xiang also smiled in satisfaction. The buzzer on the door sounded, announcing someone at the front door. They both stood up, took their pistols out, and approached the hallway leading to the front door. Mr. Xiang gestured for Emilio to stay a little back to cover him as he checked the door.

He looked at the monitor on the wall next to the door and saw it was Bogota. He undid the clamp on the massive steel security bar across the entire door and raised it up. Emilio was still behind Mr. Xiang, his back against the wall with the silenced Browning trained on the door to cover Mr. Xiang in case Bogota had company. He watched as Mr. Xiang removed the bar and unlocked the security bolts that made the safehouse more like a safe deposit vault in a bank.

She was alone and came into the suite with a portfolio and a long tube normally used for maps, blueprints, or plans. After she entered, Mr. Xiang closed the door, locked, and barred it once more. She greeted everyone with a smile, and the three of them walked to the conference room at the back of the suite. Emilio took the long tube from her to alleviate her burden, given her arm injury.

They walked into the large room. It held a long mahogany table with chairs around it, a mini bar with a stainless-steel sink, a fancy silver and gold faucet. At one side of the room was a large projector, and on the opposite wall was a retractable screen and a cork board. They got comfortable.

Bogota said, "Well, well, well. If we don't have all of it, we have most of the spider's web that we've been untangling from this diabolical international organization that they've tried to put together. This selfish man, full of dark ambition with zero sentiment, is the focus in their thirst for controlling the entire world. But a new king is replacing the old king. The old leader will be exchanged for the young Argentinian doctor who will take up the torch to follow the old plans to spread the Satanic national socialist ideology." She pulled a document out of the tube and unrolled it across the table.

It looked like a very high-quality painting. No one could doubt the artistic value of it; whoever had done the painting was an extraordinarily gifted artist. As magnificent as the painting looked, the image was diabolic, dark, and depressing. It was a man on a black horse rearing up on its hind legs. Surrounding the man and horse were six wolves, snarling ferociously. They had gray-white patches on their forehead. The horse had white circles along the bottom of the legs just above its hooves and a patch on its forehead running from above its nose, between its eyes, and up to its ears that wasn't precisely white or gray, but somewhere in between with some light brown highlights. The eyes of the horse, man, and wolves were yellow with a circle of red around the edges. The man was dressed in medieval attire with a massive full-body red cloak thrown back over his shoulders. It had black symbols, the same ones on the invitation. He wore a breastplate and leg armor, with spikes at the shoulders and on the sides of the leg armor, and the spikes were around 5 inches long. He held a two-edged sword with symbols etched into the blade, dragons and serpents adorning the hilt. It looked like an occult motif of black magic. The eyes of the man, even though his head was covered with a helmet that was the head of a black bull with short horns and ears erect, showed through the eyes of the bull's head. In his left hand he held a long pole with a three-pronged trident at the head, each point wickedly barbed. The pole was around 6 to 7 feet long. It was similar to a lance in design save for the head of the weapon.

Mr. Xiang threw up his hands in shock. "Oh, my God! This is the most vivid depiction of Lucifer I have ever seen in all my life!"

Bogota nodded. "Yes. The documents I found in my father's safe at the cabaret, though I don't know how real they might be, had a series of wax seals that looked like human blood in them. According to the documents, the young painter who did this portrait actually had Lucifer posing for him. The Devil offered to the young painter wealth and fame in return for the portrait. Some of this paint has the blood of the young painter mixed with it, for according to the account, after the man was done, Lucifer put out his eyes so he could never do one like this again." As she spoke, she pulled several documents out of the portfolio and spread them out on the table.

Mr. Xiang said, "As always, the promises of Lucifer are like those of communists and Nazis. People never realize that they are false promises. Unfortunately, people never learn, and for fame and fortune they do anything. They'll even make a pact with the Devil and instead give him in the process the most beautiful gift any human being can have: their eyes. I don't know, either, how much truth there is in all these documents you're showing us. The truth is that I can assure you, even outside these documents, after my past experience with human beings and so many evil, conniving assassins, it is possible that certain people are capable of doing anything. The most recent example we have is your own father, Juan Alberto."

Bogota and Emilio both looked at Mr. Xiang and nodded in agreement. Bogota said, "I know from my own experience that if none of this is true, it would be very close to it." She turned to Emilio, "Your intuitions have been 100% right in line. Just as you predicted, my father left the country very late last night, even before we left the safehouse. He left me this letter." She put it on the table. "He tried to justify himself and his actions, and make sense and excuse his dark ambitions, even betraying all of us and his own country along with the world, because he tried to protect me and offer me economic stability. Curiously enough he took all he could, millions of dollars, with him. He only left in the safe $50,000 with that letter so that I could continue the business."

Tears welled up in her eyes as she spoke. "At least, if we can't look the other way, he did one thing decent." She pulled another document out of the portfolio and took a deep breath. It appeared to be a power of attorney stating that everything he left behind is to belong to her: the business, the condo, all of his properties in Bogota. "I would actually prefer that he left me nothing at all, leaving me in misery by myself with the honor and decency he could not give me."

Emilio and Mr. Xiang looked at her sadly as they observed the pain and shame she was feeling at that moment. Mr. Xiang reached out and took her hand. "I'm sorry. Very sorry—even if it's the truth, and we all know how bad your father is, I should not have said what I told you before and the way I did it."

Bogota put her hand on top of his. "Thank you very much, Mr. Xiang, for your compassion and sympathy. But your apology isn't necessary at all. We should never apologize to anyone for telling the truth, no matter how painful that truth can be. If we do that, we actually cheat ourselves."

Emilio replied, "I don't know the amount of pain you're going through, but I can tell you one thing: Mr. Xiang had the best intentions when he apologized to you, but I completely agree with you. Trying to cover the truth with lies is on the border sometimes of being more criminal and more painful than how the lie originated."

They remained silent for a few seconds. Emilio tried to move past the moment of pain by saying, "I don't know about you guys, but my stomach is crying and howling like the wolves in that painting! I really have been looking forward to that breakfast from Bogota, but we should go get something outside. I cannot wait that long!"

Montauk: The Lightning Chance

"Oh!" she exclaimed in embarrassment. "I can make it in no time at all. A promise is a promise, and you should give me the opportunity to make it happen. I don't want to break my promise like the communists and Nazis do."

Emilio said, "What about breakfast tomorrow? We're past breakfast time now. Let's go and get a brunch or find a buffet. During the trip we can continue our debrief."

"OK, we'll do the breakfast tomorrow. Let's go. What do you guys want to eat?"

"Whatever you guys want," Emilio said. "You pick."

"I'm not really hungry," Bogota said, "with all that's been going on. It wouldn't be fair."

"All right, Mr. Xiang can pick. Even though we're all tired, I believe you're the most fatigued of us all with your injury, and you do need to rest."

Mr. Xiang said, "OK, how about Chinese?"

"What about that Chinese restaurant you took me to a couple of weeks ago?" Emilio suggested.

"Oh, that is great—fantastic!" Mr. Xiang said. "Not just because it's Chinese, but it's also close to here. We won't have to wait too long."

Bogota pouted. "I really wanted to make breakfast for you guys."

The men smiled. Emilio said, "You'll get the opportunity. Let's go now and check on the prisoners, and then we'll take off."

Emilio went by both doors and peered through the glass window. Both men were still unconscious from their sedatives, so he rejoined the others and they drove to the restaurant in the van in order to draw less attention.

As Mr. Xiang drove, Emilio said, "You don't have to drive that fast. We don't want to be stopped by the police for any reason. Remember what we have in the back."

"I'm sorry. Was I speeding? This little Chinaman is so hungry he could eat raw elephant meat! He's been contenting himself to sip hot tea. I've even considered eating my nails, but I know they won't taste good and are pretty indigestible."

They saw a sign that read *La Casa de Asia*[26]. Emilio said, "This was great. As I recall, the food here is excellent."

---

[26] The House of Asia

Figure 21 Chinese Restaurant

Mr. Xiang said, "We can go here, or I know another that's even better that's only a few blocks away."

"Mr. Xiang, you are the captain of this boat," Emilio said.

"Aye, aye, Admiral," Mr. Xiang said with a grin.

"This one is OK. Especially since you're so hungry, we don't want you to forget your good manners and try taking a bite out of us!"

They pulled into the parking lot and received excellent service from the moment they walked in the door. They were remembered from previous visits, and they even received a brushing of their garments from the staff. They looked through the menu, and Emilio said to Bogota, "You're the lady. You order first."

Bogota said, "Thank you." She ordered a wonton soup and fried wontons. Mr. Xiang ordered Peking duck, fried rice, and wonton soup. Emilio ordered last and asked for beef with oyster sauce, wonton soup, and fried wontons. They all agreed on wine for their drinks, and so he asked for a bottle of chardonnay. They enjoyed their pleasant meal, a great recompense for all they had missed out on during the previous day. They paid the bill and left a generous tip.

As they drove back, Bogota told Emilio that she had information that the courier Gonzales took the package early that morning on a ship to Argentina. "They were evidently in a rush," she added, "maybe because two of their assassins are missing and they have no idea what happened to them. Seeing that things were getting complicated, he took the package and immediately left Bogota. According to our information,

Montauk: The Lightning Chance

he wasn't supposed to leave the city until after they had everything in order."

Emilio said, "We should go back to Juan Alberto's condo to see if we can find anything they might have left in their rush, some evidence."

They drove back to the condo, which was the same place Emilio had gone to perform his surgery on the package. Their suspicions that this man might be Adolf Hitler grew as time passed. A mysterious individual in near-perfect disguise that was trying to reorganize his political movement in the Americas now so urgently left the city; everything in the sequence of events indicated at the very least that he was someone extremely important and not the ordinary Nazi fugitive. They parked the van in the underground garage and walked to the elevators. Bogota pulled out the special key and inserted in the slot for the penthouse. They got in the elevator and headed up. As they neared the penthouse, they all pulled their guns out and checked them, just in case Bogota's information wasn't completely accurate. They didn't want to take the chance of finding Hitler or his double and the young doctor who was supposed to be his replacement still there when they arrived. They all took a deep breath as the elevator slowed and the bell pinged. The doors opened.

When they arrived in the penthouse living room, they all got out of the elevator and carefully moved out in a triangular fashion. Mr. Xiang looked around in admiration. "Wow! I knew your father was rich, but not to this extreme. This is a lot more than I had imaged! A real polar bear skin, a baby grand piano!" They walked into the living room and he stroked the fur of the bear under the piano with his left hand. Even though he was impressed by the splendor of the magnificence of the place and the expensive paintings hanging on the walls, he did not let it distract him. His eyes were alert as he scanned the place for anyone who might be in the condo with them.

Emilio said, "Go around this place. Check everywhere, even if you think it's ridiculous. The most ridiculous place might hold evidence that they had forgotten."

As Mr. Xiang checked everything, he kept gawking at the luxury of the place, this being his first visit there. He said, "Let's hope we can find some shred of evidence here that will allow us to untangle this spider's web. We need to break the grandiose dreams of these people to control the world."

After a while, they met back in the living room and looked at each other in disappointment and shook their heads. Emilio, full of frustrated hope at finding something there, went over to the La-Z-Boy in front of the television and sat down heavily in it. He said, "Well, the only thing left now to complete our circle is to go back to the lab and get the results from the samples Mr. Xiang delivered...." He stopped as he felt something poking him in the seat. He shifted around in the seat and reached down. In between the frame of the chair and the cushions he found a bunch of promotional cards wrapped in a rubber band. He pulled them out and looked. They were the exact same cards the bearded assassin had on him from the church in Rosario, Argentina. The same occult symbols and the date of January 26th, 1955. They were even signed by Adolf Mena Gonzales. The only difference was that the address line for the intended recipient was blank.

Emilio smiled and held the bundle out to Mr. Xiang. "Bingo! Sometimes, when you're not even looking for something, you find it right in your face. That is our Lord, no doubt, sending us signals on our radios."

Mr. Xiang took the cards and passed them to Bogota, who started to examine them. She walked over to Emilio. "Where did you find these? Right there on top?"

"No, no—this is like a gift sent from God. They were stuck down in the chair. They must have fallen out of his pocket when he sat in it. When he stood up, they must have fallen in between the cushions. Many people lose their change like this."

She grinned broadly. "This is extraordinary. If you hadn't sat down there, we would have left this place without finding them."

Mr. Xiang said, "This is extremely important evidence, because this ties the bearded man we have as prisoner in with the young Doctor Gonzales."

They all nodded as they thought about that. Filled with satisfaction at this evidence, they left the condo, got in the van, and then drove to the lab. They anxiously wanted to get the results of the blood and semen samples that would conclusively prove whether the man was Hitler, a double, or just a criminal Nazi that changed his name to Adolf Schüttlemayer. He probably ran in an attempt to avoid prosecution for his crimes against humanity in South America while at the same time establishing a new base from which to spread the national socialist disease.

Montauk: The Lightning Chance

They got to the lab, and Mr. Xiang pulled over into a very small space that looked more like a pet store. He looked at the surprised expressions of his companions and said, "We've moved the lab into deeper cover now."

He went over to a glass display that had a bunch of German shepherd puppies playing in a wooden box. After a few minutes, Mr. Xiang came back out with one envelope in one hand and reading from a stapled set of three or four pages in his other hand. He had a huge grin on his face and his expression was joyful and satisfied. He walked over to the van and got inside. He handed the papers to Emilio. "99.9% positive. This shows that the individual that you took care of is for certain the Führer, Adolf Hitler."

Both Emilio and Bogota's jaws dropped. Emilio started to read through the lab papers as Bogota watched his expression carefully. He finally broke the silence. "Mr. Xiang, let's get out of here immediately. We have to go back to the safehouse in Rosales. I need a secure line to make a long-distance phone call. What I have in my hand right now will change completely what our next steps will be."

Mr. Xiang understood the urgency of the situation, started the van, and drove off to the safehouse. Emilio, lab analysis in hand, said, "It's unbelievable how my instincts never fail me and are right on target. Maybe not 100%, but 99.9%."

Bogota replied, "This is very true, Doctor. I would say even 100% true. Just thinking that I was so close to that man gives me goosebumps of terror. There's no doubt in my mind that this man is the evil mastermind for whom so many people around the world have died, because of the lust for power held by mental degenerates like him, or even worse than him. To create such ideologies with no humanity at all for their fellow human beings!"

Emilio put the papers on top of his knees. He breathed deeply and pointed at Bogota. "This might sound as ridiculous to you as when I said that I wanted to keep Ramon the sniper alive. The information he might possess could be vital to corroborate the suspicions held for a long time by me and my colleagues in intelligence that your father was not just a double but also a triple agent. For that same reason now my instincts tell me that none of the Allied members from World War II wants to see this man dead. Except, as is logical, the Israelis, for obvious reasons. Everyone else, without exception, has had a tremendous competition as to who could get their hands first on Hitler. They want him alive; I've had many conversations from the lips of the highest authorities in the intelligence community about the great value represented to whichever one of them grabs this man alive." He stopped for a few seconds, rubbing his forehead with his fingers. "As I told you before, Bogota, our work in espionage requires us to be objective and practical. We cannot allow ourselves the luxury of letting our emotions control us or we lose our perspective in our missions and the objective we're looking for."

Mr. Xiang scratched his head with one hand. "We don't always understand those decisions that come down from the high levels of government because it looks to us absurd and irrational, and that makes us sometimes go nuts and lose the perspective that we're looking for." His expression grew sad. "If the decision were all mine, I would put my pistol to the heads of each of these Nazis and blow their brains out, one by one. That's what is logical to do with the kind of human beings these guys are. My logic tells me without exception that they deserve this. Forget policy, forget diplomacy—to hell with everyone!"

Emilio looked at him and nodded. "Yes. And if I let my emotions flourish, as well, that would be the logical way of thinking for me, too. Just because it's logical, however, doesn't mean it's the most intelligent. If you still need answers to questions after doing what's logical, it's too late, because his brains are all over the floor. And then all our options and possibility for dialogue are closed. There will no longer be an opportunity, and the only thing we can do is bend over and clean up the mess."

Mr. Xiang looked down in embarrassment and then looked back up at Emilio. "That is why, my friend, we should concentrate on doing our job and let the politicians focus on doing theirs. That way we don't drive each other crazy. Of course, we will always expect to look for the best at the end when the politicians decide it will be fore everyone's common benefit."

Emilio shook his head dubiously. "Yes, we should expect that all the time, but unfortunately it isn't always like that." He looked frustrated. "Actually, I saw a gun store on this street. Keep your eyes open, please. It was on our left on the way in, so it will be on the right. I need to buy some more ammunition for those new Lugar toys I recently acquired."

Mr. Xiang smiled. "Oh, yes! It's right there. You told me in time." Mr. Xiang pulled into the parking lot for the gun store. "For a moment I thought you were going to sell your new collection of pistols."

Montauk: The Lightning Chance

Emilio smiled. "You must be kidding! That will be my legacy to my kids." Emilio got out and went inside the store. He came out with a bag filled with several boxes of bullets.

They drove to the safehouse and entered the underground lot. Mr. Xiang went around a couple of times to check every car parked there. He said, "It's better to be safe than sorry, given our recent experiences. From now on, let's always thoroughly check our surroundings."

They could see that everything was in order, and Mr. Xiang parked the van a prudent distance away from the other cars they already had stored there. They got out and walked to the elevators. Emilio pressed the button for the Tenth Floor, and they ascended. Everyone remained tensely on full alert, Emilio and Mr. Xiang exchanging glances as they put their hands on their weapons. Bogota noticed their stress. "I think we can relax, guys. I didn't see a single soul in the parking lot."

Emilio and Mr. Xiang smiled at her and shook their heads slightly. Mr. Xiang said, "Believe it or not, neither Emilio nor I, in spite of all our experience, noticed the presence of anyone in the parking lot a few hours ago. And yet when we went to our safehouse, another elevator opened, and there he was! A tremendous four hundred pound seven-foot-tall gorilla jumped out. We could not explain to ourselves how such a huge guy could be so well hidden we never noticed him. He just appeared out of the other elevator like Houdini in a magic act."

Emilio said, "We'll find out very soon. And that will determine whether we can continue to hang around here or have to abandon this location immediately." He scratched at his cheek with one hand in thought. "If my instincts haven't failed, I believe this individual didn't come from here. He was waiting for us at the El Gato Tuerto as a second hit man in case the first one failed. He sat down there like a professional and didn't interfere. He patiently kept his cool even as we were exchanging gunfire, possibly hoping that the job would get done for him without having to make any effort. When he saw that those guys couldn't handle us, he followed us all the way here, carefully, so we didn't notice him. He left his car parked outside on the street. I bet if we took our time, we would find it still there. This is what every hit man does in order to secure his exit from the scene. It's extremely possible that this man is the closest friend, perhaps even the bodyguard, to our young Dr. Gonzalez. The only reason he came here today was because he needed to finish his job before leaving this country, so no loose ends remain. This is only my analysis, instinct, and what seems logical to me. It's been several hours since that attempt on our lives and we haven't had any other unwanted visitors or violent characters."

Bogota crossed herself. "Thank you, God."

The bell pinged to announce their arrival and the label for the Tenth Floor lit up. They left the elevator car. This time, Emilio headed to move along one wall while Mr. Xiang went towards the other wall, walking backwards to face the elevator bank, just in case. Bogota kept facing forward and walked down the middle of the hall. When they reached their suite, Emilio opened the door with Mr. Xiang next to him with his pistol out while he and Bogota waited impatiently for it to open. As soon as he opened it, they scooted inside.

Emilio chuckled and said, "You can call it paranoia, but you just about stampeded me getting inside. I'll go to the conference room, but you guys go and check on our prisoners. I have to go make that phone call. As soon as you're done, meet me back there. I want you there for the call." They nodded, and Emilio walked into the conference room and to the telephone.

He sat down and pulled one of the Lugars from his back and placed it on the table. He emptied the magazine and ejected the chambered round. He went through the fresh boxes he had just purchased until he found a specific box. He filled the magazine with the bullets from the box and put it away, inserting the magazine into the pistol and chambering the first round. He carefully put the ammunition he had just unloaded in his pocket.

Mr. Xiang and Bogota returned as he was finishing his reloading of the pistol. Emilio picked up the received and dialed the operator. "Yes, I want to make an international call."

The operator's voice said, "One moment, sir."

The phone rang and another lady's voice answered. "Secretary of State John Foster Dulles' office. Code, please."

"XX021EM."

A familiar female voice picked up. "Dr. del Marmol, how are you?"

"I am very well. I hope you're OK, too."

"Yes, I'm fine, thank you."

"This call is of extreme importance and the first priority. I need to talk to John, wherever he is in the city. Please, Margaret."

Margaret replied, "Hold on. I understand and will transfer you immediately." She clearly understood the urgency and why he cut short their customary socializing.

Montauk: The Lightning Chance

A few seconds passed and a man's voice was heard. "Is everything in order, my good friend?"

"Yes, fortunately, thank God. Everything is in order, but I have a very difficult situation. The conductor of the orchestra in Berlin has left the orchestra and the city today very early, in the first hours of the morning. He left with who supposedly has a 95% certainty will be his successor."

Dulles replied, "Are you absolutely *sure* that this is the truthful and genuine conductor of the Berlin orchestra and not an imposter?"

Emilio sorted through the papers in his hand and rustled them loudly. He answered anxiously, "I have the lab results in my hand that I just picked up. I will send them to you as soon as I have an opportunity via diplomatic bag from the embassy."

He could hear Dulles pause and take a measured breath on the other end. "Do you know where the conductor is going and where we can find him?"

"Yes, he's going to: country Argentina, city Buenos Aires. The exact location I will not discuss over the phone. I'll send it to you via the diplomatic bag. I want to let you know that this almost cost not just my life but those of two of my closest collaborators. I know how this conductor is so extremely important to you guys and valuable, but he has multiple contracts. In my opinion, I don't believe he'll be able to fulfill all of them if you move quickly. In my point of view, I don't think he will be available for much longer."

Another male voice was heard asking a question of the Secretary of State and then giving him instructions. John returned and said, "Dr. del Marmol, Ike is here with me and my brother Allen. Ike wants to have a few words with you if it's OK with you."

"Sure, no problem."

Eisenhower's voice came on. "Dr. del Marmol?"

"Hello, Mr. President."

"Dr. del Marmol, what I'm about to say may sound very strange. I want this kept in high confidentiality between us. I want to ask you to please do whatever is possible in your power to maintain the conductor in a place that is comfortable and secure, someplace we can manage to guarantee his security. This is extremely important so that we can make certain he doesn't wind up in anyone else's hands but ours. Believe it or not, Dr. del Marmol, the future of humanity and their ability to live in peace for many years ahead depends on this. This will give us a way of not just preventing more world wars but also put a perpetual chain against the proliferation of the evil ideas that he represents. Imagine what would happen if he fell into the wrong hands—it will be in their best interest to continue perpetuate the cycle of conquest and persecution in every nation across the globe in order to spread that seed of domination everywhere."

Emilio replied, "Mr. President, I will do with my people whatever I have within my reach of possibilities. Remember, though, our resources are limited. This is a tremendous art auction and we have far too many competitors. They are authorized by their own governments to do anything and everything to take that valuable masterpiece to their homes. Evidently the danger of being an extinct or unique piece makes the market price very high, exorbitantly so."

Eisenhower replied, "Remember, this is our top priority for national and maybe international security, not only for the preservation of the American continent but for the rest of the world. I will authorize John right now to give you a direct line to me. All you have to do is call me with whatever you need. All embassy personnel will be informed that I have authorized this directly. There will be no interference from any other agency. I need you to succeed, Dr. del Marmol."

"Thank you, Mr. President, I promise you—and I never promise anything—that I will do the possible and the impossible to complete what you've asked me to do."

"Dr. del Marmol, humanity and our country will owe an eternal debt of gratitude to you. I know that what I'm asking isn't easy, but please do whatever you can. I'm passing the phone back to John, who is the best Secretary of State we've ever had serving in the White House. He is another gladiator like you. He had the savvy to pick you from among many people for this delicate work. God bless you, and good luck. Nice to talk to you and keep up the good work."

"Thank you, Mr. President."

John came back on the line. "Good luck to you, Dr. del Marmol. Like the President said, whatever you need, all you have to do is call him or me, twenty-four hours a day."

Emilio smiled. "I will send the documents to you tonight through the embassy. Say hello to Allen for me."

"Very well. I'll be waiting anxiously."

Emilio said goodbye and hung up with a sad expression on his face. He could not hide his dismay at having to do something he was reluctant to do. But his sense of duty told him they knew better; but to give such extreme courtesy to the man who had been responsible for the deaths of so many people was a bitter pill for him.

He looked at the others, who were waiting expectantly, as they had only heard his side of the conversation. "Well, politics. Like I said before, I completely trust John Foster Dulles, because he's a man of great integrity and extremely high intelligence. He's also on the side of God and the principles we defend. He doesn't even care that his own friends and allies around him try to ridicule him and paint him like a religious fanatic. He doesn't have a single hair on his head to be what they say, but unfortunately some people don't have enough perception to understand reality and attack us, sometimes ridiculing us as well, because the truth terrifies them. Like ostriches they believe that putting their heads in a dark hole will save them and keep them alive. To the contrary, unfortunately, it is exactly what destroys them. They only face eternal disgrace."

Bogota and Mr. Xiang both sat by Emilio's side, filled with curiosity about such a historical phone call with the Secretary of State *and* the President of the United States. Bogota was the first one who broke the silence. "What did the President say?"

Emilio replied, "As you can see, it was a very brief conversation and a little vague at the outset and difficult to understand unless you know what I meant—as you guys know. When you analyze it in detail, you'll understand it better. According to the President, this is a first priority not only for national but international security for the United States. At least from what I could understand."

Mr. Xiang asked, "What did he ask you to do that you promised him you would do the possible and impossible to make happen?"

Emilio rubbed his forehead with his fingers for a few seconds as he searched for an appropriate way to answer his old friend. "Very good question, Mr. Xiang. Here is the beginning of the first analysis. It sounds illogical to us at first glance but later, as we examine it more deeply, the result is completely logical and maybe tremendously intelligent." Instead of answering, he looked at them to make sure they were completely attentive. "How can we prevent the seed of evil and diabolic cults that completely corrupt humanity from continuing to spread around in the future, and leave open the road that leads out of corruption?"

They looked at each other in confusion and then looked back at Emilio. He continued, "That, in reality, is the question that many noble men with good principals have been asking for thousands of years." Emilio nodded with a small smile on his face. "The only way to control evil is with the knife of love and mercy at his throat." He shook his head. "It's difficult to understand that evil never will be completely exterminated. But if we can control it like a contagious disease, though it never ends, we'll remain ahead of the game." He looked at Mr. Xiang, putting his right hand affectionately on his friend's shoulder. "This is exactly what President Eisenhower asked me to do: after all this mumbo jumbo, to maintain Hitler alive at all costs. He doesn't want Hitler to fall into the wrong hands, of those who will use his evil to continue cloning more malevolence and spread it for future generations to suffer the same diabolical effects all over the face of the Earth."

Mr. Xiang scratched behind his ear with his left hand. "This is what he calls national and international security priority?"

"Yes. This diabolical being has in his head tremendous, valuable secrets that could be used for the good of the future of humanity. It could be, for instance, contact with beings from other planets, time travel, movement between certain points and times by objects and persons, super connection in communication and information, missiles, weapons of mass destruction, etc. Can you imagine whether these things are possible or not—or even possible one day, if this technology and information landed in the wrong hands? Like I said before, in a simple analysis the first thing that comes to our mind and is completely logical: when the lion attacks you, you shoot it and kill it, especially if its harmed a member of your family and friends. But what if we can sedate the lion, put it in a very secret plan of domestication, maybe we can use it as protection against our enemies? Especially an enemy that could be more powerful and sadistic in the future? And always, if this isn't a good result, we can put it to sleep eternally."

Mr. Xiang and Bogota looked at him with puzzled, dubious expressions. It was clear they weren't totally convinced about the appropriateness of what the President wanted to do, much less ethical. Emilio decided not to pursue the conversation with his friends; even though he had accepted the logic of this course of action, he also lacked moral convictions about it himself. He didn't think it was the best example for future generations. He said to Bogota, "Please, why don't you go and see if one of them has recuperated from the anesthetic?"

"Sure." She got up to go and comply. She returned a little while later, a little agitated. "The bearded man is already conscious, and it looks like he's trying to get out of bed. Though he didn't break one of the belts, he loosened it."

Montauk: The Lightning Chance

Mr. Xiang jumped up and pulled his pistol, ready to run to the man. Emilio smiled and held up his hand. "Calm down, guys. Calm down." He reached for the Lugar he had placed on the table with his right hand. "Remember, those straps had been built to support 3,000 pounds of strength. They normally use them to unload heavy cargo ships along the piers using the long cranes. Supposedly, this man has accomplished the impossible because he comes from another planet, but the doors and walls of that room are meter-thick reinforced concrete with steel bars. There is no way he can get out of that room, even if he gets free of the straps. Let's take our time. We'll be able to see him, but he can't see us. Let's see what he's doing and how strong this man really is. Not only will we find out how strong he is but also his level of IQ—which I don't think is very high, taking into consideration the profession he's chosen to be in. Unless we have between us another Nathan Leopold[27]."

They arrived at the door to the bearded man's room. They could see evidence of the immense physical strength the man had. He hadn't burst the belt itself—he had broken the metal tongue in the buckle that kept the belt tightened. He was desperately working at the other one on his left hand. The slack was enough for a small amount of movement, but not full freedom. The bed he was lying on was bolted to the concrete floor, so the only thing he had to work with were the belt buckles. No sound got through the soundproofing to them.

Emilio smiled. "Let him be for a little while. Let him try. Give him five or ten more minutes." They finally decided to open the door. Emilio stayed outside to observe while Mr. Xiang walked in. As soon as he heard the door opening, Rafael stopped moving and pretended to be asleep, trying to hide the loose belt with one hand. Emilio smiled again. He said to Bogota, "Please go and bring a syringe either with B-12 or Vitamin K—whatever you find there and fill the syringe and bring it to me. Let's terrify this guy. Bring a wheelchair, handcuffs, and leg irons."

"Very well." She turned and left.

Emilio entered the room, where Mr. Xiang stood at a prudent distance from Rafael, not taking his eyes off him. When he noticed

---

[27] Nathan Leopold and his friend Richard Loeb murdered 14-year-old Bobby Franks in 1924 in an attempt to create "the perfect crime". Both were child prodigies who, influenced by Nietzsche, thought they were supermen. Both were sentenced to life +99 years; Leopold was paroled 33 years later in 1958, dying in Puerto Rico in 1971.

Emilio enter, he asked, "What are we going to do with this beast from Hell?" He winked at Emilio as they started the first phase of their program. This was either going to be a very short or very long interrogation process, depending on the subject's IQ.

"I've already told my assistant to bring moderate doses of anesthetic and a paralytic to make our work easy. But when I cut this beast into pieces, I want him to feel exactly what I'm doing but so immobilized that he can't stop it. He'll feel everything I'm going to do to him. I believe justice will be served and we'll make him pay for all the crimes he's committed. The cleaners are supposed to show up later tonight to get the body of Ramon Valenzuela. That way they can take both bodies to the crematory, so we kill two birds with the same shot."

Mr. Xiang hid his smile carefully. "Doctor, you don't think this guy might possess some information we could use in our work?"

"No, we already know everything. We already know the other hit man was sent by Juan Alberto, and this one was sent by Dr. Adolfo Mena Gonzalez—or whatever his real name is. We also know that this stupid man doesn't know that he'll be killed as soon as he reaches Rosario, since they don't want to leave any loose ends behind. Especially loose ends that are witnesses, since we know this guy is very close to the young Argentinian doctor—do you think they'll leave this guy behind? No, sir. You know how these Nazis are. They use you, and when they no longer need you, they dispose of you. Even Dr. Gonzalez doesn't know that he's going to die the night of the ritual they plan to perform on January 26th, 1955. That will allow the old Hitler to continue in the body of the young doctor in the mission of his protector, Lucifer. Of course, that's not what they've made them believe, and by playing on the young doctor's egotism they will use just his body; the spirit and mind will be the old Hitler himself." As he spoke, Emilio covertly glanced at the man in the bed and noticed the sweat breaking out on his forehead. He continued to pretend to be asleep.

Mr. Xiang said, "If that's the case, and you don't need him, and I don't need him, let me put on a surgical gown. I don't want to get blood on my clothes when you start cutting on this animal." He picked up an electric bone saw and pressed the trigger several times. The irritating whine of the saw was quite loud in that room. "We will probably need a bigger saw for this guy. Something with a higher revolution speed, and we'll probably need Bogota to help us so we can finish in time in order to put the parts in plastic bags. He looks like he weighs at least 400 pounds."

Bogota entered the room with the wheelchair, restraints, and a massive syringe in her hand. Mr. Xiang took a sheet and covered the handcuffs and leg irons. He said, "It's a good thing you brought the wheelchair. That way we won't have to carry the bags through the hallway. We can use the chair for that."

Bogota said, "Here you are, Doctor, the anesthetic with low dosage mixed with a paralytic. I'm going to glove and mask up—even though we're going to cut this man in pieces, this filthy animal probably has a bunch of diseases that I don't want to catch."

They were silent, and Mr. Xiang looked for a more powerful bone saw. "I found the biggest one here! Yay, we'll be able to finish early!"

A loud cry broke the silence suddenly as Rafael started to sob to them, "I have information. I know who Adolfo Mena Gonzalez really is, I know his whereabouts, and I also know where he's going after the foundation and integration in Rosario!" He stopped and tried to regain his composure. "I'm only a peon, no importance at all," he said more clearly. "I just got married, my wife is pregnant with a baby boy, this was to be my last job as a hit man." He started crying once more, his cheeks apple red in panic. Mr. Xiang took the opportunity to rev the bone saw.

"I've got it!" he exclaimed gleefully as he worked to seal their little contract. It completely terrified Rafael, who began to urinate in the bed, as the liquid ran across the bed and dripped onto the floor. Emilio realized they no longer needed to intimidate him.

Emilio bent over and saw that Rafael's eyes were wide open, near to an apoplectic fit. Rafael yelled, "Please don't kill me. I'll tell you whatever you want to know. I've spent many years by his side and know all his secrets!"

"OK," Emilio replied, "if that is true, that will save your life. We'll calm down and talk about it." Rafael was so ready to talk he might actually need a gun to his head to stop him from talking. His spirit was completely broken. Emilio held up a hand to wave Mr. Xiang and Bogota off. "Rafael, if whatever you just said is the truth, and you tell me *all* the truth, this will save your life. That really makes me very happy—you don't even know how much I appreciate not having to kill you and saving us all this time and work. That doesn't even factor in that I'm a man whose profession is to save lives, not like yours that take it."

He held one hand up, forefinger and thumb narrowly separated. "But if you hide even this much from me, you can rest assured that you will die in the most painful way that any human being could ever have expired in, and that I won't just do it to you but to your pregnant wife and unborn child. You deserve all of that for being in service to such a diabolical cult that has caused so much life lost in this world." He held up the syringe and squirted a little of the contents before dropping it into the trash can. "I'm telling you this so you can examine your conscience before we begin and you lie to us, making it too late. If you do, everything here will be void and our verbal contract completely nullified." He had by now leaned into Rafael's face as he lay there in the pool of his urine.

Rafael looked up at Emilio in panic, nodding his head several times, his eyes locked on the syringe in Emilio's hand. Emilio gestured with the syringe. "Are you understanding me clearly?"

Rafael nodded. "Yes. I swear to you I will tell you all the truth, not leaving a single thing out."

"If you are honorable, I promise you that you will sleep tonight in your house in bed with your wife. I give you my word of honor on this."

"Yes, yes."

Emilio handed the syringe to Bogota. "Put the cover on the needle and put it in the refrigerator on standby." He turned to Mr. Xiang. "Take the straps off and put him in the wheelchair."

Mr. Xiang carefully untied one leg at a time, putting irons on each foot. Then he worked on the legs, then the arms, and when he got to the left hand, he noticed the tongue to the belt buckle broken. "Huh," he said. He held it up to show Emilio.

Emilio shook his head. "Hm. Must be a factory defect. This has never happened before. There's a first time for everything in life. Rafael, did you make any sudden movement with this?" Rafael shook his head in abject panic. "Very strange. I've never seen anything like this in all my years in this business." He picked up the broken off tongue and examined it clinically.

Mr. Xiang released the abdominal restraints, and assisted by Bogota, they helped him sit down in the wheelchair, tied a belt around his torso and attached the handcuffs and leg irons to the chair.

Emilio said, "All right, let's go to the conference room."

They went into the conference room and put him at the head of the long table. Emilio sat down, placing the Lugar on the table in front of him and said, "All right, are you ready? What is the true name of this Doctor Adolfo Mena Gonzalez?"

Rafael took a deep breath. "His name is Ernesto Guevara de la Serna. He's also known as Che. He was born June 14, 1928 in Rosario, Argentina. He became a member of the Nationalist Fascist Movement from its founding in 1936 until now in 1955. They call it *Frente de Fuerzas Fascistas de Cordoba*." As Rafael spoke, Emilio took notes. "The leader of this institution, and Ernesto Guevara's mentor, is General Juan Bautista Molina. Later, they changed the name to National Union of Fascists. This general allied directly with Hitler to turn Argentina into the central base for the Nazis as their headquarters for the American continent, bringing all the methods of the European Nazis under the solid control of the Führer, Adolf Hitler."

Figure 22 Argentine Nazi Organization

Mr. Xiang, Bogota, and Emilio exchanged glances as they saw that this completely corroborated all the data they had acquired over the years. Bogota asked Rafael, "Then Hitler and his allies picked Argentina as the central headquarters for their future operations?"

"No, I'm sorry. They did that in the beginning, but Hitler changed his plan, and the last minute before they arrived in Colombia."

Mr. Xiang asked curiously, "Why did they change the plan? What is the reason?"

"Because Hitler found a better and more central country in the heart of the Americas, the key to the Gulf of Mexico. It would radiate their ideology to America and then from there catapult it to the rest of the modern world."

Emilio said, "By any chance was that key country Hitler spoke of the island of Cuba?"

Rafael nodded. "How did you know that? I think you've already possessed this information, Dr. del Marmol."

Emilio smiled slightly. "Now you understand why I told you before that I wanted all the truth. I already possess some of it. All I'm doing is corroborating and putting the pieces together, verifying what I already have. Now I need to know one piece of the puzzle I don't have yet: where is Ernesto Guevara or Hitler going after the transfer of his soul in Rosario?"

"He will go to Mexico City, where he will meet with his contact, a man named Ñico Lopez, who will introduce him to the brothers Fidel and Raul Castro. They will become allies until death separates them, bound together by Lucifer. Together they will spread the national socialist seed throughout the world for the next one thousand years under the red cape of Satan."

Emilio nodded. "Rafael—don't forget that there is a white shroud that cures the sick, resuscitates men from death, and is more powerful a thousand times and more than that red cape. It has not destroyed life and is capable of forgiveness, even to murderers like you. All He asks in return is for you to repent in your heart for your past sins and not repeat those wrongs ever again. All He does is spread love and happiness over the Earth, heal the sick and protect the defenseless, and He doesn't send anyone to gas chambers to die because they have a certain nationality or religion. This is the true King, not just of the Earth, but also the Universe."

Rafael looked at Emilio in admiration. "Are you satisfied with my information?"

"Yes. I'm satisfied."

Rafael asked, "Do you have any other questions for me?"

Emilio gestured invitingly to Mr. Xiang and Bogota. Mr. Xiang shook his head, as did Bogota. He looked back at Rafael. "It looks like we've come to the end of our interrogation of you."

Rafael looked at Emilio anxiously and asked in a pleading tone, "Then I can sleep tonight at home with my wife?"

Montauk: The Lightning Chance

Emilio smiled and nodded. "It looks like it. I hope that the eye you lost is a good lesson for you to not continue in your criminal career. We'll send you back to your wife and unborn child, but you should not continue committing evil acts. There will be no second chances."

Tears rolled down his cheeks. "Thank you, thank you very much. You have no idea how much when you gave me your word of honor to not kill me returned the faith that I had lost so long ago. You've now brought back to me with your noble gesture and integrity that faith I had before I turned myself into a professional murderer. You don't know how important it is for me to be feeling this way now. You've returned my honor to me. To give you an example, when you gave me your word of honor, you might have been thinking that a criminal like me wouldn't even comprehend that concept. I have known Ernesto Guevara since we were kids. I was born in Rosario as well. We grew up together until I was 8 years old, when my family moved to Japan. I grew up there. I heard later he had moved around to different cities until he ended up in Buenos Aires. He did something to me that showed me he has no honor and is a liar. I didn't talk just to save my life; I spoke out to regain my honor. When I killed a member of the Japanese Imperial family just before the end of the War, precisely for honor, I needed the support of Ernesto. He never gave me what I asked for. They tortured me in a Japanese prison; they nearly killed me. But I never broke my vow of silence, never talked about the others involved with me. I want you to know this: I put my life and honor on the line for him, but he never did it for me. Could you please release my left hand from the chair, as a favor?"

Emilio said, "I could not only release that hand, but all your limbs. You're walking out of here, remember?" He looked at Mr. Xiang. "Release him." They looked at him in shock. "Go on."

Rafael put his left hand on the table and held up the pinky. "Would you do me the favor of holding this, please?" Emilio looked at him in uncertain puzzlement. "Put all the pressure you can." Emilio grasped it and squeezed it as hard as he could. Rafael yanked his hand away, leaving Emilio holding a prosthetic finger. "I gave that for the honor of Ernesto Guevara. The yakuza took it according to the code of their secret society."

Mr. Xiang and Bogota both recoiled in shock. Rafael smiled as he held out his hand to retrieve his prosthetic finger. Emilio helped him put it back on. "He betrayed me, even after they took that. I told him that I would forgive, but never forget. Now you tell me that they plan to eliminate me in Rosario?"

Emilio nodded. "That is what they plan to do. Just remember, the truth is never in the mouth of the Devil or his disciples. No matter how great it looks, if you look deep enough it will always be a lie." He picked up the pistol and handed it to Rafael. Mr. Xiang and Bogota looked at him in absolute shock. "Is this yours? I have several Lugars."

"Yes, it's mine. How did you know?"

Emilio held it up and showed that there was a small X in the corner. "Then you have your weapon back."

"I will never, never forget the generosity of you gentlemen and this lady. I swear on my honor that I now have regained, thanks to you, Dr. del Marmol, that anything you need, just ask." He pulled out a card and wrote a number on the back. "This is my direct number." He handed it to Emilio.

"Are you sure you can drive home?"

"Yes."

"Where is your car?'

"On the street, about a block away."

They all walked to the door. Rafael put the pistol in his waist. When they reached the door, Emilio asked him," Could you please let me see your weapon again?"

"Sure." He handed the Lugar to Emilio.

Emilio removed the magazine and handed it to Bogota. He slid the ejector and popped a bullet out. He took out the other Lugar and swapped the magazines out and handed Rafael the weapon. "Now you have real bullets. Those were blanks."

Rafael looked at Emilio in open admiration. "Doctor, you are not only smart and merciful, but you are also extremely ahead of your time. Again—thank you. God bless you."

"God bless you, too. I hope we can see each other one day again in different circumstances."

They opened the door and let him go. Emilio closed the door. Bogota looked at him and said, "I don't think I've ever seen anyone like you before."

"Thank you very much. Remember, that could go both ways."

They smiled. Bogota shook her head and smiled at Emilio in a mixture of love, admiration, and respect. "What now? Are we going to let the other sniper go free, too?"

Emilio shook his head. "That all depends on Ramon. Rafael passed the test. Now we will see if Ramon passes it, too, not only in terms of the information he already provided to us but also the information he possesses that we still need. Above everything else, the most important point is that he demonstrates to me, like Rafael did, his heartfelt repentance and that he will not be a significant danger to us in the future. If not—" he drew a finger across his throat.

Bogota looked at him wide eyed. "For real?"

"Yes, for real. He will leave this place in a plastic bag in the rear of the cleaner's van."

Bogota looked at Emilio seriously and in surprise. "For real??"

"I don't think I have to repeat myself," he replied in a slightly surprised tone. "We are noble people and know how to forgive our trespassers and enemies. When they show to us that they really have repented of the bad things they've done to us, then and only then do we offer them a second opportunity. If they abuse our nobility and try to cross the line again and hurt any of us, then they condemn themselves to death. If you don't do it that way, if they haven't repented, they have no compassion or love in their heart. To the contrary, their hearts are filled with hatred and are evil. They are the sons and daughters of Satan."

Mr. Xiang shook his head and cleared his throat three times. "In my opinion, based on personal experience, very few of these criminals ever completely reform themselves. They change their lives a little bit, but they never come full circle. They're like alcoholics: they stop drinking for a while, but eventually they return to the bottle."

"There are always exceptions," Emilio said.

"Yes," Mr. Xiang said, "I agree with you. Every rule has an exception. From prostitutes come daughters of decency and virtue. But that is an exception. If you live long enough, you find everything from everywhere in the world."

"Yes, you're right. That is the reason we have to offer, without exception, the benefit of the doubt to everyone, including the criminals that try to kill us."

They walked into the conference room, where Bogota got the projector ready to show them a roll of film she had found in her father's safe at the nightclub. Emilio sat down while Mr. Xiang went on into the kitchen. While they waited, Emilio took Ramon's pistol and started to do what he had done with Rafael's gun and replaced the live ammunition with blanks. Bogota finished adjusting the projector, and Mr. Xiang walked in with a pot of hot jasmine tea and a plate of almond cookies. Emilio and Bogota gave Mr. Xiang their thanks for his gentle gesture.

Emilio got up. "Excuse me for a few minutes. I need to go to the operating room and get something from there."

He walked into the operating chamber and opened one of the metal drawers. He pulled out a large glass and metal syringe with a thick spinal needle. He pulled out a bottle of nitro glycerin and pulled 3 ccs of the substance into the syringe—nearly half. He walked over to the medical cabinet and pulled out a bottle marked P-32. Inserting the needle once more, he pulled out another 3 ccs. He pulled out a bottle marked *biacci nitrator w. glycerin nitric acid* and *sulfuric acid*. Emilio stuck the needle into the third bottle and filled the syringe completely with it. He shook it up to mix the contents entirely, which turned the strange cocktail a yellowish color. He knew well what the consequences would be produced should that solution be injected into the human body.

He put a safety stopper on the end of the needle and placed the syringe behind the handkerchief in the breast pocket of his jacket. He returned to the conference room to find them ready and waiting for him.

Bogota said, "Everyone ready?" Receiving nods, she turned off the lights and started rolling the film.

The first images were of Adolf Hitler during his first speeches during the 1930's. They were followed by Hitler on a hunting trip with his dogs, then of him at his mansion in Poland. They were then followed by footage of large trucks filled with gold bars, 18 and 22 carats, taken out of banks and loaded into the trucks. The film narration dictated how the trucks were going to certain concealed locations (which were not shown). Then boxes of diamonds, refined jewelry, rare photos from wealthy Jewish families, carried onto trucks bearing the swastika of the Nazis, incorporating all this wealth to the Nazi looters and sent the owners of this wealth to concentration camps. It showed also scenes of Nazi dentists removing gold teeth from the prisoners just before they were put into the gas chambers. After those scenes of corpses being carted from the gas chambers to the crematories. It was unbelievably disgusting; the horror of these scenes was completely incomprehensible. This footage only incriminated themselves—they could not understand why they would document these actions.

Then came footage of wealthy Jews who bowed to Nazis and offered exquisite meals with wine and champagne hoping the Nazis would let them live and put the atrocities behind them and allow them to live in peace to live a happy life. They clearly had no knowledge that

Montauk: The Lightning Chance

this honeymoon would be shorter than they could ever imagine. Very soon after, they also wound up in the camps like the ones in worse circumstances they chose to ignore.

The next scenes were in the Berghof in the Obersalzberg of the Bavarian Alps—Hitler's private home. There was a gathering of people on the terrace, looking out over the Alps. Seated in a one-on-one conversation on the terrace was no less than Juan Alberto. A person who opened a bottle of expensive champagne proved to be Ramon Valenzuela. All three, Emilio, Mr. Xiang, and Bogota exclaimed in surprise, "What?" as they recognized both Juan Alberto and Ramon. Bogota stopped the projector, turned on the lights, and reversed it to make sure they were seeing what they thought.

She played it back, this time in slow motion, after turning the lights back off. They glued their eyes to the screen, searching it carefully. They could easily tell it was truly Juan Alberto and Ramon proudly serving the champagne to both masters, a white linen towel draped over his arm. The bottle was balanced on a silver plate held in his right hand. Juan Alberto and Hitler stood up and walked away to have an obviously private conversation. Ramon followed. Hitler whispered something in Juan Alberto's ear, evidently telling him to dismiss the butler, as Juan Alberto waved Ramon away. Ramon, like an obedient puppy walked over and sat down beneath one of the umbrellas until the two men finished sharing secrets. Whatever they were plotting, Hitler clearly didn't want any witnesses.

The film then showed parades of young Nazis in the streets of different cities around the Americas, including the United States, Argentina, and Colombia. It might have been an indication where Hitler had been eying for planting his seed of political ideology in the future. Juan Alberto was now corroborated to be a very close accomplice. It was clear he had knowledge of everything Hitler had been planning. It made sense that he would have ties with all of Hitler's associates in America. Maybe he hadn't, in fact, left Colombia out of fear of Hitler. He may have done so under direct orders to establish a new headquarters that was more appropriate to their future plans. His mission in Colombia must have come to its end. The next step should be in the final relocation and reintegration of the Führer.

The film kept rolling with Nazi symbolism and music. Bogota turned off the projector and switched on the lights. She shook her head. "Well, if any of us still had any doubts, this clears up even the smallest ones we had before."

Mr. Xiang shook his head. "Yes. There's no doubt at all the tremendous level of connection between your father and Hitler. But also, we learned just now something different, and it's good we learned it now before interviewing Ramon: what level of connection your father has with him and what level of trust he had in him. Your father isn't going all the way to see such an important figure and bring somebody off the street. It would only be someone he trusts absolutely."

They exchanged glances and nodded in agreement. Bogota said, "I don't think Ramon is a regular bird. I believe that he is like a vulture that eats even its own species when they go down just to survive."

Emilio nodded. "I believe your analysis of Ramon is very close to the truth, more even than you imagined. I will tell you something. I believe I possess a great gift from Nature that you guys have seen all these years around me: God, or whatever you want to call it from my genetic line, gave me that gift. Some call it extra-terrestrial, I call it my instincts, from what I smell and can hear—I think I have a close connection with hunting dogs. I can smell and sometimes even hear things before they happen. Of course, this sometimes can be blocked, because some people have the power to block that so that you don't smell their scent or hear them approach. But I can smell miles away the foul odor of sulfur. When that person gets close to me, the minute I sit with him for a few seconds, I can hear the evil in my ears. It's like a frequency that I cannot even explain. It's telling me I have to be very careful around that person. Like I said before, only in very rare occasions, that person is like a chameleon and has the ability to throw me off, but eventually if I hang around long enough, I'll discover who that person is."

Mr. Xiang replied, "I can only tell you one thing: in all my years around you, very few times or almost never have I seen you be wrong in your analysis when you've been examining our enemies or the people working against us. When you're not right on target, you're only a hair off of the dead center. It's hard to believe."

Emilio smiled. "Thank you, Mr. Xiang." He put Ramon's pistol on the table. "Please, why don't you guys check on Ramon? If he's conscious and up to it, I think we should proceed with him. We have to start preparing to leave for Argentina immediately to see what we can do to prevent things planned to happen down there. If he's OK, please put him in the wheelchair with all the precautions necessary, because we're also getting close to dinner time. I believe we've all earned a very elegant meal with the physical sweat off our brows."

Montauk: The Lightning Chance

Bogota rubbed her belly. "You cannot deny this child belongs to you. Remember, all four of us. Don't leave your child out of the meal. Every time you mention food, he's so well connected to you that he starts jumping in my belly."

Mr. Xiang smiled. "Well, let's see if that little boy likes Chinese food, like his father."

She smiled. "With all my respect, Mr. Xiang, I think you are in error. Emilio doesn't care about the origin of the food—he cares about the quality and experience of who cooked the food for him."

Emilio grinned and raised a finger. "There it goes!"

Mr. Xiang and Bogota laughed and left to go bring Ramon to Emilio. Emilio turned the projector on again and switched the lights off. He sat down and started to go over the film once more in order to be absolutely sure that what he saw before was Juan Alberto and Ramon by Hitler. It took him a while to stop at that point and go back and forth about two or three times. He satisfied himself and switched the projector off and turned the lights on. At that moment, Mr. Xiang and Bogota showed up with Ramon in the wheelchair.

Emilio greeted him politely and inquired as to how he was feeling. Ramon smiled a little cockily. "Like new. You are a great surgeon."

Emilio nodded. "Thank you. I adore life, and that is why I hate to waste one, especially if that life is lost for no reason at all. I despise even more when that life is wasted for a handful of money. I have never understood how someone could take another human being's life like that—what price can you put on a person's life? Especially when you figure in the sorrow that is left to the families of that person; sometimes, that person even is an innocent bystander or somebody's inconvenience in the path of another's ambition for power."

Ramon swallowed but kept silent. He knew exactly what Emilio was talking about and put his head down possibly in shame, remorse, or perhaps in playing a part. Emilio tried to look him in the eyes, but Ramon was avoiding his gaze. Emilio noticed that Ramon, from the moment he had entered the room, had not taken his eyes off the pistol lying on the table. Perhaps he recognized it as his; he might be wondering what it was doing there or what the significance of its presence was. Bogota brought the wheelchair to the table close to Emilio, and the pistol lay in the middle of the table between them. His hands were bound by the handcuffs to the arms of the wheelchair and the leg irons at his feet.

"Do you remember our agreement?"

"Yes, yes, of course," Ramon replied. "I've been telling you all the truth. Are you satisfied?" he asked anxiously.

Emilio raised the index finger of his right hand. "That's not all. I want you to repeat everything you said to me as you lay dying about Juan Alberto, not only to his daughter here, Bogota, but also to Mr. Xiang. After you finish, they may want to ask you some questions, and I might also have a few more for you."

Ramon grew very nervous. "Yes, yes—with pleasure. I will answer any question you have for me."

"Very well," Emilio said. "Begin your story. I want you to start a little earlier. Explain to us how you met Juan Alberto and why he placed all his trust in you with the life of his only daughter. How did he know you would follow his instructions so precisely? This thing he asked you to do, according to what you said to me, isn't the sort of thing you hire just any hit man off the street to do. Do you understand what I'm saying, Ramon?"

A little more agitatedly, he said, "I already told you everything I know, and that's what we agreed. Now you're changing and asking me for more stuff."

Emilio leaned back in his chair and rubbed his forehead. He calmly looked at Ramon in silence, a ghost of a smile on his lips, which made the hit man more nervous. Emilio kept trying to lock gazes with Ramon, who continued averting his eyes and locking them on the pistol. Emilio finally said, "Ramon, will you do me a favor? When you speak to me, please look into my eyes. Do you understand?"

Ramon looked at him defiantly in indignation. Emilio saw at once that this personality had dramatically changed. This was no longer the man begging for his life and asking Emilio for anything he wanted. Emilio smiled as he thought about how ignorant the man was to not realize the situation he was in, and to assume an arrogant attitude. He looked at Mr. Xiang and Bogota with marked irony. They returned his look, displaying to him their disdain for Ramon's attitude.

Emilio said, "I want you to examine yourself for a few minutes so we can understand one another here. Look at those two. One of them you tried to kill, just like you tried to kill me. The other, a woman that you shot in the arm. For myself, I should be extremely angry with you. We all should be. Now look at the arrogant attitude you're showing. Apparently, you've forgotten the situation you're in. Your life is in our hands. You might not know it, but your life might be under evaluation right now. We're not going to let you go and make the fatal mistake of giving you another opportunity to comply with your contract. Maybe you've already received some payment for it."

Ramon repeated, "But this is not what we agreed! You promised me that if I would tell you all the truth that you would take care of me."

Emilio noticed his own irritation rising, but he controlled it and concealed it. He bit his lower lip silently and massaged his forehead once more. He picked up the Lugar in his right hand. "Let me refresh your memory because I don't like your attitude at all. If there is someone in this room you don't want to anger, it's me. First of all, you're not in a position to demand anything of us. You have a lot to repent for." He pointed the pistol at Bogota's arm. He raised the pistol again and pointed it at Mr. Xiang who was looking at Ramon like a hungry wolf, ready to devour a scared rabbit. "And to me, you should not only be grateful for not leaving you to bleed to death on the stairwell of the building where you tried to kill us, and then keep you out of the hands of the local authorities. With the long record I'm sure you have, they would have put you in prison for a long time, especially once they discovered that you killed Sarita. Maybe you realize that all that I asked you in exchange that you tell me *all* the truth—not just a portion of it. Now, instead of being a little repentant, opening your heart, and apologizing to all of us for your crimes, I've just received an insult from you by accusing me of violating our agreement." He held his fingers narrowly apart. "I'm this close to losing my patience. I could at any minute totally break my agreement and put a bullet in your head." He cocked the pistol and pointed at Ramon's forehead.

Ramon started to weep. "No, please—forgive me. Please, I'm very nervous, I don't know what I'm saying. I've never been in this position before."

Emilio understood that he needed to stop at that point. He had him where he wanted, and he sat down, dropping the pistol on the table as he did so. The pistol slid a little in Ramon's direction on the polished table. He took a deep breath. "You'd better start your story before I change my mind."

Ramon began reciting his story for Bogota and Mr. Xiang. He lied his teeth out by distancing himself from Juan Alberto, indicating that they hadn't known each other long. "Juan Alberto owes me money, as well, from another job that I completed," he added.

Mr. Xiang asked, "Have you ever traveled with him outside of the country?"

Ramon hesitated and then shook his head with conviction. "No, no—Juan Alberto never trusted anyone. He sent me places, sure, but he always traveled alone. He never trusted anyone."

Bogota asked, "Then you don't know anyone in the highest ranks of the Nazi party that is associated with my father? Or any of their leaders in their movement?"

'No, no! I never saw him with any Nazi! Juan Alberto *hates* the Nazis!" They remained silent for a while. The prolonged silence made Ramon nervous. "Any other questions?"

Bogota shook her head, as did Mr. Xiang. Emilio said, "Would you sign a statement that Juan Alberto is the man behind you, that he sent you to kill Mr. Xiang and I, but only wounding Bogota? Because he wanted to use us as an alibi?"

Ramon hesitated again. "Yes, yes! It's the truth—why not?"

"Very well," Emilio replied. He looked at Mr. Xiang. "Give him a paper and pen. I want him to write in his own words a declaration how Juan Alberto contracted him to kill us and how much he was paid to do it."

Ramon asked, "After I sign it, will you let me go?"

"Of course," Emilio replied. "You'll probably sleep in your house with your family."

Ramon smiled. Mr. Xiang stood behind Ramon, looking like he wanted to strangle him. He laid a lined blank notebook in front of Ramon. Ramon jiggled his handcuffs to demonstrate his inability to write bound as he was.

Emilio said to Bogota, "Remove his restraints."

"All?" she asked. "Or just the ones on his hands?"

Emilio pretended to consider it. "No. Only his right hand. After he signs the document and we verify what he wrote, then you can take off his other restraints and escort him to the door."

Ramon smiled. "Thank you very much. I will never forget what you guys have done for me today."

Bogota released the handcuff on his right hand, leaning over him. Before she sat back down, his hand darted out to reach for the pistol. He cocked it against his body and pointed at Bogota. "Remove the other ones, bitch, or I'll send you to Hell with your friends!"

None of them moved, smiles on their lips. Emilio clucked his tongue in mock disappointment. "What a pity, Ramon. You lost your opportunity to continue walking in the land of the living."

His hand shook with anxiety. "I'm going to shoot her! You'd better tell her to release me!"

Emilio shook his head. "You, Ramon, actually wasted the opportunity that we, out of the goodness of our hearts, offer every criminal like you. You did not pass the test. Why do you think that pistol has been on the table all this time? By grabbing that pistol, you just sentenced yourself to death." Ramon clearly could not comprehend why they were so calm and nonchalant. He changed targets and pointed the pistol at Emilio.

He yelled, "You'll be the first one to die, you son of a bitch!"

Emilio smiled and said, "Turn the lights off, Bogota, and turn on the projector."

Bogota ignored Ramon's repeated demands for no one to move and switched on the projector.

Emilio said, "Ramon, the last thing your eyes will see before you die will be your masters." The projector started to roll. Ramon still hadn't pulled the trigger on any of them.

Ramon knew that all three of them had to have weapons, and he was still restrained to the wheelchair with only one hand free. He wasn't in a condition for a prolonged fight with all his injuries still so fresh. He had to be wondering what he had gotten himself into and blaming himself for grabbing the pistol too soon.

The film reached the scene in the Berghof. Emilio yelled, "Bogota, stop it!"

The image froze with Ramon pouring champagne into Hitler's glass. Ramon leaned heavily on the table, his jaw wide open. "Who are you guys?"

Emilio replied, "We are the light to the blind, and you are the darkness in people's lives. That is why you will die now. I hope I never see you again for many centuries, perverse, evil man!"

Emilio leaned over the table and reached for the pistol. Ramon opened fire, but of course the blanks did nothing. Emilio pulled out the syringe, grabbed Ramon by the shirt with his left hand, and with his right arm inserted the needle at the top of the bridge of his nose. Ramon's eyes crossed as he watched in horror the inexorable approach of the massive needle. Once inserted, Emilio injected the deadly cocktail as Bogota switched on the lights. Hitler was still on the screen.

Emilio pulled the syringe out and placed it on the table. He pulled out the box of matches from El Gato Tuerto and lit one. As he placed the lit match against the injection site, he said, "Demons of darkness, get out!" He placed the match against the skin, and like a barbeque Ramon's head burst into flames. Emilio could see flames inside Ramon's eyes. "Get back against the walls and use the backs of the chairs for protection! His head's about to explode like a grenade!"

Bogota and Mr. Xiang rushed with chairs, placing their bodies against the wall and using the high backs of the chair as instructed. They could see what would happen. Ramon's hair burst into flames, and Ramon screamed in abject horror. The explosion that followed rattled the doors of the conference room as the head vaporized. His headless body toppled lifelessly onto the table.

Emilio was the first to get out from behind the chairs. He said, "Let's hope that this demon had the chance to see the radiant light and grabbed his last hope of it before he died. If not, he's gone straight to Hell with his masters. Let's get out of here at once and let the Cleaner take care of the rest of this mess. They are the professionals at cleaning and disinfecting the scourges of society in which we live today, unfortunately. We have to leave for Argentina as soon as possible. We must make our best efforts, even if its' an impossible task, to defeat the evil forces in the Universe. Even if it's like David and Goliath repeating history again."

Believe It or Not

Declassified CIA reports detail claims about a man claiming to be Hitler, living in Colombia in 1950.

Phillip Citroen, a former SS officer, told agents a man called Adolf Schüttlemayor was living in Tunja, 85 miles north of Bogota, among a group of former Nazis in 1954.

Citroen said Hitler left Colombia in January of 1955.

A move to Argentina provided in photos a strong likeness of Hitler and characteristics in manners and facial expression showed a match with 99.9% accuracy.

FBI Declassified Documents, 2014.

Over 700 FBI documents were declassified revealing that the US government had undertaken an investigation in late 1940.

In 1950, after the report of the possibility that Hitler faked or staged his death and arrived in Colombia and later went to Argentina in 1955.

Additional CIA documents contained reports citing a man who bragged to be Hitler went to Argentina, but from orders of the highest command of the CIA station in that region, the investigation was dropped in 1955.

Figure 23 Adolf Hitler incognito

Postdated Chapter

Emilio and his friends Bogota and Mr. Xiang drove Emilio's original car after he had returned the Chrysler for his Roadster. They drove to the American embassy in Bogota. He sent the information in the diplomatic bag and was informed that it was being sent in expedited priority. The same day, as they were having dinner at a French restaurant, enjoying some Beef Wellington with béarnaise sauce, a courier arrived. He said, "The President got your package and has reviewed it. He needs to meet with you."

Emilio protested, "But I need to go to Argentina, we cannot waste any time."

"Send your friends ahead, and you'll join them in 24 or 48 hours."

They walked out of the restaurant. Emilio gave the keys to his car to Bogota and got into the embassy car that awaited him, saying his goodbyes. The car drove him and the courier to the airport and boarded the plane. As they took off, Emilio glanced at the flight plan and noticed they were not going to Washington. "Where are we going?"

The courier replied, "We're going to Montauk. The President wants you in an emergency meeting with the Secretary of State and his brother. The reason for this is because the information you delivered to the President about the conductor of the orchestra is like a bomb in the highest circle in our intelligence community. The result of the blood and semen samples you obtained could change the course of history with regards to Hitler's survival. The President wants to put together an emergency plan immediately. In his opinion, if this gets out to the public, it could create the wrong impression that all of our allies, in cooperation with the US, are trying to protect Hitler. That's both far away and pretty close to the truth. For noble purposes, we are trying to save the future of humanity, but this is a very hard pill to swallow for anyone that does not sympathize or is in the same political party as the President. His enemies, if they get their hands on this, will try to distort the facts in a smear campaign to destroy his image for re-election."

CHAPTER 10: THE PANDEMIC OF EVIL'S REORGANIZATION

Havana Cuba
January 26, 1959

Havana: the meeting of the Tricontinental, the last OSPAAAL, was founded officially in Havana in 1966. Turn the 9 upside-down and its 666. After the Tricontinental Conference of more than 500 delegates and 200 observers from over 82 countries from around the world attended this OSPAAAL, the continuation of the propagation of Nazism, socialism, fascism, and communism, based now on the small island of Cuba. Once again, they changed the name they gave to the world.

Separate from the official conference, the real gathering took place in a darkened chamber, medieval in flavor. Eighteen people were in attendance and sat around a circular wooden table with a globe on it, wearing cowled robes. The table had a circular indentation at one side, at which Che Guevara sat in a slightly elevated chair like a king on his throne. The feeling is like some kind of cultic gathering. One of them watched and listened closely in disgust, his arms crossed over his chest. A medical school ring gleamed on one of his hands.

Che stood up and stabbed the globe with a red knife with a communist symbol on the hilt. He proclaimed, "I claim Central and South America!" Other figures follow suit, each stabbing the globe with similar red knives and claimed a different part of the world for their personal control, even Antarctica.

Che went over to a pair of wooden doors, two men preceding him. He opened the door and the other two men went through to the adjoining room. They came back with a black bull

between them and led it towards the table. Two other men entered and removed the throne-like chair. The bull was brought in and secured in place, its head over the indentation in the table. Che took a needle and jabbed it into the bull's neck, using the syringe to fill a tankard. Each figure in turn came by with a tankard, filled his tankard, and then moved along. The bull grew weaker and weaker, eventually collapsing as it was drained of its blood.

All the men raised their tankards in toast. "Hoorah, hoorah, hoorah, to the Tricontinental and the conquest of the globe. To the destruction of our enemies around the world, starting with all the Christians and their associates." They drank the blood from their tankards. Then one at a

time, each figure pulled his knife out of the globe and poured blood over his region from the tankard.

Four beautiful girls came in wearing translucent robes with the emblem of the Tricontinental Union, a globe with a bald head in the middle, embroidered on them. It was evident by the candlelight of the shadowy room that they were naked beneath their robes. They bore transparent platters with lines of cocaine laid out on them as if they were serving hors d'oeuvres. Each man snorted a line. The caduceus on a medical school graduation ring flashed in the candlelight as the figure covertly brushed the cocaine onto the floor while he pretended to snort his line up.

After each person had done his line of coke, Che stood up and light shot from his eyes like a laser beam. The globe burst into flames.

Figure 24 Promotional Material for the Tricontinental

Montauk: The Lightning Chance

Havana, Cuba
Middle January, 1959

Dr. Emilio del Marmol, elegantly dressed in a tuxedo with a silk pocket handkerchief in the front, sat in a concert hall with me, his wife Melicia, and his daughter Jackie. We were all enjoying the music of Beethoven, Mozart, and Chopin at the theatre in the Galician Center, though the name had just been changed by the revolutionary government to *Teatro de la Habana*.

Figure 25 Julio Antonio, aged 11, at the buffet following concert

The powerful kettle drums made even the seats vibrate a little with the concussive power as the music poured through my body. My heartbeat blended and synched with the timpani. This was not the first time my uncle brought me to these events; he enjoyed my company, and whenever I had a long weekend off from school, he brought me along as his favorite nephew since he didn't have a son. In the strange way of nature, after his wife had his only child, Jackie, she was no longer able to bear children following a very severe surgery. My company gave him the comfort of having the son he always wanted.

They lived in a beautiful house in one of the most secluded neighborhoods in Havana, in Miramar's gated community of El Nautico. After the concert finished, my uncle took us to a very elegant restaurant not far from the theatre. There we enjoyed an exquisite first-class dinner. Like my uncle always said, one has to eat like it's one's last meal. Even though Batista had left a few weeks ago, leaving power in the hands of the new revolutionary government, it appeared that normalcy would return to the country. The reality was that the country was in chaos because the new government passed new laws each day. People lived in suspense expecting some fresh restriction from the government the following day. On top of that, the firing squad was in constant use, executing the dictator's followers without mercy. They even started to commit the exact same acts against those people who didn't sympathize with the revolution that Batista's people had done, using the stigma of being "counter-revolutionary" or other derogatory names.

They established different reforms, starting with the Agrarian Reforms, followed by the Urban Reforms, both of which allowed the government to take over the land and parcel it out however they chose. Apartment buildings were nationalized, and the rents were now paid to the government instead of private landlord/owners. Those who received land in the country had to sell the produce raised on the land only to a government agency, at the price set by the government. None of this went very well with the Cuban people who had lived under a democratic system since they had won their independence from Spain. The irony of the revolution was they only nationalized in the beginning the property of those who had committed crimes against the community during the dictatorship. But they didn't stop there; they started to nationalize all businesses, all private properties, whether or not the people had any relationship with the previous government, all because they didn't sympathize with the revolution. They annulled the Congress so there was no legislative body; that power resided solely in the hands of the new Prime Minister, Fidel Castro. Bacardi and Conchita, who had owned their businesses for generations lost them even though they were not involved in the politics of the prior regime.

That is the moment when people started to abandon everything they had and leave the country; it was also the first time the words "socialist' and "communist" started to be heard. Fidel Castro rushed to the television cameras to denounce that and announced that the revolution was as green as the palm leaves of Cuba, anything else was just propaganda circulated by their enemies, and swore that he would never be a communist nor break bread with the murderers of the Hungarian people. The irony was that a few months later he went to that same podium where he had taken that oath to declare that he was a Marxist-Leninist and would be until he died. It was a tremendous kick in the rear to those who fought to take down the dictator and a huge disappointment for many other people.

This was the first time I met Mr. Xiang and his family. As we left the restaurant, he was coming in with his two daughters. There was a brief introduction while the adults exchanged greetings and smiles. Emilio exclaimed, "The mountain came to me! Are you changing your palate?"

Mr. Xiang laughed and said, "You know I love all kinds of food!"

We exchanged bows as we said our farewells. The eldest daughter, Chandee, was an exceptionally beautiful Chinese Cuban girl and found her attention caught by my tuxedo. She kept staring at my bow, and I kept checking to see if I had spilled some food there. I had a difficult time not keeping my eyes off of the tiara she was wearing. Apparently, we gave each other a good impression, because her image remained in my mind for a long time. On her way out, Chandee turned and waved at me with a smile. Emilio gave me a sly smile, and both Melicia and Jackie noticed my flirting as well, and I turned beet red as I blushed in embarrassment. I later found out the mystic universal nature of that link when we reconnected in the future in Montauk, and it burst forth like a flame.

The restaurant was right across from the central park that was itself filled with history. We left the car in the parking lot of the restaurant, and Emilio proposed a walk in the park to aid our digestion. Melicia, always very pleasant and compliant said, "Why not, love? Let's go for a walk in the park. You're the doctor in the family, and since you recommended it as a prescription for our digestive health, we should follow it."

After we had been walking for around fifteen or twenty minutes, two very elegantly dressed individuals got in our way. One of them pointed a gun at Emilio. The other, a much larger man with a *sevillana*, stood a little off, watching his partner's back. "Where's your bag?" the gunman demanded.

Emilio replied calmly, "If you're referring to my medical bag, it's in the trunk of my car. I want to warn you, though, that I have nothing of value there, not even drugs. Just some aspirin that you can get over the counter in the pharmacy."

The one with the knife looked at the beautiful necklace Jackie wore. It was pure gold with diamonds and rubies. He went over to her, knife in hand, and said aggressively, "Take it off and give it to me, or I'll cut your head off!" He raised his knife in a threatening manner.

Jackie ran towards Emilio in panic. "No, no! This is a birthday present from my father!"

Emilio hugged her tenderly and moved her behind him to protect her. Maintaining his calm, he said "That's OK, Jackie. It's not worth your getting hurt. Give it to this man and I'll get you another one much more beautiful."

Jackie put her hands behind her neck to unclasp the necklace and obediently did what her father had asked her to do. She fumbled a little bit in the dark. I had been watching everything in silence without losing my calm. I had a handful of marbles in the right pocket of my pants that I had been fiddling with as the situation developed. When I saw my cousin's tears at her sense of impotence and reluctance to yield her necklace, I felt my blood rush from my chest into my head, ears, and cheeks, which began to burn. I could not contain myself any longer. With all the strength of the rush of blood I pulled out the handful of marbles. I yelled fiercely with all my might as I threw the handful into his face. Both men were taken completely by surprise at my attack and roar. The man with the knife turned towards me as I screamed, catching all the marbles full in his face.

He yelled back angrily as he backed away from us, forgetting the necklace. He wiped his forehead and his hand came away bloody, as some of the marbles had cut him. He took some steps towards me and tried to intimidate me. "You little piece of shit! I'm going to cut you into pieces and grind you up to feed my dog with your shitty meat!"

I stood my ground as he advanced on me, trying to lock his eyes with mine. I raised my right leg high and spread my hands like a crane, which took him by even greater surprise. My hands were open like bear claws and I screamed like an animal again, simulating the growl of an angry bear. He stopped and froze a few steps from me. He let the knife fall to the ground and looked up in terror, as if an immense animal was about to bite his head off. He fell to his knees and, crying like a baby, asked for forgiveness. "Please don't kill me, forgive me!"

Montauk: The Lightning Chance

Even my relatives were startled by this, along with his partner, who could not understand how his large friend could be begging for forgiveness from a skinny little boy, who still was poised with his leg upraised and hands spread out in a dragon claw fashion. At that moment, Mr. Xiang rushed out of the restaurant, pistol in hand. "Drop that pistol to the ground if you don't want a bullet in your head!"

The man with the pistol turned and saw the Chinaman pointing a gun at him and prudently dropped his weapon, raising his arms in surrender. I realized that neither one of these bandits represented a threat any longer, and dropped my aggressive position, relaxing my body. The crying man at my feet had his head between his arms. As if he were recovering from a nightmare, he raised his head and looked at me. He looked around, as if searching for the animal that had terrified him. He stood up and started to run away as fast as he could without even saying goodbye or picking up his knife. The other one, seeing his partner taking off, ran as well, leaving behind his firearm. Possibly he was going to leave his questions for his partner later.

Jackie drew close to her father and hugged him. With a big smile as she fingered her cross, she said, "Thank you, father. I didn't want these bandits to take your beautiful birthday gift."

Emilio let her hug him, enjoying her expression of love. A few seconds later, with a smile on his lips, he parted from her and said, "I don't think I'm the one who deserves these thanks. The ones who deserve it the most are your cousin Julio Antonio and Mr. Xiang. They actually are the ones who prevented those thieves from taking your necklace."

Jackie smiled and came over to me, hugging me and kissing me on the cheek. "Thank you, my cousin." She walked over and did the same to Mr. Xiang, and then returned to her mother.

Melicia hugged her. "Honey, I'm sorry you had to go through this."

Mr. Xiang came over to me and lowered his voice so the others couldn't hear him. "Who taught you that tiger kung fu style?"

I smiled. "The two ladies in white, or my angels—whichever you prefer."

Mr. Xiang looked at me in uncomprehending surprise. Emilio took a couple of steps to us. "Mr. Xiang, you probably remember the two ladies from his nightmares a long time ago."

Mr. Xiang threw his arm up as it all came back to him. "Oh!" he exclaimed.

Uncle Emilio asked me curiously, "What did you do to that man to make him kneel before you and react the way he did?"

"Nothing. All I did was demonstrate to him how small he really is. I took him out of this reality to another one and another dimension." Mr. Xiang and Emilio looked at each other in confusion. Both of them looked me in the eyes uncomprehendingly, so I said, "Remember my nightmares? They're not nightmares any longer. They're now very beautiful dreams, and those ladies in white transport me to another dimension in my dream where I go to a very nice school. They taught me many nice things, but I don't think you would understand if I explained."

Emilio rubbed his forehead with his fingers. "But you haven't explained what you did to that man to make him cry and grovel."

I shook my head. "I didn't do anything. I just took him to another reality. I put him right in front of a very angry, very hungry bear, so that I could show him how small he is by comparison to that beast." I smiled. "That is why he looked up and then put his head down to beg for forgiveness. He wasn't asking me—he was begging to the bear!"

Mr. Xiang asked, "Those ladies in white, or your angels in your dreams, they taught you to do that?"

"Of course, yes. And I knew you were coming towards us as well." Mr. Xiang's confusion grew. "You saw my uncle's car in the restaurant parking lot when you were preparing to leave with your family. You were worried, and my angels sent you towards us." I raised my index finger and added with a small smile, "Oh, oh." I pointed to his back. "I think your wife and daughters are coming behind you, looking for you."

They both turned, but no one was there. They exchanged glances and smiled. After all I had just said, however, they weren't surprised and shrugged when not even a few seconds went by and they heard the voices of the two girls calling for their father. They came running towards him out of the darkness. Mr. Xiang looked at Emilio and shook his head with a wondering expression.

We said goodbye to the Xiangs, got back in my uncle's car, and drove back to his house in Miramar, across from the Country Club, which would be nationalized few years later. That was when they turned it into the National Institute for Arts, Cubanacan, where, ironically, I would spend a few years learning music for symphonic orchestral percussion, as well as dramatic arts and cinematography.

Montauk: The Lightning Chance

The next day, early in the morning after a delicious breakfast of fresh orange juice, a slice of mango and a glass of *café con leche*[28]. I said goodbye to my aunt and cousin, we got in my uncle's car and he drove me back to Pinar del Rio to take me home. The trip took around two and a half hours. Emilio always enjoyed taking these long drives to talk to me.

He turned the radio off and said, "You know what? I know you are very young to understand some things, but you actually are a very, very old spirit. For your age you understand many things that maybe many adults cannot understand. I think your spirit is probably hundreds if not thousands of years old, based on your reactions when you face a daily problem. It's as if you had already been through it and solved it before." I sat next to him listening attentively and respectfully. He smiled. "You should never be scared of anything, but you should be prudent and careful. Some people can hurt you. There are very bad people on this Earth. I want you to remember that we are human beings, we have a spirit and body that are separate from each other. I'll give you an example: fruit has both pulp and seed, like a mango. We eat the pulp and then we drop the seeds on the ground. The seeds bear another tree and thousands of other mangoes come from that single seed, with each one having the potential to create many thousands more. This is the cycle of nature."

He reached out to me with his right hand and mussed my hair affectionately. "From the day you were born I have seen in you the seed not only from my grandfather but also from my father. Something that is extraordinary, because they both have the same name. Evidently your father, Leonardo, sees that in you like I do—you are the only one of his boys named Donato. Maybe it's because his rebel spirit tried to break the tradition of the family, he never calls you Donato and calls you Julio Antonio instead. Julio Antonio is the name of one of the sons from our grandfather, the Major General who was decapitated by the Spanish during the war of Independence against the Spanish Crown in 1871. You should be as proud of that name as I am of Donato. But I'm not Donato del Marmol, I'm Emilio. Unfortunately, we cannot pick our names; that comes from whatever member of the family who suggest the names."

I shook my head a little uncomfortably and put my hand to my throat. I looked at him. "You're not going to believe what I'm going to tell you; I haven't told anyone else because I don't want people to think

---

[28] A typical Cuban breakfast with bread and butter

I'm crazy. In my nightmares, I feel like I'm the one being decapitated, and I feel the tingling in my throat when you said that to me, like I have it in my brains. I experienced the same sensation many times before of my head rolling along the dusty road beneath the hooves of horses, as if my head is not on my body but rolling along the road." Two tears welled in my eyes as I went back to 1871 at that particular moment.

"I'm sorry. I shouldn't have brought that up."

"No, no—I don't fear it anymore. I'm the master of it and control it; my ladies in white taught me."

Emilio reached out and squeezed my shoulder a little hard, as if he were feeling my own pain. In a voice thick with emotion, he said, "Unfortunately the evil men can do to other men is associated with Satan. That is what made the Spanish kill your granduncle." He might have been trying to soften the pain he knew I felt at that moment at the recollection of those horrible nightmares that had plagued me since my birth. "I want to tell you something that I don't want you to repeat to anyone, not even your father, OK?"

"Another secret?"

"Yes. But this secret is more important. You're not a normal kid like others, even your brothers, and you've probably come to realize that already. I know the level of your intelligence is unprecedented, and I don't want you to even discuss it with your father. If he makes the mistake of telling anyone else, he could put your life in danger." I looked my question to him. "The highest tested IQ in the whole world has been until now 228. Perhaps someone will be born tomorrow with a higher one. Yours is ten times higher, up to the point that it looks fictional. Whatever you have in your brain, it is like it works at maximum capacity while the rest of ours works at 10% capacity." He shifted a little towards me so he could glance in my eyes before returning them to the road. "Do you understand what I'm saying?"

I nodded. "Of course. That is why you don't want anybody to see the results from the tests you and your colleagues at the university ran on me for nearly a week."

"Of course. People tend to be afraid of what they don't know. In many cases they try to destroy what they don't understand or have the capacity to assimilate for themselves."

I nodded in agreement. "That is the reason you made me promise you not to tell anyone what I had heard there. You made every single one of your colleagues destroy all the analyses they performed on my brain and swore to you to keep secret until they die. They probably belonged to a secret society that you are a member of. You told me that only you and I could know it."

He nodded, looking at me in surprise. He shook his head. "You never cease to amaze me. Yes, you're right. This other secret I will entrust to you now is more delicate than the one before. Do you understand?"

"*Claro*, of course. I've never told anyone the first secret, not even to my Mima. I feel guilty about that occasionally, because you made me break my promise to her." I tapped him on the arm. "I promised her that I would never keep any secrets from her. Because you told me how dangerous this could be for my life and my entire family, I never even dared to tell Mima. I considered it *your* secret and priority, and that is the reason I never told a single soul what you relayed to me."

'Very well," he replied with a small smile of satisfaction on his face at hearing from my lips that he could have complete confidence in me. He had told me before that he could trust me more than his wife because her intellectual level didn't allow her to digest some of the things he could talk about. "It's a great satisfaction for me to be able to communicate with you, like I've told you many times, seeing how young you are. It's unbelievable that you can understand me and what I'm talking about even better than intellectuals, doctors, and brain surgeons that have tremendous intelligence and capacity for understanding. Let's move on," and he grew very serious. "The world in which we live today is divided into two forces: the forces of good and those of evil. The forces of evil have been controlling our country recently to a very great magnitude. They have plans to expand around the world, destroying religions, established institutions, and personal freedom for everyone who doesn't join them. This is not an ideology, it's above that. It looks like one, but when we open that can, it's the real evil, Satan. This evil will cost Cuba, the Americas, and the world, millions more innocent lives than it already has."

I looked at him, without understanding completely, in surprise at what he was trying to tell me. In my mind, the actual world government, the revolution in Cuba, was precisely intended to destroy evil. The tyrant, in his ambition for power, tortured people, plucking out eyes and pulling out nails of anyone who went against his government, even students. After cutting people up, they dropped them in the gutters of cities, sidewalks, in the middle of streets, all over the country. I didn't understand why he was referring to evil as being present now rather than before. I interrupted him, "With all my respect because I love you like my father very much, I want to ask you, are you maybe referring to all these firing squads to execute the criminals in order to create justice? The torture and murder of the people who sympathize with Batista's regime? I do consider it excessive; like Papi has said many times, when you are bitten by a dog, if you get in the ground in the same position and bite it back, all you do is become another dog. Is that what you mean, that we're going overboard?"

He smiled. "Not quite. But you are close. In my opinion, as you saw, we're not just executing criminals from the dictatorship. Now, like a good Cuban sandwich, between those criminals we're putting innocent people who disagree with the revolution, losing their property even though they had no association with the tyrant, simply because they are opposed to the revolution. In consequence, the people are enraged at the injustices being committed against them by the leaders of this revolution. They've started to fabricate charges they pull out of thin air to justify the expropriation of houses, yachts, cars, and jewelry from the wealthy."

I thought about that for several seconds. He took me out of my thoughts by saying, "Whatever I tell you, and this is the secret I wanted to tell you, don't believe anything I or anyone else says. Do like you always do, which is one of the things I admire in you: listen and exactly like I told you before, investigate. After your investigation, if you can corroborate what I or anyone else tells you is close enough to the truth, then you can draw your own conclusions. Follow this golden rule and you will never be a victim of gossip, propaganda, or personal vendetta from someone who wants to use you and instigate by using you for political or some other multiple reasons. Remember, like I said before, this is a secret that I want you to keep in mind, even if you don't agree with me at this moment. I know your father is very devoted to this revolution, I will tell you something right now that I want you to digest, but don't ask me how I obtained the information. Even though I absolutely trust you, it would not be prudent to put you in that tremendous risk. But I know all the plans that these leaders have in their minds. I know one of them very well. I've been tracking him down for years. This man is associated with Satanic cults and is their main symbol that almost destroyed all of Europe. He is infiltrated among the leaders of this revolution. That is how much danger we're in. They promise to help the poor and give people housing for free; only the ignorant will believe that. All the wealth they take from the rich will become their personal possessions. Everything your Papi worked all his life for—

business, properties—all of it will end up in the hands of these bandits. They don't give two cents that your father fought against the dictator to bring him down and almost lost his life in the process, as well as using his status as Grand Master Mason to convince those Masonic brothers who followed his revolutionary ideas into putting millions of dollars out of all their combined pockets."

Once more I remained silent out of respect for my uncle. I still could not believe that what he was telling me would become reality, so I replied, "I will not repeat a single word of what you just told me to my father or anyone else. I will also do what you told me to do and initiate my own investigation. If in the end whatever you've said has any shred of truth, even if it's just close to the truth, I will be the worst enemy that these leaders of the revolution will ever have. This I promise you from the bottom of my heart. I also promise you that unless I have irrefutable proof in my hand of what you just told me, I will never confront my father or tell him a single word of what you just told me. I know for sure that this will break his heart into pieces. His deception will be so great that it would probably destroy him for the rest of his life. You know him better as his brother—he's never voted in his life for any President in this country because he hated the corruption that's infested our system since the beginning of the republic. Now if the leaders of the revolution that he's completely trusted are becoming more corrupt than the politicians who came before—imagine what that will do to him!"

Uncle Emilio nodded. "This is not political corruption—that can be fixed with an honest election. These are disciples of Satan. This is a vastly different animal. When these people put everyone under their control and take power, many times through intimidation and terror, decades will pass before we can take that power away from them. This always comes at an extremely high price where hundreds of thousands of innocent lives get sacrificed in the process. They are not only protected by Satan, but they follow to a T all the rules of the Satanic rituals. They are brutal without any consideration of any kind for human life. They have no care, no remorse, even if they must eliminate an entire population to maintain power. If you think about it, such a sadistic, unscrupulous enemy must annihilate all opposition, even though, like an old tree with deep roots, a new branch sprouts and comes back. But in such cases that normally wind up being isolated groups that can work only in the dark in clandestine manner. Public opinion never dares to support them much less defend them openly out of the fear that is injected into people's minds that not only will supporters be exterminated, but so will their entire families."

Emilio grew silent, his face long in his sorrow. It was an unusual expression for him. I remained silent, deep in my own thoughts running through my head at the speed of light. I had so many questions then. Was it possible that my Papi was wrong? Was his friendship and admiration for that young attorney, Fidel Castro, and his best friend Eddie Chibas[29] misplaced? Seizing this opportunity, Castro became the Number One in the Ortodoxo Party. Eventually, all the members crossed the line and joined the new movement he created, the Movement of the 26th of July. Some said that the evidence pointed to Castro as having orchestrated the theft of Chibas' documents.

Figure 26 Eduardo Chibas

Deep in my thoughts, I didn't realize that we were passing by the military regiment at Rio Rivera on the edges of the city. They had several trailers by the main Central Highway, with bulldozers and tanks, creating a vast improvised parking area for the vehicle storage of those who got arrested during their searches of those coming in or out of the city. The red soil was not packed at all, creating massive clouds of nearly blood-

---

[29] Eduardo Chibas used to be the primary leader who used a radio program to broadcast his views to the public. He tried to reveal proof he had recently obtained about the corruption of the government from high level contacts. When in 1951 the opportunity came to expose it during his radio program, he discovered that his enemies had stolen the documents from his briefcase just a few minutes before the program. He had no time to think, and as a man of honor took his own revolver and said into the microphone, "I kill myself in shame before my nation because I'm breaking my promise. Some unscrupulous individuals from the government stole my proof out of my briefcase a few moments ago. Shame against money!" He shot himself in the stomach and died three days later.

red dust. The length of time some cars had been sitting there could be attested by the amount of red dust that lay over them.

Several cars were in front of us. A group of soldiers walked along the line to expedite the searches, and anyone they cleared they waived on ahead in the line to go through the checkpoint. Emilio was apparently annoyed at this. He said, "You see, Julio Antonio? Just use your head. What is the reason for these searches in the middle of the sole highway that connects two important cities in our island? The only obvious reason is to implant psychological terror in the people, intimidating them into submitting to their new government and get used to this kind of conduct."

I didn't agree and shook my head. "Well, my uncle, with all my respect, only a few weeks ago there were some people hung from the light poles along the streets in our city. Nobody knew where they came from or who did it. Maybe that's the reason they have this checkpoint up at the entry of the city, to find out who was coming in and out."

Emilio shook his head in irritation. "It's very possible that the people from this government didn't have enough time to fabricate proof to justify executing those people by the firing squad, and used the light poles of the city to eliminate those they couldn't prove guilty and at the same time terrify 100% of the opposition."

Not wanting to contradict him, I smiled and nodded. "Maybe you're right. When the people we sometimes have suspicions of become the real perpetrators of those horrible crimes, like in the mystery movies. I've watched a lot of Dick Tracy."

Emilio could not hold it in and smiled at my having an answer for everything. He reached over and affectionately mussed my hair. "I'm sorry I've been a little cranky. Thank you for your patience with your old uncle."

I turned to him and said, "Uncle, please—you're just beginning to live. How can you call yourself an old man?"

He smiled and shook his head as two soldiers approached our car. We rolled our windows down. The one on my side looked in the car and kept walking. The one of the driver's side asked Emilio for his license and registration. My uncle handed the requested documents to the soldier and answered his questions about who we were, were we were coming from, and what we were doing. The soldier was very tall with a long beard, and behaved in a nasty, rude manner. He also stank so badly that I could smell him on my side of the car. It looked like he hadn't taken a shower for several weeks.

He said in a disrespectful tone, "You're dressed too nice. You probably worked for the Batista team or the mafiosos in our nation who like mosquitoes have been sucking our blood." Evidently this man was an illiterate peasant in a uniform and held resentment for my uncle's immaculate attire. He opened the door. "What are you waiting for? Get out of the car! I need to take you to my sergeant. You look suspicious to me."

Emilio touched my left knee and looked in my eyes. "Please don't do anything. I will resolve this. The last thing we want to do is give this individual an excuse to do anything to harm us. I'll be right back. Stay in the car." We were about six cars back in the line. Emilio got out. The other soldiers were doing the same thing up and down the line. "Follow me." The soldier jumped in the car behind the driver's wheel.

My uncle patiently walked behind the car as the soldier drove to the bulldozed parking lot. It was obvious the soldier was trying to anger my uncle. All the other cars in the area were filthy with dust and dirt. I noticed we passed several available spaces, but he kept driving farther off, much farther than need be. I kept watching my uncle in the rearview mirror, patiently walking behind, far away from the highway.

I poked my head out of the window and held my arm over my nose to hide myself from the soldier's stench. The soldier smiled. "What happened? You have a delicate nose like a little rich girl?"

That was a blow below the belt to me and produced a reaction I normally experience when I see someone abusing another unjustly. I felt a heat coming from my stomach to my head and ears. I kept looking in the rearview, hoping my uncle would get close soon and defuse the situation. As I watched him walking along behind and remembered his request that I not do anything. Even though this man was filling the glass of my impatience to overflowing with that comment, I did not answer him at all. I tried to contain the volcano I was feeling in my ears and chest, beating like drums, and then had an acute contraction in my stomach, like when you need to go to the bathroom badly lest you have an accident.

The soldier leaned towards me after stopping the car in the last spot of the entire lot, right next to a cornfield. I didn't know what his intentions were but caressed my cheek. "Are you a boy or a girl? You have a very pretty face."

That was the straw that broke the camel's back. I raised both of my arms, grabbed him by both shoulders and squeezed as hard as I could

Montauk: The Lightning Chance

so that I could disable the muscles in his legs. Then I moved my hands along to his jaw, my fingers reaching up for his temple. He looked at me in panic, clearly not expecting this. With all the force I had in my body, I vomited full in his face, mouth, nose, and eyes, all the orange juice, mango pulp, milk and coffee, and finally the bread and butter from my breakfast that morning. He was blinded by the stomach acid and screamed. The vomit covered his face, down along the shoulder strap for his machine gun and onto the weapon itself.

He reached for his machine gun to defend himself, but the goop and saliva made it too slick. He yelled, "I cannot see, I cannot see! What did you do to me, you little shit?" The stench of the soldier grew worse from my vomit, and he desperately scrabbled for the door handle without any success. I turned and braced myself against my door and kicked him with both feet repeatedly. He hit his head against the window frame and yelled in pain. "What are you doing to me?"

I kept my silence. I opened my door and got out. I walked around and opened his door. To my uncle's astonished eyes, I grabbed the soldier by the neck and threw him out of the car onto the ground. His legs still immobilized, he rolled in the dirt on the ground, turning it into mud and vomit, and getting it in his mouth. He tried once more to grab his machine gun, but the strap was still too slick, and it continually slipped out of his grasp. I took a handkerchief out of my pants pocket, wrapped it around my hand, and grabbed the strap of his weapon. I pulled it off his neck and threw it away while he continued to scream about his blindness. He was also still unable to stand. Since he had brought us so far from the other soldiers, he could yell all he wanted, as there was also an electrical generator nearby, and its noise completely drowned him out.

I looked around and saw that nobody was nearby or paying any attention and decided to give him a hard time. I picked up the machine gun and tossed it into the bed of a dump truck that appeared to be filled with salt lick blocks for the cattle ranches. It would take them a while to find that weapon. I walked back to the soldier. Emilio only saw as he walked up my occasional kicking of the soldier, directing his rolling into the corn field.

My uncle came up and stopped me. "I believe that's good enough. We should leave this place at once before his friends notice he's missing and come looking for him."

"OK," I said, "let's go. That's a good idea, even though I don't think anyone's going to notice this moron. His own people probably don't like him."

We used our handkerchiefs to clean the vomit residue off the car's seats and left that place. As we drove off, Emilio asked, "What did that man do to make you so mad?" I told him what happened. "He did *that* to you?" he asked incredulously. "What is wrong with him?"

"I don't know. He knew you were behind us, so even if he thought I was a girl, I don't know what he thought he would be able to do."

Emilio shook his head. "I don't think you'll be able to survive inside this political system. It's designed to abuse the weak, and as it's impossible for you to contain yourself now, you will find it even more so in your teenage years."

"I think as long as I have God and my angels on myside, I can survive anything. Whatever circumstances come up with me, I'll deal with it."

"How can you induce yourself to vomit? And it's been several hours since breakfast. It should already be digested—and especially with the force it came out of your mouth that you described. You blinded that guy!"

"With the help of my angels. They're never too far away from me, even when I'm sleeping."

"My worry now is what is going to happen when they find this man and he tells them what you did."

I smiled and shook my head. "I can assure you that this man will invent his own story, but he will never admit that a skinny little boy with long hair like a girl kicked his ass so many times to the point of taking his machine gun away from him and that such a big guy could do nothing to defend himself. I don't' think even his superiors will believe that story."

Emilio was silent for a few moments in thought, his worry clearly on his face. He might be thinking what would happen on his way back out. His look of preoccupation disappeared and was replaced with an immense smile. He patted me on my left shoulder and shook his head again. He burst out laughing, startling me.

"I can't believe it," he said, tears of mirth rolling down his cheeks. "I can't get the image of that big soldier with a thick beard, and you kicking him into the corn field. What did you do to him that he couldn't see? I understand he couldn't see initially because your stomach acid temporarily blinded him. As I approached you, I couldn't even believe my eyes at the way he could do nothing to defend himself against your kicks." He wiped the tears from his eyes and paused. He pointed at me with his right hand. "You are in reality an extremely dangerous weapon, especially to somebody who angers you. Can you explain to me why he couldn't get up? What did you do to him? I saw him try several times, and he kept falling down." I reached out and put my hand on his shoulders. "No, no—you don't need to demonstrate."

"No, I'm just showing you what I did." I tapped at the spot in his shoulder. "I dug my fingers deep into the nerves there and created a temporary knot in that muscle that obstructed the flow of blood to his legs."

He looked at me incredulously. "How, if you never studied medicine, did you know that?" I smiled and opened my mouth to answer, but he held up his hand. "Yeah, yeah, I know—the ladies in white. Right?"

My smile grew. "Yes, my uncle. You bet your ass." He was swerving in the highway and I hit him hard in the shoulder. He corrected his driving and he turned to look at me in surprise. I thought I might be in trouble, first because I shouldn't speak to him that way, and second because of the strength of my blow. "I'm sorry, Uncle—I'm sorry. I think I got carried away." He looked at me seriously. I looked at him guiltily. "What's up? I already apologized."

An immense smiled showed in his face. I felt better at that. The last thing I wanted to do was end my weekend with my uncle being angry at me. "No, no—you don't have to apologize at all. First of all, you're a young man already. Between us, we can speak man to man. You can use those words with me; of course, not in front of a lady."

"Of course. I know the golden rule of being a gentleman."

He smiled and nodded. "And your hitting my shoulder, even though it was a little too hard for a young man your age, you just caught me by surprise. I didn't know you were so strong. You're still so little and skinny, but don't worry about it. There's nothing you need to apologize for." I smiled, more at ease, and he added, "I'm the one who needs to apologize. This is the second time you really saved my ass. I told Jackie to give you a thank you and a kiss, but I forgot to do it myself. I have to give you thanks not just for yesterday evening but now today this morning."

"For me it is a pleasure to help people I don't even know. It's a double pleasure to help my family and in your case, who I love as much or more than my own father, the satisfaction multiplies a hundred percent. You don't have to thank me—for me it's not just a duty but an extraordinary satisfaction."

Emilio touched my shoulder affectionately. We were pulling up to the front of my house on 116 Avenue Cabada in Pinar del Rio. I picked up my travel bag and walked into the house. Mima, Majito, and Papi received us with great joy. Majito and Mima hugged and kissed me all over. Papi shook my hand and he and Emilio exchanged a strong, warm hug.

I looked at Mima, "Where are my sisters and brothers?"

"They're at a birthday party a few blocks away."

Mima and Emilio hugged each other, and she kissed him on the cheek. "How did he behave in your house?"

Emilio answered, 'You don't have to worry about it. You have a properly educated young man, and it's always a pleasure to have him around."

"You're just in time for lunch. I hope you're hungry." Majito put out some extra plates in the formal dining room.

After some small talk around the table, Majito began to serve what Mima had prepared. She continued to ask, "He didn't do anything inappropriate? Tell me the truth."

"Why are you asking that? You know how proper he is. Not only that, I'm going to add that it's not only a pleasure, but it's a measure of security to have him around. He is extremely smart, and he knows how to handle everything. Actually, when I take him on the weekends it's like mental therapy. I know he likes to come with us, but for me it's a great pleasure to have him around."

Papi smiled. "Well, I don't know about him being a young man. Here we call him 'the Old Man.' His brothers and sisters call him the Attorney because nobody can win a single fight or argument with him." He pointed to me with his right arm. "Imagine it—look at him, only 12 years old. I don't want to see what he's like in another ten years with a lot more experience." He shook his head proudly. He looked deeply into my eyes. "I think, as I've said several times, he is the direct reincarnation of our grandfather." My father looked at Emilio. "Don't you think so?"

Emilio grinned broadly. "I don't know, my brother, whether he is the way you say or maybe something more complicated, Julio Antonio has an extraordinary level of intelligence that we cannot comprehend sometimes. In my criteria and according to yours, too, following the reincarnation theory of our grandfather, I think as we analyze him, he is like two different reincarnations: our grandfather and *his* son, the old Julio Antonio who was decapitated by the Spanish in 1871."

Both Mima and Majito crossed themselves anxiously. Majito brought in a large piece of medium rare Beef Wellington. She nearly dropped the ladle of glaze for the dish. A little splashed out of the pot. She and Mima crossed themselves. She said, "Look what you made me do!"

"I'm sorry," he apologized, "we were just talking."

Mima said, "This is the part you'll like the most: the rare part."

"Yes, Verena, thank you," Emilio replied.

Majito rushed to clean the beautiful white linen tablecloth. Both women continued to cross themselves. Mima wasn't happy with the commentary said, "Please, Emilio—why don't you guys change the subject? Julio Antonio is still too young to understand what you're talking about, and the last thing especially you would like to see is him regressing to those horrible nightmares that disturbed him for so long."

I interrupted, "Please, Mima—I don't want you ever, ever to be worried about me again with those nightmares. That's in the past. Now, instead of the nightmares controlling me, I have learned to control them, and they're now beautiful dreams of learning experiences. I have infinite opportunities to learn whatever I want: music, science, even walking in space."

Papi had just opened his mouth for a piece of beef. "What?"

All the adults exchanged glances. He had started to eat before the rest of them, forgetting his good manners. I looked at Emilio who with a warning glance made me remember what we had spoken of in the car about things people didn't or wouldn't understand. I realized I had overstepped the boundaries, and so said, "Mima, this is the best bearnaise sauce you've ever made."

"What craziness is that about walking in space?" Papi demanded.

"It's fantasy, Papi. Don't worry, I haven't lost my marbles yet—they're still in my pocket."

Emilio smiled and nodded wordlessly at how smoothly I got out of that, even though my Papi was a very smart man. He had never completed his university studies—although he had left the university it had never left him. Similarly, some people who completed the university found that it had never been even entered them. He had noticed how Emilio and I had been exchanging looks and how we were communicating. He might have been a little jealous about it and was wondering what was not true and what was.

Emilio did not sympathize with the new regime and had profound doubts. He was looking out for our best interests and wanted to protect us from the huge disaster that was coming. He had not in fact tried to convince me of anything; he only did the good spy work of planting doubt and putting the seed in my brain. He let me develop my ideas and not impose his own, leaving me to find out on my own as I investigated if it was true or not what he had been telling me.

But my Papi was completely fanatic about the promises of his supposed friend Fidel Castro; he was not prepared at that moment to listen to anything that looked critical of his dreams of so many years of sacrifice that they worked to achieve in that revolution. He had worked very hard against the political corruption and this frustrated dream of the majority of the Cuban people, to have a free Cuba, independent of foreign interference, with respect and rights for everyone without regard to race or religion. Of course, that is the Kool-Aid of false promises the new leader of the revolution and his group of followers: to convince the rest of the Cuban people and then to control the world under Satan's ideology.

We had finished our lunch. Majito and Mima picked up the plates and began to bring in clean plates for dessert, a typical custom in every household in Cuba, even the poorest one. The high economic standard the country still enjoyed even under the years of the dictator the Cuban people had lived in. The dessert consisted of a mango pulp made at home, cooked with light steam, and mixed with cream very close to the French *crème brulee*. Added to this was some ice cream. Then they poured Grand Marnier over it and lit it off. Then they finished by scattering some nuts over it. This dessert was frequently made because of its distinguished flavor. Emilio's palate was ecstatic.

As he ate his ice cream, he said, "Thank you very much, Verena. You have divine hands and are professional to the extreme. This is not a typical lunch." He lifted a spoon of ice cream high and put it in his mouth. "This is a gift to the palate." He savored the spoonful and swallowed. He looked at Papi. "My brother Leonardo, there is no doubt in my mind that you are an extremely lucky and intelligent man, not only blessed by God with all your success in business, but also with the wife you have."

Mima smiled. "Oh, thank you!"

Montauk: The Lightning Chance

My father smiled. "Thank you for your compliments to me and to Mima." Full of satisfaction, he picked up his tall glass of wine he had been sipping. "Let's toast for this fantastic and wonderful day. Thank you very much, Emilio my older brother, and let's also cheer for your beautiful medical career as the surgeon, gynecologist and obstetrician you are, for you are the best. You bring so much tranquility and healing and make us fathers and mothers like family to be at ease when you are around."

Majito and Mima, who didn't drink wine, toasted with their orange juices. Emilio said to Papi, "Leonardo, as your big brother and also a member of this family, I give you my most profound and sincere thanks for your compliments. I don't know if you are prepared to swallow or assimilate what it is my duty to tell you today. Because I didn't want to disturb you, I've been postponing this for the past month on every single visit I've made to your house. This is to me like appendix pain. As you have the first pain or symptom, you should immediately remove it. You will save problems that could be created in the future and even prevent death."

Mima saw what was coming and looked worried. "Is anyone in your family or you sick, Emilio?"

'No, it's not about that. It's about you guys." Mima opened her eyes wide and looked over at me anxiously. She held her cross and fiddled with it between her fingers. She kissed it but stayed silent in worry. Emilio took a deep breath and leaned forward. He looked directly into Papi's eyes. Papi still held his glass of wine in his right hand. He returned the look, possibly concerned about a big brother lecture about something. Everyone stopped eating, letting the ice cream melt on the plates. Emilio looked down at his plate regretfully, pondering whether he should have waited until everyone had finished. But it was too late. He put the small spoon down by his plate. "Leonardo, I know how you feel about this revolution and its leaders. But please, don't interrupt me and listen to me, whatever I say, to the end. I would appreciate that."

Mima heard that and leaned back, this time biting her lower lip worriedly. Clearly, she was expecting a bad reaction from Papi. Nobody was authorized in that house to make any criticism about the revolution, and Papi had refused to hear any comment, even in jest, that touched that subject. Whatever bad or ugly had happened during the revolution at that moment, in his mind had no comparison with what Batista's regime had done for some many years before. To everyone's surprise, including mine, all Papi did was gesture with his wine glass for Emilio to continue and sipped his wine.

Emilio leaned back. "My brother, you know better than anyone that I'm against any dictator or totalitarian system or regime. You and I together, helped by so many others, some who have unfortunately died in the process, have been fighting to eliminate precisely this kind of system for so many years. You also are the only person on this Earth that knows my most delicate secret about for whom I've been working all my life. I communicated that in absolute trust many years ago when we were transporting that coffin from Guane all the way to the capital to save Nolberis' life from Machado's henchmen." Papi nodded his agreement but remained silent.

Emilio continued, "These same forces of intelligence that I've worked for almost all my life have all the details about the leaders of this revolution and how they want to conduct and where they want to take this country. The future of Cuba doesn't look good at all. You know I don't take things lightly; I confirmed this recently with my own eyes in a very dark meeting. They have formed an alliance with Satanic cults."

Mima and Majito looked shocked and crossed themselves. Majito had been standing by respectfully, waiting to collect the plates. The ice cream over the delicious dessert continued to melt, threatening to overflow the plates. But Emilio touched the subject that was in Mima's heart from the beginning of the revolution, practically killing her. She always felt that they would be governed by bandits, but my father in his fanaticism could not see what the leaders truly were doing, and he was further blinded by the huge investment he had made into the revolution, both personally and through his Masonic brothers.

Papi raised his hand with the glass of wine. "I'm sorry, I don't want to interrupt you, and I won't do it again. But I want you to understand and remember something: the North Americans have never been our friends. They've been our allies; and as is completely logical to me as a businessman, they will look out first for their own interests, not ours or a better future for Cuba. I just want you to remember as we agreed before, not to believe anything of what anyone tells you and only half of what you see. Your own eyes can betray you and lead you to foolish conclusions. Even though you've been working for them nearly all your life, your duty, your honor, and your heart should be with your country, because you are a Cuban. Your priority should be your country before anything else. It's very difficult to be loyal to two different flags. I don't know where you are going with this conversation, and I out of courtesy and love to you as my brother, will let you conclude and finish like you asked me without any more interruptions." He took another sip of wine and put the glass down on the table and looked at Emilio.

Emilio looked Leonardo in the eyes. He realized at that moment that he was not going to make much headway in his conversation with his brother. He decided to take the last shot Leonardo had given him, but he wasn't going to waste it. He snatched hope in the deepest side of his heart and continued. "My brother Leonardo, please listen to me. I've been bringing you an opportunity to save not only all you've acquired all your life, your money, your properties—all the sweat of your brow from the last thirty years. If you listen carefully and open your heart, because you know my love for you is unconditional, maybe you can save from these bandits if not everything then a large amount of what you have before it's too late, before these unscrupulous leaders nationalize the treasury and all the banks in the country. Think of your sons and daughters. This government won't allow you, if you change your mind in the future, to let them leave the country. This will happen in a very few months. This is not a moment to be fanatic, my brother—you have to think clearly and be focused. We have created a clandestine operation with the Catholic Church. The name of that is *Pedros Pan*[30]. They will get all your children out of this country while you put your financial affairs in order and salvage everything you can before you get out of here. They'll put them in Catholic schools all over the United States." He pointed to me. "If you don't do it for any of your children, for yourself, or for Mima, do it for this kid. You know why, Leonardo? Because we both know this kid possesses extraordinary gifts. You and I can both bear witness to it; this gift isn't just for us, it's for all of humanity. Imagine, Leonardo," he spread his arms, "the horror of him being indoctrinated and utilized for these disciples of Satan, not for good, but for the destruction of all of humanity.

---

[30] Operation Peter Pan was conducted between 1960 and 1962, resulting in the mass exodus of over 14,000 unaccompanied Cuban children of between the ages 6 and 18 to the United States. Their parents sacrificed to send them out of the country in order to prevent the communist regime from indoctrinating their kids: the wonders of socialism, communism, and Marxism!

Dr. Julio Antonio del Marmol

Figure 27 Pedro Pan Children

Maybe you don't even believe it, even Fidel Castro has no idea who in reality this individual is that is actually inside the body of Ernesto Guevara de la Serna. The same man that for many months right here in Cuba had a macabre party, killing thousands in his euphoria for quenching his thirst for human blood in the prison of La Cabaña. I saw with my own eyes this same sadistic, unscrupulous murderer change bodies in Rosario, Argentina in a very dark cult with his body dripping in blood, nothing less than what the worst murderer humanity ever produced, the man who killed millions of Jews in Europe and around the world, Adolf Hitler. He then left for Mexico to meet, who do you think? The Castro brothers, especially Fidel. This is the man Castro has in his ear to keep himself in power."

Leonardo stood up and raised his arms in exasperated incredulity. "Emilo, my brother! Do you realize what you're saying? I'm sorry to interrupt you and break my promise to you, but what you just said is so outrageously over the top that I beg you, as your brother, not to repeat this to anyone. Nobody will believe a single word of what you just said. It's very possible that maybe they'll assume you're losing your mind and put you in a psychiatric hospital. For God's sake," Leonardo shook his head in clear irritation, "my brother Emilio, you are a man of science!" Papi opened his arms again and asked, "What happened to you?" Before Emilio could answer, he continued, "Who has brainwashed you?"

Montauk: The Lightning Chance

Mima and Majito had been quiet all this time but had watched Emilio very carefully. They both shook their heads as they saw the two tears escape Emilio's eyes. I had never until this day seen Mima and Papi have a single argument about anything at all. But evidently this went too far for Mima to digest. She was a very smart woman and knew Emilio's feelings very well. She knew that he was not a man to invent tales, much less believe in superstitions. To the contrary, as a man of science and a doctor, he was so devoted to the process of scientific inquiry that he always made sure he had his feet on the ground and his information accurate before he would ever comment on anything. She had no choice but to come to his defense.

She said with a sweet smile, "Leonardo! You asked what happened to your brother, and I ask what's happened to you, my love, that you would lose the capacity and manners that made me fall in love with you so many years ago. How can any political idea turn you to such an extreme viewpoint that you're not even capable of listening to someone you know in your heart that has shown you love, loyalty, and has been by your side all your life. Your own blood! As you've told me yourself, he's protected you ever since you were kids whenever some older kids tried to abuse you because you were the smallest one in the whole bunch."

Everyone was silent, shocked at Mima contradicting her husband in front of others. Ordinarily a Cuban wife remained neutral before others in any dispute. She stood up and walked a few steps over to Emilio and put her right hand on his shoulder. She said to him, "I believe you. Majito probably does, too." Majito nodded. "You probably won't even believe it, but your brother Leonardo believes you, too!" My father glared at her. "Even if he doesn't want to admit because of his extreme political ideas, pride, or whatever it is that's keeping him blind to the truth. He must resist believing that maybe what you just brought to him today is a message from God, not only for him but also his brother Masons. They try to be different than everyone else without realizing that they've been little by little moving far away from God. Everyone without exception, even the love of my life, Leonardo del Marmol, is becoming very easy prey for Satan and his followers!"

My father interrupted her in extreme irritation, trying not to raise his voice or aggravating a very tense conversation that caused everyone to leave their dessert untouched. He forced a smile. "Mima, Mima—please, don't join yourself with this kind of idiocy! You don't know what you're talking about. All these things Emilio just finished saying—"

Emilio said, "I wasn't finished yet."

"OK, all that he was saying and I interrupted, are nothing less than the political maneuvers of the enemies of the revolution who connive to demoralize and destroy what cost so much blood to take the dictator down. Nothing more than lies and fairy tales!"

Mima interrupted Papi this time, raising her right arm high. She actually raised her voice. "Leonardo del Marmol! How many times has your older brother Emilio told you anything at all—*anything at all*—that came to be a lie or a deception? Never! True?" Papi nodded silently. "Then, Leonardo del Marmol, since you don't want to hear me or anyone else, why at least don't you listen your brother, who has been by your side all these years, working with you in your rebellious craziness, and Heaven and God knows what else?" She shook her head in disappointment, her face redder than I had seen in a long time. This time, her eyes were filled with tears. She sat back down, and Majito came over to her. She put both hands around her neck and began to massage her to relax her. A prolonged silence ensued, but Mima was not finished yet.

She took a small sip of orange juice. She nodded. "You men! You have in your heads that we women are all idiots because we decide to be silent many times and swallow our feelings and emotions for love, for harmony, and in an attempt to prevent friction in order to keep our families in good function. You have no idea the suffering a woman goes through when she puts her head down and cures your wounds when you have bullets in your body due to your stupid fanatic ideas. Many times, we don't sleep due to our agony, turning in our beds and wondering when the secret police or army will knock on our door in the middle of the night to take our husbands, sons, or brothers. For what?" She sniffled and repeated in a cracking voice, "For what? To take one little dictator down and replace him with a bigger one." She nodded and looked directly in my father's eyes. "Yes, yes, sir. We've invited Satan into our country. I have no doubts about that at all." She took Emilio's arm and looked into his eyes this time. "I know you are a man of honor and you have no reason to invent any stories. I don't know for sure what you've been doing all these years, even though I have a very vague idea that you've been involved in something really huge all your life. You seem to know things before they happen. But you have to be convinced that right here," she tapped her breast with her right hand, "in the deepest part of my heart, that whatever you've been doing is for the common good for everyone, not only for you, but for your family and all of humanity. You are a clean and good man. There's not even a hair of badness on your body." Her voice grew thick with emotion. "God probably picked you to bring this good message to your brother Leonardo and our family. Whether he listens to you or not, remember, this will always be your house. You will always be welcome here."

Majito spoke this time without directing her comment to anyone. She pointed upwards with her right hand. "I'm only an ignorant black woman, nothing else, but I want to let you know something I've read lately, and it's in the oldest book in the world, the Bible. Satan will put all his energy in making sure that he makes brothers fight brothers, sons fight with fathers, spouses and against spouses. That is the Devil's mission and every single day that goes by, I see that agenda growing bigger and more effective with this revolution. I see more and more clearly the hand of Satan." Majito had never been involved in any conversation with the family out of respect. It looked like after spending so many years with our family that she could no longer keep her mouth shut after observing that friction in the family. Majito then asked respectfully, "Can I remove the plates of the delicious dessert that you guys are so upset that you didn't finish and let the ice cream melt all over the plates? That was a real tragedy! Emilio, you only got a taste, but you didn't touch it."

We gestured that she could take them away. We were too tense. Majito began to clean the table. Papi stood up abruptly. What had started to be a nice, pleasant family lunch ended with an embarrassing for him and tense conversation for the rest of us, not just with his brother but also with Mima, and then to close it with a golden brush, even Majito. I was only one who hadn't spoken a single word out of respect to both of them, even though I had doubts in my mind. I believed that there was a shred of truth to both sides. Unfortunately, they let themselves get wrapped up in their emotions and failed to be able to communicate with each other in a pleasant way. Of course, I knew for a fact that Mima never sympathized with the revolution, and she despised the leaders because she considered them menaces to society. This time, there were no hugs and a smile between my father and my uncle, but my father at least was civilized enough to extend his hand coldly and wished my uncle a good trip back to the capital.

Uncle Emilio said as his last attempt while they shook hands, "Remember, my brother Leonardo, we can be loyal to two flags but also to multiple flags. The proof of that is to look at history, when those flags are united in the good will of people and God during World War II.

How many flags united to bring down the common enemy? That union gave us victory."

Papi smiled a little at that. "Well, well—let's hope that it will be like that in the future in a better world."

That is the last time I saw my Uncle Emilio for a long time. I felt inside me an extreme sadness as he said goodbye with tears in his eyes. After he left the house, I followed him to his car. He gave me a warm, strong hug. "Remember,' he said, "keep your eyes open. Investigate. Later, make your own conclusions."

I was filled with distress because of what just happened. There was a little resentment towards my father, though I didn't understand that until much later. I only wished that with all the love and respect that these brothers had for each other, at least my father should have let Uncle Emilio finish what he had come to say. But my father, in his fanaticism and ignorance, not only lost his opportunity to see all the truth that his brother knew firsthand but also the most valuable treasure he had: the trust and respect of his big brother who had all his life been protecting him. From this moment onward, for pride or whatever reason, they never spoke again to reconcile. When my uncle left our home that afternoon, I knew that I would not see him again for an exceptionally long time. Whatever Emilio had in his hand could have been provided to us. I looked down at the tile mosaic on the floor of our porch, playing back my mental tape of the conversation we had, specifically that what was happening in Cuba could not be fixed with honest elections, that what had happened was more complicated on a different level, more delicate. All these individuals that were now in power had turned around that beautiful revolution at the beginning and put it in the hands of Satan.

My father touched my shoulder, pulling me out of the deep train of thoughts I was immersed in. I would never forget this for the rest of my life. He said, "Julio Antonio, come with me into the library. I want to talk to you in private."

"OK, Papi." I followed him into his library, thinking seriously that he might question me about my conversations with his brother over the weekend. I prepared myself mentally and decided to try and tell him the closest to the truth without betraying what I had promised Uncle Emilio to maintain in silence. I knew it was a complicated situation, but I determined to do whatever was best in my power to not separate them more than they already were and reconcile them if the opportunity arose.

Montauk: The Lightning Chance

My father sat down behind his desk and I sat in one of the comfortable chairs in front of it. He looked into my eyes, very worried and a little guiltily, probably wondering what I had been thinking. "Why are you so serious? Is something bothering you?"

"Yes. I have to be honest with you. I'm a little disappointed and also sad. I cannot say that my uncle was mad, but very, very sad and wounded. He wanted to communicate with you. It looked like it was something extremely important, and he failed in his intent because you didn't want to listen to him."

Papi smiled slightly, knowing he had read me well. "That is the reason you are sad, and that is the reason you are disappointed."

"Yes. Very, because I believe in my heart that we will never see my uncle again in our home, and I also believe in my heart if I know you a little bit that we will never be in his house in the capital."

Papi turned serious. "I have to tell you something, my son. Because what you just said and the way you reacted to other things in the past, that is the only reason I call you my Little Old Man." He shook his head. "I'm sorry, very much so from my heart, that everyone, especially you, had to witness this with me. This was not a pleasant conversation. But let me tell you something: I love my brother Emilio probably more than you do, and more than I love any of my other brothers and sisters. But there are certain things you have no knowledge of, and those things I cannot reveal to you about Emilio. Those things I don't sympathize with, but out of respect for him, I never shared that with him. He is more worried about the rest of the world, especially foreigners, than he has been about his own country. We should all be concerned with that first, all Cubans. Perhaps he lost his perspective along the way and has forgotten the most serious priorities we should have: our own people. Of course, in his blindness he allowed himself to be filled like a chorizo by the propaganda by the capitalist North Americans, who are only looking to exploit our natural resources to pay back at a low price. It's logical that they protect their own interests. They don't care about *our* interests."

I looked at him slightly confused. "Why would my uncle Emilio protect the interest of the North Americans and not our own, when he actually is a citizen of our country?"

Leonardo couldn't answer that question and grew angry at his inability. He abruptly said, "Because he's working for them."

"My uncle Emilio works for the North Americans?"

Not realizing what he was saying, he just said, "*Claro!*" He raised both arms over his head with a look of discontent on his face.

I shook my head, still not understanding. "But I believe my uncle works with the university and the medical school."

My father, realizing that he cannot answer me without revealing the secret that had been entrusted him, tried to get out of the trap I had just put him in by trying to change the subject. He looked me in the eyes and said, "I'm sorry, Julio Antonio, but that is something only Emilio can answer. It's something extremely confidential and personal. Do you understand?"

"*Claro.* It's something like a secret between the two of you."

He nodded his head. I stayed silent for a few seconds. From that moment on, I was full of curiosity at what my father had just hinted. Out of respect and discretion, I decided I would never repeat that question or bring up the subject. At the same time, I felt tremendous peace in my conscience to know that the two of them shared secrets, which is perfectly all right between brothers. Besides, I had a secret with my uncle Emilio, too.

Papi asked, "Do you still like this revolution, Julio Antonio? Tell me the truth. I won't be upset."

"Yes, *claro*. I really like the revolution. You've been telling me that Fidel, his brother Raul, Huber Matos, Camilo are all like Che. They want to help their countrymen and the poor and end all the abuses in our country."

"Did you tell that to your uncle?"

I nodded. "Yes." I scratched my head a little. I hadn't exactly told him that, but I wanted to soften the tone of the conversation. "I believe that my uncle Emilio has got great intentions. He's just very worried about all the deaths by the firing squad. It looks like they'll never end. Now it's not just the criminals left over from Batista, now they're expanding it to those disaffected by the new laws of the revolution."

Papi scratched the back of his head. "I don't like that, either, believe me. Not a bit. You know how I feel about killing another human being. That is something that belongs to God. But if you go around and start shooting the police and the soldiers of the revolution, of course they'll do the same to you. They have to defend themselves and the revolution from its enemies." I looked dubious at that. "What?"

"Well, that is exactly what the soldiers and the police of Batista were telling us. They also thought they should defend themselves and their President. Don't you believe that, Papi?"

Montauk: The Lightning Chance

He looked at me incredulously as he scratched his forehead. "Well, the situation is completely different."

"Really, Papi?"

He shook his head with a dubious expression. He didn't know how to answer me. Finally, he said without much conviction, "Well, remember, what we had before was a dictator. What we have today is different—we're defending our democratic revolution."

I looked unconvinced. "Well, that's not what Mima and Majito think. Both of them told me many times that this revolution used to be a democratic one, but now every single step, laws, and actions indicate that they will go to a socialist or communist totalitarian regime."

Papi raised both arms. "What do you think these women know about politics?"

I smiled. "I don't know too much about politics either, Papi. Only what I've heard you say since I got out of Mima's belly, that politics is very filthy. All politicians should be hung by their testicles from the highest streetlamp in town."

He couldn't help but smile at that. "That is true. And I haven't changed my way of thinking."

"Well, Papi, changing the subject for a minute, I wanted to tell you an idea I've had for a long time which will change your mood to a happier one. I've been turning this over in my head for a while, and I think this is the perfect time to bring it to you. I want to organize a military youth army, the Juvenile Commandos. They will replace the formal army, with only young men who have pure revolutionary ideas, no communist or socialist ideas, with morality and good intentions towards people. They could be an example for everyone to create a beautiful new Cuba for the future without hatred, grudges towards anyone, nor revenge for what others did in the past. Just looking forward to happiness and harmony when everyone lives in peace with respect that every human being deserves without taking care at all what race or religion that man comes from."

Papi looked at me filled with pride. "I think that's a wonderful idea. Put it down in a letter. I'm meeting my friend Fidel in a couple of days in the capital and I'll give it to him then."

"Very well. I'll do that right now." Excitedly I jumped out of my seat, happy at seeing my father's smiling face. "Then we've finished this conversation? I think we've had enough sadness for one day.'"

He smiled again proudly. "Yes. I agree. Enough sadness for one day, and this will bring me joy, to see what you're going to write for me to bring to my friends."

I excused myself and left the library. I paused in the doorway. "I'll go write it right now."

I smiled as I walked away from him. Even though I knew he was proud, the negativity from Mima and Majito that I had heard from their lips didn't influence me to take me away from his side. I was still loyal to his ideals and devotion for the revolution. I took a lined composition book from my school bag and started to write a letter to Fidel Castro. I didn't even know at that time how that letter would radically change my life but also open my eyes and mind, taking me to a very unknown world until now: the world of intrigue and espionage that many times nearly cost me my life.

A few weeks later, after a long interview with Castro, who was fascinated not just with my capacity for eloquence in how I expressed my ideas, I was named the Commander-in-Chief of the Juvenile Commandos of the Rebel Army. Castro personally presented me with a .38 pistol and gave me documents that authorized me to form this juvenile army throughout our entire country with the highest clearance in the civilian and military organizations, top secret only to the level of the President of the nation, Manuel Urrutia Lleo, and Fidel Castro himself.

Figure 28 The Juvenile Commandos

Figure 29 The Commandantico

Dr. Julio Antonio del Marmol

CHAPTER 11: THE LIARS AND DECEIVERS FINALLY LOSE THEIR COVER

It didn't take much time after Fidel introduced me to the other leaders of the revolution. It took me a few months to conduct my own investigation with great scrutiny, not basing my analysis on hearsay or maybes. I only considered the personal testimonies of all of those leaders as they answered my questions. The majority were practically in agreement with my Uncle Emilio, Mima, and Majito. They didn't support the socialist or communist ideologies that Fidel, his brother Raul, advised by Che, wanted to establish in Cuba. For this reason, the purges began: arrests and prosecutions of many leaders accused of being traitors, even the highest leaders. Many were sentenced to the firing squad; the lucky ones, like Huber Matos, were sentenced to 20 or 30 years in jail. Others, like Camilo Cienfuegos simply disappeared. Like my uncle told me, all opposition disappeared. Those that remained who didn't agree survived by keeping their mouths shut. Then the leaders were able to start enacting arbitrary laws using nationalization as an excuse to take control of *all* the industries and private businesses. Castro would use the word *gusano*[31] to scapegoat and accuse *them* of being communists that were trying to paint our beautiful revolution as being red. The newspapers and TV stations were not yet "nationalized," and he painted his opposition as traitors in media; the reality was that Castro and his friends were the traitors and the ones responsible for the destruction of the democratic principles that hundreds or thousands of young Cubans gave their lives for. These new leaders had only one

---

[31] Worms

ambition in mind: to keep themselves in power. Satan's personal emissary, Che Guevara, advised Fidel and his brother to pursue that one goal. They continued the pandemic of evil that was already marching to spread its seed to the rest of the continent and eventually the rest of the world.

Now they searched for an alliance with a stronger nation aligned with their same ideology and the conversations reviewed the possible candidates: the Soviet Union, China, and North Korea—all communist countries. I want to let my readers know that I have recordings of the conversations between Fidel, Raul, and Che and leaders of other totalitarian regimes around the world in my possession still today. I not only have my personal copies—I transmitted other copies of this evidence a long time ago to my uncle, who passed them to his courier and then into the hands of the intelligence community through the US Navy Base at Guantanamo.

Several months later, I was completely disappointed because of all the lies, intrigues, manipulations, and entrapments from these three pestilent musketeers. My father used to say, "Tell me who you're walking with and I'll tell you who you are." I began to be so uncomfortable around any of them that I started to feel asphyxiated merely by their presence. I realized that coming into their circle hadn't really taken much trouble. But now that I wanted to leave them, I started to feel like a fish out of water. I felt the danger of what they would do to me because I knew too much. I realized that I couldn't withdraw all at once. I had to plan my exit very carefully. It could cost not just my life; it could cost the lives of my entire family. The magnitude of the information that they had entrusted me with was that significant. I would become a suspect involved with anything that could happen to any of them due to the information I had. I realized all of this during one of my trips to Santa Clara with the cynical Che when he blew out the brains of his supposed best friend, bodyguard, and confidant. They had known each other since fighting in the mountains. We had suffered an attempt on our lives, and Che was convinced that since his friend was the only one that knew the itinerary for the trip, he had to be the traitor who told the worms who tried to take our lives.

A few days later, in the Prime Minister's office, I decided to come and visit my father's youngest brother, Francisco del Marmol. He was an attorney who lived near the *Castillo del Principe*[32] on Avenue Carlos III. Unfortunately, I never made it to his house because I was intercepted by Che and his escort that arrived in three separate Oldsmobile cars. They signaled for us to stop, and my driver Daniel (who was both chauffer and orderly) asked me, "Do you want me to stop or ignore them? What do you want me to do, Commander?"

I nodded. "Just pull over and see what they want."

He pulled over and brought our jeep to a halt. It already had the logo for the Juvenile Commandos of the Rebel Army and had been provided me by the military from the main headquarters of the army. Che stepped out of one of the Oldsmobiles and approached us. "Hey, Commandantico! How are you doing?" he said.

I smiled pleasantly, "Great, Che! What's up?"

"I saw you and wanted to give you a surprise that will be a good learning lesson for you."

"No problem. I was just going to say hello to one of my uncles, it's nothing important."

"Oh, this will be a great experience. Come on over. Send your driver back to Fidel."

I turned to Daniel. "OK. Go ahead and go back to the Prime Minister's office and wait for me there."

"OK, Commandante," Daniel said. He saluted me and then Che before driving off.

We walked with four escorts back to the middle car. Normally Che traveled in the middle Oldsmobile. Depending on the risk assessment, he sometimes switched and rode in the end or front car. The escort closed the door. Che asked, "Do you have enough ammunition for your pistol with you?"

"Yes. Why? Are we going to meet any enemies along the road?"

"No, I just want to make sure you have everything you need."

"Oh, Fidel gave me so many bullets that I don't think I'll run out even if I live to be 80."

He smiled broadly. "Let me tell you something. I know Fidel likes you very much, and I told him last night that I want to endorse you, for saving my life, for a medal for valor, loyalty, honor, and courage for your act of altruism and bravery. You put your life in danger to protect

---

[32] Castle of the Prince—converted into a prison for common criminals by the revolution.

mine on that Santa Clara highway a few days ago. Remember that very unpleasant attempt we had on our lives?"

I smiled. "Who could forget that?"

He laughed. "Thank God my intelligence and prompt instincts detected the traitor." He pointed at his temple. He smiled as he remembered that incident with satisfaction. I thought perhaps he was trying to convince himself that horrendous crime that he committed right in front of my eyes was justified. I remembered how my stomach churned nastily as fragments of skull, pieces of brain, and drops of blood hit my face when he shot that poor man in the head just on suspicion. He didn't care about finding any evidence at all. It was as if he was killing a chicken for lunch on the patio. He put his right hand on my left shoulder. "Thank you very much. I will never forget what you did for me."

I tried to smile but only managed a half smile. "I think you would have done the same for me. You don't have any reason to thank me for it, much less give me a medal for something I did instinctively. All you guys were completely distracted by the breasts of those beautiful women and weren't paying attention. All I did was keep my eyes on their hands as well as their lovely breasts. When I saw one of them pull a machine gun out of a grocery bag, all I could think at that moment was to grab you by the shirt and pull you down onto the floor of the Oldsmobile so you didn't get shot and yell my warning about the machine gun."

He interrupted me with a smile on his face. "Yes, yes—if you had not acted that way at that moment, I wouldn't be in this world right now."

I stood there for a few seconds thinking, nodding my head. Tremendous remorse filled my mind. If this individual, like my uncle had told me, was the possessor of Hitler's soul, how could I do something like saving the life of that monstrous Satanic individual. I suppressed an urge to shudder throughout my entire body. Not only was it because of remorse but also impotent frustration. Che noticed my shaking.

"What happened?"

"Nothing. Just remembering how all that transpired gives me chills." I breathed deeply. Che's eyes still bored into me, and I could see his hatred for all of humanity. It was like he was trying to scan my brains. It was like he was trying to discover what the real motive for my saving his life was, and it was like he couldn't penetrate my thoughts. What he didn't realize at that moment was that my natural impulse to saved the lives of another human being was only a noble gesture beyond his ability to comprehend. Nobility didn't exist in his character, much less in his personality, especially if he in reality was the spirit of the beast, Adolf Hitler.

I didn't know if what my uncle had said was reality or fiction, but as Mima always had told us, my uncle Emilio never had told us something that wasn't true. From Che you could only expect the worst. The Argentinian had become infamous in Cuba because all he brought to Cuba was tragedy and death. He had earned the hatred of everyone for the hundreds if not thousands of murders he had committed in the political prison of La Cabaña. I heard all of a sudden, a very small whistle, something like a radio frequency from far, far away, like tuning in a short-wave radio. Strangely enough, I didn't hear it in my left ear, which was next to Che—I heard it only in my right ear.

I heard the sweet voice of one of my protectors. "Julio Antonio, don't have any fear of this man. He is the Beast and the darkness, but you are the light and the sword. Remember, he cannot hurt you. You are much stronger than he is. That is why he is trying to court you, because he is afraid of you much more than you can ever be afraid of him. Remember always, Julio Antonio, fear is a nasty companion that you should not keep in your life. Fear is the mother of all insecurities, preventing you from using your clear mind, destroying your heart, and ruining your life. Fear also is the origin of all the weakness, horror, and darkness that can come into your life."

I smiled. At the same time the voice slowly disappeared into space like an echo. Filling the emptiness of that frequency was celestial choral voice that floated in my mind and filled my ear. Again, it was interesting to me that this was heard in only one ear—it was as if they wanted to make certain that Che heard nothing of what was being communicated to me. My face was radiant from the tranquility and happiness they left me with and the security I felt. Che looked at me in confusion. I saw a little fear in his eyes unless I was much mistaken.

Very abruptly he grabbed my shoulder and shook me, as if I were sleeping and he wanted me to wake up. He demanded, "Commandtico! Are you OK?" I looked at his hand on my shoulder and then looked up at him in his eyes. He snatched his hand away. My face was long as I questioned his actions with my eyes. I spoke no word, but he could clearly understand my meaning. "I'm sorry," he apologized. "It wasn't my intention to hurt you. I wanted your attention. I called your name several times, but you never responded. I thought something had happened to you, like maybe you were having a seizure."

I shook my head. "No," I replied calmly. "Don't worry. You didn't hurt me. I'm OK. I just floated to another dimension in my thoughts. I never even heard you calling me." I kept my tone friendly and pleasant. I added, "I'm sorry. It wasn't my intention to ignore you."

He smiled again. "Don't worry about it. That happens to me frequently."

I smiled, thinking *Yes, maybe when you connect your brain with Satan. The dimension you probably go is the route to Hell.*

Che continued, "I want to show you something that I believe you'll learn a lot from. It will be like a window into the progress of our plans that we're implanting in Cuba. We'll expand around the world in the future."

"It must be something you've been planning for a long time."

"How do you know that? Are you a mind reader, too?"

I smiled. "No. All I need to do is look in your eyes and you can immediately notice that you are full of satisfaction. That tells me there must be something you've been working on for a while and is finally coming to a completion."

Che shook his head. "Well, this is only the beginning. It will take a lot more time to come to completion."

We reached a tall office building on the Vedado. We entered the parking lot and parked the cars, walking to the elevators. We took one and went up to the penthouse. Four men in civilian clothes, elegant suits with nice ties, looking like the perfect bureaucrats with folders of papers under their arms and documents in hand came over to us as soon as we stepped off the elevator. They greeted Che, who introduced me to all the men. His first question to them was, "How much longer?"

The one who appeared to be the leader replied, "I believe three to four weeks more."

Che shook his head angrily. "Unacceptable, *compañero*.

"Commandante, to prepare all these people efficiently takes a very long time. Not months like we've been trying to make happen for you. Sometimes it takes years."

Che replied in impolite aggression, "I don't give a damn, *la concha de la madre de nadie*[33]*?*" He hit the aluminum filing cabinets so loud that it sounded like a bomb going off. Everyone, perhaps two or three hundred

---

[33] Pussy of the mother of anyone

people at various tables, in the room stopped what they were doing and looked towards us in surprise. The bang echoed throughout the room. Che ignored them, possibly enjoying the attention, yelled, "Pancho, you told me it would be ready this week!" He held two fingers in front of the man's face. "I'll give you two weeks for this goddamned job to be done, finished and complete. It's already cost us one *palo verde*[34]! If you don't deliver in that time, I assure you that you'll take a very long vacation in La Cabaña!"

Pancho looked at him, terrified. Sweat broke out on his bald head, even though the air conditioning was on full blast in that building, so much so that I was feeling chilly. He removed his glasses and wiped the lenses nervously. He put them back on with trembling hands. He nodded. "We'll do the impossible to comply with you, my Commander."

Che didn't even look at him again. "It's better for you to do the impossible. We have already done the possible to give you this revolution, and you bureaucrats never lifted a finger to help us." Extremely angered, he turned around and stormed back to the elevators, the rest of us following, without even saying goodbye.

I wondered why he had brought me here. It was what we would call in Cuba a medical visit—quick in and back out. We spent more time on that trip than we did inside the building. Even though I had no clue why he brought me along, something really seemed a little strange to me. They not only had guards at the entrance to the building but also uniformed guards on the doors to that penthouse room. Most of the people were men, a few women, and it looked like they were receiving training for something.

After we left the elevator, we walked towards the cars. Che tried to apologize to me. "I'm sorry—I thought we had everything ready to go, and I wanted to show you something as a surprise that we're supposed to start tomorrow. Evidently this program they made be believe was ready to fly like a bird was, unfortunately, still growing feathers. But the most important thing is that very soon it will be complete." With a small smile, possibly with a little hint of mischievousness, he asked, "Do you know who those people are?"

"There's a lot of people there, and I only saw a few faces."

"No, I don't mean that. What do you think they were doing?"

I shook my head. "I don't have the slightest idea."

---

[34] Green case, a term for one million dollars

Montauk: The Lightning Chance

"Remember, this is completely confidential, but they are the executives that will be in charge of the whole economy of this country in two—" he hesitated, "or maybe three weeks. When we nationalize all the banks and all kinds of private businesses, the entire economy of this country will be in our hands."

I felt like a bomb went off in my stomach. Pretending, however, I made all the effort necessary to not allow it to explode, I gave him a small smile. "Good. Very good! More money for our government. If we are the government, this is fantastic! More money for us!"

He looked like I had just taken him completely by surprise. I realized then that maybe he had brought me there with another purpose. I didn't know if he had taken me seriously, but he might have had other intentions and it could be that he was trying to test my loyalty to all of them so he could run to Castro and report what my reaction was. He had no reason to entrust me, at my age, with such delicate information, exposing them and corroborating what they had been for so long denying. He asked me in a cynical voice, "Does not your father own a beer factory?"

"Let me clarify something for your information. My father is not the owner of that factory. He's one of the investors. The factory never has been profitable yet. It's an investment, but it's not a business yet. Maybe it's a dream that will end just as that: a dream. With all his other businesses, I'm sure that we as a good revolutionary government will indemnify him in a fair way. That great compensation my father can use, after 30 years of hard work, to a good, good retirement and a great vacation. I'm going to tell you something more: I believe in my heart that my father, at his age now, really needs a vacation. He's earned it, but never taken one. He's been such a great revolutionary, and I'm completely convinced that the next time he sees you, mark my words, he'll probably give you a big hug, because you're taking finally that tremendous responsibility that he's carried on his shoulders for so many years."

Che looked at me as if he had seen in my face another being from another world. He was completely shocked and surprised. "Are you an extra-terrestrial animal?"

"Maybe I am, but not an animal!"

He grew serious. "Are you sure your father won't be pissed off with all these crazy laws we're making?"

I smiled and raised both arms outwards. "*Claro, chico!* I'm not only sure, I'm absolutely sure." I moved closer. "Let me tell you something else. My father doesn't allow anyone in my house to even make a joke against this government or the revolution. No criticism at all is allowed. There's something else," I added pointing upwards. "I heard one of my father's closest friends tell him that this government is going at 100 mph on the highway to becoming a communist totalitarian regime." I paused. "How do you think my father replied?"

Che looked at me puzzled and shrugged. "I don't know. What did he say?"

I grinned broadly and put all my emphasis in making a proud face of my father's reply. "He said that if we're going towards communism that we have to open a bottle of champagne to celebrate. At least it will be a communism that belongs to us and not to foreigners. We've already had enough of the intervention of the North Americans in our economy and all the internal affairs in our nation, from the time they imposed on us the Platt Amendment, for almost a hundred years now. They've maintained their imperialist boot on our necks, practically not even allowing us to breathe. It's time now for us to take the reins of our own country. At least we won't be puppets anymore."

Che burst out laughing. He started clapping like he was applauding a masterful performance. "Bravo! Bravo for Leonardo del Marmol, a true revolutionary! Even forgetting that Fidel said on national television to the Cuban people and all over the world that the revolution will never be communist and break bread with the Russian communists, the murderers of the Hungarian people." He continued to laugh and built up to a euphoric hysteria. "Yes, yes!! This is what we're going to do and what we're going to be!" He opened a can of worms and started to declare what they were planning to do from the first day they took power.

I had just won my battle with him, and he didn't even realize the damage that I could do with that information. Forgetting that all of that was supposed to be a high-level secret, he put at risk all their plans to control the country's economy by revealing it to me prematurely. Perhaps he reflected a little bit what he had been doing. He raised the fingers of his right hand and said with a little worry in his face, "Remember what I said before. This is completely confidential and classified to the highest level of the government. Only Fidel and a small group of us knows about this. If this escapes our hands and ends up in our enemy's hands, they can use it against us to create massive rioting all over the country. Not only the professionals but regular workers throughout the island could destroy in a single day what we've been working so hard on for so many years. Remember, again, this is classified from the rest of the population."

I shook my head. "Everything I heard with you today or hear from Raul or hear from Fidel, for me it's all classified. I won't even repeat among you guys what is said about each other. I'm not the official newspaper to make public comments and ideas." I put my thumb and index finger to my mouth and mimed sealing it with a zipper. "I learned that from when I was a kid: you don't repeat anything you hear, or you will be labeled a gossip, and that's not a good role for a man."

Che grinned from ear to ear and gave me a thumbs up. "That is the difference between being all a man and only being a clown."

I nodded. "My father told me repeatedly that a man is not distinguished by his sex; he is distinguished only by his dignity, loyalty, and decency. When he loses one of these attributes, it's comparable to losing one of his testicles."

Che smiled, but this time half-heartedly. I might have made him ponder whether he had any of those attributes, and whether or not he had any testicles at all. We had by now arrived at the Prime Minister's office, who I now knew was the biggest liar in history, Fidel Castro Ruz. After I said goodbye to Che, I went over to the jeep where Daniel had been waiting for me. He was very happy when I told him we were leaving immediately for Pinar del Rio, because I had something of extreme importance to share with my father.

As we traveled, I knew that this would be a tremendous pain for my father, one he certainly never expected. But he had taught me from when I was a very small child that the truth should always be revealed naked even if it brought tears and temporary sadness, because the lie in the end would produce the same results with a prolonged pain and scar when we inevitably discover that one had not spoken the truth. That scar covered the wound of betrayal from the realization that the truth had been willfully concealed. If it had been openly proclaimed in all its ugliness, by now that pain would be gone and additionally no scarring would exist.

Daniel noticed that on the almost two-and a half-hour trip I had spoken scarcely a word, which was unusual for me. But out of respect he didn't ask me any questions. When we passed by the Rio Rivera regiment, I remembered the incident with that odiferous soldier, and it occurred to me that he had smelled much like Che. I had tried to find him all these months but had never seen him again, even during the visits I made weekly to the regiment. I was looking for an opportunity to find him, look him in the face, and see his reaction; that would be extremely rewarding. Thinking of that allowed my mind to stay away from different subjects and distract me, which is what the subconscious does sometimes when faced with an unpleasant situation. Heaven only knew what Papi's reaction would be. It could be like it was with Emilio; by now it had been six months since last, they had spoken or visited each other.

We arrived at my home on 116 Avenue Cabada. I got out of the jeep and saw the 1959 Ford Ranch wagon my father drove in the driveway. I said to Daniel, "Go to the regiment and refuel the jeep, check its oil and all the other stuff. Go and spend a few hours with your family. After that come here and pick me up. We'll have to go back to the capital to attend some unfinished business I have back there."

Daniel thanked me for giving him a little free time with a big smile on his face and said goodbye. I picked up my travel bag and the box of pastries I had bought in Artemisa for Mima. It always gave her a big smile. I walked into the house. My sisters saw me first, and the three of them came up to hug and kiss me, since they had not seen me for months. Then Majito did the same, and Mima came out of the library. She approached me with a big smile and yelled, "Julio Antonio! Bless my eyes to see you safe and sound!" I smiled and handed the box of pastries to her after she gave me a hug and kiss. She had already kissed me several times but did it again after I gave her the box. She said close to my ear, "You never forget your Mima."

"*Claro*, Mima—how can I forget you, the most beautiful and intelligent woman in the universe?"

Mima said, "Oh!" She kissed me on both cheeks. She gave the pastry box to Majito and took me by my right hand with her left and practically dragged me, putting a finger to her lips, back to the dinette by the kitchen, where she always brought me when she wanted to speak to me in private. We were followed by Majito, who went to put the pastries in the refrigerator and then into the kitchen. We sat down at the dinette table. I had never seen her so happy and her face was shining. "I believe your father is finally waking up from his hypnotic dream of this revolution. He is in the library with one of his best friends, and I heard him having a political conversation when I brought them coffee and some hors d'oeuvres. His brother Mason, Emilio Huerta, evidently is extremely worried that he and his other brothers have heard rumors that the Castro brothers, advised by Che Guevara, is going to turn the democratic revolution in to a communist one. To my surprise, your father not only didn't defend the brothers," she said with a satisfied smile, "on the contrary, he told Mr. Huerta that it would be a big tragedy and a very great deception for everyone that considers himself a true revolutionary. I saw your father rubbing his forehead with his fingers, really, really worried, almost with tears in his eyes, he said to his friend that it would be the worst treason anyone could ever commit. He said that he would live the rest of his life in shame and remorse because he convinced all the Masons to put not only their financial power but also their hearts in such a tremendous traitor."

After Mima gave me all these details to this conversation, I told her everything that had happened with Che and how I had managed to get out of him the truth that he wasn't even supposed to utter. They only nationalized so far, the big giant foreign companies and the utilities, but no smaller or local businesses. I told what I had seen with my own eyes and heard directly from Che Guevara all the details.

She crossed herself. "Oh, my God—we'll lose everything we've worked for all our lives."

"Mima, it's OK. Material things can be replaced. Our lives are the only things we have to thank God for. Let's stay grounded, stay true to God, and see what we can accomplish."

"You should not stay silent. Tell your father. This is the best opportunity. Either he'll blow up, or you'll convince him that what his brother has been telling him is nothing more than the truth, the whole truth, so help us God."

Full of joy, I believed it would be an easy thing, since the other man had already done my groundwork. Because of the encouragement I received from Mima about what had been going on, the minute I saw Mr. Huerta leave the house, Mima and I marched to the library to reveal to my father the full truth I discovered in all my investigations over the past months. I had even been neglecting my schooling, optimistically having faith that my father would listen to me and take my word as solid proof of the treason of the Castros and Che Guevara, not only to him personally but to the entire Cuban people and the democratic world.

I thought that this was *la grand estafa*[35]. Now it would be up to me to get my father to view these people as I did. We entered the library and my father looked up at our approach, his eyes looking at us over the rims of his glasses. He had been reading a document that he still held in his hand. He smiled in satisfaction and said, "Hey! What a great

---

[35] The Greatest Political Fraud of the 20th Century

pleasure, my great Commandante! I saw you the other day on TV at the Plaza de la Revolucion on the podium with Fidel and the other leaders. You looked good on there, and I have to tell you that you made me very proud to be your father."

Figure 30 *Fidel with the Commandantico*

"Thank you, Papi," I replied.

Mima didn't smile. She said, "Leonardo, there is something that your pride, Julio Antonio, shared with me and wishes to communicate with you as well."

My father leaned back in his chair, laid the paper down on his desk, took his glasses off, and crossed his arms, holding his chin in his left hand. His smile disappeared and he grew serious as he looked at my face. I immediately detected his intimidating and aggressive message he was sending with that gesture. Perhaps he was thinking ahead and assuming that whatever I had to tell him came from Mima, something that would be unfavorable to his political ideas. Even so, his predisposition and physical stance didn't dissuade me. I had come all the way from the capitol to sit in front of his desk at that moment to convince him and let him see the truth through my eyes of what I had discovered from my investigations. I couldn't let his crossed arms and long face intimidate me. I didn't want to take the chance of having the same luck my uncle had, that my father wouldn't even allow him to finish his message.

So as I sat in front of his desk, I looked him straight in the eye and, like the old saying from Spain, grabbed the bull by the horns, I crossed my arms over my chest and caressed my chin, mirroring him. My expression changed from pleasant to harsh and firm. Papi stayed silent but scrutinized me and could not contain a small smile at my imitation. He uncrossed his arms. That was my signal that he received my message that I wasn't there to allow him to intimidate me. I was completely determined that neither he nor anyone else was going to turn me away from my intent. That was probably the reason that he, being an intelligent man, tried to get Mima out of the library to take her far away from the discussion. He probably calculated that it was not going to be a favorable conversation, and he didn't want to have two on one. He nonchalantly said to her with a smile, "Mima, when you go out, please close the door. I want to have privacy with my son."

Mima stood by the door near the wall. She glared at him; if looks could kill, Papi would have died immediately. However, out of respect to him, she moved to leave the library with a long face. Reacting quickly, I intervened and stopped, "No, Mima. I prefer you stay here and partake in this conversation because whatever I have to say to Papi, it affects the entire family. Not just our family, but all the families in Cuba." Papi crossed his legs and leaned back to the other side of his chair uncomfortably. I added, "But let's start by fixing our family problems. Later we can try to fix those of our neighbors."

Papi looked at me in confusion. "What is the problem in our family? Can you explain that to me, please?"

I looked at him very seriously as Mima sat down in the other chair before his desk. "Unfortunately, Papi," I said after she had sat down, with a small smile on my face, "it is you. I know how painful this will be for you, because nothing is comparable with the pain of a betrayal, especially when it comes from somebody or an institution that we have deposited complete and absolute trust in."

Papi knew where I was coming from for sure now. He looked at me in irritation and distrust. He asked again, "You've been talking with your Uncle Emilio in these past weeks or months?"

I smiled. I raised my right arm. "I promise you and give you my word of honor that from the time Emilio and you had that unpleasant conversation, as you call it, right here in our home over six months ago that I have never seen or heard from my Uncle Emilio again. Have you?"

Papi shook his head. He said abruptly, "No, I haven't." He seemed to me a little guilty at that moment, possibly at the premature assumption he had made and just expressed. He raised his right arm without saying anything and shook his head with an embarrassed expression.

"I want to let you know, Papi, as a promise I made to myself, that until I possessed absolute proof of what this government planned, I would say nothing. I've learned that not only have they no intention to comply with any promise they've made to the Cuban people, I've discovered that their motivations were corrupt." I tapped my breast with my left hand. "I didn't want to bring to you any unnecessary pain bigger than the pain I feel right here inside of my chest today. I want you to have this very clear in your mind. Whatever I'm going to tell you now is very classified, only to the highest level of the leaders and top ranks of the military or counterintelligence in our country. I had managed to bait Che in a way he hadn't even noticed. Our supposed friend, Ernesto Guevara in a moment of euphoria told me just this morning what I want to share with you now. I wanted to let you know this before I go into that unless you want to see me front of the firing squad in spite of my youth, don't tell anyone what I'm going to share with you now."

He shook his head gravely. "If that's the case, I don't think that we should continue this conversation. I'm pretty sure that Che, in order to share that with you, probably made you promise silence. I don't think you should break that promise with him or any of the other leaders of this democratic revolution."

I looked at him and smiled sarcastically. I remained calm and said, "You are absolutely on the right track and have all the reasons." I went silent for a few seconds to make him wonder. As he waited, Papi kept looking at me to see if there was anything else or if this was the end of the chat. I leaned back in my chair and assumed the position he had at the beginning of our dialogue. "Do you know where Che took me this morning?"

Papi shook his head. "I don't have the slightest idea."

"He took me to a very tall office building in one of the most opulent zones in the capitol, where he showed me hundreds of executives that will be in charge of all the businesses they intend to nationalize in the next few weeks. Nationalize what? We're not talking about foreign businesses—nationalize *you*, Papi. How can they

Montauk: The Lightning Chance

nationalize you, who are a national?" Papi didn't know how to respond to that. "Every single private entity, without exception, from movie theatres to jewelry stores to gas stations to hardware stores like you have, even hot dog wagons in the street. I asked Che that directly, and he said, 'No one should own any business here but us.' Is that what you call a 'democratic revolution', Papi?" I made air quotes with my fingers as I said that last. I continued them as I said for emphasis, "'Democratic?'" I leaned back so he could see them clearly. "Do you still believe that I should keep my silence and respect whatever promise I made to Che? Do you keep the promise you make to a thief to wait there for a while before you call the police? Do you believe I should not tell anyone what this diabolical character confessed to me in his euphoric attempt to conquer my heart and be a little devil next to him? These people, Papi, not only have lied and cheated you but also your brother Masons, the Cuban people, and the entire world. Do you want your son, me, to become an accomplice to all these criminals, thieves, and perverse individuals?"

Papi looked at me with sincere disappointment in his eyes. In spite of what I had just said, he didn't want to see the ugly reality. It was too hard for him to swallow and admit that he had been wrong and that my uncle Emilio was right. He boiled over in exasperation, too irritated to notice that I wasn't backing down. He yelled, "I know for a fact that you've been visiting my brother Emilio in the capitol. He is the only one capable of brainwashing you this way!"

Mima could not hold herself in anymore. "If you weren't so blind, Leonardo, as you've been with this group of pestilent bums and political criminals, and you listened to your brother months, *months* ago when he tried to warn you, we might have saved part of what we've been working all our lives for." Tears filled her eyes and she began to sob. In between sobs she said, "Leonardo del Marmol, what a pity that an intelligent man has been doped and duped by these imbeciles, and you with your inflexible fanaticism that your entire family will be paying for, because according to what Julio Antonio shared with me, it's only a matter of weeks before we lose everything! Everything!" She broke down and cried uncontrollably. "They will leave nothing for us, Leonardo! These bandits have no mercy. It's the jealousy, envy, and hatred against those who have worked all their lives and have something to show for it, and you cannot take a pause in your stupid fanaticism and you resisted first listening to your brother and now you cannot listen even to your golden child!" Mima crossed herself. "You let Satan take control of your spirit!" She pulled a bottle of holy water out of her brassier. She sprayed Papi in the face. He sprang up and tried to cover his face with a book he snatched up from the desk. But Mima didn't stop. "In the name of the Father, the Son, and the Holy Spirit, leave this body! You cannot live in the body of this noble man, Satan! Depart this confused but good man at once! He is confused, but on the side of God, not you! Demons, go away!!" She stopped and began to mumble a prayer aloud.

I took the opportunity to pick up a piece of blank paper from his desk. I tore it into small pieces. I walked over to my father and said, "You are contributing to the destruction of the Americas. If you keep supporting these maniacs, the American continent will be shattered in pieces just as I've done with this sheet of paper." I opened my hand and allowed the pieces to flutter down over his desk and onto the floor. "Unfortunately, by the time you realize your mistake it will be too late, for they will no longer have any need for you. Those who will not share in these communist ideas will have done to them what I did to that sheet of paper. I heard them, and you have not, Papi. Castro's idol is Adolf Hitler. That is what Che Guevara is! He is the reincarnation of Hitler—imagine what they will do, Papi, with this ambition for power. They will not stop with the Americas. They will continue until they control the entire world unless we stop them."

He stood up for the first time, his book still in his hand, still trying to protect himself from the sprays from Mima as she continued to pray and cross herself. Heaven knew what else was in the water she and Majito had prepared with the priest. Mima raised her voice a little. "Satan leave this body! It is not yours!" She found at that moment the perfect opportunity to put into motion her exorcism. It was possible that she and Majito had, in association with Doña Carmen, prepared without any doubts that I would give them this opening for her. By now my father was extremely angry from what had occurred. Mima did not stop yelling at him and spraying him with the water.

He yelled louder than ever, *"Stop this nonsense!* You're both nutcases!" Mima pretended she had heard nothing and continued her ritual. He yelled at me, "You lied to me! You gave me your word of honor that you had never met with my brother Emilio!"

I nodded and said with strong conviction, "I never, ever told you a lie. Exactly what I said before is exactly the way it happened."

Papi looked at me. "Then who told you about that crap about Hitler and Che Guevara?"

Montauk: The Lightning Chance

"They told me through their actions, but also it was corroborated by the ladies in white." My father froze momentarily in shock at that. "Che Guevara told me that he wanted to put all homosexuals into re-education camps, along with everyone who doesn't sympathize with the revolution. By the way, the ladies gave me a message for you since they've come up." My mother stopped for a few seconds to pay attention to what I said. "They told me that you should remember that you have a special mission to accomplish. That is the only reason they've been protecting and saving your life on more than one occasion. You have been derailed from the light and walking in the dark, fascinated by the lies dressed in golden dresses. They've blinded you with a dark veil covering your eyes now for a long time. Only you can find yourself again and the beautiful light."

My father lost his marbles at that and yelled at Mima, "Stop that nonsense!" Mima crossed herself and ignored him, pacing from one wall to the other, continued to pray and spray him for nearly the entire time. The bottle was now nearly empty. Papi slammed the desk with the book. "Quit making stupid remarks! This is my home, and everyone has to do what I say! Enough is enough! You are not only talking like a traitor; you *are* a traitor!"

I replied, "If that is the way you think, very well, Father. This is your home, and you are the boss, but only to those living under your roof. I will be moving today, and you will probably not see me again." I kissed my tearful Mima. "Don't worry, Mima. God is always on the side of the truth." I looked at Papi for the last time. "I hope you think it over and please come back to the light." I walked to the door and left. As I left the house, I could hear the sobs of my poor mother still screaming to Satan to leave my father's body.

I closed the door and went out into the street. My once-happy home had turned into Hell. I walked the streets of Pinar del Rio for a while. I didn't want to cut Daniel's visit with his family short, so I waited until several hours passed before walking to Daniel's house. I didn't want him to go through the embarrassment of coming to my house and discovering that disturbing situation I left behind with my family. For many years, every time I think of that day, unwanted, uncontrollable tears fill my eyes—not only from the pain and deception from my father that day, but my worst and greatest pain was the game played by Satan in his diabolical breach of my family. It made me think, deep in my heart that day, that he had won and taken with him the spirit and heart of my father. That thought left me with a profound emptiness in my soul.

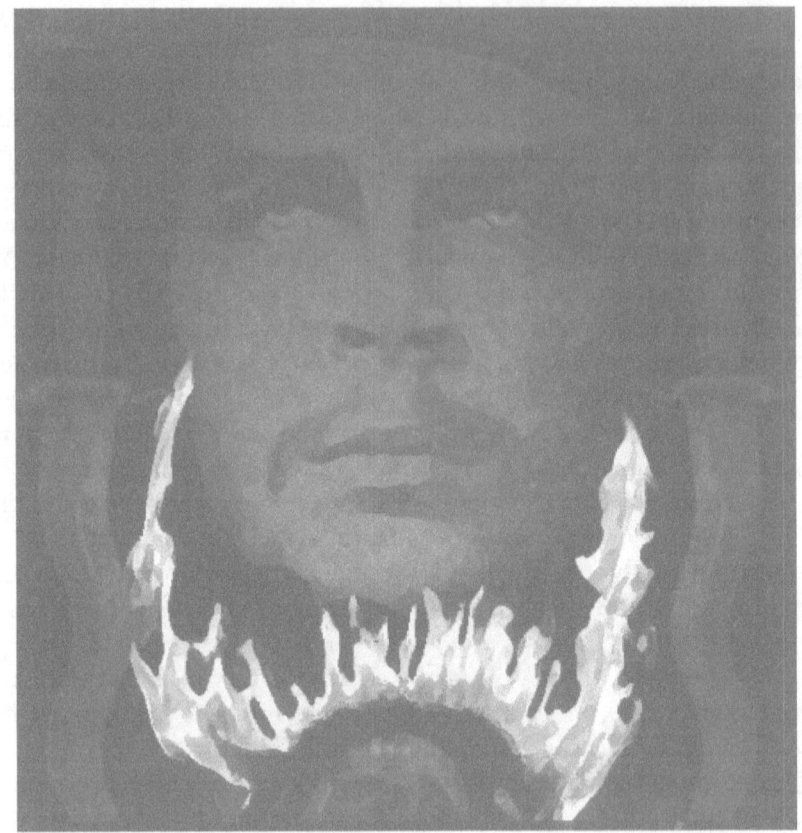

Figure 31 Satan's Agent in the World

CHAPTER 12: THE SPY HIDDEN IN PLAIN SIGHT

Daniel and I drove back to Havana. We stopped along the way to pick up my good friend, a big black man named Cisneros. Despite his youth, he was already six feet six inches tall and very muscular. He saluted me; I had given him the rank of Sergeant-Major in the Commandos, which made him very proud. Characteristic of that pride, he liked to show off his insignia to everyone. After we entered the Capital, Daniel asked, "Prime Minister's office, Commandante?"

"No," I pointed the way. "Go along the Malecon and into Miramar. Go to the Nautico development. I want to have a heart-to-heart conversation with my uncle, my father's older brother."

Daniel nodded. "I know. I've only seen him once, but he looked very distinguished. He was a very nice and pleasant man, not a racist hair in his body. Maybe he'll even invite us to lunch."

I replied, "No one in my family can have a racist hair in their body when my great-grandfather burned his hacienda and his sugar plantation to free you guys. It would be a disgrace to our family to find anyone to be like Che. What I'm about to say to you is completely confidential; I know you've heard a couple of comments, but I want you to know what Che says behind your backs. All he does is talk about how the blacks should go back to slavery, how they don't have the brains of a mosquito, and why I have the two of you around all the time. He's questioned me several times why I couldn't find a couple of white guys to be with me, why I was always going around with you two gorillas. If I had a problem in finding the right white driver and white bodyguard, he would find them for me. I told him 'no, but no thank you.' Knowing him, he probably just wants someone around me all the time to keep track of what I'm doing. That wouldn't be pleasant for us, since we don't agree with everything the revolution is doing."

Cisneros said, "My mother thinks the same. That means we're not the only ones who think like that."

Daniel said, "Well, in my house neither my mother or my grandmother are fans of the revolution, but my father is one of the big union leaders on the piers here in Havana. *Mi padre es come candela*[36] for the revolution. He says he's a socialist, but I think he's more a communist to his bones. He told me that he's very proud of me because you picked me as your chauffer. He told me that several times."

I smiled slightly. "What and irony! That is exactly what my father told me only a few hours ago, because he saw me on TV with Fidel, Raul, Camilo, and Che." I shook my head. "What a coincidence! Isn't that true?" I turned my head away so they couldn't see the two tears that ran down my cheeks. I didn't want my two good friends to see my weakness. I pulled my handkerchief out of my pants pocket and pretended to blow my nose to cover my wiping the tears away that resulted from the horrible discussion with my father.

As we arrived at Emilio's house, I told them it would be most prudent for them to remain in the jeep until I explored the grounds. I was a little afraid of the potential rejection from my uncle; I had had enough embarrassment for one day, especially wearing the military uniform with the Commander's stars on my shoulders from the revolutionary government I knew for a fact he despised.

Pulling together all my courage from my guts, I drew the strength to face him. I walked through the gardens to his beautiful residence right in front of the ocean and rang the doorbell. I breathed deeply and asked God to give me enough strength to convince my uncle of my sincerity. I hoped he would be better than my father and at least let me start and finish what I had to share with him.

I waited patiently, but nobody came to the door. I rang the bell a little more insistently. I came to realize that somebody had moved the curtains in one of the windows by the side of the house, just slightly, as if they didn't want to be seen peeking out to see who was there before opening the door. I saw as the curtain was pulled a little more to see better, in between the crack in the curtain my uncle's face. I took my Commando's beret off so that he could recognize me. It had, after all been six months and I was at an age where change occurred quickly. I

---

[36] My father is a fire-eater

saluted and said, "It's me, your nephew Julio Antonio." He gestured to me that he would be there in a minute.

A few seconds later, the door finally opened, but not completely. He greeted me with some reserve. He pointed to the military jeep where Daniel and Cisneros sat in complete uniform. He asked, "Who are those soldiers there?"

I smiled. "They're not soldiers. They're my chauffer and assistant."

He looked at me from my boots to my head, taking in my uniform. He said with a small smile and a nod, "Yes, yes—the youngest Commander of the revolution. I've seen you many times on TV with Fidel and the other leaders of the revolution and was wondering when you would come say hello to your old uncle. To what do I owe the honor of your visit?"

I felt a little rejected by this, but I decided to swallow my pride and give him the benefit of the doubt. I beckoned him closer with my index finger. I put my left hand to my mouth as I put my right hand on his shoulder and whispered in his ear, "I've come to discuss with you the results of my investigation over the past six months. Can I talk to you in private, or do we have to conduct this conversation here in the doorway?"

He jerked back as if struck by lightning and opened the door fully. I respectfully removed my beret and put it under my arm. After I entered the house, he closed the door and double locked it. I noticed he was acting very nervous and reserved. He tried to hide it from me quite well, and he asked, "Are you sure you don't want to invite your friends in?"

I shook my head. "No. What I have to say to you is something very personal and confidential."

He nodded and smiled pleasantly. He said uncertainly, "I believe you've picked the ideal moment and day for this. Jackie and Melicia both have taken off not long ago to the hair salon. Neither one of them will be back for several hours."

"God always works in mysterious ways."

"You're right," he said with a small smile.

I followed him into the living room, and we sat down in a couple of leather armchairs facing each other. He opened a small box which contained his pipe, took it out and filled it. He then lit it and leaned back in his chair as he took a deep puff on it. He exhaled and asked, "Are you sure you don't want anything to drink? I have your favorite, fresh-squeezed orange juice. Melicia squeezed some oranges this morning before they left."

I raised my right arm and waved dismissively. "No, thank you very much for your offer."

Emilio leaned back, shifting his position uncomfortably. He continued his scrutiny of my attire, boots, epaulettes, my eagle-hilted Commando's knife, pistol, and the stars on my epaulettes in silence.

I broke the silence. "Do you remember, months ago, when we made the trip from here to Pinar del Rio, the last time we saw each other?"

He smiled and took the pipe out of his mouth. "Yes, of course. Who can forget that scene? Every time I think of it I burst out laughing and how you kicked that huge soldier into the corn field." He smiled as he was reminded of it at that moment. "I never saw you so pissed off before, ever since the day you were born."

I nodded, remembering the incident myself. My face, however, remained serious. "If you remember that, you probably remember as well what you said to me during that trip, that whatever secret you revealed to me in that conversation which came to be the second and most important secret that I've maintained very close to my heart for all these long months. That is extremely important that I maintain complete confidentiality." He nodded his head dubiously and gulped. He shifted his position again. He looked me up and down distrustfully again. It occurred to me that he might be afraid that I was recording the conversation. That distrust from him, even though I understood it, was offensive and unnecessary. I had no knowledge of his clandestine activities at that time and so truly did not understand fully. I thought of myself at that moment as his favorite nephew, which is why I believed I deserved his trust because of our tie of blood. It shouldn't make any difference what uniform I was wearing at that moment.

I put my head down, swallowing that bitter flavor of his distrust. Trying to maintain my calm, I looked him in the eyes and said, "You should remember also your words: you told me that in order to avoid becoming a victim of gossip or misinformation or derogatory propaganda, I should investigate and uncover my own information, not caring where it came from or who has been bringing it to me. After I confirmed the result of my own inquiry, only then could I make my own proper conclusion of whatever truth I find. That truth, of course, cannot be distorted or changed or manipulated by ill-intentioned people that are only looking to protect their own political agendas or personal interests."

Montauk: The Lightning Chance

I stopped and this time kept my eyes in his silently. We stared at each other for a few seconds.

Emilio asked, "Well, do I get to know what the results of that investigation are? Now I see very clearly the reason for your visit to me today."

I nodded. "Yes. You're right. My information is based on personal testimonies of every one of the leaders of this revolution. The majority agree with you that this revolution is going directly and inevitably to a communist society and they are preparing the ground to change and destroy the established culture and form a totally totalitarian regime. But, unfortunately, the most important leaders who have taken the reins of this government don't care about what the other leaders think. In a macabre maneuver they have already decided the destiny for the future of our country. The principle one responsible that all this ideology is exactly who you pointed to: Ernesto Guevara de la Serna. This morning I got him to admit in his euphoric sense of triumph that in a few weeks the Cuban government will proceed to completely expropriate all the private property from the rightful owners' hands, and everything without exception will pass into the government's hands. In other words, to the hands of political delinquents." Put my hand on the handle of my pistol and gripped it. "We have another way of seeing things. I and a group of my friends will take one of the planes at the airport and use our weapons to force the pilot to fly us out of Cuba before this becomes the same inferno that I witnessed in my house today when my father accused me of being a traitor just a few hours ago. All I did was try to communicate with him and prevent him from losing everything that he worked for all his life. Unfortunately, his fanaticism has blinded him."

Emilio stood up abruptly. He held his pipe still in his hand. He said to me excitedly, pointing at me with the stem of his pipe, "You know better than anyone that you should not tell these things to me! Why are you telling me all of this? Who told you to come and tell me these things? You know better than anyone that an armed attempt against this government is considered high treason against the motherland and the revolution, and the penalty is death before the firing squad. Did you tell Che Guevara about my discussion with your father?"

I grew agitated. "No, no—please, hold on! I never repeated anything you told me, and it never crossed my mind to betray anyone in my family, much less you that I love as much as my father, or maybe even more!"

He stepped toward me a little more aggressively. "Are you sure, Julio Antonio, that your friend Che hasn't put you up to this and put a recorder on your body?" He came over and patted me down. "To take your uncle before the firing squad?"

I looked him in the eyes silently. I said quietly, "Do you truly believe that? Is that how you feel about me? What sort of concept do you have of my person? Where is the love you supposedly have for your preferred nephew? Or were those all words? If that is the way you feel, my uncle, we have nothing more to discuss. God forgive you this injustice you committed against me today!" I spun on my heel, snatched up my beret up, and headed towards the door rapidly. I fumbled with the multiple locks on the door in my anger.

My uncle finally broke the silence while I fumbled. I heard his voice broken in emotion. "Julio Antonio, please stop right there." He composed himself and said in a stronger voice, "Don't leave. There's something very important I want you to know before you go. Please come back here." He beckoned me to follow him with his index finger. We walked into his library together, which had a huge window facing the ocean. We could see the waves breaking against the rocks along the coast before the neighboring house. We sat down and he asked, "Could you please wait for me a few seconds here? I have to make an urgent phone call."

"Sure."

He walked away, looking at his wristwatch. He left the door open, and I could see him pick up the receiver on the wall telephone near the living room. He dialed a number and had a very short conversation with someone on the other end. "Yes. I want you here as soon as possible. Yes. My nephew is here, and as you know he's inside Castro's first ring. Yes. I want you to hear how he feels and the great things he has to tell us about the revolution and the new leaders." He hung up and came back. He sat down next to me. My old uncle returned to me as he put both hands on my shoulders affectionately.

"I'm sorry," he said, "but I needed to be sure these guys hadn't penetrated your brains and given you the power to let me live or die. And not only my life but the lives of my wife and daughter." He looked straight into my eyes. "I am part of an intelligence cell from World War II of the most elite international intelligence community. My mission was to keep the Nazis from taking over Central and South America as well as the Caribbean Islands. You entrusted your secret to me, putting your life in my hands, because if instead of calling my contact, I could have called our enemies the Cuban G-2 intelligence, and your life would last less than a chocolate candy in the school door. It would have ended in a very short time, like the hundreds of thousands of young lives that have been taken in these past months in our country, arbitrarily accused of being agents of the CIA. They probably didn't even know what the hell it signifies. I'm returning your favor and revealing to you the most precious secret that I have in my life."

I'm also extending an invitation for your consideration instead of abandoning Cuba. That is to come and work with us. Don't abandon Cuba when she most needs you. Unite with our resistance against this government that will come soon to be a very dictatorial totalitarian regime. You will be trained by me and others, the best of the best. If possible, due to your high position in this government, you could become the youngest spy in our history. With your talents and the extraordinary qualities you possess I promise you that you'll never get caught. Not simply because of the training we'll provide you, but also because I'll assign a code for you that no one will ever know who you are. It will only be known to you, a couple of people I absolutely trust, and me. Let me repeat to you today that you have my entire faith that everything will be ultra-confidential information. I will swear on our ancestor's legacy that I will protect your identity with my life, if necessary."

I smiled in complete surprise. At the same time, I was overjoyed at the tremendous level of confidence and trust that my uncle returned to me. I understood many things now about my uncle who had been a puzzle for many years. The enigma for me to all the questions I had before been clarified in a short period of time in that conversation. I asked, "I have only one question to ask you."

"Go ahead."

"Does Papi know this secret about you, too?"

He smiled and nodded his head. "Yes, you're right. Your father knows. Now this secret is between your father, you, and I. Nobody else will ever possess this information outside our intelligence circle."

I smiled this time. "You can rest in tranquility. Like I said before, when I discovered the truth about these leaders and discovered all their lies and deceptions, I will become the worst enemy that this group of political thieves ever, ever could imagine. Today right here in your house that enemy is born and delivered by your own hands, the best obstetrician and greatest man that I have ever known."

My uncle grinned broadly. "That means you are accepting my offer?"

"Yes, I am. And I will be honored to be part of your team."

"Then we have to give the welcome to you in your new life as a spy. We will have a toast for that." He walked a few steps to the bar and took a bottle of orange liquor. He brought two small shot glasses. "I know you are very young and have never had any alcohol in your life, but I also know your favorite beverage is orange juice. This is a special occasion—after all, this liquor is made by fermenting oranges. I will introduce you to the first alcoholic drink, but we will toast with the best liquor in the world: Grand Marnier." He filled half of the shot glass with the liquid, and we touched the glasses. We toasted to a long life to my career as a spy. That was the first taste of alcohol I had ever had, as a spy or anything else.

My uncle smiled afterwards. "I have to give you my most sincere thanks. First of all, for your opportune visit, also to being yourself and maintaining your integrity by not allowing these people to steal your spirit with bribes and temptations. I'm absolutely sure that you've had more than one offer to bribe to you with material things. That is the most common approach Satan uses. You resisted that temptation, and they couldn't conquer your soul or even a centimeter of your heart. You've been loyal to your true feelings and this has only one name: Divine Love and His power. There are a lot more powerful things than all the temptations that Satan can put before us. I want you to remember the biggest temptation is still to come. Especially now that you have decided to help us. You will be walking into the circles of the real evil and the temptation will be enormous. As others fail, they will keep putting greater temptations before you. That is why I advise you to not let your guard down and sleep with one eye open. Evil never rests."

I smiled, putting my right hand on his shoulder. "My uncle, I can assure you that I can sleep very peacefully with both eyes closed for two reasons. The first one is because from the instant that I fall asleep the ladies in white take my spirit to another dimension where Satan will not dare to enter because he knows if he gets in, there will be no way out for centuries and centuries, amen. The second reason is that I never walk alone. I have always at my back day and night the most powerful guardian angel that exists, and even Satan cannot imagine it. Starting today, I'm going to walk under His absolute direction. The Holy Spirit can be seen only by blessed eyes but is absolutely invisible to the evil eyes of Satan and all his disciples."

Montauk: The Lightning Chance

My uncle looked at me very seriously. He stepped closer to me and embraced me. Almost in my ear he murmured, "And the last thanks are for Jesus, the Son of God, for bringing you back to my house on this beautiful day."

I felt that in that very sincere hug a combination of feelings: joy, gratitude, love, and peace. It produced a great tranquility in my soul. There was absolute reassurance to know for a fact that his adopted son had come back to his side with the disposition to help him and his fight against evil and the strong forces of Satan all around the world.

At that moment the doorbell rang. It didn't take us by surprise since we were both expecting the arrival of his contact coming to meet me. The urgency certainly was there in the phone call, since my uncle had a premonition that I would wake up and come back to him. He had been waiting for this moment. I wasn't expecting that he would show up so quickly. For that reason, before Emilio opened the door, he looked through the window as he had before through the curtain to check who was outside. As soon as he was sure he rushed to open the door.

A very tall man, young, dressed elegantly with a lantern jaw, black, wavy hair and a muscular frame entered the house. His face was very serious. He came over and shook my hand. "You are absolutely sure that you want to partake with us in our clandestine work? Remember, you don't have to do this. It's only up to you if you choose to do this."

I nodded. I replied without hesitation, looking into his eyes, "I not only am willing to do this, but I will also enjoy every minute. Like I told my uncle, if I'm willing to risk my life to steal a plane, I will do this with the greatest pleasure to stop these three sulfurous musketeers of pestilence, the sons of Satan, to prevent before it's too late the destruction of our beautiful Cuba and swallow with their diabolical ideas the rest of the world."

He grinned broadly. "OK. You are welcome. I also was recruited by your uncle quite a few years ago during my trip to Ecuador. Since then, I believe I have earned with my hard work his complete trust. Now, as you see, I'm his right hand. I'm very proud of that." He held out his hand. "My name in the clandestine world is the General. My real name nobody knows. I think you will be one of the few I will ever reveal it to in intelligence. I believe that you should know since you and I will be working closely together from this day forward. I will personally supervise your training."

Dr. Julio Antonio del Marmol

I nodded and took his hand. "I'm Julio Antonio del Marmol."

He smiled again. Clearly, he already knew my name. He put his left hand on my shoulder. "My name is Canen Hernandez. The pleasure is all mine, and I will be at your service." I could hear the sincerity and emotion in his voice. "I'm so proud of you." He looked at my uncle. "I know your uncle, Dr. Emilio del Marmol, is full of joy to see that the work he did with you was not in vain."

My uncle smiled from ear to ear. "Not proud—*extraordinarily* proud. That is how I feel. I was already thinking that my brother Leonardo took my jewel and turned him around completely. Unfortunately, I will never have another opportunity to turn him to our side and bring him to the light."

I thanked them both. "Very well. When do we start my training?"

My uncle smiled. "Right here and right now, at this very moment you will have the first lesson. And that first lesson is to not believe anything that anyone tells you, even myself, and only half of what you see. That way you will never be the victim of gossip or a useful fool of someone else to further his agenda."

I nodded. "Good. What else?"

"The next one," he said as he pulled a ring off one of his fingers. He showed me how the ring functioned as a weapon. He handed it to me. "Use it only in extreme circumstance. This is an extremely dangerous weapon. Remember, it can take the life of a human being. Use it only in extreme circumstances when your life is in danger. You only have five minutes to inject him with the antidote or the person will die."

"OK. I will take that into consideration. I don't like to hurt people, only when it's absolutely necessary to defend myself or somebody I love."

Canen put his hand on my shoulder. "I've heard a lot about you, and the more I hear the more I like you. You speak like my father, despite your age." He took a pen out of his sportscoat pocket. He took his coat off and put it over the back of a chair. "OK, sit down here and I'll explain how this works." He showed me step by step the functions hidden in that tiny object. It was a camera. It also had a microphone to record conversations. More to my liking for non-lethal means of defense, it had an alpine power beam that could blind someone momentarily to put them out of combat. It also had a small button to self-destruct in case I got caught in a situation in which I didn't want it to fall into the wrong hands and so prove that I was a spy. I had to push it three times and drop it, and then it would blow up and disappear.

After several hours with my uncle and Canen, Emilio gave me a box with different colored pens. I put one in the cargo pocket of my uniform. We set another meeting with Canen in Pinar del Rio for a week following. We exchanged bear hugs, and I said goodbye. I left my uncle's house through the small garden, where I watched the waves crashing over the reefs along the coast in front of the house. I was full of optimism, joy and hope, thinking that after all the evil and destructive forces that I had encountered with the Castro brothers and Che, God had placed a solution before me with maybe the opportunity to not have to abandon my country—something I didn't take lightly. It was the last thing I wanted to do. After all, I could be part of something bigger to clean those rotten apples that were only a small minority in the revolution. And maybe we could accomplish after all to save our democratic revolution.

I felt joyful also now knowing who my uncle really was. I was extremely proud of the tremendous trust placed in me not just from my uncle, but also his organization that was willing to bring me in to work with them in spite of my youth, which I knew could be an impediment to them. It made me feel great and I swore to myself to be honorable and put my life on the line if necessary before I ever revealed that to anyone. Both had put their lives in my hand that day. Those pens were undeniable proof if anyone in the government questioned me. I remembered what Canen told me: those pens were invaluable to survival in a spy's life as well as my effectiveness as a spy.

I bit my lower lip with a smile on my face. I squeezed the box in my pants pocket with my right hand as I jumped into the jeep. Daniel said, "My Commander, your face tells me that your visit with your uncle came to be very pleasant."

I replied, "Yes, Daniel. Extremely pleasant and fruitful."

Cisneros said, "I'm really glad that happened, my Commander, because there's nothing in this world that substitutes in our lives for the love of our family."

I nodded in agreement. "You're both right. Whoever says to the contrary is not on the side of God. It is the work of Satan: divide and destroy the love between us and our family and friends. You probably are hungry. You've been waiting for me for hours and it's nearly two o'clock in the afternoon." They both rolled their eyes as they nodded vigorously. "OK, let's go and celebrate with a great lunch in the Hotel Capri restaurant with the great French cuisine they have there."

Daniel exclaimed, "Ooh-lala! One hundred points for the Commander for best suggestion for today's meal!"

Cisneros rubbed his belly and grinned. "You don't even know, Commander, I've had a dog and cat fighting in my stomach for over two hours."

We all smiled. Daniel stomped so hard on the accelerator we almost got whiplash. "Hey, hey! Slow down! The food's not going anywhere," I exclaimed.

Daniel smiled. "Well, you never know—maybe we get to the Capri and we find the government has nationalized it. That would be a tragedy."

I smiled. "Don't worry about it. You guys forgot that we represent the new government."

Daniel smiled and nodded. "You're right, Commander. No reason to rush." He took his foot off the accelerator. He added in a lower voice, just perceptible to our ears, "Sometimes I forget that fact." He shook his head.

We arrived at the Hotel Capri Cabaret Restaurant and Casino. As we entered, we ran into a local celebrity: Jose Maria Lopez Lledin, best known in Havana as the Gentleman of Paris. He was having an argument as he tried to convince the manager to allow him in. The manager didn't think his attire was appropriate for the place. Though he was elegantly dressed, his clothes were very ragged and dirty, though his manners were excellent, and he was trying to point that fact out to the manager. Though he didn't smell bad his beard desperately needed a trimming and he also needed a haircut; his hairstyle looked more like something out of Biblical times.

I couldn't avoid feeling sorry for him. As I drew near, I asked the manager, who already had two bouncers ready to kick Jose Maria Lopez out of the place, "What's going on here?"

Jose Maria looked at me with great joy. With refined manners he saluted me in a military fashion, but his thumb wiggled at me beneath the plane of his hand. That is when I noticed that he had a ring very much like the one my uncle had just given me. I didn't know if he was trying to send me a signal or if it was his mental derangement. With a broad grin he said, "It's very nice to see you again, Commander."

"What seems to be the problem here?" I asked.

Montauk: The Lightning Chance

Before the manager could reply, he rushed to say, "No, no—no problem at all. Just a little lack of proper manners and communication on the part of the management of this establishment that this gentleman, Jaime, represents." He pointed to the manager. "He requires his own extremely strict protocol. I understand this is a beautiful and elegant place, but as you know, Commander, look at the requirements." He gestured to a sign at the top of the door. It read *Proper dress is required: coat, tie, and shoes. No tennis shoes, please.* He pointed at his shoes. Even though they were filthy, they clearly weren't tennis shoes. "Are these tennis shoes? No—correct, Commander?"

"Yes."

He held up his ratty floral print tie. "I have a tie, yes?"

"Yes."

"As you can see, it's a beautiful tie." You could barely see the flowers for the food stains as faded as they were. "I not only have a jacket; I have a trench coat! It's even more elegant." He opened his trench coat to show his jacket. He began to raise his voice to attract the attention of new customers. He raised both arms above his head. "Commander, is this not the reason for our making this revolution, to end racial discrimination? I'm a French Cuban—does that make me in any way or manner different from any one of these guys?" He pointed at random customers.

Figure 32 Jose Maria Lopez Lledin, the Gentleman of Paris

I raised my right arm. "OK, let me talk to the manager." I turned to Jaime. "Do you have any objection if he sits with us? Each table has four chairs and there's three of us."

Jaime looked at me in resignation and shrugged his shoulders. "OK. Only because of you, OK, Commander?" He turned to Jose Maria and shook his finger. "Don't do this anymore, OK?" He dismissed the bouncers and said to the maître d, "Take them to a table." He looked at Jose Maria in revulsion, who was smiling ear to ear.

"Thank you very much, Commander," Jose Maria said. "I know you were sent by God to help me. Thanks God or fortune for this dim light."

The lights dimmed fully, and an announcer on the stage said, "This afternoon we will have a promo show of the Italian American singer, the fabulous Francis Albert Sinatra, actor, singer, producer, the international raconteur." He announced the other artists who would take part in the show and then finished with, "The show will conclude with the piano composer and conductor Gonzalo Roig Lobo. He will begin with the famous piece of his own composition, *'Quiereme Mucho,'* accompanied by the famous orchestra of CMQ Television."

Gonzalo Roig came out to a huge round of applause to direct the orchestra. The melody they played was beautiful, and a waiter came over to us to take our order. As a courtesy, I allowed Jose Maria to order first. He only shyly ordered an onion soup. I realized immediately that this was the cheapest item on the whole menu.

"Are you sure you don't want an entrée?" the waiter asked.

He took out his wallet and looked twice. "No, no—that's all I need right now."

I smiled. "You can order whatever you want. Whatever we have here, you and my friends, will be picked up by the government. Don't worry about it. If you don't have an appetite and only want the soup, that's fine. But if you're hungry and want a real meal but aren't ordering because your wallet is on a diet, don't worry about it. You're my guest today. You can order whatever you want."

He looked at me in surprise. "Really?" He grinned ear to ear. "Commander, I don't want to abuse your courtesy. You've already done a great thing for me. I've been trying to get in here for a while and finally accomplished that because of you." I nodded. He snatched the menu up and opened it like a little boy in a toy store. "Chateaubriand." He said decisively.

Montauk: The Lightning Chance

The waiter said, "The chateaubriand is 8 pounds and meant for 8 people. Let me explain that that plate is $99." He looked at me his doubt. "$99!"

I asked my friends, "What do you prefer to eat? Would you like chateaubriand? That's not a bad choice at all." I turned to him. "The roast creation of the chef Vicomte Francois-Rene de Chateaubriand."

Jose Maria gave me an OK sign. "Very well, Commandante! You know your business! You have a culinary education—I'm very proud of you."

"Thank you."

Daniel and Cisneros were used to asking for whatever I asked anyway as they trusted my palate. Even though it wasn't actually my choice, they both nodded. "We'll order whatever you do, Commander. If it's good for you, it's good for us."

I smiled. "Thank you for your confidence." I turned to the waiter. "You heard my friends. Chateaubriand for everyone."

"Ooh-lala!" he said, getting into the atmosphere. "Can I have a piece too, Commander?" He continued jesting with us. "I can add another chair to the table." The positive atmosphere was contagious. "I will promise you I will bring you a huge jar of orange Sangria and I will baptize it with a little touch of the splendid Grand Marnier." He put his index finger to his lips as three of us were underaged. Only Jose Maria was of age.

"OK," I replied with a big smile and a wink. "You got it, Phillipe."

Phillipe smiled because he knew I always left a generous tip, even though the revolution was criticizing tips of any kind as denigrating the wait staff. The rhetoric was that they were already paid a salary. It was an absurdity, but this was the beginning of the socialist campaign to get to people whether it was politically correct or not. That is the beginning of the destruction of the democracy within any country wherever these ideas were applied, there or anywhere else.

This time it was Jose Maria who said something that surprised me. He spoke in a natural way. "Commander, the next time I see your uncle I will tell him that you're not only a genuinely generous gentleman but also definitely you have a great heart, big as an elephant, like only the best of the del Marmol family."

I looked him in the eyes without saying a word. Phillipe was returning with the jar of Sangria. As he had promised us, Phillipe with a broad grin on his lips put the jar down on the table. Again, laying his index finger on his lips and a mischievous expression, he murmured, "Take it easy, OK? This Sangria is really, really loaded with Grand Marnier liquor. It has almost half a bottle, a few orange slices, orange juice that I personally squeezed."

We thanked him, and he left smiling. The orange slices inside the jar were mixed with pineapple, cherries, mangos, and some other fruit I didn't know where they had come from. We tasted it and it was delicious.

Jose Maria raised his cup. "Let's toast the youngest Commander of the revolution!"

I said, "I think it's a better toast for a free Cuba and a very, very smart Gentleman of Paris."

He recoiled and put his finger to his lip. "Shh!" He lowered his voice. "OK. To a free Cuba from all kinds of tyranny." He pointed to himself. "But me?" He circled his finger along the temple. "Cuckoo, cuckoo! I'm not right in my head. And I think it's better that everyone, especially the members of this new government think that I was brought to this island by a UFO. That's why my head is not in order."

I understood immediately what he was telling me in very few words. To change the subject, I replied since Phillipe was coming over with plates laden with the beef, "Phillipe deserves an extra bonus in his tip for his efficiency and speed in serving us."

At that precise moment, Frank Sinatra began his act, making a few jokes in Spanish and English before singing "Love Is a Many-Splendored Thing," partly in Spanish and part in English. The place was by now very full, and when he finished gave him a standing ovation. At the request of the public, he continued singing other songs from his repertoire. I stood up and said since I had almost finished my meal, "I have to go to the restroom. Nature is screaming at me." They continued devouring the exquisite meal. I put one of the plates aside for Phillipe. It was served with fresh asparagus and mixed vegetables of split peas and mashed potatoes with gravy. "You guys eat the rest." I covered my unfinished piece. "You can eat everything but leave that plate for Phillipe. I don't know if he was joking, but we have so much we should give him that courtesy."

On the way to the bathroom I ran into Fidel, Camilo, Piñiero[37], Che, and their escorts as they walked into the place with another

---

[37] The head of the G-2 Counterintelligence, also known as *"Bajaroja,"* the "Red Beard."

celebrity: Ernest Hemingway and his entourage. Fidel introduced me to Hemingway and said, "When you're finished your business in the bathroom come over to our table. I want to tell you something."

Figure 33 Piñeiro and Guevara

"I will see you there in a bit," I replied.

I finished up in the bathroom and stopped in the lobby before the placards with the pictures of Frank Sinatra and Ava Gardner—I hadn't noticed them before. Ava Gardner's photo caught my attention. She was wearing an exceptionally beautiful, low-cut, and provocative dress. It was translucent enough that you could see the nipples of her large breasts beneath the sequined gown. She wore a tiara of a color matching the golden dress and what appeared to be a white furred animal on her arm. I looked at this beautiful woman and her long, elegant gloves that went up her arms past the elbow. I thought at that moment of my girlfriend in Pinar del Rio, Sandra. Perhaps when she grew up completely in a few years she might look like her. There were certain resemblances. For a few seconds I imagined myself in Frank Sinatra's place with Sandra's face over that of Ava Gardner's. This daydream lasted very briefly in the middle of the cabaret lobby because a very refined, delicately perfumed white female hand covered my eyes. Her voice asked, "If you guess who I am you will win a kiss. On the cheek," she added with marked irony.

Even with the help of God I could not imagine who it could be. Most of my friends and family were in Pinar del Rio. I had family in

Havana, but in a city that large, it could be literally anyone. It didn't take me long to find out that it was a young girl that lived close to my house in Pinar del Rio who had a great crush on me. She had big blue eyes, wavy golden hair, and she was only a couple of years younger than me. As I saw her, my face filled with shocked surprise, and I asked, "Yaneba, what are you doing here in Havana?"

She wasn't very happy with my reaction and looked disappointed. "Well, well, Julio Antonio del Marmol! At least you could pretend a little bit of joy to see me at your side in this beautiful cabaret?" She didn't give me a chance to answer. "You've already forgotten your good manners after becoming a Commander in a communist army!"

"Hey, a little more respect, OK? First, I'm not a communist. Second, lower your voice. What mosquito bit you in order to be in such a bad humor?"

She looked me in the eyes, and I could see tears welling up in them. "These degenerate communists want to execute the younger brother of my father." She made an effort to control her feelings. "That's why I'm in Havana, Julio Antonio. Not just me, the entire family. Tomorrow is the final trial. It's very possible they'll put him in the firing squad. Or maybe, if we're 'lucky,' we're all praying, even my father who isn't very religious, that he'll get 30 years in prison. 30 years in a political prison." She shook her head. "Can you imagine—30 years? And that's if he's lucky and gets out alive, he'll be an old man. His whole life will be gone. Is that why so many people fought to take down Batista? To put up another dictator who is a lot worse, Fidel Castro and his gang of bandits?"

I felt her deep pain in my chest. I took my finger and held it to my lips to indicate silence. I put my security at risk because I knew for a fact that this converted me into an accomplice of whatever she had been saying, or at least agreeing with her. She looked at me in confusion from my action and involuntary gesture to protect her. It never crossed her mind that I didn't sympathize with those individuals who were communist, socialist, or even Satanic—whatever somebody wanted to call them. At that moment I could see Che out of the corner of my eye leaving the room with two of his men from the restaurant and heading in our direction. I was afraid Yaneba might say something more that would put us both in danger since her back was to that door. I didn't even know why I did it, I stepped over to her and hugged her. Perhaps it was instinct. I murmured in her ear. "Don't say a single word more.

Montauk: The Lightning Chance

I am in complete agreement with everything you said, but Che is right behind you and coming in our direction."

Yaneba, acting on impulse, tried to turn to look back but I held her head in place. As she moved her head, though, our faces practically touched. Without thinking twice at having her mouth in such proximity, and to distract her to prevent her from turning around and getting Che's attention, I kissed her on the lips. This not only took her by surprise but prevented her from looking back. It was what she had been looking for in the past months after she had told me how she felt about me. Despite her youth she was extremely mature and old spirited. Her body made her look a lot older than she really was, a teenager of fifteen or so. Her figure was curvy like a woman's, but her breasts were still on the small side. The rest of her body was blooming; it was a precious, well-formed body to look at. She looked at me with teary eyes that contrasted with the satisfied smile on her lips.

After a few seconds we separated. We stood there gazing into each other's eyes. This time it was she who stepped forward. She kissed me on the lips with a little more passion and sweetness. It not only confused the escort walking with Che, it completely threw off Che as well. They stopped momentarily to observe us with grins on their faces. To this day, so many years later, I remember that sweet and extraordinary kiss, full of sincere, pure love that had just started with the motivation of saving our lives as a staged kiss due to our dangerous proximity to the assassin Che Guevara, Adolf Hitler, or whoever was wearing that body at that moment. He was the worst emissary of Satan—or perhaps he was Satan himself in that supposedly human form. Even though I had enjoyed that moment intensely I had not abandoned looking out of the corner of my right eye for a second the movements of Che and his guards. I wasn't about to drop my guard and I looked at them to see what they were doing.

I saw they started to move again in our direction. I pretended that I didn't' see them. I told Yaneba in a nearly imperceptible whisper, "Keep your mouth shut, please. We have the Devil himself coming up behind us. Just keep looking me in the eyes with that beautiful smile and think of good things. That way God takes us away from this danger."

A few seconds later I felt Che's hand on my right shoulder. Immediately I smelled his unbearable odor of sulfur. His voice said, "Hey, Commandantico! Aren't you going to introduce us to your beautiful girlfriend?"

I turned slightly. "Of course, Che. But let me tell you before I do that, I should clarify that she is only my friend. My neighbor from Pinar del Rio."

"Ahh," Che said knowingly. He held out his hand to Yaneba. "*Mucho gusto*. Ernesto Guevara de la Serna, also known as Che."

Yaneba hesitated briefly but looked at me in recrimination. She did exactly what I expected from her. She held out her hand and said, "*Mucho gusto*. My name is Yaneba. I'm not his girlfriend. His girlfriend is a mulatta and her name is Sandra. She also lives in Pinar del Rio in our neighborhood."

Che smiled. "Just Yaneba?"

"Just Yaneba."

Che didn't insist. He could see she wasn't smiling or bubbling like other girls. His ego was bruised, and it was clear he didn't like her at all. He ignored her for the rest of the conversation as he turned to me. "Don't forget we're waiting for you at our table."

I nodded. "Yes, I know. Thank you for reminding me. I'll be there in a little while."

Che bowed with his head slightly, and said to Yaneba, "Good afternoon, young lady."

Yaneba nodded her head to him. "Good afternoon, sir."

Che turned and left with his entourage. Yaneba held my right hand with her left and squeezed her stomach. "I'm sorry, Julio Antonio. It's exceedingly difficult for me to be present before these criminals and control myself, especially with what I feel right here in my belly."

"You did great. Remember, you only show your true sentiments to your friends and your loved ones. To your enemy absolutely nothing, no emotions, if you don't want them to take advantage of you. But I must congratulate you again because you held yourself from insulting him and maintained civility. That's your prerogative. We have to take into consideration what you're going through with your uncle at this moment. Taking that into account, you did fantastic. Later, I'll give you more details and tell you what that stinking devil did to his best friend, the one who was supposed to be his most trusted driver and friend from the mountains. He blew his head off right in front of me just because he was suspicious that he betrayed us. I have to be honest with you, every time I have him in front of me, I have an unbearable impulse to spit in his face."

Yaneba could see my sincerity. She smiled. "That's exactly how I felt at that moment."

Montauk: The Lightning Chance

This time I was the one who smiled. "That is why I congratulated you twice. I believe you would be a great spy if you wanted to."

"Oh, no! I could never be a spy because I'm too emotional."

I smirked. "Remember what we say here: never say that you will never drink from that well. Destiny might obligate you to drink from it not much later."

She looked at me. "You know what? You will be a great writer one day. You find logic in everything that has no logic at all. I should go back to the table with my family before my mother comes looking for me and says something embarrassing in front of you about me taking so long in the bathroom."

I smiled in understanding and walked her towards the door back to the restaurant. We said goodbye a short distance from her parents' table. I waived to them, but the only one who waved back was her little sister, Elena. Her father, ironically, was sitting near Castro's entourage. He took in my uniform. If looks could kill, I would be dead. Her mother had a little more pleasant look towards me, but she still did not return my wave.

I left Yaneba with her family and returned to my table. Jose Maria stood up as I approached. In his refined manner thanked me once again and said goodbye to us. He lifted his right arm high and raised his voice so that the other tables noticed him. As if he were in a theatrical performance, he bowed nearly down to the ground in an exaggerated fashion. "I wish I could stay and spend more time with you, my great friends. But unfortunately, the universe claims my attention in other, more exotic places, in other worlds and dimensions. I've already made them wait too long. They are very distinguished individuals, the ingenious gentleman Don Quixote de la Mancha and his friend Sancho Panza, not counting my great and noble countryman Napoleon Bonaparte and his beautiful wife Josephine." He thumped his breast. "That is why, even though I have great gratitude to you, my young Commander, and the immense gratitude for that exquisite meal you shared with me, I have no other alternative but to leave you now with sorrow in my heart." The interlude music stopped completely, and his voice echoed throughout the space. "I'm sorry, my Commander, but I have to retreat from this battle tonight, even though your beautiful and elegant company and that of your friends has touched my most delicate feelings in my heart."

Everyone started to pay attention as his voice grew louder. Even Castro started peering in our direction. Some of the people who couldn't see us clearly stood up at their tables, craning their necks to peer at us. He continued in his dramatic declamation, "With the pleasure invested by my power as the good Samaritan of this revolution, I implore all of you beautiful ladies and gentlemen to excuse my retreat! *Salud, salud, salud.*[38]" He held his glass up to toast us. Not wanting to leave him in the air, we clinked our glasses with his. He set his glass down and covered it with a linen napkin. He carefully moved the plates from the meal out of the way, leaned down and removed his right shoe, and then smashed it down on the glass like he was the groom at a Jewish wedding. Then, picking the napkin up by the corners, he stood up, hand on his hip like a flamenco dancer, and began to pirouette as he whirled it over his head, the tinkling sound of broken glass providing an accompaniment to his loudly shouted, "Ole! Ole! Ole! Leave our Motherland, Spain, for a thousand years, amen!" Placing the napkin and its contents down on the table, he started to walk away, shaking his trench coat comically. Everyone in the audience, including Fidel, Che, and Hemingway, started to applaud. I wondered why they were clapping. I thought maybe some of them recognized him and went along with it, while those who didn't know who he was thought he was part of the show.

Completely in awe, I watched the Gentleman of Paris depart in his classic walk, holding his top hat with one hand and the other holding his London Fog. Even Che, Fidel, and the others stood to give him an ovation. I thought that I could perhaps learn a few things from this guy. I sat down when everything was calm and stroked my chin, thinking about what he had just said. I concluded that perhaps the Gentleman of Paris was not there by coincidence. There must have been a purpose that I was at that moment unaware of. I did, however, confirm it later that indeed my uncle had sent him.

Using the commotion he created as cover, I stood up and told Daniel and Cisneros that I would return shortly. I walked over to the table where Fidel and his group were sitting. When I reached them, Fidel cordially said to the waiter, "Bring another chair, please, and put it right here by me. Che, move our chair a little bit, give the Commandantico a little space between us."

---

[38] Batista frequently ended his speeches with this repeated toast.

Montauk: The Lightning Chance

Che looked sourly at Fidel. Hemingway said to me, "Well, I heard that you have extraordinary powers. I want you to show me those one of these days."

The waiter brought the chair accompanied by the maître d, who whispered in Fidel's ear. Fidel nodded and said, "Sure, sure—bring them on over!"

I replied, "I don't think what I have is extraordinary. I am simply able to do things other people are still searching for. Probably they are just looking in the wrong places."

Fidel grinned from ear to ear. He said to Hemingway, "I told you this kid is more than a handful. You want to eat something, or something to drink?"

"No, thank you—I just ate."

"Yes—I saw you had a second, more entertaining act there. Your friend the Gentleman of Paris got a standing ovation. I think the people liked his performance more than that of Frank Sinatra."

Che reached across me and nudged Fidel in the elbow. "Hey, careful—here he comes."

I looked up and saw Frank Sinatra approaching us from the edge of the stage, Ava Gardner on his arm. They came over and introduced themselves and asked Fidel if they could take a picture. After a few minutes of taking pictures, they thanked Fidel and left.

Figure 34 Frank Sinatra and Ava Gardner at the Capri

Fidel tapped me on the arm. "I want you to come with me. I'm going to show you the new little toys we just got from our friends the Chinese communists. They just recently brought it to us, and with this technology we'll be able to kick the gringos in the ass. We'll break the myth that they have the best and greatest technology. We'll confuse them for braggarts because they won't know where this came from. I believe this will be a great experience and reassure you that what we're doing is right in detaching from the gringos and being allied to new friends in communist China and Russia."

"OK, Commandante." I nodded and tried to make myself the most convincingly pleased expression on my face that I could. This was my first lesson about how I could make him believe I was his firm friend.

The maître d came over to us and gave Fidel a copy of the pictures. He stood up, not bothering to sign the check. One of the escorts did, without leaving any tip. Fidel said, "Follow me. You're going to have a very pleasant and great surprise."

On the way out I stopped by the table and said to Daniel and Cisneros, "Follow us to wherever we're going."

They followed the entourage. I saw Phillipe and said, "The money I've left you on the table is the tip. Add our tab to Fidel's. He already signed it."

Phillipe said, "Commandante, this is too much money for a tip."

I smiled and raised my right arm high and said in a very low voice, "You deserve that and a lot more. Don't tell anyone if you don't want to get either of us in trouble. Don't worry about it. The rest is for you. The tab is paid by the same entity: the government."

"OK, OK. Thank you very much," he said with a sincere grin of gratefulness. "God bless you and protect you for your generosity."

I smiled once more and said goodbye. As Daniel, Cisneros, and I joined Fidel and his entourage on the way out of the restaurant, I looked over at the table where Yaneba and her family were seated. I waved my farewell to them, and Yaneba and her sister enthusiastically waved back. Whether it was because they felt badly about before or out of fear or being impressed that I was so near to Fidel, this time I noticed that her parents also waved. I smiled in satisfaction.

Hemingway said goodbye in the lobby. I noticed that Che reminded him that they would see each other in a few hours on his yacht, *Pilar,* in Cojimar. We left the lobby and encountered Commandante Huber Matos on our way to the cars. He and Camilo exchanged warm hugs. Fidel coldly greeted him, as did Che and the others. It was apparent to me that Matos was not in Fidel's best graces at that time. I could see Fidel's scowl as soon as he saw him. When Camilo invited Matos to come with us, Fidel shook his head, "No, no, Camilo. There's no more space for anyone else in the cars, and it's too hot to make you guys suffer."

I saw an opportunity and said, "Perhaps my assistant could go in the car, and I could bring Camilo and Commandante Matos in my jeep with me."

Figure 35 Camilo Cienfuegos

Fidel clearly didn't like that suggestion, but he had no choice. Making it a patched job, he said, "You see, guys? That's what I like about the Commandantico. As young as he is, he always comes up with a solution to any problem." Che and the others gave us a fake smile. They all knew how Fidel felt about Huber, but like hypocrites tried to hide it.

Dr. Julio Antonio del Marmol

CHAPTER 13: THE ULTIMATE FEAR OF THE SPY

We all entered our respective vehicles and departed towards a location known only to Fidel and probably Che. We drove deep into the heart of the city. Camilo was seated in the front by Daniel, while Huber and I were seated in the back. Huber asked Camilo with a hint of worry about my presence there, "Are you sure we can talk here, Camilo?"

Camilo replied with a friendly smile, "Yes, with complete assurance or holding back." He reached back and grabbed my knee with his left hand. He spoke again with an assurance that surprised Matos. "Huber, this Commandantico is very young, I know, and you don't know him well, but let me tell you something: there are very few people that have all the qualities of being a gentleman like this kid has. I've already tested him several times." He lifted his left hand and pointed up. "Never has he repeated to anyone whatever he hears in our conversations." I remained silent, listening. He continued emphatically, "Not even Fidel or Che have ever been able to get a single word of what I've told him, no matter what kind of pressure they apply. Always with the savvy and good conduct of a very mature man, he replied to all of us, even me on several occasions, 'If you're interested in what Camilo told me in confidence, please don't ask me. Ask *him*. I'm absolutely sure that if he wants to communicate it to you guys, he'll have no reason to not tell you, so there's no reason for you to ask me.'"

Huber looked at me admiringly and put his left hand on my shoulder. "Bravo, Commandantico! You should always continue to embrace those principles, and you will win the admiration and affection of everyone that is around you, even the ones you reject."

"Thank you," I said. "I don't like when someone asks me questions about other people's comments, either looking to create gossip or controversy between people. The best thing is to not say a single word. If you speak up, they can turn what you say around to their own version of what they want to say but lack the courage to say themselves. That's why I learned to do this." I made a motion over my mouth with my index finger and thumb, like I was closing a zipper over it. "It's a lesson I learned from my father. Don't say anything—that is the best method. Flies don't enter a closed mouth. They cannot say later that you said anything because everyone knows you never do. You close off that gossip before it's ever born."

Matos relaxed as he smiled and realized that Camilo had good judgment about me. "OK, I will talk in front of you, and I hope you give the same respect that you've done until this day regarding my conversation. It's extremely delicate for our eyes and ears only."

I zipped my mouth shut again, and he patted my shoulder in approval. He turned to Camilo. "Camilo, you know better than anyone that Fidel convinced me to leave my teaching profession behind and the last thing I wanted to be in my life to become a guerilla for the freedom of our country. I did it because I put my full trust in Fidel. You also know that I'm a man of peace. I don't like wars. I've been in this war for almost ten years because it was absolutely necessary in our fight against the dictator Batista." He took a breath. "You also know, Camilo, of my grand friendship with Celia Sanchez. Because of the intimate relationship she's always had with Fidel, she is the one who brought me to him, and that's how I got involved in this revolution, depositing faith in her and Fidel. And even though I don't like his brother very much because he's a wimp wannabe, I will respect him out of respect for Fidel. And all that sacrifice to return the freedom of Cuba and give to the people the gift of clean and democratic revolution from which we've all been robbed by the dictator."

Huber crossed his legs. He said emphatically, "But never, never did it cross my mind that Fidel wanted to implant a totalitarian socialist or communist regime in our country. That is complete treason not just to all the people who have been fighting with us and offering their lives for this democratic fight but also to the revolution itself. He has come to be a traitor even to his own principles. He's told the Cuban people all these years and most recently the entire world that he would never break bread with the killers of the Hungarian people—what happened to this man, Camilo?" He leaned back and supported his forehead on two fingers. "What caused the metamorphosis in such a short time and defecate all over what he even said in his speeches and to all of us?"

Camilo turned around to look at him. "El Che Guevara, my friend."

Huber couldn't hold back. He shook his head and said angrily, "Yes, I know, I know. This damned sulfurous Argentinian is nothing less than a disciple of Satan."

Camilo turned back again sharply. "In my opinion, you come short. I believe he is more than a disciple. I think, if I tell you what I feel in my heart, I think he is a professor of Satan, body and soul. I tell you this because I saw with my own eyes the number of teenaged kids that have been executed in prisons around the country." He wiped away the two tears that threatened to escape his eyes. "These things are extreme and unnecessary, this bloodbath he has taken from one corner to the other across the island. We have more deaths than Batista ever dreamed of having on his list." Camilo took his Stetson off and wiped the sweat from his forehead with a handkerchief. "I think this man enjoys killing people. I can see it; it is like the satisfaction you have when you take a lick of ice cream. He has that same satisfaction." He ran his fingers through his long hair. "I'm getting sick and tired of telling Fidel that if he doesn't stop Che's massacres all over the country that history will bestow on us the greatest death toll, even above the French revolution. But Fidel always responds with the same crap, 'I'll talk to Che' or 'I'll talk to Raul.' But the bloodbath continues unabated. When we run out of Batista's government, then we go after others for stupid little things, then our own youth because they violate our arbitrary laws." His face was pale and filled with concern. He reached back and grabbed Huber's knee. "My friend, I'm coming to think that Fidel has the same morbid pleasure to see all these people killed as Che. Children, women, old men, they have no mercy with anyone. Maybe he's motivated by Che or possessed by him."

This time, Matos removed his uniform cap and put it on his knee. He shook his head. There were a few seconds of silence. He took his handkerchief to wipe the sweat from his forehead and face. This conversation had raised the temperature of both men, and their gestures, voices, and demeanor revealed their mutual frustration.

Matos said, "My friend Camilo, I have tried several times to communicate my worries and the concerns of most of my officers and troops. Not only my officers, but also the civilian organization of the province of Camagüey that I was put in charge of. I have a duty and obligation to attend to all the complaints and the voices of the civil organizations as the military governor. I have exhausted my excuses with these people during our weekly and monthly meetings, trying to defend against the accusations that Fidel Castro and his advisor Che Guevara are trying to turn the democratic revolution into a socialist or communist one. Then the next day Fidel passes a new, extremely left-wing law that completely contradicts himself and destroys all my arguments with those organizations. They contradict what he himself said before. What can we do?" There was desperation in his voice as he pled with his friend.

Camilo breathed deeply and sighed. He took his hat off again and wiped his brow once more. He shook his head. With a very troubled face he replied, "My friend Huber, to be honest with you, I don't think there's anything we can do. Like the good friend you are, I'm going to give you some advice, for your own good and the well-being of your family and friends. Don't do anything that can irritate Fidel and Che any more than they already are. I won't repeat what they say behind your back, like our friend the Commandantico said, but what I heard Fidel and Che say is not beneficial to you at all. I don't want you to become one more victim of this revolution." He said emphatically, "Remember, revolutions are famous for devouring their own sons. I believe that what you should do is what I've been thinking and planning to do for several months. I will renounce my military position and leave this career. Maybe with a little luck and some friends I have in Costa Rica, I can get out of Cuba for a while until things return to normal. I don't want to be another victim of the revolution, either, like so many of our friends have. Unfortunately, Huber, we created this revolution and like a beast it can now be unleashed against us by others for their own self-interest."

Huber shook his head, his worry deepening. His face clearly reflected his sorrow at what he had just heard from his best friend in this group. I had remained totally silent without saying a single word, either agreeing or disagreeing with them. I couldn't contain myself any longer, however. It was clear that these two top leaders didn't know themselves what was going on. I didn't know whether I should speak. I might blow my cover, and I looked out the window on my side of the jeep and looked up at the sky. The white clouds seemed to form the faces of both my ladies in white, smiling as they gave me the green light to go forward with what had just crossed my mind to do.

I smiled and said, "Excuse me, both of you. There's something here that sounds very, very odd to me. I think you've both been duped. That is something a gentleman cannot keep silent about. I'm violating my promise to Che not to repeat it to anyone, but I think I can do so with certain restrictions provided you maintain this in complete confidentiality. I don't think you have any idea of what's been going on or what Che showed me just today. My good friend Camilo, that the people of Cuba love even more than Fidel, and you, Huber, are both talking like outsiders that have no idea what's going on. You're such high leaders of this revolution and I listen to the worries you're sharing and your rational concerns for your troops and country. I think you actually don't have any idea of what's going on." They both looked at me. I raised my right arm and said, "The destiny of this country is already decided and is in motion as to what the future of Cuba will be." Now they looked at me like I was from outer space.

Camilo's expression grew harsh with anger. "What in the hell are you referring to, Commandantico? Please!"

I opened both arms wide and shook my head sorrowfully. "I want to make clear once more that what I'm about to say is classified and extremely confidential." They both acknowledge almost simultaneously. "Very well, now it is clear that this should not be repeated to anybody, and I will tell you where Che took me this morning. We went to a beautiful, huge building in Vedado's opulent district. There almost two hundred people have been trained to nationalize every single private property in the country in a couple of weeks. Maybe three at the outside; there will be no one that owns anything in this country. All will be in the hands of the government. You guys tell me what that is."

Camilo and Huber exchanged worried glances. Camilo said, "Fidel promised me that this would only be done to foreign enterprises and factories." He looked at me, his temper rising. He said a little more loudly that I didn't like a bit, "Why did Che take you to show all the things you *say* he showed you?"

I leaned back in my seat. "Did you just forget what you told your friend Huber a little bit ago, that I don't exaggerate and can be trusted, or are you changing your tone now?"

"Don't take me wrong! I'm not angry at you—I'm angry at *me*! How could I be so stupid?"

"That is exactly what I went through with my father today." Two tears escaped my face.

"You told your father?"

"Yes." I looked at him angrily and emphatically. "This is my first priority. Before anything else I have to be a good son, and I have to tell the truth. Believe it or not, he called me a traitor and kicked me out of the house. Can you imagine the pain I have in my chest right now? Do you think I have any reason to tell you anything that's not true?"

Huber squeezed my shoulder. "Calm down, Commandantico. We are all disappointed and betrayed by these vindictive, destructive bandidos."

I nodded. "If I have to be honest with you, I don't even have an answer for the question why he took me over there and not you guys. At least, not until I heard you guys talking, because I had assumed until now that you guys knew what was going on."

Camilo controlled his irritation and asked, "What did Che tell you when he showed you all that?"

I smiled again, stroking my chin with my right hand. I shrugged and shook my head. "I already told you what Che showed me this morning. But if you want to know what he actually *said* to me this morning, that you will have to go and ask Che yourselves. Remember, when you do this don't even mention my name for anything. You heard not a peep out of me about it. I cannot be more surprised and shocked that both of you high leaders of this revolution, being born Cuban citizens are kept in the dark while Che who is not even Cuban, a foreigner, has more information about what is going to happen and the changes they're implementing in our country. It's very evident after listening that neither of you knows that Fidel's on a honeymoon with communist China and Russia and now I understand why Fidel doesn't want you, Huber, to come with us to wherever we're going. I expect when we arrive at the place that you, Camilo, will be sent away with whatever excuse they can fabricate because he doesn't want you to see the new toys the communist Chinese government just gave him. You're in the town, but you don't see the buildings."

Camilo's face turned red. I had never seen him like this before. I must have touched a very live nerve during the root canal of a deep, dark cavity. He shifted in his seat like he had phosphorus inside his body, ready to blow up. He was silent for a few seconds, and then said almost imperceptibly, "These sons of bitches think they're so smart."

Huber asked, "What did you say?"

When Camilo turned, his face was still red. "Huber, I believe we're both been the last ones to know what these sons of bitches are plotting to do." He touched my knee. "I'm sorry, Commandantico, for losing my temper a little bit."

"No problem," I said.

He turned back to Huber. "My advice to you, my good, old friend, whatever your next decision is when you return to your province, do it quickly. As we've heard from the lips of our young friend here, these conniving individuals are moving swiftly. If you wait until tomorrow, you'll end up in front of the firing squad for treason. You'll regret in that minute that you didn't do something beforehand."

He said, "I've heard enough to return to Camagüey immediately. Thanks to what you said, Commandantico." He patted my shoulder. "I've been a teacher all my life, and I've learned my best lesson from you. Thank you."

"You're welcome. I couldn't remain silent with the knowledge of something so morbid and conniving in my heart."

"I know what my next step will be Camilo."

"Good luck, Huber. Walk with leather soles on shattered glass."

We arrived at a military hospital. We passed through the entry gates and exchanged salutes with the soldiers there. We drove behind the three Oldsmobiles of Che and Fidel into the rear left side of the compound, far from the regular population. We followed them until they stopped before a vast building and got out of our vehicles. Che and Fidel parked a little farther in, sending their escort of four soldiers and Cisneros to intercept us as we exited the jeep.

The escort leader said to Camilo, "The orders of the Commander-in-Chief are for us to take you guys wherever you want to go. They'll be here for a while. Something's come up that was unexpected, and they'll be here longer than planned."

An Oldsmobile approached to take Camilo and Huber to wherever they were to go. They both looked at me in mild surprise at the verification of what I had told them. I saluted, "A pleasure, Commanders."

"God be with you," Huber said.

"God protect you," Camilo added.

I shot each of them a cautionary look. I started to get into the jeep with Daniel and Cisneros. The escort leader called out, "No, Commandantico. I was told not to let you go and escort you back to them."

Montauk: The Lightning Chance

Figure 36 Huber Matos

Figure 37 Huber Matos and Julio Antonio

Huber and Camilo exchanged looks and then looked at me. I gave them a thumbs up sadly. I will never forget their own sorrowful expressions. Both of them stroked their beards and nodded sadly, silently affirming the truth of my words to them.[39]

---

[39] That was the last time I ever saw my friend Commander Camilo Cienfuegos. Only a few months later he and his pilot disappeared in his

Dr. Julio Antonio del Marmol

I followed the leader of the escort into the building and rejoined Fidel and Che in a subterranean room that looked like a massive research facility's laboratory. They started to give everyone lead aprons to don and protective helmets also made of lead with dark tinted lenses that looked much like welder's masks. Everyone wore white robes with navy blue nuclear research emblems on them. Clearly, we were being protected against some form of radiation. We went into a room that had a wall of thick tempered glass, probably thick enough to be bullet proof. The other room we viewed through these windows looked like a surgical room that held a machine which looked like something out of a science fiction movie, a pulsing intermodulation microwave frequency emitter. There was a table with straps to totally immobilize someone lying on it, and then some kind of machine with a cone that pointed the narrow tip towards the subject while the researcher could presumably look into the wide end. A brand label on the side read Alpine Light Ultrasonic Encephalogram Machine.

According to the description Fidel gave me, the machine was not completely perfected, but it could extract every single memory a human being had in his or her brain. These memories were then stored on a computer. Unfortunately, it would cause brain trauma in some cases, but they were working to perfect that aspect. He said, "This technology means that we'll never need to send spies anywhere. We just have to catch their spies and then scan their brains and we'll have all the information we need. It will affect how we conduct chemical and biological warfare."

---

plane without any trace. Commander Huber Matos was arrested for high treason a few weeks after this conversation, after he presented his resignation in a letter to Fidel, pleading with him in that letter to abandon his intention to create a communist state. He was sentenced to 20 years in La Cabaña for the crimes of resigning and refusing to be by the sides of the Castros and Che Guevara. Nearly 30 years after his release I was able to reunite with him in a meeting in California for a political resistance group he had created to free the island named Cuba Independent and Democratic. He gave me the honor of assigning me as the Chief Advisor of Intelligence, in charge of the organization's intelligence. He died several years later with the same spirit of a warrior and decency that he left for posterity. Unfortunately, he did not live to see what I expect to see one day, a Cuba free of a socialist dictatorship.

Montauk: The Lightning Chance

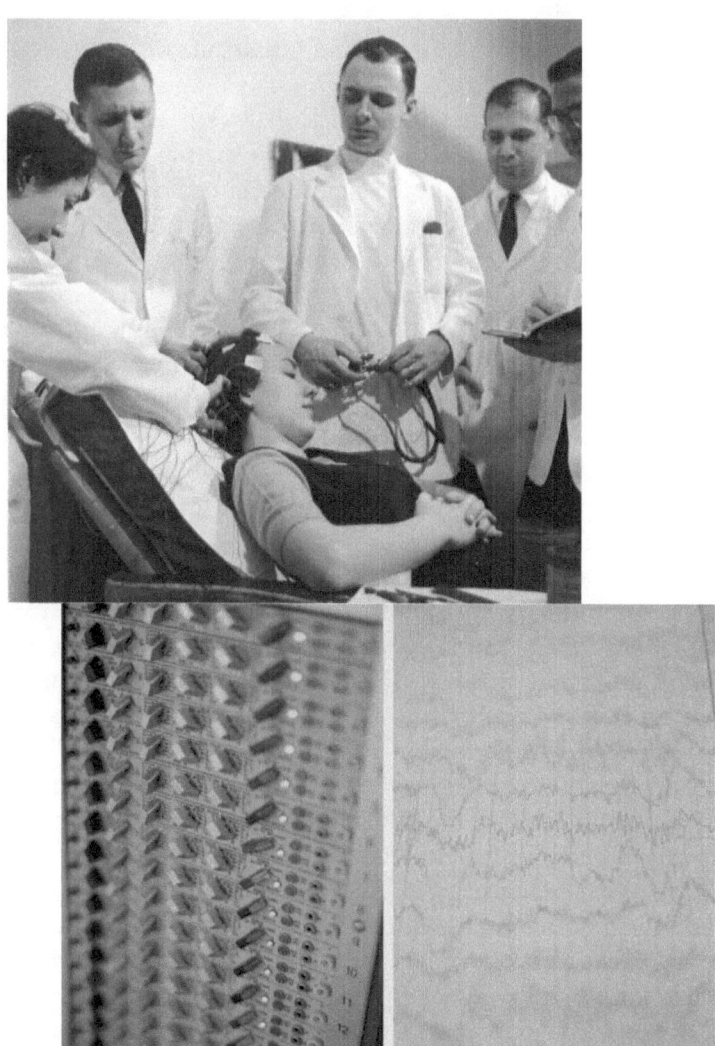

Figure 38 The Experimental Sonar Machine

The enormous artifact sat like a grim behemoth. The man who was giving the orders for the project I had met once before; he had been Fidel's personal doctor. His name was Commander Renee Vallejo. His hair and beard were nearly white, making him appear much older than his age of forty. He wore a white robe over his commander's uniform with a surgeon's cap. He was apparently Fidel's most trusted person, since he accompanied us everywhere we went. I hadn't seen him for several weeks, and now I knew why. Fidel had put him in charge of the new toy and overseeing the research. There was certainly no better individual to be in charge of this new strange machine than his personal doctor.

We saw some computers on wheels that were connected to this strange machine. Four men walked into the room, one on each side to a man handcuffed between them, the last walking behind. The men on either side of the prisoner wore the white robes and surgeon's caps. In addition to the handcuffs, the bound man wore leg irons and a green patient's gown. He struggled a little, as if he had a suspicion that what was going to happen wouldn't be pleasant. The man behind took a metal syringe and injected something into the prisoner—I hoped it was a tranquilizer, since the prisoner offered no more resistance. He was a tall mulatto, but not a typical Cuban one. His features looked more European. They laid him down on the table. They tied him down, starting with his legs and finishing with his neck, utterly immobilizing him.

I watched all of this behind the thick glass. It would be my perfect opportunity to use the pen that my uncle had given me. As a cleansing measure, they shaved his hair with electric clippers, a plastic container catching the hair as it fell. After they removed all his hair and his head completely cleansed, they put cream on his head and face and used a straight edged razor to shave any remaining hair as well as his eyebrows and facial area down to the follicles. This was not just for hygiene but also to prevent any interference with this high frequency machine. Hair is electrically conductive, and they wanted to eliminate any variance in their experiment.

Fidel came over to me and proudly put his arm around my shoulder. "What you're about to see is a pioneering invention that will revolutionize the way we conduct espionage in the future. As I told you, we won't have to send our spies anywhere. All we have to do is catch *their* spies and take the information directly out of their brains. This spy you see inside the room is a confessed agent for the American CIA. We caught him red-handed bringing weapons and technological communication equipment to the counterrevolutionaries in Santa Clara that was supposed to go into the mountains of Escambray, where the main focus of the resistance is located. This spy has been renewed even though he confessed to be the contact with the rebels to give us information as to who his accomplices here in Cuba are and who the people in charge in the urban resistances are." He stroked his beard with an evil smile. "Now when we connect him to that scanner this machine

Montauk: The Lightning Chance

in his brain will be cleaning up all the information we need." He pointed at the computer on wheels. "And then it will be sent to that computer and we'll be able to read everything, even that which is in his subconscious. Every single thing he has in his memory we will extract like we would a molar tooth from someone. With the printout the computer will give us we will confront him. He doesn't even know how the hell we got the information that he's not even aware he has."

As Fidel spoke, I wrote in my notebook with the special pen. I looked at my wristwatch, marking down the reactions this individual had before and after he was connected to the machine. I also recorded the details of the experiment. In so doing, I accomplished two things: first, I disguised the use of the pen and drew his attention more to the notebook in which I was writing the information down, while at the same time I was covertly taking pictures with the pen. Fidel was accustomed already to this habit I had whenever we got together. On more than one occasion when somebody questioned me why I had been writing everything down, I had explained that this was a habit I got from my father. He had told me that great friendships and relations between people get lost because they lack the memory of what they said or didn't say before. Even worse, wars between countries happen because of this lack of communication or the leaders who partake in the meetings failing to remember agreements reached later. That is why I didn't ever depend completely on my memory. Before I made any statement about previous discussions, I always consulted my notebook. Fidel praised me several times for conducting myself properly because of that.

As the man was connected to the machine and the cone was pointed at the head of the supposed CIA spy, everything looked perfectly normal at start. We heard a strong, irritating whistle. It was like an acute version of a steam train's whistle departing from the station, warning travelers of their last chance to get on board. It wasn't pleasant, but it was tolerable. Of course, we were separated by that thick glass, and I had no idea what kind of acoustics that room had. They were completely isolated—if we could hear it, it might be unbearable to those inside the room.

I had been writing in my notebook since the beginning, starting with 00100s. Then 002, 003, 004, 005, and so on, until I got to 035. The computer printer started to operate, and the paper rolled down onto the floor. The individual at that mark started to convulse. At first, they were mild; but they continually built in rapidity. He began to vomit and the man conducting the experiment looked at the computer printout. He picked it up off the floor and saw that there were no more printouts, indicating the brain had stopped sending signals to the computer. They rushed and switched the machine off and then took the man's pulse. The EKG machine whined a single tone and the line measuring his heartbeat turned into a straight, unbroken line. His heart had stopped.

I continued observing this commotion, writing in my notebook without stopping. Two new men entered the room. One appeared to be a cardiologist, who ordered the others to remove the restraints across the patient's chest. He hurriedly opened the man's gown and began to apply the defibrillator paddles, or AEDS—also commonly called a heart shock machine. They tried unsuccessfully to revive him three times. Finally, the EKG started to beep rhythmically, and they stabilized the heart's rhythm once more. Fidel and Commander Vallejo were very agitated. They walked away, concerned about losing the subject. Some more men left the room and brought the computer printout to them. They looked over their results of the 35 seconds that the man's brain had been connected to the computer. They looked out in the hallway as they went through the IBM printout, and Vallejo explained to Fidel what they had extracted.

I felt something strange at my back, and I heard a strange whine in my ears, which usually indicated danger. Normally, I had it in one ear, but this time I was getting it in both. I knew I had to be extremely careful, so I turned the pen off and put it away in my shirt pocket. Without stopping I counted by tapping my finger against my watch. I finished the counting, pulled out my pen, and made a note of the time I had just counted to (without activating the pen). I pretended to read my notes, checking the previous pages.

I heard Piñiero's sinister voice behind me. Evidently, Fidel had brought him to this location as state security to maintain the deepest secrecy on the toy he had from China. From the moment we met neither of us had liked the other. To make matters worse, Fidel even joked that I would be the one replacing him in the future, because the psychological capacity and natural gifts I possessed would make me suitable to be in charge of the state security once I reached a certain age. The morbid, stupid individual took it seriously, because from that moment his purpose every day was to not take his eyes off anything I was doing and try to discredit me in front of Fidel at every opportunity that presented itself. He wanted to get back in Fidel's good graces. He asked in an authoritarian manner, "Don't you know it's prohibited to take notes in this restricted area?" I turned my head slightly and smiled without replying. I turned back and continued reading my notebook. He grew indignant at my attitude of indifference, which stung his ego. He nearly yelled, "*Quien carajo*[40] do you think you are? Do you think that just because you're by Fidel's side you can ignore me as if I were a piece of shit the dog dropped in the street?" He took a step towards me and abruptly snatched the notebook out of my hand.

I turned towards him, momentarily losing my cool. "What the hell did you do that for?" My face was red, and my ears pounded with my indignation. I put my right hand on my pistol, and he did the same, as if we were about to have a duel. I unsnapped my holster cover and put my finger on the trigger. I held my other hand out. "Give me my book back!"

He shook his head. "No. What are you going to do about it?"

"Please return my book if you don't want to end today in a coffin. Somebody is going to die now, and it's not going to be me. You are the one who will die on this beautiful afternoon."

He yelled, his tone tinged in fear, "What the hell are you going to do? Are you threatening me?"

Everyone turned around and looked at us. Che was the first to assess the situation and walked over to us rapidly. He saw Piñiero's pistol half drawn and yelled, "What the hell are you doing, Piñiero?"

Piñiero didn't even look at Che. He said to me, "You are a spy, and I'm going to shoot you in the head."

I locked eyes with him, my hand still on my pistol. I furrowed my brow and unfurrowed it, my ears moving in time with it. He drew his pistol, but found himself unable to train it on me, like he was paralyzed or didn't have the strength to raise it fully. I had frozen him mentally, and Che got to us in only a couple of steps. He screamed, "Are you *crazy*, Piñiero?"

Fidel was only about ten feet behind with Commander Vallejo. He said, "Manuel Piñiero, what the hell are you doing?"

Piñiero could not even speak. His pistol still stubbornly pointed at the floor. That attitude and image sent the signal to Che and Fidel what his intentions were toward me quite clearly. Without taking my eyes off him or moving a single muscle in my body save for those in my face and skull, my hand remained on my pistol and my left hand extended for the return of my notebook.

---

[40] Who the hell

Commander Vallejo looked at both of us and motioned Fidel and Che back. He walked over to Piñiero, who began to urinate in front of everyone there. The notebook remained firmly clutched in his left hand. Vallejo pried my notebook out of Piñiero's hand. He walked over to me and held it out to me. "OK, my son. This belongs to you. Calm down now, please." He patted my shoulder. "We're all friends here. OK?"

I took my eyes off Piñiero and smiled as I took it from him. "Yes, it belongs to me. Thank you very much."

Vallejo asked, "Who are you?"

"To whoever can possibly understand, I am the full vessel. I have a mission ahead." I pointed to Piñiero. "He is an empty vessel with no moral compass. This is my psychological and behavioral analysis of myself."

Vallejo smiled. "You have nothing to worry about anymore. No one will harm you. Relax, and come with me." He took me over to Fidel.

Everyone looked at me in surprise, including Piñiero, who was still recuperating without understanding what had just happened. He looked down in shock at his wet pants. In total embarrassment, he holstered his pistol and held his hands over his crotch. As Fidel moved towards him, he edged away from the puddle of urine, trying to put some distance between himself and it. He didn't even realize that while he was in the hypnotic state everyone had seen what had happened. Like the dog he had mentioned in his comparison, he had soiled himself in front of his idol, Fidel, as well as the others.

Piñiero tried to yell, but his voice cracked. He cleared it and pointed at me. "That kid is not who you think he is. What are those symbols in his book? I know my business in the spy world, those are spy notes about everything we've been conducting here. I have no doubts in my mind that he is infiltrating us."

Fidel shook his head and came over to me. Pleasantly he asked, "Commandantico, would you please allow me to look in your notebook?"

"Sure, Commandante," I said as I gave him my notebook.

He knew I would have a rational answer for it, as this is not the first time Piñiero had tried something like this, and that once more *Barba*

Montauk: The Lightning Chance

Roja[41] would be far off in his accusation. As I gave Fidel my book with the same pleasantness and cordiality he showed me, I said, "Commandante, do you notice these numbers that Piñiero refers to a spy code? Would you like me to explain them to you?"

"Please, Commandantico, explain it."

"Did you want me to do it in private or before everyone here?"

"Here, so everyone can see how wrong Piñiero can be. I know you'll give me a very satisfactory answer."

"You're right, Commandante. I intended to show this to you, but I didn't have time because Piñiero confronted me in a derogatory way and very rudely took the book out of my hands. Very disrespectfully. These are my conclusions from my analysis of the experiment you conducted with that machine. Could you please give me my book back?" Fidel handed it back to me, and I showed him in the book. "All these numbers, 001, etc., indicated the number of seconds the spy was connected to the machine and his subconscious was feeding your computers without any side effects and under very normal conditions. As you can see in the book, when you reach 035 and put the stars, that is when he started to have convulsions. That was the first symptom that his subconscious sent to the computer that something was going very wrong. If we knew that previously, that man would never have had a heart attack. But because this is the first time you conducted the experiment, you didn't know that, which makes the data I have here very valuable. You don't want to kill him; you want him unharmed, or you'll lose the opportunity to extract more information from him. These previous signals here show when the brain started to overheat and marked the exhaustion point where the brain cannot provide more information. When the brain surpasses one hundred and four degrees in this case, the central nervous system becomes confused, agitated, and dizziness are the effects and the signs that a heart stroke is coming."

Everyone looked at me in shocked awe, especially Commander Vallejo. Piñiero started to say something but Fidel held up a hand. "Shut up! Continue, Commandantico, please." Piñiero stepped back, moving farther away from the puddle of urine.

"If you see, Commandante," I continued, "if we pass this data to your friends the Chinese communists, not only will they perfect this machine but also you can continue using the machine in the time being,

---

[41] Red Beard—a nickname he was given because of his red-haired beard

knowing already from my data that you have to stop it before you reach 35 seconds, give the brain time to cool off, five minutes or whatever, and then recycle the test for another 35 seconds. Using those breaks, you can extract all the information from the subject without harming him. Even though he's a CIA agent, you don't want him to die of a heart attack before you complete your research." Naturally, I was telling them this not to perfect the machine but to save the man's life from their stupidity. I also needed to destroy Piñiero's argument that I was taking notes as a spy.

It worked; I had not even finished speaking before Fidel gave me a bear hug. "This Commandantico is a genius!" he exclaimed. Piñiero writhed, and Fidel turned to him. "Manuel Piñiero, you come here right now! I won't ask you to get on your knees and kiss this kid's boots, but I am going to demand that you give him a very sincere and honest apology. Right now, I don't want to hear anything else! I want to warn you once more, the next time this happens and we come to this tremendous stupidity that one of us is a spy, I'm going to take your goddamned stars off your shoulder and send you on a long vacation to the Mazorra Psychaitric Hospital!"

Piñiero walked towards me. I looked down at his wet pants. He hung his head in shame and extended his hand. Fidel yelled, "*Carajo*! Look him in the eyes and mean what you say!"

He looked me in the eyes. "I'm really very sorry. You're a good kid. I've got kids like you."

I glared at him for a few seconds, letting him hang with his hand extended, my own hand still on my pistol. I looked at him in disgust, but as soon as his eyes met mine, I took my hand off my pistol and took his hand. I could feel all the negative energy consuming him and snatched my hand away. I knew that this would not be my last encounter with this sinister individual. I felt how empty he was and the hatred he had in his heart, fighting with my good energy. It crossed my mind that Che had already converted him to that Satanic cult.

Fidel started to make fun of Piñiero. "I've told you many times that you leave the Commandantico in peace. This time and the past times we've been around, but one of these days you'll be with him alone. You see this skinny kid without much muscle? He'll kick your ass completely out of your headquarters in Villa Marista with what he has in his brain."

Everyone laughed, and Piñiero hung his head in shame at the way his master humiliated him in front of the others and enjoyed it. I separated from Piñiero, and Che took me a little distance away. I heard Commander Vallejo beg Fidel, "Please, let me have him for a little while. If you ask him to come spend at least a couple of weeks with us, he could be a tremendous help with the research programs we have right now."

"I don't know. I don't think it's a good idea," Fidel replied with a shake of his head. "I'll tell him. He has his hands full putting the juvenile military commandos together."

Vallejo replied, "I know, I know. But this young man possesses extraordinary gifts with the power of psycho hypnosis, something that I've never seen before that brings the seen and unseen around you."

Fidel replied, "OK, if you think it's so important for you, I'll ask him. But I don't want to push him if he doesn't want to do it. The last thing I want to do is piss him off. We'll lose him completely for everything."

"I understand. Just talk to him. He likes you." As an old fox, Vallejo wanted to sweet talk me and find out where I got that energy. "Take care of this Commandantico. He is a diamond in charcoal. He doesn't even know how valuable that gift he has is. If we show him how to polish it, it will be integral in our plans to control the world."

Fidel smiled and nodded. "Why do you think I have him by my side, Vallejo?"

Vallejo smiled and patted Fidel on the shoulder. I could no longer overhear them because Che put his hand on my shoulder. The whine I got when I was near him disrupted my hearing completely. I could only hear the repeated observation by Fidel. Che said, "Hey, Commandantico—you want to come to the Cojimar Beach? It's a beautiful day today, and maybe you need to cool off. Your ears are so red. That asshole Piñiero isn't just like that with you; he's like that with all of us who are close to Fidel. Let's give a visit to the old writer, my *tocayo*[42], Ernest Hemingway. I promised Fidel to bring him some *tobacos* from our special reserve. We only smoke the flower and the cream of the industry."

I replied enthusiastically, "Che, I will always go to the ocean with the greatest pleasure or without any objections at all. I love the ocean with all my heart."

Che raised his right arm and yelled to Fidel, "I'm taking the Commandantico to Cojimar for a while onto Hemingway's yacht. Did you want to come with us?"

---

[42] Name twin

Fidel replied, "Are you taking the cigars with you that we promised him?"

"Yes, yes."

"OK. Say hello for me and we'll see each other in my office a little later."

"OK." I walked with Che out of the underground room, followed by his escort. Piñiero had vanished already like magic. After we walked a few steps we saw a janitor cleaning up the urine from the floor with a bucket and towels. Che asked, "Tell me one thing I'd like to know: what did you do to Piñiero to make him urinate in his pants like that? I've never seen anybody do something like that, and he looked like someone who had been demoralized."

I shook my head. "I did nothing. I only showed him that he's not as strong as he thinks he is."

A little malice reflected in his face as he smiled. "You showed him the scorpion under the rock. Without even moving a finger on your hand. Hey?"

"Something like that, close enough."

We left the military hospital. I indicated to Daniel and Cisneros to wait for me at the Prime Minister's office, and that I would meet them there later. Che told me that we had to stop off at the National Bank, which was on our way down to the beach at Cojimar. After a long while in the bank the escort returned and loaded metal military containers in the trunks of all three Oldsmobiles. We finally started on our trip towards Hemingway's yacht.

When we arrived at the *Pilar*, Che yelled, "Ahoy! Can we come on board, Captain?"

A different voice from Hemingway's replied, "Welcome aboard." It was a thirty- or forty-foot yacht. A man with a Spanish nose and large ears who wore a first mate's hat introduced himself as Gregorio Fuentes. He received us with a broad smile and embraced Che as if he saw him frequently, perhaps on daily visits. He had a huge Havana cigar in his mouth. He said to all of us, "Ernest is not going to take too long. He's changing his clothes."

Gregorio was a man of medium height and had a great sense of humor, as I discovered later on. He had been by Hemingway's side for many years. He was of Spanish origin, born in Lanzarote in the Canary Islands. He started his life as a fisherman at the age of ten, next to his father. He emigrated to Cuba permanently when he was 22 years old.

Montauk: The Lightning Chance

When Hemingway finally came up on deck from his cabin, he walked around with a bottle of Cinzano Vermouth.

Figure 39 Ernest Hemingway's Yacht **Pilar**

He yelled to Che, "Come over, I have an ice-cold double daiquiri for you and me," he held up the bottle. "We have to celebrate today."

Che abandoned helping load the boxes from the trucks to the yacht. He said to me, "This old man is always looking for a holiday to celebrate to excuse his drinking. These capitalists think they have everything in life all with a simple bottle of liquor." He turned and left us as we unloaded all that stuff and climbed the stairs onto the yacht.

It was my intention to continue helping transfer the heavy metal munitions boxes. It made me think twice when I tried to lift it but found I could barely lift one corner. This caught my attention. Havana cigars indeed! Unless they were all made of lead, there was no way they could be so heavy! One of the guys smiled. "It's too heavy for *me*, let alone a young guy like you!"

There were six bodyguards and they made it look routine, like they knew exactly where they were going. They were continually looking around to make sure there were no curious eyes watching as they worked. I detected something sinister in all of this. I became curious to learn what this old writer had to do with this cargo.

Che yelled for me. "Commandantico, come on over!"

I lost my opportunity to open the one box at that moment, since I was alone. I had to go as he beckoned. I went up on deck, and Hemingway offered me a virgin daiquiri. I asked him if he had any Grand Marnier on board. He looked at me curiously and smiled. "Of course! I have every kind of liquor on here. You are fancy, Commandantico, and you've already educated your palate!"

"I don't want to brag. I lost my alcohol virginity today when my uncle, the doctor I told you about, Che, and I had breakfast this morning. We made a toast for a free Cuba with a better future for all. He knows I love orange juice, and he suggested that, since I was a minor and it was fermented oranges, it would be OK for me to have."

Hemingway said, "Well, if your uncle allowed you to drink that, let's make a Grand Marnier daiquiri!"

"That could not be a better drink," I said. "Daiquiris are made from lemons, and Grand Marnier's from orange, they're both in the citrus family."

Hemingway grinned. "Your analysis, Commandantico, is perfect. Even I will try that delicious-sounding cocktail. Shall we call it after you?"

"Whatever you wish, sir. You're the host here."

"Perfect! I want one for myself. Gregorio, make three. No, make a whole pitcher, so you can give some to the bodyguards, too!"

Gregorio looked at him in surprise and slightly confused. He smiled and said, "Hiyo, Captain! I'll be back in a few minutes." He saluted Hemingway. He looked over at a black man, possibly Jamaican from his looks, who was in his late 40's with a white beard and similar build. "Hey, Dagoberto—give me a hand with this, will you?"

He smiled. "Sure thing, man. Right behind you." He turned to me and said, "Commandantico—I'm a huge fan of yours. I have a boy about your age who would like to join your Commandos. Could you please give me a recommendation?"

I said, "Sure. Let me know his name and I'll make arrangements for him."

Dagoberto smiled and saluted me. He saluted Hemingway as well and followed Gregorio below.

Montauk: The Lightning Chance

"I feel like you guys, because even Gregorio has a military attitude towards me all the time. He never did before."

Figure 40 Hemingway and Gregorio

Gregorio returned a few minutes later with the pitcher of Grand Marnier daiquiris. He started to leave, and Hemingway said, "Wait—what did you put in these?"

Gregorio hesitated. "Well, I added the pulp from the oranges I squeezed to get the juice and mixed it in the whole thing."

"Oh! That is delicious, Commandantico! That is exquisite. You made an extraordinary discovery today." He turned to Che. "This kid is a genius!"

"Oh, don't say that! Fidel said that a little while ago. Soon he'll have an ego we can't fit on your yacht!" I grew embarrassed.

I said, "No egos allowed in my head, sir."

Hemingway asked Gregorio, "Did you take care of the escort?"

Che noticed my embarrassment and touched my shoulder. "Hey, man—I have to grant you something. You don't have to be embarrassed. I was just joking about all those compliments. Enjoy. Wherever we go, if you make this impression on people, keep doing it. That will open a lot of doors."

They both smiled and pointed at me. Che said to Hemingway, "We cannot deny that the new generation is better than us. This kid possesses the fountain of youth! We have to hang around him more." Che took my beret off and mussed my hair. That was the first time Che made such a friendly gesture with me. I didn't know if the alcohol was working on him or if it was all the compliments. I never saw him be so familiar with anyone else. I looked at the jar of Grand Marnier daiquiris and started to think that it might be creating a good effect on him as it was putting his guard down. I contemplated carrying a small bottle of Grand Marnier with me to pour into his drinks.

I kept my glass half full all the time. Every time Hemingway or Gregorio refilled it I surreptitiously poured half the contents overboard when they weren't watching. The fish in the sea would have a good time dancing Jamba and sleep well that night.

An hour or two passed, and Che passed out, snoring as he leaned back in one of the deck chairs. I asked Hemingway, "Where is the bathroom?"

"Right there," Hemingway said as he pointed overboard. "Oh, no—I don't think it would be either appropriate or comfortable for me to defecate over the side of your yacht."

"Oh!" he said, raising his arms high. He pointed to the stairs down towards the cabins. "Your friend Che is sleeping like a hibernating bear." I smiled and stood up. I walked towards the stairs and Hemingway said, "Che is a lightweight! He's snoring like a train."

I smiled and shook my head as I looked at Che snoring away with a cigar dangling from his mouth. Gregorio took it gently from his mouth and put it in the ash tray. I emptied the remnants of my cup overboard while they were distracted. Then I went down to use the bathroom, thanking Hemingway again for his kindness.

I looked through all the cabins, but I could not find the boxes that had been loaded in. All I knew for certain was that they didn't contain cigars. I opened one door and found myself face to face with one of the bodyguards. He was a little tipsy as the daiquiris had their effect. I wondered where they had hidden them, and asked the soldier, "Where is the cleanest bathroom?"

"The cleanest one, of course, Commandantico, is the Captain's bathroom. Over there."

I went where he pointed towards. I went in but held the door open a crack to watch his movements. I watched him go up on deck. I jumped out of the cabin and went straight for the door I saw him putting the small vanity in. I didn't close the door completely as I went in. I saw a sign that read in red and white letters "Electrical Room." I thought that it was no wonder I couldn't find the boxes. I was checking the cabins and it was in the Electrical Room. I opened the small vanity and saw it was full of large, beautiful diamonds. I pulled my pen out and

Montauk: The Lightning Chance

took pictures. I opened each of the other containers, which had no locks, just spring latches. One was filled with bars of gold. Another was full of golden tableware and goblets. I wondered why a famous writer like Ernest Hemingway would have anything to do with this.

I was closing the last container, pen in my right hand, when I heard the door behind me creak open. Hemingway's voice said sternly, "What the devil are you doing here, Commandantico?"

I turned fast as lightning and said quickly, "I just encountered one of the bodyguards when I left the bathroom. I was wondering what he was doing in the electrical room. My curiosity was sparked and thought it didn't make any sense for them to be in this particular room."

He was taken by surprise. He couldn't understand how I could fabricate a story so rapidly, so he figured it must have been sincere. I used the confusion to put the pen away in my shirt pocket to hide it from his view. I thought I had convinced him, as he had remained frozen in silence.

He surprised me by stepping forward rapidly and snatching the pen out of my pocket. Without saying a word, he began to examine it with a sarcastic smile on his face. After a few seconds of silence, he looked me in the face seriously. "This purpose of this pen isn't just writing. You can fool anyone else, but not *me* specifically. This is the most advanced technology possessed only by very sophisticated assets that exist within the intelligence community. Do you have any logical explanation for your having one?"

I smiled and returned his gaze with the same level of seriousness. The only difference was that I frowned slightly. "Oooh! I don't know where you have pulled this out of, maybe a theory from some spy thriller you are writing now? Do you intend to release it soon?"

He didn't smile in the slightest. But he was distracted by my taunting oohs, and I was able to snatch it back out of his hand even faster than he had taken it from me. He was taken completely by surprise. He lunged towards me but stopped as I stepped back and went for my pistol with my right hand, unsnapping the bond as I did so. At the same time, I stowed the pen in my campaign pants with my left hand. He realized that I was faster than him and was already prepared to draw. He paused and shook his head in wonderment with a tinge of admiration at my audacity and the quickness of movement that surprised the old writer. He nodded and smiled. "What you just did confirmed to me that you really are a spy and very well trained in that business." I smiled and did not reply. I wasn't about to admit to this. He asked, "Who are you working for? Maybe we're working for the same entity. Are you working for the KGB? CIA? Or MI-6 British intelligence?"

I said, "Are you?"

He grinned at me broadly. He shook his head and changed his aggressive tone to a more persuasive one. "You know better than anyone, I believe, that I cannot let you get out of here with that pen full of evidence. Right?" He nodded to encourage my agreement.

I smiled again. This time I put tucked leather peace bond on my pistol on the inner side and let the pistol ride half-drawn in my holster. I stepped back once more and said with strong conviction, "I don't believe that you or anyone can prevent that happening. In order to satisfy your curiosity, I should tell you that the answer is 'no' to both questions you asked me before. I don't work for anyone, only for my conscience in defense of my democratic principles and the freedom of my country. The second question is no, too. I've never been trained by anyone. Believe it or not, today is my first day. As you know, I'm very young, possibly still in diapers in whatever you call the spy business. Of course, this is me assuming, as you just did, about me being a spy, but in truth you are the real spy here. That's called diversion, and that's why you tried to put the blame on me to detour my attention." Hemingway reached into the right pocket of his white guayabera that half-covered his white linen shorts. He took out a pen identical to the one I had. I immediately pointed at him with my left hand and exclaimed, "Ah, ha!" My right hand remained on the handle of my pistol.

He scratched his forehead with his left hand in a gesture of deep worry. "I think we're both in a dark cul-de-sac. I can't allow you to get out of here with that pen. This will put my life in danger as well as the lives of my family. It will destroy my cover. Do you want to be responsible for my death?" I said nothing but looked at him seriously. "And you, on the other hand, could simply be a patriot that is defending his country and need that evidence to expose the corruption within this supposedly-moralist socialist or communist, whatever the devil you want to call it, government. I cannot explain to you why I'm doing what I'm doing for the same reason I know you cannot trust me and tell me who you really are, your reasons, or motives."

I smiled and replied, "I think you are in a very tremendous error. I will manage to get out of here, one way or another, for sure, whether you want it or not, with this pen. I have several weapons to make that happen. Some of them you don't even have a clue of what they are. Don't think this gun is the only weapon I have." I patted the handle of my pistol. All I have to do is put a bullet in your head right now, and the rest of the evidence is in your own hand. I can say that I discovered that you were really a spy for the CIA. Who do you think is not going to believe my story, with my reputation and the absolute trust and confidence I enjoy from the most important leaders of the revolution? Remember that your part in the story will never be heard, just like a book that was never published, because you'll be dead. Of course, that is the last alternative I would want to use. I enjoy life, embrace it, and the idea of taking the life of any other human being to me would be unpleasant. I'm not like Che."

"I know." He nodded.

"And I don't really want to stain my hands with your blood unless you leave me no other choice on such a beautiful day like today. Especially not after all the beautiful beginning to our friendship in which I introduced you to a new cocktail, an orange daiquiri a la Marmol." My voice grew grave in my sincerity. "That would fill my spirit with tremendous sadness. But que sera sera. What will be will be."

He looked at me and saw both the determination and sincerity in my face. His expression changed as he stroked his forehead with his left fingers of extreme worry. "I believe I have a solution if you want to hear it and decide to help me."

I looked deeply into his eyes. "Everything depends on you now. It also depends on the solution you want to propose to me. Of course, I agree with you in one thing: it is like a cul-de-sac. But you are mistaken in that it is not so for both of us; only for you. From my heart I tell you this now: I would prefer it tremendously if you stayed on deck, guarding the sleeping, Satanic Che. Not long ago he put a bullet in the head of his best friend right in front of my eyes. A few minutes later he was eating a sandwich like nothing had happened and dropped his friend's body with the corpses who had tried a few moments earlier to kill him. Can you imagine if he would do that to his best friend and confidant what he would do to you if it even remotely crosses his mind that you are an agent for the CIA?"

He looked at me, his worry increasing as he turned white. He looked me up and down. Finally, he realized that he was not going to be able to deceive me as well as the seriousness of his situation. What had initially looked to him like catching me red-handed now had turned against him entirely. He now felt like he was a mouse caught in a trap. He could see no exit that would be of benefit to him. He was an intelligent man who loved life and its pleasures, especially young, beautiful women and delicious cocktails, so he said, "My solution to this problem is to ask you for us to both be rational. Of course, I don't want to die with a bullet in my head on this beautiful day. What I've seen here I can ignore like it never happened. You can take your pen, but I need to ask you for a big favor. Please hold on that information for the next seven days. That way you give me the opportunity to cover my bases without putting the lives of myself or my family at risk." He grew melancholy and added, "This is a big favor, I know. When you need to ask me one in return, I will be more than glad to return it to you in any circumstance that you ask for."

"Seven days? Beginning today?"

"No. Beginning tomorrow. Today is almost over."

I stroked my chin with my left hand and thought that over for a bit. I needed to make sure I didn't compromise myself. But I thought I had plenty of information from the Chinese present in a different pen. "I can delay this," I said. "I don't want to break any records on my first day." I definitely didn't want my uncle to feel ashamed. "Not a single word about this to anyone, absolutely."

"Of course."

"You give me your word of honor that you will fulfill our agreement here?"

He smiled a little. "Of course. For your security and mine, it will be stupid and improper of me to repeat anything that happened here today."

I nodded. "Very well. This is a pact of honor between you and I."

He held out his right hand. "Thank you very much. I will never forget this. I see now that everything that has been said about you, in both the good circles and the bad, accurately describe the caliber of the great young man you are. I would be grateful if you could consider me your friend one day."

"I assure you, if you honor our pact to the end of the seven days, I might consider you my friend. To me, nothing is more important in life than loyalty and honor in any person, man or woman. In my eyes, a person who is disloyal and cannot keep a secret or an agreement has no value as a human being."

Hemingway looked me in the eyes this time with gratitude and respect. I could see his sincerity. "The enemies of my enemies aren't always my friends. But at least sometimes they can come to be my associates. In your case, I believe I will break that rule. I think that you and I can be great friends. Between us are certain feelings and principles of decency. To prove that to you, I want to meet with you at the end of the seven days at the address I will give you now in Old Havana: La Bodeguita del Medio. I know the Minister of the Interior, Piñeiro, has been harassing and bugging you for a while. I will put in your hands the information about something horrible that he's done behind the backs of Fidel and the other leaders. They have no idea about it. I assure you that after you let him know you have something detrimental to him, he never will bother you again. That is what we in the intelligence community call a very solid insurance policy. Piñeiro, knowing that you possess that information is your security that he will never—listen to me carefully—*never* bother you again." He had a sarcastic smile on his face and attitude as he spoke.

I smiled this time. "You don't have to admit anything to me. Now I know for a fact, after what you just said, that you work with intelligence. I don't know if it's CIA or some other agency, but you work with American intelligence, whatever name you want to give it. Not too long ago I heard that expression from the lips of someone I have great respect and trust for, and he's an old fox, a master spy in the arts of intelligence." Hemingway started to speak to correct himself, but I raised both arms high to stop him. "You don't have to worry about it, I assure you of this, and I understand perfectly. We just met and don't know each other. The principal business of intelligence is to verify, verify again, and then before you trust, verify one more time. I learned this in the past months as I told you before, from somebody I absolutely have confidence in. You don't have to worry about anything—your secret is safe with me as if you had just put it in a safety deposit box."

He stayed silent, understanding what I had been telling him. He knew he couldn't take back what he had said. I wouldn't accept another false excuse. With a smile he said, "Commandantico, I have to tell you something. No matter who your teacher is, he has taught you very well."

I smiled again. "I'll repeat to you that I just lost my virginity very recently. I've had only one lesson. I'm in my first grade of elementary school."

Hemingway shook his head rapidly and emphatically. "Well, taking what you say for granted and accepting it, I will have a great and wonderful pleasure to have you by my side when you graduate from high school. Of course, never as an enemy, but as a good friend!"

We both smiled at each other in friendly fashion. He said, "In seven days, the carnival will begin right here in Havana. We will meet at 8 pm in La Bodeguita del Medio in Old Havana."

"Very well. I will be there as I always do with meetings, a little early."

He put an arm on my shoulder. "I know. You don't have to swear to me. I assure you that I am the same way."

"I believe that we should go on deck. The last thing either of us want is to create any suspicions in the sinister mind of Che. This sulfurous character has the sense of smell of a jackal and the mind of a poisonous snake. The last thing we want is for one of his diabolic nightmares to cross his mind, especially after what Fidel showed me today. It will be exceedingly difficult to keep any secret even in your mind. The Chinese have created a machine that they have either copied or stolen. More properly they stole it because they never create anything. Probably from some capitalist country, that is of course what they do all the time. The communists steal our work, our ideas, our freedom, they are masters in the art of stealing, hypocrisy, and deception."

He looked at me in surprise. "What do you mean when you talk about reading minds? You're telling me that they can read your mind?"

I looked at him. I understood it wasn't appropriate for me at that moment to talk about, neither the time nor the place. "I don't believe that we should talk about this here. I understand your curiosity." I looked at my watch. "I repeat—we should go up on deck immediately."

He understood both my rush and worry and said, "OK."

We went up the stairs onto the deck. We were in for a surprise. Che looked like he was just waking up and was furious. He screamed obscenities at the top of his lungs at Silvano, the man who was presently in charge of his escort. He screamed about being an hour late to a meeting he was to have with Fidel and other leaders in the beautiful, opulent Russian embassy.

We said our goodbyes to Hemingway since Che didn't want to delay further because of his nap. The victim came to be Silvano, even though the only one at fault was Che himself. He was the one who drank too much. Even an illiterate who lacked even the most rudimentary education without medical studies in his life knows when you drink alcohol to excess you fall asleep for several hours. That allows the lungs and blood circulation to have enough time to remove the alcohol-contaminated blood from the brain. I wondered where this man had studied medicine. Maybe, like his friend Fidel who never attended his law classes (as my uncle and Dr. Sayaz-Bazan told me), he always got 100's in his courses at gunpoint. I also pondered something more sinister, if it could be when the change of bodies took place during that diabolic ritual, maybe since Hitler had no medical training something had gotten lost in the brain. In the end, I could not make any sense regarding this sinister assassin because his own life had no logic or meaning at all.

On the way back to the Prime Minister's office, Che continually talked bad about the old gringo capitalist though he had spent almost all afternoon drinking and enjoying the orange daiquiri. But his egotistic personality made him act in a very strange manner. He was completely humiliated just because he had fallen asleep. Maybe he blamed the writer for his own weakness to drink to excess. He was worried about the impression in his mind that it had given the rest of us when he woke up and realized that his cigar was perfectly placed in an ashtray. This told him that somebody had taken his cigar out of his mouth while he slept, and it was killing him inside. I had never seen him drink so much alcohol before, especially to the point of passing out. He was very meticulous about his image and what was presented to others. He only drank in moderation wine or maté. It looked like the sweet cognac in the Grand Marnier didn't let him realize how much he was drinking. He lost count as to how many cocktails he had. I was myself a little tipsy, but was in control, like Hemingway; but it was an unfair comparison since the author had been a drinker all his life.

Figure 41 The Vedado

When we finally reached the Vedado, I stepped out of the Oldsmobile. I felt a profound release, not just from the ugly smell that always accompanied Che, but also the agony of his repetitious obsession about the whole incident which had been unceasing since we left the yacht. He rolled the window down and said to me, "I'm sorry, Commandantico. It was not my intention to fall asleep like a perfect idiot."

I smiled. "Don't let that bother you so much. If you want, the next time I see you like that, I'll wake you up. I didn't do it this time out of respect because I believed you might not have slept well last night, and I wanted to let you rest to recuperate your energies."

"Thank you. The old Hemingway probably burst out laughing as I was snoring there sleeping like an imbecile," he said resentfully. He went silent, looking me in the eyes, waiting for an answer. I seriously shook my head but maintained my silence. That's all he got from me. After a few seconds, he gave up, and raised his right hand and said, "I know that you don't like to repeat what you hear in conversation with other people when we're not present." He scratched his head with his left hand. He pointed at me. "But you should remember that everything in life has exceptions, and your loyalty should be with me, OK? Not with that damned old man or anybody else."

I raised my right arm and pointed at him. "You should also remember, because this is extremely important for me, that is not to confuse loyalty with gossip. I resent that, because I am very loyal, but no one, without exception, ever will convert me into a gossip."

Che was struck mute by that. He stroked his mustache with the back of his left hand. "OK. See you later."

I replied in the same tone, "OK, see you later." I turned and ignored him completely.

As I left, I heard him say to the driver, "Go ahead, move!"

I paid no attention and went directly to my jeep where Cisneros and Daniel were patiently waiting for me. The sun was beginning to set, and the first shadows of the night were encroaching on us. I said, "Let's look for someplace to get something decent to eat. We'll be staying in the Havana Hilton tonight and will go back tomorrow to Pinar del Rio. I have to attend a military training there."

Daniel started the jeep and drove the few blocks from the Prime Minister's office to the Hilton. It was on 23rd Street and L Street at the corner, called La Rampa. This hotel practically was where Fidel and all his entourage slept, ate, and even conducted international business.

Since the first days at the beginning of the revolution, they took it over and served themselves like kings in the most luxurious hotel in Havana, even before it was nationalized. At the same time, the revolution criticized its opulence and luxury. It was not only the most expensive hotel in Havana, but also in all Hispanic America.

Figure 42 Havana Hilton, Later Havana Libre

No matter how much they criticized luxury, they loved it. They sold the Cuban people on their rhetorical slogan of taking them from the hands of the foreign imperialists and gringos. Nobody would ever get to know that it was nothing more than another communist lie to convince the useful fools. The 25-story hotel boasted 512 rooms and was built with money from the worker's union of the CTC[43] in Cuba. It was an investment the CTC made with the retirement funds for the national workers in the Cuban Catering Workers Union pension through the law firm of Wilton, Backer, and Associates along with the Cuban firm Arroyo and Menendez. Fidel, from the first day they entered Havana, grabbed the best suite, 2324, the Continental Suite, and never left it.

It was 3 kilometers from Old Havana. The Hilton company was only a licensee because of its international fame as a manager of luxury hotels around the world. When the communist government took this hotel, they didn't take it from the Hilton company. They took it from

---

[43] *Central de Trabajadores Cubanos,* or Central Cuban Workers

the workers and the retirement funds of the Cuban people, stealing from the CTC's retirement funds (and therefore from all the members of the syndicate) to enjoy for the personal use of all members of the government.

As I looked at all this opulence when we walked into the hotel, I said, "*Arriba los pobres del mundo y los esclavos sin pan. Y que viva la internacional.*[44] But yesterday, today, and tomorrow, if you don't have the dollars, you won't live in the Havana Hilton. Only the high entourage of the communist government can stay in this luxurious, beautiful hotel while the Cuban people don't even have the most necessary essentials for living, including toilet paper. This is the proletariat paradise of Cuba and the new Paradise on Earth that the communists promise to everyone!"

As members of the government elite, we got one of the suites that could easily sleep ten people. The Cuban government had taken two complete floors. If any of these suites weren't sufficient for the Soviet embassy, then the changing alleged alliances were now evident. The state and its name eventually changed to Havana Libre in 1960. History had been changed by a group of bandits with no scruples and the worst intentions right in front of my eyes.

We went to the cafeteria to check the menu. They had several luxury restaurants, but since in the cafeteria one got served quickly with still-delicious menus, we decided on that as our first choice. If we didn't care for the menu, we would go to a restaurant. We sat down and opened the menu. It had everything to satisfy even the most refined, discerning palate. I asked for scallops in garlic butter with congri and fried yucca, and asparagus salad with tomatoes, onions, and avocado. Daniel asked for fried chicken with French fries and a spinach salad with avocado. Cisneros settled on a huge T-bone steak fricassee style, white rice, and black beans.

After we finished our exquisite meal, we went across the street to the Cinerama movie theatre on 23rd Street. They were showing *Casablanca* with Humphrey Bogart, Lauren Bacall, and Ingrid Bergman. We enjoyed it very much, and after it finished, we were tired from the long day. We went back to our suite to retire for the day and rest.

I woke up around 5:30 in the morning. I had been tossing and turning the entire night as I thought about my conversation with

---

[44] Leave the poor of the world and the slaves without bread. Long live the international communists!

Montauk: The Lightning Chance

Hemingway and what I had found on his yacht, *Pilar*. An idea had been rolling around my head all night. I jumped out of bed and took a quick shower. I left a note for Daniel and Cisneros that I would be leaving with the jeep. They were to take their breakfast and do whatever they wanted to do. I would be back for lunch and meet them at the suite then. I left and took one of the elevators. By chance I encountered the Soviet ambassador and his bodyguards, who I had already met on different occasions. They greeted me in a friendly manner.

I was shocked because I had to cover my nose discretely with the back of my hand; those men smelled exactly like Che. For a minute I started to think they had a meeting with him and their proximity to his unpleasant odor of rotten garlic and sulfur mixed with rotten fish had impregnated their clothing. When I got out of the elevator and could breathe again, as they filed past me one at a time and said goodbye, I realized that my theory was incorrect. There was no way they could have that odor cling to them so perceptibly simply by being in proximity to him. Each of them, without exception, had that same odor. I wondered if those men could be possibly disciples of Satan as well, like my uncle Emilio had told me. I thought anything was possible, especially after what Che had shown me the day before and how they were taking billions of dollars from the national treasury. Though it was supposedly taken from the wealthy and super rich in Cuba but the undeniable thing in my mind was the fact that this wealth was not being redistributed to the poor as they had promised to do. Now it had been put into the hands of this old writer from North America, Heaven knew for what purpose, The useful fools like my father had let themselves be brainwashed and served as the ladder to obtain the vast political power they enjoyed now. I wondered how it was possible that the less than one percent of the population enjoyed now all the fruit of the work of everyone in the country without working themselves for even a day. They never bothered to consider that their extreme left-wing ideas had never properly functioned in any part of the world where they had dared to change the political system for a socialist or communist one.

I shook my head as I jumped into the jeep and drove towards my uncle's house on Carlos III. I could fulfill the visit that Che had interfered with the day before. They possessed an enormous residence that his wife had inherited. Since he was an attorney and highly intelligent, like my uncle Emilio, I had a plan that had been rolling around in my head all night. They might be able to help me put it in motion. I had a mischievous smile on my face as I thought about it.

Dr. Julio Antonio del Marmol

I arrived at the house and parked the jeep in the street. They had a few cars in the driveway, and I didn't want to block anyone in. All the residences on that block looked opulent. With their colonial style construction, they looked like they had all been built in the 18th century and designed by the same architect. The one my uncle lived in was different because of the two large lion statues at the entrance to the porch of the house. They were the Marmol lions, and whoever the sculptor was who made them there could be no doubt in anyone's mind that he was extraordinarily talented. The lions were made from marble but looked like real lions that sat on the porch to protect the inhabitants from intruders. I smiled because the significance of those lions didn't end as decoration for that beautiful residence. There was something deeper in the emotional structure of the family. They signified the union of the two families Marmol and Lion. I rang the colonial bell, which was so loud you could hear its clanging clear out in the back porch. My uncle Pancho opened the door with a genuine smile of joy on his face. My aunt Violeta embraced me as did my uncle immediately—much differently from how my uncle Emilio had received me. It felt good to be loved by my family again, even if they didn't sympathize with the revolution.

I was immediately invited inside. It had been a while since we had seen each other, and after we sat in the living room for a time, being recounted about my mischievous life as a younger kid, the things I had said, some of them unbelievable even to myself. This was like something out of a science fiction story. Initially, they thought that I had a great futuristic imagination. Later they discovered, like the rest of the family, that I truly possess very deep and powerful gifts from Nature and God. I could see things before they happen.

As an example, Aunt Violeta related a tale from when I was about five years old. My Aunt Violeta was holding me in her lap after I had eaten. I fell asleep with my head on her belly. Nobody knew that she was pregnant at the time as it was in the very beginning of her term. When I woke up, I started to cry unconsolably. The entire time I was sleeping my head had been pillowed on her belly. She pled with me to say why I was crying so badly, she wanted to know what I had been dreaming and what would devastate me so profoundly. I resisted telling her, saying I didn't want to make her cry like I was. That was simple and short but the only answer she got from me. Every member of the family had tried to calm me down, even Mima and Majito.

Montauk: The Lightning Chance

After they left the house that day, I confessed to Mima that she would have a baby boy, and they would be very happy with that. When Mima asked how I knew, I said that I had played ball with him, but that he wouldn't live very long. He would die a little boy. Mima tried to console me by telling me in concern not to worry and that it was just a bad dream. Even though I was only five years old, I stood up angrily and I replied firmly that it was not a bad dream or anything like that. I *had* played ball with him, and he told me that he would die. I saw him die. Both Pancho and Violeta would try to protect him by isolating him in his room far away from everyone, covering their mouths with masks each time they walked into the room. This was all to protect him from any virus or bacteria. They forced every member of the family who came to visit him to wear masks before entering his room. With this excess of care, they both without realizing it wound up depriving him of bacteria in his body and just a simple cold would kill him. His immune system wasn't allowed to develop, and so he couldn't survive, and that was the reason for his death. At that young age and with that tragic incident, I had my first lesson to understand how nothing extreme was good. If the temperature is too high, you melt. If it is too low, you freeze. An excess of love killed my cousin.

After I spent a few hours with Pancho and Violeta, they invited me to have breakfast with them. We finished and my uncle and I went back to the living room because I had said I wanted to discuss something I needed his help with in private. We sat on the long colonial sofa and he turned his record player on so that no one could listen in on our conversation. "The only way we can speak in confidence is to play the music loud," he explained

He put Chopin's "Revolutionary Étude" on. I explained to him what I needed from him, and the del Marmol gesture with the fingers of his left hand rubbing his forehead was displayed for a few seconds. Without hesitation he raised his right hand and said, "I'm willing to help you, but the only thing I'm going to ask you is not to tell me wants inside those containers."

He took a key from his keyring and handed it to me. "This is the gate key. You can come in the back without knocking on the house and no one will know what you're doing. You can enter through the entry on the left gate, which I will leave open. Go all the way to the back of the patio, to the maid's quarters. Of course, they're empty since, as you know, I lost my job because the revolution needs no more attorneys. They nationalized the firm I worked at and let me go. I was offered a job as the tender for the elevator for an alternate job. What a change from being the senior partner in the firm! Of course, I could no longer afford servants anymore, but don't worry about us. We'll survive as long as we can with our savings. You can put whatever you want in that room. The only condition is that I don't want to know what's in them. That way I have no responsibility for what's there, as it belongs to you."

"OK, fair enough. I give you my word of honor not only to not tell you but no one what I have in there. Whatever I put in there will be my sole responsibility."

"Very well." He extended his hand as he stood up. I stood, we shook hands and embraced.

"Thank you. I have to go. Time passes quickly in great company, and it's already noon, and I got up at 5:30 this morning. I can't believe it." I shook my head and smiled.

He said, "It's true. Time passes very quickly when we have a great time. It passes very slowly when we have problems or unpleasant company in our lives. If you think the time passed fast now, at your age, wait until you get to be my age, and you'll see that time is like a supersonic jet."

I smiled. "Thank you again for your trust. After I finish moving the stuff, I'll return this key to you." I showed him the key.

He shook his head and waved it off. "That key is yours. No one else has any copies, not even me, so make sure you don't lose it. That place is yours from now on. Whatever you put in there is your property, and no one has any business going in there from now on. Only you should have access to your property."

I smiled and thanked him once more for his generosity. Aunt Violeta came to the front when she saw us walking to the door. She said, "Remember, Julio Antonio, I don't care what you do with your life, whether you want to be in the military or be a minister. This is your house, and no government, political ideas, or religion can ever break these beautiful ties that are stronger than anything—our blood. Because this is the indestructible love tie that God and Jesus Christ offer to us."

I nodded and smiled as I embraced her in a bear hug. I murmured in her ear, "I am a hundred percent in agreement with you. God bless you both and thank you for your trust and love. That includes the exquisite breakfast you offered me today."

We all three laughed and I left the house. I jumped in the jeep and waved to them once more as I drove off. As I drove back to the Hilton, I stopped at a liquor store near the Theatre Astral on Infanta

Montauk: The Lightning Chance

Street. I got out of the jeep and walked by a group of teenagers by the liquor store that kept looking at me strangely. They waved to me, at least pretending to be friendly, except for the largest, most muscular one, who looked me up and down jealously. I paid him no heed; I was already accustomed to this behavior in other kids my age or even older. Even though we were close in age, they had different ideas about the revolution. Most of them at the beginning of the revolution, admired the heroes who wore their hair and beards long. They had made the dictator leave Cuba and were supposed to return freedom to the country. They weren't used to seeing a young kid like me in a military uniform, my shiny, ostentatious pistol on the right side at my waist and the massive Commandos knife I had on the other side, along with my long hair. They might have assumed I was a son of one of the big honchos in the revolution or that I had been in the mountains. Some of them looked at me with admiration and curiosity. I wondered what they would think if they knew how I felt about the admired leaders of the revolution who had actually sold their souls to the Devil in order to keep power forever.

They might not look at me with admiration now if they knew that. They would look at me with the same look of revulsion I wanted to show after being by Fidel and Che's side for all that time. I looked on them as thieves of that beautiful idea of the great revolution to turn it around and make a communist one. I walked into the liquor store, the small bells at the top of the glass door tinkling to announce my arrival. I greeted the man cordially as he welcomed me courteously. I asked him if he had any Grand Marnier.

He was about thirty years old with a receding hairline; what hair was left was salt and pepper. "How many bottles do you want? I have to keep it locked up, so the kids don't walk out with bottles hidden in their clothing. It's very expensive."

I smiled and shook my head. "We still have juvenile delinquents like that, eh? I thought by now the revolution would have cleaned them out."

"No, my Commander. Look at the bums outside. I have to hose them out like flies around the pie."

I smiled. "Two big bottles, please."

Even though I was underage, he didn't dare contradict me. He started to fold the bottles into some paper to cushion them against breakage. Very nonchalantly he asked, "A present for your friends, eh?"

"Yes, sir. One for Fidel, the Commander-in-Chief. The other is for Che."

The man gulped, extremely impressed. He looked like he was glad he hadn't given me a hard time. "My store is one of the few not yet taken by the government."

"You're lucky. Maybe they won't take small businesses away."

He crossed himself. "I've been praying that to God every night." He didn't dare ask me for age or ID. I paid the amount he told me.

I picked up my package and walked toward the glass door. I stopped for a second. There was a brick wall about four feet high outside the store. A car had pulled up in the street right outside, and the sun shining on the glass of the window turned it into a mirror. In that reflection I could see the muscular boy hiding there, holding something in his right hand. It looked very much like a sap to me, like the gangsters used in movies to hit someone in the head to rob him. I smiled. I put my bag on a pile of boxes that advertised Bacardi Añejo at a reduced price.

Very slowly, I opened the door. As I walked out of the door, as I expected, the boy lunged out towards me to hit me in the forehead. My left hand darted out, grabbing his wrist while my right wrapped around his neck. I spun halfway to put his body over my lower waist. With incredible speed, I twisted around, using his own strength and momentum against him, and he went flying through the glass door, skidding towards the boxes of liquor. He rolled around as some of the boxes fell on his head right before the eyes of all his friends, who were surprised at what they saw. The attendant of the store was also surprised. The boy was still stunned, cut from the glass of the door. I ducked through the shattered door and walked over to him. He looked at me in terror, his hand still clutching the sap. I took it from his hand. This time he offered no resistance. Tears filled his eyes.

He asked in a quavering voice, "Where did you learn that, kid?"

I looked at him angrily and said, "In my crib, idiot." I turned my back on him and went back to the attendant. I dropped the sap onto the counter. "Please call the police. They should give a lesson to this juvenile delinquent. He should be put in jail for a while. Maybe he'll learn a good lesson that could one day save his life in the future. If he tried that with someone like Che, I assure you that instead of you calling the police you would be calling the coroner to pick up his body."

The other seven or eight kids were looking through the broken door. Some of the teens looked proud that the bully learned a lesson. He might have been the leader of the group and had put them through some humiliation. Others, who perhaps sympathized with him, had

Montauk: The Lightning Chance

looks of terror. I picked up my bag with the Grand Marnier bottles and stepped through the broken door. I put it in the passenger's seat of the jeep. Some of them came over to me and gathered curiously behind me. They were close enough for me to feel uncomfortable, and I watched them in the reflection of the car's window. I unsnapped the peace bond on my pistol and noticed them jump back away from me. It could be they were the ones that sympathized with him, so I decided to give them a hard time.

I spun around. I had noticed a snake coming out of the sewer grate heading towards a tree to the left of the liquor store's door. I grabbed my Commando knife in my right hand and threw it in the direction of the kids. It hit in the center of the snake's body just below its head, pinning it to the tree it was climbing. It flopped around wildly, trying hopelessly to escape. The other teens were petrified, their mouths gaping open. The only motion they made was to step back away from me. Their eyes had been glued on me, and so none of them had seen the snake. As soon as they saw the snake pinned to the tree by my huge knife, they remained with their backs against the wall in terror. I walked over to the tree, passing by them, took the knife out of the tree, and I flicked the snake off the blade in their direction at their feet. They ran in different directions to put some distance between them and the reptile, which still weakly flopped around on the sidewalk as it died. Those who weren't against the wall before were now welded to it.

I walked over to them and said, "These summer days we have to be extremely careful and keep your eyes open. All these reptiles come out of the sewers and holes looking for fresh air. We never know when one of those could be poisonous and could hurt us."

They had no answer for me. Two police cars arrived on the scene at that moment. The sergeant in one of the cars got out and saluted me. He asked me, "Who of these delinquents tried to rob you?"

"No, no, officer. These kids had nothing to do with what happened." I pointed at the door of the store, where the attendant was bringing the boy out with his hands tied behind him. The attendant handed the sap to the officer.

He said, "This delinquent tried to attack the Commandantico right here in front of my business door. Look what he did to it! Evidently he took the wrong trolley."

The teen looked at him despitefully. "When I get out of jail, I will burn your business down, *hijo de puta*[45]!"

The sergeant grabbed him by the arm and shook him. "You stupid idiot! You just added several more years in prison by saying that in front of us. I now have the obligation of including that in my report."

I walked over to the big bully. "If you use that energy for something more positive and your brain for something more productive than the violence you have inside, maybe you can have something better in your life in the future."

"Fuck you!" he spat at me.

I put all my strength and with one hand grabbed him by the testicle while with my other hand I grabbed him firmly by the chin. I looked into his eyes, bring my face close to his. His eyes were bugging out of their sockets from the strength of my grip on his testicles. "You don't have any manners or decency at all. You are a royal jerk. You had better take care of these in prison. It's very possible that when you get out of there you will want to change your sex. I know what kind of people are in prison. Let's hope that doesn't happen to you. After you get out of there, pray that I never find you in front of my favorite liquor store in Havana. Because if I do, I will cut your testicles with this big knife and hang them around your neck with one of the laces from your shoe. Especially if you are so stupid as to start a fire in this store." I released his face and testicles at the same time, and he sighed in relief.

Most of the other teens were laughing at him. Those who had been his victims enjoyed seeing him get a taste of his own medicine. The sergeant looked at me and grinned. "Thank you, Commandantico. I think we'll need you around these areas some more."

The owner of the liquor store also thanked me. I said to the sergeant, "I will stop by later to sign my testimony for your report. Where are you guys taking him?"

"To the First Precinct."

"OK. I'll be there a little later. I have to attend to something important right now."

"Very well, Commandante. Take all the time you want. This jerk isn't going anywhere." He handed the kid off to one of the other officers, who handcuffed him and put him in the back of the car. "I completely assure you, wherever this kid goes, he will spend a long summer and winter vacation."

---

[45] Son of a whore

CHAPTER 14: THE GENTLEMAN OF PARIS AND HIS CONNECTIONS

After I said goodbye to the sergeant and his officers and thanked the owner of the liquor store, I signaled to the teenagers with my hand. Some looked at me in gratitude—at least those who were smart enough to realize I had just kept them out of trouble with the police. They saluted me like they were themselves in the military. That gave me a great feeling of satisfaction because I knew I had reached them. The rest were a lost cause, and there was nothing I could do for them.

I remembered what Mima once told me when I had been nominated to be the Commander-in-Chief of the Commandos. Something happened with an old friend of my father's who was stopped because he drove through the street work we were doing without listening to me or my Commandos. He was arrested, and I interfered to get him out of trouble with the police without knowing about his relationship to my father. That man later investigated the family I came from and felt really embarrassed to discover whose son I was. He paid my father a visit at our home to thank him so much for having raised such a great, fair man. He wanted to apologize to me again for being so abrupt in such an unnecessary fashion. Mima was very proud of me and said, "Never do any damage or hurt anyone, and never abuse your position of power. This will keep you always clean. It doesn't matter what government you're in, and no one will ever hate you. You will always be loved and receive sincere gratitude because you're not vindictive even when they do something wrong to you. Just as you did with this man by defending him against the criminal indictments the police wanted to charge just for a traffic violation. He was disrespecting you in front of the lieutenant in charge of the traffic in this province without knowing who you are. He let his hatred for the revolution blind him because it had taken away all his properties and businesses."

I shook my head and smiled. I thanked God and His Son, Jesus Christ, for giving me such decent parents, even though my father had such a hard head that not even the rails for the trolleys could compare to the thickness of his skull. I still loved him; in the end, nobody, even God isn't perfect. Even God made the mistake of creating Lucifer. God spent centuries, if not millennia, regretting the one mistake in calculation made by Him as the Supreme Architect of the Universe that brought so much suffering and damage to His masterpiece in the world, humanity.

I continued my trip back to the Hilton in thought. Even though I had absolute trust in Daniel and Cisneros in everything and every decision I made, I always liked to avoid involving my personal friends in things that were extremely risky, and what I intended to do was very dangerous and put their lives on the line. I never had any fear for my own life; perhaps it was an imbalance in my personality. Maybe God made me this way so that I could do the things I do. One day I might have an answer to that. One thing I know for certain, and that is that every problem I get into I will find a way out of, no matter how complicated the situation, sometimes a few scratches and broken bones; but they're *my* scratches and broken bones, not those of my friends. The last thing I want on my mind is even the idea that my friends could be arrested, harassed, create problems for their families, or at worst wind up before the firing squad because they were implicated in something that I decided to do. That to me was a huge responsibility. Unfortunately, what I had in mind to do I could not do myself because I did not at that age have the physical strength to move the boxes I intended to smuggle off Hemingway's yachts.

I shook my head in sad resignation. I made the decision that I found most appropriate and so when I arrived at the hotel, I took the elevators up to our suite where I found them luxuriously enjoying room service for breakfast. There were still two large jars, one of orange and one of grapefruit juice, on the table. They were watching a movie on TV direct by Billy Wilder and starring Marilyn Monroe, Tony Curtis, and Jack Lemmon: *Some Like It Hot*, the black and white romantic comedy.

I smiled and said, "Well, well—life is good in Havana, eh? While the Commander sweats his eyebrows off in the hot sun you guys, like the super-rich slaveowners, make the poor kid work his butt off while

Montauk: The Lightning Chance

they enjoy the lives of the rich and famous." They looked at me and started up. Daniel jumped up and switched the TV off. "For God's sake," I looked at my wristwatch, "I'm not in any rush at all. I had an exquisite, nutritious, and very happy breakfast with my aunt and uncle on Carlos III. If you prefer to continue watching that movie, we'll go to lunch later. I'm still full anyway. Our plans have changed a little. We're not going back to Pinar del Rio today. Probably the day after tomorrow. OK?"

They both nodded, and Daniel hurriedly put the TV back on. They looked at me with happy smiles. Cisneros said, "I'm not hungry at all."

Daniel agreed. "We ate breakfast very late because nobody woke us up."

I smiled. "You guys are getting spoiled. You're so used to me waking you up, and you're supposed to wake me up!"

I didn't want to bother them anymore. They were fascinated with the movie. They were like kids with a new toy and enjoyed it like kids loved Mickey Mouse. Both were large boys but were still very innocent-minded. Both came from broken families through divorce, and everything surrounding them now resulted in their viewing it as extraordinary and fascinating, something well outside of their wildest dreams given their extreme poverty. I thanked God in my heart for my being born in a happy home where we had everything we needed thanks to the effort, hard work, and sacrifice of my parents. I learned that in the last months of the revolution that not everyone had the fortune and blessing from God to be born with these privileges in their lives.

They made a space for me and I sat down between my good friends to watch that unusual movie with them. Our differences in race, social class, and education didn't matter. My two good friends, maybe because of the religious upbringing they received in their home from their mothers and grandparents and without any father figures since early childhood, had hearts the size of elephants in their way of conducting themselves and the feelings they had towards others. That is why I considered both of them my best friends. It is also why I had complete trust in them and was grateful for their friendship. We sat like the Three Musketeers as we watched the movies, and I put my arms around their shoulders. They smiled at me in gratitude for my gesture of affection.

For the next two hours, though I had missed the first twelve minutes of the movie, we sat in front of the TV laughing. When the movie finished, they told me the small piece at the start that I had missed.

Neither of them had a television in their homes, and so they were a little overwhelmed. We were hungry by now, so we left to get lunch.

We entered one of the elevators and headed to our favorite place in the hotel. We sat down and ordered the plate of the day, a *paella valenciana*. I brought them up to speed about what I had in mind to do. I told them that they could join with me in this or not. I needed them, but if they didn't want to, I would find someone else to do it. This would not involve a small risk—it involved serious, dangerous risk. They didn't even think twice. Without hesitating, they offered to help me in my next mission.

After we finished that delightful lunch we joked, Daniel especially liked to joke with Cisneros, and said, "Negro, did you enjoy that paella? The next month might be bread and water!"

Cisneros said, "Ah! Don't be such a pessimist!"

I said, "Guys, keep your mouths shut. You never know who might be listening."

Daniel said, "Sorry."

We went back up the elevators to the suite to go over the details of my plan to make sure everything was prepared accordingly. The sun was going down and night started to show her eyelashes. We left the hotel and drove towards Cojimar and the *Pilar*. By the time we arrived it was completely dark. We drove through the small marina and realized that not far from the yacht was the parking lot designated for the owners of the vessels moored there. We passed near a beautiful 1955 Ford Fairlane sedan with whitewall tires strategically parked two hundred feet away to watch the yacht. Inside were four men: members of Che's escort. It looked like these men were maintaining strict vigilance over the loot Che had deposited on Hemingway's yacht. I shook my head.

I said to my friends, "This looks like it's going to be a little more difficult than what I had imagined."

Daniel and Cisneros also noticed the car. They nodded. Daniel said, "Difficult, but not impossible."

I grinned. "Daniel, you made my evening. I'm very happy with your attitude."

Cisneros, to not sound like a pessimist, added, "You're right, Daniel. I'm in absolute agreement with you guys. Some things can result in difficulties, but nothing in life is at all impossible."

We all smiled. I said, "These guys should be a little more discreet and not be in a car so shiny that it can be seen for miles."

Montauk: The Lightning Chance

We drove by them and they recognized us. They waved and I saluted in return. We stopped near the yacht in the assigned parking spot for the owner of the vessel moored there. We left the jeep behind and approached the yacht.

Gregorio was walking around the craft on his routine and recognized me. He called out affectionately, "Hey, guys! How are you doing?"

I replied to his greeting. We walked onto the deck to have a new surprise there. Beneath the canopy, two more men of Che's escort lounged in deck chairs. They also recognized and greeted us. They were dressed in civilian clothes, white shorts and flowered tropical shirts. I smiled and put my arm around Gregorio and led him away from them in a friendly manner. I needed to do my job and get the details we required to get done what we had planned to do.

I asked him, "Where is the old wolf of the sea?"

"Ernest left very early this morning with Che. He told me he wouldn't be back until tomorrow evening. That's when we're scheduled to set sail for Costa Rica. You know, Santo Domingo, *Republica Dominicana.*" He grinned. "Thank God for these two guys Che left here, because I was going to take the night off. I'm supposed to stay here all the time, but I'm going to spend this beautiful, starry night with my wife at home." He pointed at the guards. "These poor sons of bitches have to stay here in the mist. They're here until we leave tomorrow evening. I'm going to rest up tonight so that I'll be reenergized for the trip. Those long voyages can take a toll on you."

"Yes, take your well-deserved rest. I see you work a lot here all the time. I've got something for the old man here." I opened the bag I had in my hand. I pulled out the 750 ml bottle of Grand Marnier. "Tell your captain that this is a little token of gratitude from me for his courtesy and good manners he showed me yesterday during my first visit to his yacht."

Gregorio clapped his hands twice rapidly. "I am in debt with you and very grateful to you. You took something off my shoulders. This large bottle you just brought will I think provide enough liquor for many orange daiquiris a la Marmol. Ernest has already added this delicious cocktail to his favorite and preferred drinks."

I smiled. Gregorio made it sound like it was a great honor to have my name added to the list of cocktails that Captain Hemingway preferred. We smiled at each other. "Why did you clap like that when I showed you the bottle?"

"Because he asked me to buy the biggest bottle of Grand Marnier I could find. You took one of my errands off my list. When I tell him it's a gift from you, he won't be able to say anything." We grinned and laughed.

I said goodbye to Gregorio and the escort, and we disembarked from the yacht. We walked along the marina towards our jeep silently. What had looked before to be exceedingly difficult appeared now to be almost impossible. Those two gorillas were sitting directly before the entry door that led down to the cabins where Che and Hemingway had their containers of loot stowed. I wondered how we were going to get anything out of there. I had no idea what the purpose they had for all that money. I just knew for a certainty that nothing good could come from it if Fidel and Che were involved. Hemingway continued to be a question mark to me.

As we walked along the pier, I said to Daniel and Cisneros, "In order to make this job work efficiently, we'll need all the help we can find."

They nodded. Cisneros said, "I'm going to suggest something, if you don't mind. I think you should leave me here with binoculars so I can check these people and keep my eyes on all their movements. I could find the Achilles' heel in their security to penetrate them and make this happen the way you want. I know, with the privileged mind God gave you, that you'll come up with something that will make sense and work out."

"Thank you, I really appreciate that. But this is a difficult one, I assure you. I have an idea, but I don't know if it will work. It's an excellent idea you stay here. We have to find out how they communicate between the yacht and the car."

"Very well," he said.

"Let's get out of the marina. If they're watching us, I want them to see all three of us leave here. After we get out of here, I'll leave you a few blocks by the coast. You come back using the coastline. Don't get too close to them because if they see you after we leave now, we'll have no excuse at all for you to be around here. That will compromise all my plans."

"I understand, Commander. Don't worry, I'll be invisible."

"When we come back, stay in a position to see us when we enter the marina again. I don't want to come fully in—I want to leave the jeep here, where we're dropping you off now. When you see us, you can reunite with us. Remember there are very thick mangroves to hide in. I don't want them to notice our presence. That will be the end of what we want to do." I gave Cisneros my military binoculars with night vision lenses. "Be very careful. The most important thing in all of this is to appear like we have nothing to do with what happens here tonight. That is the only reason I bought that bottle of Grand Marnier. It justified why I came back here and look at how much valuable information we got in the one shot. We've been extremely lucky so far."

"You don't have to worry about it, Commandante," Cisneros replied. "I'll be extremely careful."

"Remember, your only job here is observing to report to us later."

Before Cisneros got out, Daniel grinned and said, "Black man, no matter what you do or whatever happens around you, under no circumstance should you open your mouth to smile. Those white teeth of yours in that black face will be like a spotlight for our enemies to find you immediately in the dark!"

Cisneros playfully hit Daniel in the shoulder as he got out. I said, "Concentrate now! Later, we'll have time for jokes. Go, Cisneros."

He disappeared into the darkness. I said to Daniel, "Go to the Capri Hotel. That is where the Gentleman of Paris is accustomed to hang around. He could be a great help for what we're going to do."

Daniel said, "Good thinking, Commander. I noticed that he's not what he appears to be."

"Oh, you noticed too, eh? Cisneros is already the 'black bear,' you'll be the 'white bear,' OK?"

"All right, it's settled."

On the way back, I looked up at the sky. It was a beautiful, star-filled night. I felt the evening breeze that brought the distinctive smell of the sea close by. I thought that it was such a beautiful, prosperous island that had been for so many years the preferred resort of Europeans, North Americans, and the rest of the world to enjoy great vacations with their families. I imagined that all of it would be in ruins in just a few years. It was a pity. It was precisely what Satan looked to do: to ruin the peace and harmony without leaving any room for happiness among human beings. This was what was happening to my Cuba at the speed of light, step by step, with the plan these Devil's disciples had put into motion. It was a distraction to my train of thought.

We reached the Vedado very quickly. It was amazing how fast the time had flown during my distraction. We arrived at the Capri Hotel and Cabaret. We parked the jeep at the entry, a distance from the front door, declining the valet parking to save time. I was well-known for my generous tipping there.

One of the valets came up to me. I asked if any of them had seen the Gentleman of Paris lately. One said, "I saw him earlier today. As always, one member of the staff kicked him out."

Another chimed in as he finished parking a Mercedes Roadster for an elegant, beautiful woman. She left and he came over. "I heard you guys asking about the Gentleman of Paris. What do you want to know?"

"Yes. I need to talk to him. It's very important. Do you know where I can find him?"

"I know where he sleeps."

"If you take us to where he is, I will make sure that I gratify you generously. I'll also be very grateful to you." I pulled a $20 bill out of my pocket.

"No, no, my Commander. You are too generous to me all the time. This is a favor."

He was about 20 years old with dirty blonde hair. "We can go in your jeep and I'll take you to where he is."

"How are you going to leave your job?"

"I'll tell the others and they'll cover for me."

"OK, thank you very much."

We got into the jeep and the young attendant asked, "Do you remember me?"

I turned my neck to look at his face. "Yes. You are the only one here that, when I give you a tip, that replies that it's too much. I always say that it's money from the government."

He grinned. Daniel said, "Remember, everything the Commander does for this government he isn't paying for. When he gives you a tip, receive it with gratitude and joy. We've all been sweating for it."

"Thank you," the young attendant replied. He held out his hand to shake my hand. "My name is Modesto."

I took his hand. "My name is Julio Antonio. Remember, I don't like to be called Julio. Julio Antonio."

"I better call you 'Commander.' I don't want to get into any trouble."

"No, you won't get into any trouble. But you just honored your name."

Montauk: The Lightning Chance

We laughed, and Modesto pointed out the way as Daniel drove. We wound up behind the Hotel Hilton in a dark alley perhaps two or three hundred feet from where the Hilton's trash bins were in an empty lot with weeds growing up through the pavement. It was right next to a scrap yard with old, abandoned cars.

We left the jeep in the street. Behind all of that I saw next to some debris and some tents a VW minibus painted in multiple colors. It looked like the painting had been done by the hand of some Bohemian painter of Havana, or perhaps the Gentleman of Paris himself. Modesto led the way and parted the fence to enter the lot. We followed him closely. It looked like a scene out of a European city that had been bombed out by the Nazis. It was out of place, right in the middle of the more opulent section of Havana, behind the most luxurious hotel in the city.

The strangest creatures began to appear and disappear in the shadows. They looked like most bizarre characters I had ever seen, like something out of a fantasy novel. From under a tent next to these wrecked cars, an incredibly tall woman who looked to me about 9 or 10 feet tall, wearing thin clothing like a gypsy emerged. I could see by surprise that she only had one large eye in the center of her forehead right above her nose. Where she was supposed to have her other eyes, she had two small ones that looked like rat's eyes.

Daniel looked at me without saying a word. His eyes were wide with incredulity. The woman came over to us, ignoring us utterly. She sat down next to another woman and what appeared to be children around a bonfire. We continued going deeper into the darkness of that place, going past cars covered with canvas secured by ropes. I later realized that what I had thought were children by the woman were midgets. We continued in that paradoxical encampment, deeper into this new experience for Daniel and me. It appeared that Modesto had been immunized against its strangeness. His expression did not change.

A curtain extended from a bus to another car, suspended by ropes. An exquisite smell wafted from behind it. Somebody opened the curtains to come onto our side, and we could see a group of men, women, children, and older men sitting around a pit with small piglets on a rotisserie that looked to be their dinner. The lady who came out had a very thick, long beard. She smiled as she walked by us. She went to one of the abandoned cars. She held the handle of one of the doors like one holds the handle in a toilet stall. To our surprise, she raised her skirt up to her breasts, revealing to us she wasn't even wearing underwear. She shamelessly began to urinate. She was a large woman, it seemed to our young minds a half ton in weight. This was the straw that broke the camel's back for Modesto. Even though he had probably seen things like this before, he looked at us and smiled in embarrassment.

"These people are free spirits," he said lamely by way of excuse. "They have nothing at all to lose. That is why they live here and in this manner. They have no material possessions from when they arrive until the day comes when they leave this cruel world. They have to live like this as outcasts because of their physical and emotional deformities."

Daniel shook his head and said to Modesto, "Whatever. With all my respect, Modesto, I want to let you know that though I'm poor, black, and maybe not the brightest mind in the bunch, even if I were born with five legs and four eyes and a couple of ears on my neck extra, I will never live as these people do. I'm not going to go in front of someone, pull out my ding-a-ling with a smile, without caring a fig, and begin to urinate without any kind of discrimination. I'm a man, and if I need to urinate somewhere in the country without a latrine, I'll still turn my back on my friends." He tapped his temple. "This is not normal behavior. It's a courtesy to my friends so they don't have to look at my black ding-a-ling. I'm sorry, but what this woman just did in front of us was like Liberace in his most flaming moments. We got to see a theatre of terror with that immense horror and showed us her fat-assed, black Jack the Ripper opera!" He shook his head in disgust and shuddered in revulsion. "Madre mia! I believe that I've been traumatized for the rest of my days with that grotesque vision."

Modesto and I couldn't hold it in any longer and burst out laughing. It looked like the creatures living there weren't used to hearing loud laughter like that. We saw them coming from everywhere as if we had stepped on an ant hill or hit a honeycomb of bees with a stick. If we had thought before that we had passed strange beings, now truly we had stirred them up. Truly, the ugliest creatures came out of their caves. One woman, probably at least 90 years old, had four arms, two on each side. Half of her face had no flesh over her right jaw. Her mandible and teeth were completely visible. Half her hair was gone, and it appeared like she had at one time had brain surgery, as a metallic plate covered part of her scalp. A man in a small platform on four wheels who appeared to be cut in half with what seemed to be lead holding his intestines in appeared. One midget with large eyes, long beard, and a massive afro (we didn't know if it was a deformity or hair) looking like something out of a horror movie came out. The worst was they started

Montauk: The Lightning Chance

to form a mob and followed us with knives, machetes, and pitchforks. I wondered where they had gotten these weapons and implements.

They started to yell obscenities at us. Even the deformed children threw cans at our feet. One of them yelled, "*¿Que carajo hacen ustedes aqui?*[46]"

Modesto was mute at first and a little panicked. He finally reacted and turned to a midget that appeared to be the leader of that community, who appeared to be around 60 years old, completely grey haired and bearded (but no mustache). He said, "My name is Modesto and these are my friends." As he spoke, he approached the man. "I'm a great friend of the Gentleman of Paris. I've been here several times with him. My friends asked me to bring them to him because they have something of great importance to tell him."

One of the younger girls that looked somewhat normal, albeit filthy, looked up in surprise at what Modesto said and ran off into the darkness toward the back. The old grumpy midget yelled at Modesto, "The Gentleman of Paris never receives anyone here! You are a liar!" He took a few steps towards Modesto. He pulled a switchblade nearly as big as he was out. He opened it. "We have a punishment for those who are liars and deceivers with poisoned tongues. We cut their tongues out!"

Up until this point, Daniel and I had remained silent. The mob started to chant, "Cut out the tongue! Cut out the tongue!"

Like a movie in my mind, I relived something fresh in my mind—how the mob in Pinar del Rio during the first days of the revolution's victory encouraged something horrible and disgusting. It was so bad that it made my friend Tite lose his power of speech for a long while. He was the son of the man who provided charcoal for the whole town. When he was able to speak again, it left him with a speech impediment from the psychological trauma that followed him for the rest of his life. All those horrific memories flooded my brain, and I could feel it on my face and ears as I grew extremely upset. I began to feel nauseous; my face started to spasm as I looked directly at the old midget closing in on Modesto with that long knife that looked more like the straight edge razor my father used to shave with. It was clear he was going to cut Modesto's tongue out of his mouth, like Tite had told me that the woman did with scissors in front of him, cheered by the mob, when a young man was accused of being an informant for Bastista's

---

[46] What the hell are you guys doing in here?

police. The truth was that he was a revolutionary and a decent human being against the dictator. In the end, he was innocent of what he had been accused of.

My face grew warmer and warmer as I felt the blood pumping into my cheeks and up to my temple. I raised both of my arms high and yelled with all the power in my lungs, "Stop! Stop!"

The midget halted as if paralyzed. Before everyone's surprised eyes, he started to levitate off the ground without being able to do anything. Sparks surrounded him like miniature lightning bolts. He dropped the large weapon as he was lifted higher into the air, trying to fight the electrical energy that surrounded him. I made a circular motion with both hands, and he inverted upside down. Forks, spoons, knives, and other silverware fell out of his pants. All of them had the Hilton logo on them.

The young girl returned with the Gentleman of Paris by her hand. He came over to us and began to pick up the tableware. He looked up at the midget and said, "Oh, you're stealing this from the Hilton, eh? You're stealing from the revolution, too! You know what that means?" He drew a finger across his throat.

I said, "No, he's not stealing from the Hilton or the revolution. He's stealing from the workers' pension plan of our people!"

The fat lady said, "How do you know that? You're so young!" The crowd was now silent.

The Gentleman of Paris said, "You ignorant people! I've tried so hard to educate you. You don't know who this kid is? Have you not watched the television I gave you guys? This kid is the favorite of Fidel Castro and Che Guevara!" The crowd gasped and took a step back.

The midget pleaded, "Please, put me down. Please, Gentleman of Paris, tell him to put me down!" The midget looked down at the ground below his head and realized he was between ten and twelve feet off the ground. He added, "But slowly, please."

"This will teach you that you cannot threaten people and treat them with disrespect because you can see now that this doesn't always work the way you think it will with some people. Maybe it will work with those who allow themselves to be intimidated, but not this time, eh?" The midget urinated himself at that point. "What, did your nuts get loose?" The rest of the crowd began to laugh; as ever, the mob turned against its leader as soon as someone stronger came along.

A loud noise erupted from the pants of the midget and the little girl covered her mouth to hide her laughter. His state of terror was so great that he began to beg me. "Please, Commandantico, forgive me. Please!" He looked around and said to the Gentleman. "Please, they are your friends. Please bring me down, I'm still too young to die." He began to cry like a baby.

I understood he had been punished enough and I slowly let him down. When he was near the ground, I twisted my arms like before to rotate him back right-side up, and his feet touched the ground a few feet from the Gentleman of Paris. He hugged Jose Maria around one leg, this time crying with happiness as he saw himself safe and out of harm. Jose Maria, feeling bad for him, caressed his head. "Don't give thanks to me, but to the Commandantico. He is the one you should be grateful to. You should apologize to all of them. Yes, they are my friends." He put his arm on the little girl's head and caressed her hair. "According to Maca, you actually have been a bad boy. You didn't behave well with my friends. To make it worse, you insulted Modesto."

Maca nodded vigorously. "You were very nasty and out of line, treating them with disdain." Maca smiled at me and waved hello. I returned her wave. Thanks to the intervention of her and Jose Maria, that situation hadn't turned into a violent one, especially with all the strange beings around us that certainly didn't look like they came from our planet. The white-bearded midget hesitated for a few seconds, still afraid. He slowly edged over to my side. His voice cracked as he extended his hand with his head down, "Please forgive me, it was not my intention to offend or disrespect you. I was only trying to protect my community. You don't know how many abuses we've endured from the juvenile delinquents and the dictator's discriminatory police."

I let him finish in silence and then said to the little thief, "I accept your apology. What you just said though, is an excuse that I cannot accept. You cannot treat all the people you meet in your life the same way you've been treated by your worst enemies. This attitude will never conquer the hearts or friendship of anyone. Besides, who you really have to apologize to isn't me. You got me upset, and you received what you get when you do that. But you really insulted Modesto. You called him a liar. As you can now see, you were completely wrong. All he told you was nothing more than the truth."

The white-bearded midget stood there with his hand still extended. He nodded and repeated, "Yes, yes. You have all the right to tell me whatever you want, and I have to accept it. I'm sorry. I've been a jerk." Everyone exploded in laughter and he whirled on them angrily. He turned back to me and said, "I'm sorry again. I've behaved like a perfect imbecile." His eyes grew moist with tears that he tried to contain. He wiped them with the back of his hand. I understood he was sincerely remorseful.

I took his hand with sincere affection. It was clear that he had at least enough integrity to apologize from his heart. To me, personally, it took a lot of courage and a strong character for an individual to recognize his own mistakes and then publicly admit them. He accepted responsibility for his inappropriate conduct and deserved sincere forgiveness. Daniel and Modesto did as I did and took his hand.

Trying to start with us anew, the midget said, "My name is Solitario." We gave him our names. It was getting close to dinner, so he said, "Since it's nearly time for our meal, why don't you stay with us? Every good friendship starts and is sealed with a good meal."

I didn't want to disappoint him. Since we had all night we weren't in any hurry, and I believed after all that all these strange characters that we had met in this camp could come to be a blessing and a great help. If we could get them to agree to it, they would serve as perfect distractions for us to successfully complete the work we wanted to do. I accepted the invitation of the miniature Solitario.

With genuine joy, he replied, "Very good! We have a great menu tonight. We have *arros congri*, plantains, and *puerco asado*. We also have avocado salad with tomatoes, onions, and black olives." He spoke as if he were a maître d convincing us that it would be worth it to stay. He extended his small hand to the Gentleman of Paris. "May I get my silverware back?"

With a smile, Jose Maria gave the silverware back. Solitario smiled. "I want to clarify that I'm not a thief. These haven't been *stolen* from the Hilton, as my great, famous friend the Gentleman of Paris implied. They have just been *borrowed*. I can read the future and I knew that very important guests would be arriving in our camp. Of course, I wanted to offer the top quality that we don't have here for my guests."

Everyone looked at him with extreme skepticism. It was clear nobody believed a word. Jose Maria laughed loudly and clapped Solitario on the shoulder. Everyone began to laugh as well. He said, "Solitario, *carajo*! You little midget—you actually see me as the face of a *chorizo*? You think you can stuff all that past my face and down my throat?"

Solitario looked ashamed but had a small smile on his lips as he shook his head and shrugged. "You cannot blame me for trying."

"Yes, I do! You little rascal!"

Montauk: The Lightning Chance

"Oh, well." Solitario walked a little ashamed ahead of us past the curtain.

Beyond it was the bonfire we had glimpsed before. The piglets were still on the rotisserie. It looked and smelled finger-licking good. What he had described as being on the menu, even though it was very typical for Cuban cuisine, it also was very much to my preference as well as the palates of the others. I tried to put the bad moments just now out of my mind. It looked like we started off on the wrong foot, but perhaps in the end of all this we not only resolved what we had come to get from the Gentleman, we might be able to cultivate some new friendships among these people. They could be a great help in my new line of work.

There were several tables with umbrellas on the patio, and we took one of them. I looked at the umbrellas. They all looked alike, which meant they were probably stolen as well, with multicolored floral print. Modesto excused himself to get back to work. I gave him a generous tip and he said goodbye to us. "Thank you very much, Modesto," I said.

Solitario told us that it would take at least another hour before the pigs were ready to eat, but he would try to rush it a little. I used the opportunity to give the Gentleman of Paris the details of what I had in mind that prompted my visit to him. I told him of my need to create a distraction, some kind of decoy, so that I could get off of the *Pilar* something that I didn't think should remain in the hands of our enemies. I didn't give him any information as to what was in the containers. "All I need to do is to get those containers off of the yacht, and I need someone to distract the soldiers."

"How many men are there?"

"In total, six. Two are in front of the door to the cabins of the yacht, up on deck. The others are inside a car perhaps two hundred feet from the yacht in the marina parking lot."

I gave him a few more details on my plan. He interrupted me. "Hold on here for a few minutes. I need to go to my little cave and bring something I think will be useful and necessary for what you plan to do."

He stood up and headed back to where he had emerged, followed by Maca, who grabbed the skirts of his trench coat. After he left, Daniel asked me in worry, "Do you think you can completely trust this guy? He doesn't look all together."

"Did you notice the ring he has on his right hand?" I showed him the ring I was wearing.

Daniel nodded and smiled. "I got it."

We looked at each other and nodded wordlessly. Solitario came and sat down next to us with two beautiful tigers tied like a couple of dogs to leashes with thin chains and leather handholds. He smiled and said to the tigers, "Sit." They sat next to him obediently. "I want to introduce you to my two best friends, Elma and Paco." Both tigers raised their heads at the mention of their names and roared. He tapped them lightly with the leather end of the chains on both their head. He added in a firm voice. "You be quiet. I'm talking about important things now." Both tigers put their heads on his lap. "Put one of your hands very slowly close to his nose. I want them to get to know you, get your smell, and become your friends." I hesitated for a few seconds. But I looked Paco straight in the eyes and then slowly I extended the back of my right hand towards his nose. After a few seconds of smelling it all over he began to lick me. In the same manner I made friends with the female, Elma. At the same time, I rubbed Paco's head with my left hand.

I said in a very low, calm voice, "Good boy. Good boy." I started to do the same with Elma. She started to enjoy my scratching her ears. To Solitario's surprise she rolled over like a cat to expose her belly to me. The only problem here was that I wasn't her master, so he looked at me and smiled.

"There's no doubt that you have good energy in you. We can fool each other, but not the instincts of an animal. Nobody can do that. This is the first test that I do with new friends. You passed it with 100 percent and multiple colored ribbons. My tiger, Elma, never shows her belly to anyone for scratching. She only does that with me, and I've had them since they were cubs." He hadn't even finished before Paco not only rolled over to show me his belly as well but started to bat my arm with one huge paw, as if demanding that I let Elma alone and concentrate entirely on him. Solitario scratched his white beard and shook his head in surprised admiration. "This is incredible! Paco *never* lets even me rub his belly!"

I had a tiger's belly in each hand, and they were in Heaven. From the back of the encampment the Gentleman of Paris reappeared, followed by Maca. He held what appeared to be a wooden cigar box in his hand. He looked at Solitario and shook his head in surprise. Solitario spread his hands as well and nodded his own astonishment.

Jose Maria said, "Now you are probably completely convinced that the Commandantico is not just any twelve-year-old boy like you and I are accustomed to dealing with."

Montauk: The Lightning Chance

Solitario, still shaking his head, said, "From the moment I saw my feet levitated off of the firm ground I realized that no matter how hard I tried to get myself free of the electrical energy that was holding me and lifting me up in the air; the more I tried to free myself instead of letting me go free he raised me up even more. It was as if that energy were using my own strength against me. I understood then that the Commandantico was not the boy we thought he was. Definitely not one from our planet."

Jose Maria nodded and grinned. "Well, I'm very glad that you made friends very rapidly with him. I can assure you that the last thing I want to do is have him as my enemy, not even for five minutes. I believe that you as his friend now should offer to help him in what he intends to do tonight. That is the only reason he came here—he was looking for help." He pointed to the tigers. "I believe Elma and Paco could be a great help in what we're trying to do in order to create a good distraction to complete our plans tonight."

Solitario raised both of his small arms high and turned to me. "You can count on me without any hesitation."

"Thank you very much."

Solitario smiled at me. "You are very welcome. Let me go and put Elma and Paco back in their cages. We'll probably have dinner shortly."

"Very well," Jose Maria replied. "Let me go over a few more details with the Commandantico. After the meal I will update you on all the minor points. You also can get the others that are willing to participate with us updated as to what we're going to do on this nocturnal venture."

"Right," Solitario replied as he walked away with the two tigers. The Gentleman of Paris put the small wooden box on the table. I could see when he opened it what appeared to be large marbles. He showed me one of them. There was an imperceptible button that, when you pressed it, showed a multicolored light display. They moved in different directions with a beautiful rhythm, like ballerinas dancing. He turned it off.

"They're not lethal," he explained, "but after twenty seconds they explode and a green anesthetic gas powerful enough to put an elephant to sleep for multiple hours erupts. To activate it, you need to press it three times. To deactivate it you have to press it four times."

I laid out the plan to him and what I needed from him. We finished and started to enjoy the great meal that Solitario prepared for us. I said, "Who is the cook?"

The immensely fat lady said, "It's not a cook, it's a chef. It's me, Aleida." She smiled at us from her table. "What—you don't like my food?"

"No, no—it's all exquisite. I had been thinking I could even recommend you as a chef for the Hilton. I believe Fidel and the rest of his entourage will fall completely in love with you."

Aleida came over to me slowly, a big smile on her lips. With difficulty because of her size, she leaned over, put her hand under my chin, pulled me towards her, and gave me a big smacking kiss on the cheek. "That is very well deserved, a present for you in exchange for your beautiful complement to my cuisine." She pointed around at the others. "These low lifes swallow my food every day but never once gave me a complement, much less a beautiful one like the one you just gave me. That's called 'class.'" She nodded and waddled back to her table, which was especially constructed to support her great weight. Her chair even looked like a throne. She proclaimed loudly, "You should all learn from the Commandantico. But I doubt any one of you could ever learn because class is something you're born with, not something you can learn in universities or any other school."

The others protested with murmurs. She picked up one of the plantains and threw it like a frisbee at the midgets, who were protesting louder than anyone else. The plantain flew over, and one of the midgets ducked, only to allow it to land in a pitcher of lemonade in the center of the table, lightly splashing all of them at the table. They protested and one yelled, "Hey, cut it out, OK?"

Aleida laughed gleefully at the reaction she provoked while the midgets wiped their faces with napkins. The Gentleman of Paris disappeared for a bit and returned with an accordion. The midgets pulled out musical instruments, violins, trumpets, drums, and guitars. Within only a few minutes we had an orchestra assembled. Aleida began to sing the beautiful song by Ernesto Lecuona, "Siboney." She was a mezzo soprano and had an incredible voice. After she finished, she sang 1940's hit "Besame Mucho" by the Mexican composer Consuelo.

There was no doubt in my mind that everyone there possessed tremendous gifts from God due to the extraordinary natural talents they had. I thought about how strange it was that all those creatures there, for one reason or another, picked the Bohemian lifestyle; but maybe they preferred to live their lives free from social responsibilities that normal life requires of every human being. The option the capitalist system offered in a democratic society was that one could be integrated into society or remain on the margins of it, like they were. But no one there, I was certain, knew that was a privilege that would end very soon in Cuba for all of us. The leaders of the revolution would very soon establish a totalitarian system. Anyone who didn't conform with it would be condemned through arbitrary laws because the right of a human being to choose his or her own destiny would no longer exist. Everyone would live their lives as the government dictated because their personal rights would be suspended and substituted for the rights of the communist state government. My thoughts at that particular moment distracted me from the harmony and happiness that these strange creatures seemed to enjoy. These odd societal misfits illuminated my views on life and taught me that night that even living the way they did was an expression of freedom. Those of us who have the greatest privilege to live in a capitalist society and surrounded by the precious democracy don't appreciate the options we have each day to live as we please. Because we're actually predisposed to be more critical the little imperfections in our democracy, we forget to appreciate the grand virtues of democracy as well as the enormous advantages it offers.

After the enjoyment of that precious moment with these strange people, I realized that I would carry away a great moment of happiness in my soul that I would never forget for the rest of my life. These strange Bohemian artists were odd in their physical appearance but like jewels, diamonds, and uncut gems, possessed extraordinary beauty under the skin. We gave them our plan of action in mind and like a good team of new recruits had a long interchange of ideas with the group that had decided to partake in our venture.

It was already past midnight as the loud sound of the closest church indicated by its chimes. We left the camp, followed by the Gentleman of Paris who drove an ancient school bus painted with all kind of astrological symbols. Behind him was a huge caravan of the strangest automobiles that you could possibly imagine. The first one behind him was the painted VW bus that belonged to Solitario, carrying Aleida, the two tigers, and a bunch of midgets. Behind them came different cars, every one of them more bizarre than the previous, as if they had a competition between them as to who possessed the most existentialistic vehicle of them all. If that were the case, the Gentleman of Paris won the contest—his was the most unusual and bizarre of them all. Half the tail section of an airplane was welded to the roof of the bus.

Daniel smiled and looked in the side rearview mirror of the jeep. He shook his head as he watched the line behind us. He said, "Commander, if what we're looking for is a distraction, I think we've won the jackpot. I think your idea of asking the Gentleman of Paris was brilliant."

I smiled. "The opera just commenced. We should not sing victory yet until Aleida sings the last notes. Then we will all sing a great chorus of victory together."

We both smiled. Daniel said, "I will be carried into the audience on those notes from her with anxiety."

"Me, too."

We arrived at the entry to the marina where we had dropped Cisneros off. He was waiting there for us and waved both of his arms at us. Daniel pulled over and Cisneros jumped in. He looked at the caravan behind us in concern, and asked, "What's going on? Where did all these cars come from?"

Daniel smiled. "Hello! How are you doing? Did everything go well?"

Cisneros shook his head unhappily. "Cut it out, Daniel! Can't you give me a break once in a while? This is no time for joking right now."

I reached under the seat and brought out a plate and silverware as well as a bottle of jupiña and handed them to Cisneros. I said, "I thought you might be hungry after so many hours, and whatever we brought you would be a joy to your palate."

He lifted the cover on the plate. "Thank you, Commander, I knew you wouldn't forget about me. Even though the night is very old, your mind is always on my tummy." He smiled pleasantly and his disposition improved.

Daniel used that opportunity to give him a further hard time. "Oh! What happened to your worry about the cars we have behind us? Poof! The roast pork wiped your memory by the power of the Holy Spirit!"

Cisneros smiled as he chewed a piece of pork. With his mouth full, he exclaimed, "Ooh! This is homemade! Delicious! My favorite: roast pork."

"Yes, it's homemade and the cook is behind us in that weird van." I pointed back behind us. "She's coming as a companion with the

Montauk: The Lightning Chance

Gentleman of Paris." I pointed at a turnoff and said to Daniel, "Turn here. It's a good place for us to hide the jeep. We cannot be seen, remember."

Daniel pulled off and concealed the jeep in a good spot behind the mangroves and bushes. Some of the vehicles stayed on the highway and parked. A couple of them pulled in behind us, and several of them got out to come meet with us. In the meantime, Cisneros shared his observations as he ate. I went over the plan once more and updated Cisneros with the new additions. I told Daniel to go with them so he could pinpoint the car we wanted to distract in case it wasn't the only one parked there.

I said, "When I'm done, I'll shoot a couple of flares so that you guys know I've done my job with the two men on the yacht. When you see the flares, the Gentleman of Paris should come alone to meet me on the yacht." We agreed on the finalized details, and I said, "OK, Cisneros, we saved the most important detail for you. Go sit in the jeep and eat in peace until you see the flare. When you do, drive towards the yacht. We'll all meet there."

Dr. Julio Antonio del Marmol

CHAPTER 15: THE CLOSE ENCOUNTER OF THE FIFTH KIND

Our arrangements made, I took my clothes off and pulled out a pair of shorts from the back seat. I took a snorkel mask and fins out of the storage compartment. I walked to the coast barefoot, wearing only my boxers and a couple of the decoy toys the Gentleman of Paris gave me, sealed inside a plastic bag. I didn't have to walk far to reach the water. I put on my snorkeling gear and entered the water to swim towards the *Pilar*.

When I got close to it, I could hear the two guards on deck talking about UFOs and extraterrestrials. One of them was evidently fascinated with the subject, while the other one was dubious. He said, "Well, it is possible that all this exists someplace. After all, the universe is immense, almost infinite, and it's logical and natural that other beings exist in it. The reality is, in my opinion, all these phenomena we see in the newspapers and hear on radio and TV, are nothing more than decoys by different governments by different countries around the world. They're using these excuses to cover up scientific experiments, especially new, modern weapons, and supersonic vehicles to divert the attention of the public to cover up what they don't want their enemies to know about. They simply are trying to fill our heads with fantasies and make us believe that these are different beings from other worlds. Until I see something with my own eyes, I don't fully believe in anything at all. Not until I can corroborate it."

As they talked, I had reached the vessel. I took a couple of the little glass balls from the bag. I shoved my mask up on my head and let the snorkel hang by my side. I oriented myself to determine which direction they were facing as they sat there, looking for the most strategic point to toss the decoys and put them in the hands of the guards within the twenty second span. As I swam around the yacht seeking that best point, I could hear the other guard's reply to his partner's question.

"Let me ask you something—something very peculiar. Do you believe in God?"

The other man said, "Of course, *chico*. Though lately I've been having my doubts because of all I've heard from our political orientation officer. According to political scientific theory, nothing exists outside of the material."

"Well, have you asked yourself where the hell this political theorist learned astronomy or the occult sciences of the universe? All these individuals know is how to wash your brain with their political theories. Let's say that you have doubts now. But you have believed in God all your life. Is that not true?"

"Yes."

"Well, did you ever see God?"

"No. Absolutely not. But this is completely different. What does God have to do with beings from another planet, like we've been talking about, and astronomy?"

I smiled as I listened to this debate. I found the spot I was looking for so I could drop my little bombs. I was only a few feet away from them and I started to count silently to ten. Then I activated the devices, tossed them high in the air and watched them drop on the deck. They rolled out, the wild flashing of lights illuminating the deck. The two objects rolled right to the feet of the two guards who looked at them in fascination. They hesitated briefly. "What the hell is that?!" asked the disbelieving guard.

"A test for your incredulity," the other replied. "Maybe it's sent by Providence. Hurry up—you grab one and I'll get the other before they disappear. We'll have evidence of what we're seeing, and no one else will say as you did that we're just hallucinating."

I kept counting, starting at eleven. When I reached twenty the two balls exploded in the faces of each guard. I started to count to five.

I reached four and heard a double thud as the two guards fell to the deck, sound asleep. I climbed onto the yacht by the ladder on the stern. I went through their pockets, knowing that one of them should have a set of keys. I found not just the keys to the cabins but also the set for the medical cabinet and the emergency storage box where I would find the flares. I opened the door to the cabins and went downstairs. I checked to make sure the loot was still there.

I went to the captain's quarters, went through his clothing, and found a decent shirt that was easily five sizes too big. I grabbed the lace for a laundry bag and used it as a belt to tie the massive guayabera to my waist. Looking like a clown, I peeled off my wet shorts and dried myself off with a towel. Passing by a full-length mirror I saw my reflection and felt that I looked like I was part of the team of strange creatures brought by the Gentleman of Paris. I said softly to myself, "Apparently, Jose Maria has recruited me. No one will recognize me."

Daniel later told me that at that same moment, they parked the VW bus right in front of the Ford. They then released the two tigers, and the other vehicles pulled in to surround the car. The four men started to open their doors, but two of them got confronted by the tigers, and they quickly retreated back inside, slamming the doors shut. They had the windows rolled down, and a mysterious, manicured hand dropped some more balls in through one of the windows. The voice of the Gentleman of Paris said, "Sweet dreams. At least until Che finds you guys sleeping. Then your nightmare will start."

Meanwhile, I found a container that held the flares. I went up on deck and shot one flare to my right and another to my left. As soon as the Gentleman saw the signal, he said goodbye to the others and dismissed them. He and Daniel came onto the yacht, and a few minutes later we were joined by Cisneros. After a while, we pulled the containers out and loaded them onto the bus. He then left and drove to the house on Carlos III.

When we had finished our work, we went to the *El Parador*, a coffee shop on the road to the airport in Havana on the Avenue Rancho Boyeros, far away from the city. It was a place we normally met when we wanted to be out of the eyes of others. This place was accustomed to visits by truck drivers and all kinds of different people on their way to the airport. I believed this place was more prudent since I didn't want anyone to see the Gentleman of Paris in case something happened later. He couldn't be seen early that morning having breakfast with us. He passed as one of the normal clientele, and so would create less attention for himself. We had to make sure that none of us would be remembered in the company of the other. It wasn't that we expected anything to happen; it was just a precaution.

We thanked him for his invaluable help. We said our farewells and returned to the Hilton to rest from that crazy, fruitful night. We had, in total silence, destroyed the morbid plans and Hitlerian ambitions of Che and Fidel to use Cuban money to enslave the rest of the world with their own adventurers disguised as revolutionaries. I smiled with great satisfaction. After several hours of sleeping quite soundly, we woke up to find it was nearly 6 pm. We all shared that satisfaction, showered, and went down the elevator to the coffee shop.

We took an early dinner: some great lobster thermidors and Daniel had his usual New York steak with mushroom sauce. I used the opportunity to debrief Daniel and Cisneros what had happened the day before at the liquor store.

We finished dinner and drove to the police station so I could sign the charges and the sergeant's report. We arrived at the First Precinct and I walked inside while they waited in the jeep. The first man I saw was the sergeant. He smiled when he saw me, a large folder in his hand. "Oh, we've been waiting for you!" He shook the folder, and something caught my attention. He seemed to be a little too joyful at seeing me. It was odd. "This young delinquent has no previous arrest, but he is of age according to the Ministry of Interior to be transferred to the Office of Health and Research."

Dr. Julio Antonio del Marmol

Figure 43 Central Police Station, Havana

"What is the age required for that?"

"Fourteen to seventeen. We are authorized to treat them as adults. Everything is done: blood tests, and everything else. All we need is your signature to transfer him out of here."

I held out my hand. "Please, will you let me see the charges in that file and the record?"

He hesitated. "Yes, yes—of course!" He handed me the folder with a nervous smile. There was a strange gleam in his eyes I hadn't noticed before. I examined the file and looked over the charges they wanted to stick him with; I noticed they hadn't exaggerated very much. The most serious charge he had was to attack a figure of authority; this could be considered an act of terrorism which would lead to a long term in prison or even execution before the firing squad.

I finished reading the file and I felt a chill go all over my body starting in my feet and finishing behind my neck. I felt a strange sensation as my conscience called to me. It screamed to me that I should reexamine what had really happened before and what appeared to be in motion now. Technically, he had indeed tried something against me—but his attempt had failed miserably since he hadn't laid a finger on me before I beat him up. Given the facts, it seemed a little extreme to me. Something in the back of my mind told me that something sinister was

Montauk: The Lightning Chance

cooking here involving the young delinquent. And it looked like the sergeant had complete knowledge of what was being planned. I asked him, "Has the juvenile delinquent shown you guys any remorse for his previous actions?"

The sergeant raised both arms high and in a very disapproving expression said, "No, no—remorse? Not at all! On the contrary, this morning he was singing rock and roll in his cell."

That sounded very strange to me. This kid was supposed to have no previous arrest record and just spent the night in jail, probably with even worse delinquents than he dreamed of being himself. Singing rock and roll—he must either have been tougher than I imagined, or he was cynical. It made no sense to me. "Please, will you take me to him? I want to talk to him and remove some doubts I have in my mind before I sign these charges against him."

At that moment the corporal in charge of the cells approached us. "Sergeant, Lieutenant Mendoza needs to talk to you immediately in his office."

The sergeant snatched the folder out of my hand and handed it to the corporal. "Take the Commandantico to the prison. He wants to talk to the prisoner. I don't know why he wants to talk to him; he just needs to sign the paper." His expression was harsh, and he shrugged his shoulders. "Go ahead."

I looked at him in disapproval without saying a word. His manners were not good, and the way he conducted himself sent an even louder signal. I put on a long face and stared him in the eyes. He got my message. Before he left, he added, "He is your prisoner. You can do whatever you want with him, whatever you think is more appropriate."

I didn't reply but nodded slightly at this obvious statement. He gave me a sloppy salute as I left him in the company of the corporal. He turned his back on us and walked towards the offices. I walked next to the corporal who looked through the folder as we did.

He said, "Last night we had to change this young man's cell assignment. He didn't stop crying all night. We had to separate him from the others because he got into a nasty fight with four huge prisoners, all career criminals. I don't know why the sergeant put him in that cell unless he wanted him dead. Four on one would be bad enough for an adult, much less a kid. We never would put these young kids at the mercy of these hardened felons—but that happens sometimes. When it does it usually winds up in death for the kid. It could start with an insignificant argument, and at least one of these other prisoners have a knife they managed to smuggle in." He shook his head in disgust.

As he opened the interrogation room, I asked, "Corporal, you tell me this boy has not stopped crying all night?"

"Yes, sir. That is what I said."

"I cannot understand that. Something is not right here." I bore a mild expression of disgust. "Sergeant Sardiñas told me a few minutes ago that this boy was heard this morning singing rock and roll in his cell."

The corporal said, "No, no!" He shook his head violently in disagreement. "The sergeant is completely wrong. He wasn't singing rock and roll this morning. It was his cellmate, a skinny, young kid they brought in last night for driving under the influence of alcohol. We put him in there because he was inoffensive. We had no other place to put him. Last night was terribly busy, even more complicated than the weekends—several arrests, some shootings, it's been crazy!"

"Maybe it's possible the sergeant was mistaken when he told me that."

The corporal nodded, considering it. He didn't look very convinced as he thought about what I had told him. He started to scratch his head with his left hand. "I cannot understand why Sergeant Sardiñas told you that. He spent almost all morning bringing him to an interrogation room and back to his cell with different doctors from the Ministry of Health and the Ministry of the Interior. They were in and out almost ten times."

"Is this a normal routine here?"

"No." He shook his head violently once more. "I assumed it was because the kid had been banged up, maybe some broken ribs from the fight last night. Normally when they do that it's only once or twice with the youngest kids brought in here. What caught my attention, Commandantico, was that after the doctors from the Ministry of the Interior examined this kid and transferred him from here, the records disappeared. It's happened before. A friend of mine had his boy here. We tried to locate him, and he appeared later in the Missing Persons list. It had never been processed by any civil or criminal court—it was like the Earth had swallowed him." I could tell he thought something was fishy.

"Did you report these irregularities to your superior?"

He nodded with conviction. He pointed with his right hand to his corporal's chevron. "That's why I lost one arrow." He smiled sarcastically. "I used to be Sergeant-Major and Chief Auditor of this

Montauk: The Lightning Chance

precinct. They demoted me to a simple corporal and made me the Chief of Guards."

I nodded. "Ah, ha! I see. And I understand now."

He nodded as well. "If I have to be honest with you, Commandantico, I don't think it came from this level. It came from the higher ups. The only reason I'm entrusting you with this is that I know you're close to Fidel, Che, and the other leaders. Maybe you can bring this to their ears and find out what's going on here and in other police stations here in Havana. My friends, of whom I have many in other precincts, have shared with me the same irregularities. My intimate friends in other units noticed how strange it was, too. This started to happen after we took the reins of this new government."

I nodded again, lost in thought for a bit, analyzing what the corporal had just entrusted me with. I thought that the least this corporal could even imagine was that Fidel and Che knew what was going on everywhere. They were eliminating all opposition to their plans. Whatever was going on, they already knew and were accomplices. They had already placed themselves at the service of their supreme teacher, Satan.

I said, "What is your name, Corporal?"

He hesitated. "Aurelio. Corporal Aurelio." He sounded a little nervous as he spoke. "Whatever you need, my commander, I'm at your service."

"I'm going to ask you a favor. I want you to disconnect the recorders here in the interrogation room. I want to speak with him in complete confidence, that whatever I say to him will be completely off the record. That way he'll be more candid with me."

"Very well, Commander. Whatever you ask. That's not unusual. It's the way Sergeant Sardiñas conducted his interrogations this morning with this same prisoner."

"Very well. Another thing I want to ask you: whatever you confided in me just now, even though I'm going to bring it to Che and Fidel's attention, for our mutual security I don't want you to repeat it to anyone."

His face was long as he nodded. He gulped nervously. "OK, Commandantico. I will do as you instruct."

"Another thing. Tell your friends, the ones who entrusted you in reporting these abnormalities elsewhere to walk very carefully. Be very sure of whoever they share this information with. For their security as well as that of their families."

"OK." He was getting more nervous as he perceived this was getting more complicated than he had anticipated.

I smiled as I observed his stress. I patted him on the shoulder. "I will assure you that I will find out what's going on with these young men and who is responsible. I will update you with whatever I discover. Maybe you'll recover your bars as a Sergeant-Major, but possibly even a higher promotion."

He smiled in satisfaction. He looked a little embarrassed then. "No, no—I'm just trying to do my duty, Commandantico. It's not necessary. Of course, getting my rank back would be much appreciated, as it's been an embarrassment to my family."

"You're right, my friend. That wasn't nice at all. But remember not everybody does what they're supposed to do in complying with their duties. Those who do should obtain recompense for their actions."

"Thank you very much," he said, still a little embarrassed. "All right, I'll bring you the prisoner so you can continue your work."

"Thank you." He left the interrogation room, leaving the door slightly ajar. I sat down in the reclining chair on one side of the table and took the folder the corporal had left. I started to examine the contents again, this time in greater detail. Sergeant Sardiñas had been so quick to take it out of my hands, I wanted to see what was in it. As I pulled the folder towards me, it fell onto the floor accidentally as I shifted position in my chair. A small envelope fell out of the folder that had been concealed behind the folder's cuff. I organized the papers that had fallen out and replaced it on top of the table. To my surprise, when I opened the envelope and read the note signed by Che that said, "Transplanted organs don't transfer their DNA to the host any more than the host makes genetic changes to the implanted organs. The genetic instructions in the cells of any organs stay the same after transplantation. The most organs in demand are kidneys and livers. The ideal age for the donor for our projects is between the ages of fourteen and seventeen years of age." On top of the note, large letters read, "Human Organs for Transplant."

I could see quite openly what the sergeant's orders from his masters were regarding this unfortunate young delinquent. To make matters worse, when they had the first blood test it must have matched one of the subjects. That was the reason the doctors came so many times to take additional blood tests to corroborate what they had found. When they knew that he was the right individual, whether for experimenting with him or removing his organs for sale, they decided that they needed a cause. The trigger would be my signature on the paperwork for his transfer.

I wondered what Che had to do with all this. But immediately the answer to my question, using my own common sense, lit up in my brain like a light bulb. The Devil had everything to do with anything evil or destructive in every part of the world. It was what made the Devil efficient.

Corporal Aurelio returned with the young delinquent in handcuffs and leg irons. He sat him down on the opposite side of the table from me, his left hand cuffed to the chair while his leg irons got attached to the table. He remained behind the boy. With his right hand he drew a finger across his throat and circled around the room. "Did you want me to stay here or remain outside?"

"Please stay outside. I want the subject to answer my questions as truthfully as he can."

"Whatever you say, Commander." He left the room and closed the door.

The young delinquent hung his head, staring at the floor. He looked remorseful to me. He looked like he had been in a serious car accident. He had stitches above his right eyebrow, and that eye was blackened. His swollen upper lip also had a small cut. He clearly was terrified and had no idea what to say to me. I maintained my silence for a couple of minutes. He finally raised his head and I saw two tears rolling down his cheeks. I looked at him wordlessly, trying to control my own emotions.

He said in a broken voice, "Forgive me. I've been a stupid-assed moron trying to get the respect of my friends. Instead, I got the greatest humiliation in my life for my stupidities and created a huge problem for myself. I realize that it could even cost me my life now. The Sergeant told me this morning that intending to make an aggression against you was like making an attempt on Fidel's life. All they have to is accuse me of terrorism, being a counter-revolutionary, or even worse, working with the CIA as one of the special foreign agents they discover all the time. Those get executed on the spot without a trial. If not hundreds, then thousands of them every month, he says."

I looked at this boy, so tough before, and thought to myself how many of those kids were patriots but still wound up being arrested for minor things, accused of working with the CIA, and not even having an idea of what those three letters signified. I asked, "What happened to your face?"

Dr. Julio Antonio del Marmol

He grew a little resentful. "The sergeant put me into a cell with four gorillas yesterday. Killers! When he pushed me in and took my handcuffs off, he yelled, 'Fresh meat for the lions today!' I had no argument with anyone. The four immediately started to beat me up like I was a punching bag in a boxer's practice ring. While they beat me up, the sergeant left whistling an Elvis Presley song." He raised his right hand and touched his forehead. "I believe in my heart the sergeant previously arranged this with those four in order to kill me last night. As he was walking away, he said, 'Let me know when you're finished with him. I will have an ambulance ready at the back door.' Thank God Corporal Aurelio showed up. He wasn't even supposed to be working last night. Apparently, the man who was supposed to be on shift was in a car accident, and he substituted in. He heard my screams, saw what was happening, and sounded the alarm. The other police came in and rescued me from being beat to death." He turned a little in the chair and lifted his shirt, showing plainly the black, blue, and green bruising he had over his abdominal area. "The doctors who examined me this morning said I have eight ribs broken and several other fractures."

I noticed his difficulty in moving without pain as he turned back to sit normally in his chair. I leaned back in my own and said in genuine pity, "I'm sorry about what happened to you, my friend." I knew well the type of individuals I had been dealing with as one of the revolutionary leaders of the new government, but it never crossed my mind the kind of abuses they would carry out against these teens. They had accused the previous dictator of these exact things to get the support of the Cuban people to take power, and now they were doing it even worse. And all under the guise of being the benefactors of the poor people, that the government would redistribute all of nation's wealth to the poor! Without hesitation, I stood up and walked over to the door. I opened it and said to Aurelio, "Come in, please."

He took one look at my indignant face. "What happened?"

"Close the door, please, and remove this kid's handcuffs." He looked surprised but did as he was told. I asked the young man, "What is your name?"

His voice cracked with emotion. "My name is Andres Martinez." He extended his right hand as the corporal removed his restraints.

I smiled a little as I took it. "It's a great pleasure to see you have remorse and that I will be able to let you go free. You will sleep in your bed at home tonight. But one thing I want to make sure of: I don't ever want to see you by that liquor store ever again." He nodded and looked remorseful. I said to Aurelio. "Go to records and fill out the necessary forms to release this young man."

Aurelio smiled and gave me a salute. "Immediately, my Commander!" He left the interrogation room, dropping the chains at Andres' feet with a smile.

After he left, I said to Andres, "You don't even know the danger you were in. Not just what the sergeant told you about the firing squad." I shook the folder in my hand. "Somebody is interested in your organs. You know what that means? How many blood tests did you have today this morning?"

"I don't remember, several. Yesterday, they conducted a few. That's when all those doctors came to see me. I began to get suspicious. They had already examined me and took me to get X-rays. According to Sergeant Sardiñas they found that I have hepatitis A. They had to remove me at once to a military hospital's isolation unit."

I shook my head. "Every single test I have here says you were negative for everything. It's a flagrant lie, maybe with the excuse of getting you out of here for whatever purpose. It could be several things: to get your organs, perform experiments, Heaven knows what. When you leave here, I advise you to go straight home and not stop anywhere for any reason. Maybe for a while you should watch your back. If this Sergeant Sardiñas is associated with the people I think he is, your life is in greater danger than you can imagine. These members are all members of a Satanic cult that eat human flesh." He recoiled in revulsion. "And drink their blood in social celebrations." He shivered in horrified shock.

He looked at me with his eyes bugging out. Still horrified, he asked me in wonder, "How do you know all these things at such a young age?"

"Andres Martinez, the body is only a vessel for your spirit. Some of us have spirits that are thousands of years old. Obsession with image and time stimulate the economy, but it never stimulates human harmony. On the contrary—it fixates on competition and creates pain out of the ensuing battles when the body is limited to this road; life and living have been replaced by a concept of life and concept of living. It all seems quite empty. This is called progress, but sadly it is in truth a regression."

Andres looked at me without understanding everything I had just tried to communicate. He scratched his head. It appeared my words sounded in his ears as if it were in the Taiwanese form of the Mandarin language called Guoyu. I understood that my new young friend had a very young spirit, even more so than his vessel. He would not be able to understand, even if I spent a whole month with him. I decided then to change the subject.

"Please don't move from here. Don't even stand up from that chair until either I or Corporal Aurelio return. I have to go to the restroom to discharge my strategic weapon."

He got that and smiled. It appeared that perhaps his spirit was a little older than I had thought. He didn't look into my eyes as if I had been speaking in Chinese or pulling his leg. He said with a smile of gratitude, "I want to again apologize to you and ask your forgiveness for my earlier stupidity."

"Please—this is old news, like salt in water. It exists but when you put the salt in the water it disappears without a trace."

He smiled again, understanding me once more. I left the interrogation room and headed towards the rest rooms. As I walked through the hallway, I passed Corporal Aurelio who smiled at me. He said, "Commander, I've almost finished filling out the forms."

"No rush. I'm going to the restroom and will see you when I'm back in a few minutes." I continued walking down the hallway as I heard the typewriter keys clack once more.

As I walked along, several policemen and detectives saw me, recognized me, and greeted me cordially. As I nearly entered the restroom, the lieutenant commanding the precinct intercepted me. He said, "I'm Lieutenant Mendoza." He gave me his hand. He showed me a picture in his left hand a picture of Fidel with the other leaders, and me in the center. "Please, can you autograph this picture for me? You are the idol of my son, Manolito. He's only eight years old, but he puts my police hat on and salutes the mirror. He wants to be like you and join the Commandoes as soon as he's old enough. His birthday is in a few days, and I want to surprise him of this picture of you with all the leaders of the revolution."

"Of course, Lieutenant." I signed the picture and handed it back to him. "Say hello to your son, Manolito."

"Thank you very much, Commander. I've heard a lot about you, but you confirmed the legends with this gesture." He saluted me and returned to his office.

I went into the restroom. I finished discharging my weapon and went to wash my hands, something I had noticed not everyone there did. I was nearly finished when I heard an explosion that sounded like a car backfiring in the street. But it was followed by two more—this now sounded more like actual shots being fired. I unsnapped my peace bond and drew my pistol quickly as I spun my back to the sink. I walked to the door and very slowly opened it. The first faces I saw were my two friends, Daniel and Cisneros. Weapons in hand, they had entered the building.

Both of them were worried, their faces puzzled. Daniel asked, "What happened, Commander?"

I replied with a shrug, "I don't know. I just got out of the bathroom."

Everyone was walking at a rapid pace towards the end of the corridor. We followed the crowd. As we neared the interrogation room, I saw the door was open. Corporal Aurelio held the release papers he had been working on in his hand. A dark cloud filled my thoughts as if I had seen what happened. When we arrived at the door, the picture in my mind was identical to what we saw. A large pool of blood was on the floor surrounding the body of the young Andres Martinez, a gunshot wound in his forehead, one in his temple, and one in his right leg. Sitting in the chair I had been in a few moments before was Sergeant Sardiñas, his pistol still in his right hand as it rested on top of the table.

He cynically said, "He attacked me. When I entered this room, I don't know how, but he didn't have his restraints on. He hit me with the chains and handcuffs." He showed a bruise on his left hand to the Lieutenant. It could easily have been self-inflicted. He added, "I shot him first in the leg, but he acted crazy, and so I had no other alternative than to shoot to kill, hitting him in the head."

I was outraged, trying my best to contain my frustration. I was completely convinced that what he had just performed was an execution, not self-defense. It crossed my mind the possibility existed that the organs of every one of us could be such a valuable commodity to all these murderers that no one was safe any longer. For the first time, I was concerned for my life. I had so much information in my head now that I never would be able to sleep soundly unless I had my gun close to me. Especially with these diabolic creatures of Lucifer roaming freely in our country with the absolute power of the totalitarian regime they had prepared.

I was shaken tremendously. It started in my feet and worked its way up my body to my head. Corporal Aurelio tried to show the release forms that I had not yet signed, explaining that what Sardiñas had said didn't hold water. Mendoza cut him off, glancing at the papers Aurelio tried to show him. He snatched them and violently ripped them to pieces and tossed them in the trash can. He clearly didn't want to hear it.

I knew nothing that I could say or do at that moment would return that innocent young man to life. I commended my soul to Jesus and all His forces in the universe that kept me safe when I was born and survived my entry into this world. I could not stay silent in the face of this horrendous crime.

I excused myself as I pushed my way through the crowd with Daniel and Cisneros following me. I entered the interrogation room wordlessly. I picked up the trash can next to the table and violently emptied its contents onto the table. I silently reassembled the pieces. Everyone watched me work in surprise, including the corporal, the sergeant, and the lieutenant. After I reassembled the release forms on the table, Sardiñas tried to alleviate the tension, as the silence was so great that one could hear a pin drop. No one dared say anything to me given the black fury on my face and the pistol at my side.

He joked, "What's up, Commandantico? Did you lose your power of speech in the trash?"

I looked him in the eyes. "No, I haven't. But I believe that some of you might have lost your decency and dignity."

The sergeant and lieutenant looked at me in surprise. Mendoza tried to calm the situation. "Commandantico, please calm down. We're all very tense here with what just happened. I believe it's better to look at everything with calm head before we say anything offensive or do something that we'll regret later."

The sergeant looked at me with a hate-filled expression. I took one of the pieces of the torn-up document. One could clearly see it said, "The subject is to be freed immediately by the authorization of the Commandantico." I put the piece of paper in front of Mendoza's eyes, then Sardiña's, and then the other officers assembled. I yelled, "Freedom!" I tapped the paper. "This document shows that I asked Corporal Aurelio to free this prisoner." I showed it to Aurelio, raising it slightly so he could see.

Aurelio spoke up immediately. "I don't know what business the Sergeant had in this interrogation room since he passed the case to me and told me to handle it together with the Commandantico."

Sardiñas yelled, "I passed by the hallway, and through that small window in the door saw the prisoner was freed of his restraints! I assumed he was trying to escape—that is why I entered the room, to put him back in handcuffs and return him to his cell."

I asked, "Sergeant, did you not tell me that this young man had never been arrested before?"

Montauk: The Lightning Chance

"Yes." He spoke with a challenge in his voice. "What the hell does that have to do with what we're talking about here?"

I shook my head. "Then why did you put that young kid in a cell with four gorillas of career offenders, say to them before you left for them to let you know when they were finished with him, and that you would have an ambulance in the rear ready to take his body?"

Sardiñas stood up violently and drew his pistol as he shoved the chair back behind him. He yelled, "Where the hell did you get that from, you snot-nosed piece of shit?"

Before he could even train his pistol on me, I cocked mine and braced it over my left arm, as did Daniel and Cisneros, who took up positions to my left and right. I had it trained right on his head. "Blink, and you die! Put your pistol down slowly, or you will die in a worse manner than your execution of that kid. Using your own foul language, Sergeant Shit! There will be two bodies to pick up at the back door of this station in a very few seconds, one being this one and the other will be you."

Daniel and Cisneros spread out on either side to make it more difficult if he tried to snap off three shots to get all of us. He hesitated indecisively.

I yelled, "You want to die today? Or do you want to leave it for some other day?"

Sardiñas was petrified and looked at Mendoza for support. Mendoza looked at him dubiously, shrugged his shoulders, and stepped back. It was clear from the expressions on the faces of the assembled police and detectives that Sardiñas was not well-liked. It was clear he was on his own. I looked at Corporal Aurelio. "Corporal, disarm the Sergeant. Do me a favor—put him with the same four criminals he put this kid with. I will go in a little while to tell them to let me know when they get finished with him. I'll find out if there's anything else the sergeant hasn't told us yet. I'm sure they'll be happy to tell me everything when I speak with them one on one if they have a deal with the sergeant to not let that kid leave the cell alive."

Aurelio took his weapons and handcuffed him. I said to Cisneros, "Go with him and make sure nothing happens."

Mendoza asked me, "What are you going to do with him?"

"For the moment, put him where he belongs—behind bars like an animal. I will ask the highest authorities in the Ministry of the Interior to begin an exhaustive investigation of what's gone on here, the criminal activities he's been involved in and who his accomplices here are." Mendoza paled and swallowed nervously.

A little while later, as I was preparing to leave the station, I said my farewells to the officers there (none of whom had a good word for Sardiñas), Mendoza came over to me. "Commandantico, can we have a word in private?"

"Very well," I said with a small smile in a friendly tone. I didn't want to let him know that his attitude in defense of the sergeant had in my mind given me very serious suspicions about his involvement in these activities as well. Aurelio had told me when he tried to report what he had seen he had been demoted as a punishment. Mendoza, in my mind, was the only one who possessed there the authority to do so.

As we walked towards his office, he noticed my silence. To break the ice, he said, "You are very intelligent, Commandantico, and everything I've heard about you I can corroborate today. Without any doubts in my mind, you possess a superior power above all of us, probably not just mentally but also a gift from Nature to be able to maintain your balance of law and order and your good conduct with us human beings." He nodded. "I am convinced and in my criteria that you have been picked to be a great leader, or maybe a future President or Prime Minister, if not in our country than in some other place in the world." I smiled at his words, full of empty gossip. I understood that he didn't even believe it himself. He was just pumping up my ego to inject in my brain a sense of grandiosity in order to overpower me. That might have worked on a weak mind indeed, and on people like Che and Fidel who already had grandiose dreams of conquering power beyond anybody's imagination. Mendoza had no idea that I already was aware that this is the oldest weapon to be used in order to control a man's mind. It was called personal vanity. It corrupted and destroyed the most beautiful minds with noble ideas and great dreams through the temptation of that vanity and the thirst for power for absolute control over other human beings.

We arrived at his office and entered. He opened a small refrigerator and offered me something to drink. I replied, "No, thank you."

He opened a small bottle of Coca-Cola he pulled out for himself. He took a glass from behind his glass, put in a few ice cubes, and then opened one of the desk drawers. He pulled out a bottle of Bacardi rum and began to prepare for himself what used to be called a Cuba Libre (now called a mojito). What he wanted to tell me, my intuition said, that

Montauk: The Lightning Chance

he required a boost of alcohol to encourage himself because he needed to substitute what he lacked: courage. Finally, after taking a long sip, he looked at me and asked with a small smile as he raised his glass, "This is my medicine. Have you never drunk alcohol before?"

I nodded. "Yes. I drink Grand Marnier daiquiri a la Marmol."

He looked at me in surprise. He shook his head. "What is that?"

I smiled this time. "You don't know? This is most unique, preferred cocktail to the famous writer, Ernest Hemingway."

This time he was even more surprised. "Who is the creator of this cocktail? Your grandpa?"

I smiled again and crossed my arms. "No. My grandpa only drinks *guayabita del pinar*. The creator of this exquisite cocktail was me, I can say in all modesty. Just a few days ago."

He looked at me in awe this time. There may have been a little admiration in it, too. "Now I understand more clearly the admiration and fascination my Manolito has for you. You're so young and yet you have all this experience. It would be the envy of many men multiple times your age. They don't have not just your experience but also your intelligence."

I smiled and thanked him for his compliment. I understood that this compliment was for real. I leaned back in my chair. "You mentioned you wanted to talk to me about something. What did you want from me? I have an idea that this is about Sergeant Sardiñas. True or false?"

He looked at me mischievously with a small smile. He nodded. "Definitely your intuition is in line with reality. As reasonable, it appears that you once more are right about the topic I want to discuss with you concerning Sergeant Sardiñas."

I smiled. "Very well. That conversation will be very interesting to me. I might learn something from it, especially as I want to study to be an attorney and learn civil and criminal law. Of course, that will be at the age when I'm prepared to enter the university. It will be fascinating to hear from your mouth, who looks like an educated man, proper manners, and eloquent enough to defend the worst delinquent or criminal. Especially if that delinquent or criminal happens to be your friend or associate. That will be a strong incentive for you to fight in your argument."

Mendoza smiled and shook his head. He looked at me in surprise. "How did you know I was an attorney?"

"Even though I have a strong intuition that seldom fails me," I looked him in the eyes and reclined in my chair as I shook my head, "I didn't know you were an attorney until you told me so. As I said before, my intuition and capability of reading people's demeanor rarely gives me a wrong reading. Its screaming in my ear from a little while ago that you're not a common ignorant individual as most people involved in this revolution that follows the crowd to obtain personal benefit from the movement. If I'm not wrong, you follow this movement because of your patriotism and internal feelings that determine for you what is wrong and right. I believe you want to return your country to democracy and freedom. This country that you love in your heart. And if I'm not wrong, I believe you are a good man."

"Thank you. What else?"

"Well, I believe that the good man has a conscience. He tries very hard to fulfill his responsibilities and duties without contradicting the new norms and rules that have recently been established by the new leaders of this government. In that process that good man has been derailed, has wandered a little from the basic principles of the universe and the divine forces that give form and life to every human being. Those principles are basically decency and respect for other peoples' lives and the right to be free and exist, the same cause so many people died for in order to depose the dictator. Unfortunately, as that man compromises his integrity, he walks down a dark alley he wants to get out of desperately. His conscience doesn't allow him any longer to live in peace. But he cannot find the exit, and as time passes it gets worse, to the point he can no longer breathe. That is how uncomfortable that man feels."

I had told him all this like a psychic reading someone's future and past. I kept my eyes locked on his without blinking. His face turned red as a tomato as I finished. At the same time his face spasmed as his emotions warred inside him. I could see how disturbed he was thanks to two tears that escaped his control and ran down his cheeks and his bloodshot eyes. I had enunciated exactly what he had been suffering for quite some time now, but he had lacked the courage to confront it for himself. Now this skinny underaged kid's words brought back all the remorse he had been feeling and suppressing. He was overwhelmed.

"Who are you?" He looked at me intensely.

With a placid, serious expression in my face, I replied, "Maybe I'm the voice of your conscience that wants to set you free from your spiritual pain, which is more unbearable that any physical torture."

Montauk: The Lightning Chance

He didn't take his eyes away from mine. "Yes. It's true. Yes, it's true." I maintained our locked gaze, but he dropped his eyes so that he could wipe away his tears. He picked up the glass and took another long sip as if he were trying to drown his pain and insecurities in that alcohol. When he raised his head again, I could see two fresh tears escape his eyes. This time he pulled a handkerchief from his pants pocket and dried his face without any shame. Those tears were for him a release from his pain. As he dried his eyes he added, "They say men don't cry, but that is absolute crap and ignorance. The man who cannot cry, unless he has a physical impediment that blocks his tear ducts, completely lacks any human sentiment. I believe the only being that is capable of this and probably enjoys it is Satan, because he has no conscience or feelings."

I nodded in agreement. "I believe tears in our eyes is like an escape valve for the pressure cookers of our brain and hearts. It removes pain from our bodies and conscience. Without those tears, I believe that our hearts and brains would blow up like those pressure cookers without a release."

Mendoza nodded and looked at me once more in the eyes, this time with a small smile that contradicted his red eyes and tears at what I just said. He blew his nose with the handkerchief. "Whatever I'm about to say to you, I want you to keep in confidence between us."

"Of course. If that's the way you want it, I give you my word of honor, that unless you give me the green light after consulting with you first, I will never repeat it to anyone."

"Very well. I know that, and you don't have to swear it to me. Everything started a few months ago. Sergeant Sardiñas was transferred over here on the direct orders of Che and Commander Piñeiro." I shook my head at that but continued to respectfully listen. "They started to take our youngest teenaged boys that we had in custody for driving under the influence of alcohol or getting into street fights or disturbances in night clubs. Minor infractions. They said they found in the records of these accused that they were mixed up with high crimes like attempted assassination of the main leaders of the revolution—usually Fidel. They had different accusers and witnesses on file to testify to it. Unfortunately, Commandantico, after Corporal Aurelio—who used to be a sergeant—brought this to my attention and examined these kids' records, I found that none of these accusers existed. They either had already been killed by the dictator or had already abandoned the country when the revolution won last January. After I exhausted the investigation, I followed my duty and dug deeper before passing it to my superiors. I discovered some of these kids had been executed by firing squad. I took copies of the birth certificates of these supposed accusers and I realized they had been charged by ghost witnesses. One way or the other, I could not find anyone. How could these people be witnesses to attempts on the life of the Supreme Leader when they were one of the first ones who wanted him dead? It didn't make any sense at all."

I shook my head and squeezed my chin. It was very disturbing, but I continued to listen to Lieutenant Manolo Mendoza's narrative in silence. I could see him getting more and more disturbed. He took another long sip from his drink, leaving very little left among the nearly melted ice cubes. He put the glass down again and scratched the hairs of his left sideburns a little. He continued, "After I presented my report the next day Che and Piñeiro were in my office. No previous appointment or notice. They came in several cars with their entourage, perhaps with the intention of intimidating me. They first took Aurelio to an office, which they locked themselves in for several hours. Apparently, Aurelio didn't agree to sweep it all under the rug. Saying that this was a matter of national security, top secret, they said this had to be completely sealed. It would be detrimental to the political process and ideas of the new socialist ideology they wanted to implant in the country. When they gave it up with Aurelio, they came to me. They offered to promote me to Captain and put me in charge of the entire district in the Central Police in the capital if I agreed to their demands. If I didn't, they promised me they would demote me for being not in the spirit of the revolution and transfer me to one of the provinces out in the hinterlands."

I smiled. "Of course. As is logical, an intelligent man like you, you had no other alternative but to take the deal."

He looked at me indignantly, but it seemed more directed inwards. "Of course I had no alternative!" He fiddled with the glass in his angry agitation, turning it around with his fingers of his right hand. "I could have sent them both to hell and assumed the dignified position that Sergeant Major Aurelio had taken. I was ordered by them later to demote him, and I've been so ashamed since then that I cannot look in his eyes even now." He raised his glass and slammed it down on the desk. It shattered in his hand. I noticed a small trickle of blood mix with the remnants of the liquor and melted ice running across the desk.

I looked at him calmly and offered him one of my handkerchiefs. He declined it, pulling out another one. He stood up in silence. He

Montauk: The Lightning Chance

picked up the trash can, grabbed some paper napkins from the minibar, and swept the pieces of glass into the trash can. I remained silent, waiting for him to regain his composure after he had released all the internal pressure with that one violent action. I needed to see what his next reaction would be. I thought that he might perhaps turn out to be the decent individual he had been for many years before. I didn't know him, but normally people who confront their inner demons and overcome that pain return to being the person they once were. I didn't want to aggravate the situation. Even though I knew the low levels of indecent behavior these men could stoop to, especially Che, nothing would surprise me anymore. They were followers of Satan and all he had told me proved what I had initially been debriefed by my uncle Emilio and the young Captain Canen.

Lieutenant Mendoza poured and mixed himself another cocktail. At the same time, he apologized. "Commandantico, I'm sorry for my previous reaction. It was kind of violent." He showed me the cut he had on his hand. "Even though I only hurt myself, I realize it was utterly stupid. I should damage those who have abused their power and have obligated me to lower myself to their level." He raised his glass high. "Cuba Libre! What a joke!" It occurred to me right then that I might be able to make an ally of this man. He said with complete conviction, "I assure you that this will never happen to me again, even if I have to swim to Miami with my wife and son riding on my back."

I looked at him and saw his sincerity as I looked into his eyes. After a brief pause in which I consulted with my angels, I smiled as I watched him take another sip of his refilled drink. "I would like you to answer two questions for me if you can. What can I do for you? And why have you so openly entrusted me with this? If it's possible for you to reply to those two questions, I would really appreciate it."

He looked at me in surprise. He hesitated before answering for a few seconds. "I like your personality. You go directly to the lungs. You don't go around to any other organs to get what you want, which I assume is oxygen."

I smiled. "Yes, you're right. And we just happen to be talking about organs and psychological manipulation in which our enemies possess PhDs."

Mendoza replied, "I'm 100% in agreement with you. We are the stupid ones if we allow them to intimidate us. Let me answer your first question—what you can do for me." He nodded. "First, I beg of you when you make your report, don't implicate me in anything that happened here today with Sergeant Sardiñas. OK?"

"I will try to do that. And my other question?"

He scratched his sideburn hairs, fiddling them with his fingers. "Well, thinking about it carefully, for me to ask you to not involve me, I knew I had to come clean with you, or you wouldn't take me seriously. I know you haven't even a single hair of being a fool. That is why you're around all these leaders and Fidel keeps you so close to him."

I leaned forward in my chair to get closer to him. "Bravo! You passed two questions of loyalty very well. To me, loyalty is a virtue and one of the most important ones a man can possess. Without loyalty, no one qualifies to obtain my friendship. The other important quality for a man to survive in the world against this diabolic cult and their intrigues is to listen to those who have an older spirit, who can explore and get to know very deeply the universe. They have had the opportunity they get to know very well Satan and his tricks, hypocrisy, and his multiple personalities and faces. This is the only tool that will save you from him destroying you. It will teach you how to survive multiple attacks from him from the moment he starts to plan them some of which can be fatal."

He looked at me and leaned back in his chair. "In that case, what is your first recommendation to me?"

"I see you paid attention and put your ear to my words. Very well, I say to you right now that my first advice is to throw away that cocktail you have in your hand. You've already had one, and it can relax you, offering you a way to see things in a calmer way. But the second one could be your death sentence. Your enemies have studied every move you make and weakness you have, and those weaknesses can be a blessing to those seeking weapons to destroy you." I stood up. "You are on duty right now, aren't you?" He nodded. "With the modern technology we have today, all anybody has to do is take a few pictures of you at this moment, in uniform, drinking alcohol in your office, and they have more than sufficient evidence to demote you if not even arrest you to be more severe with you. Or they could recommend a dishonorable discharge in which you'll lose your pension and all your benefits…" Before I had finished, Mendoza stood up and dumped his drink in the trash can. "I was only starting with the minor things and was going to build up, but apparently that wasn't necessary. To those with understanding, few words are necessary."

"All officers do the same," he said lamely.

Montauk: The Lightning Chance

I sat down. "Not all the officers are under the microscopes of Che and Piñeiro. Got it?"

He nodded. "You are 100% right. I'm sorry."

"No need to apologize. If you don't make a mistake, you don't have to apologize. But don't try to justify it, or you'll look like a fool. But pay attention so you don't make the same error again. My second recommendation, to bring peace to your conscience, I want to say what you did with Che and Piñeiro which is exactly how I've handled them and would proceed in your position. You'll ask how it is possible, and I'll tell you. It's very simple: what Corporal Aurelio did was without doubt the dignified position and the right thing to do, but it's not always the most intelligent thing to do. He not only endured the humiliation with his family and friends of being demoted, but he also blew his cover before all these miserable men. They will never let him get even an inch close to them, ever. This means, in order to destroy those enemies, water doesn't always work with fire. Sometimes you need a bigger fire to stop it. We don't have to be evil, but we have to be strong and clever to destroy it, or they'll continue doing damage to others. What Aurelio did was castrate himself. That doesn't sound good and rather painful in the end. They will continue to do their evil things to other people, and he has no power to stop them now."

Mendoza leaned back and ran his fingers through his hair. "Where did you learn all these things? Where do you come from?"

"Maybe from previous lives. Maybe in the womb of my mother." I said that last with a tiny smile on my face. "I want to ask you one more thing."

"Go ahead and ask whatever you want."

"When are you to be transferred to the new position that Che and Piñeiro offered you?"

"Tomorrow."

I smiled. "How would you like to get back the great grace of Corporal Aurelio?"

"I would do whatever is necessary. I'm so ashamed of what I did to him."

"You'll be able to look at him, and he'll look at you with even greater respect than he had for you before. He'll also look at you with infinite gratitude."

Mendoza grinned in satisfaction. "Commandantico, you actually made my day and caused it to end with shiny gold ribbons. If this really happens, I will recover my self-esteem."

"Who will be the one who replaces you here?"

"Sergeant Sardiñas."

He hadn't even finished saying it as his face lit up as he understood what I was hinting at. He put his left hand to his mouth and then opened his arms. "Oh, my God! You are either His greatest angel or a little devil! That is a brilliant idea!!"

"What idea? I haven't suggested anything yet."

"I know where you're going. The only one authorized to name my successor is me. After what Sardiñas did by killing that kid today, he's no longer qualified. All I have to do to excuse myself to Che and Piñeiro is tell them that Sardiñas made the stupid mistake of doing that in front of everyone else. It will be a hard pill for them to swallow, but they can go to hell. I'm not the one compromising what they agreed to—he did it! I'm transferred tomorrow," he said joyfully, "and then I'll not just put Aurelio back in his duties, I'll promote him to the Lieutenant in charge of this precinct!"

"You read my mind."

"You already told me in very few words."

"Well, you also have the intelligence. Like I said, only a few words were necessary."

He stood up joyfully. He ran over to me, opening his arms, and before I could do anything, he motioned me to stand up and gave me a bear hug. To this day I remember the strength of that hug. He was around 6' 6", very muscular and about 300 pounds, and I was a still-developing kid of perhaps 60 pounds. I screamed, "*Carajo!* Let me go, I can't breathe!"

"I'm sorry. I forgot you're only four years older than Manolito."

I breathed deeply. I looked at him sternly and pointed at him with my left hand as I put my right on my pistol. "If you want to live, don't ever do that again! You nearly asphyxiated me!" I took several deep breaths to regain my breath. It took a few seconds to recover from that killer hug. "Why don't you call Aurelio? We can tell him together."

He snapped his fingers. "Good idea." He picked up his phone and called the corporal on the front desk. "Please tell Corporal Aurelio to come to my office immediately." He looked at me still massaging my ribs. "You OK?"

I nodded. "Please don't do that again. I thought I was going to die. I realize you were ecstatic in your great happiness. Man, you have tremendous strength in your arms." He smiled and apologized again, but I waved it off in dismissal as I continued to regain my breath. Several days later, I still had muscular spasms. Mima had said that some love could be deadly.

A few minutes later a respectful tap was heard. Mendoza yelled, "Come in, the door is open!"

Corporal Aurelio opened the door timidly. He walked in. "Excuse me, Lieutenant. The corporal at the front desk said you wanted to talk to me."

"Yes. Close the door behind you, please." Aurelio looked at me sitting there and misgivings entered his mind that I had shared his information and was now in deep trouble. He looked at me in worry mixed with reproach. His dilemma was to either deny he had said anything to me, appearing in front of me like a coward, or admit that he had told me and accept the consequences. He looked at me again nervously, kind of the way a gladiator might look at the spectators in the Colosseum in Rome after being thrown to the lions with only a small knife to defend himself on the sands stained with the blood of their previous victims. He stood before us timidly, not even daring to sit down until Mendoza said, "Corporal, please sit down and relax."

He looked at me once more in agonized uncertainty in his eyes. He clearly wanted to ask me what was going on and what I had said, but he knew he couldn't. I understood his frustration and anxiety, so I smiled and said, "I think Lieutenant Mendoza and I have come to a very pretty arrangement. You will benefit the most in everything and will be compensated for your previous honesty and all the inconvenience, harassment, and suffering you went through in the humiliation of your demotion. It was completely unfair, and I know from my discussion with Lieutenant Mendoza without any doubts agrees with me."

Corporal Aurelio, as he listened to what I was saying, could no longer control his emotions. He swallowed the knot that was forming in his throat and blinked back his tears. His voice cracked and was thick with the emotion of his joy. "Thank you," was all he could say.

"You don't have to thank me," I said. "It's called justice, and I have to be the one to apologize for the injustice you suffered. I have to thank you for your courage in taking the risk you did to tell me all the things you said without knowing what I would do with that information. I can assure you that I will make my best effort and use all the resources I have at my disposal to alleviate every single hassle you've been going through. I will try to expose those responsible for all the injustices you suffered."

Lieutenant Mendoza swallowed and said in a guilty tone and expression, "I should be the one to apologize to Aurelio, Commandantico, not you. All you've done is open both our eyes and try to remedy whatever immoral acts that have occurred here and in other precincts from the beginning of the new government until now." He halted to correct himself and pointed at himself. "At least, I am guilty as well because of my cowardly character by converting myself into an accomplice to these criminals. Even though we cannot restore life to Andres Martinez, we might at least be able to prevent a repetition of this to others like him in our country."

Corporal Aurelio listened to Mendoza in shocked surprise. "Thank you, Lieutenant. You did what you had to do to survive. I understand and have no grudges against you. You're a decent, good man."

Mendoza and I exchanged looks, and I saw fresh tears in his eyes. I said to him, "Remember, it's never too late to remedy our bad actions in the past. Especially when we know how to recognize that our actions were not the most dignified and took away slowly our tranquility. It makes us evil, destroying our spirits and conscience."

Lieutenant Mendoza looked at me and shook his head. "You don't even have the slightest idea, because for many weeks I could not sleep more than a few hours each night. They took away my self-esteem. I could not look in my wife's eyes for a long time out of fear she could see my terrible actions. The man she married and loved had become one more criminal out of the bunch." He looked me in the eyes. In the same way he looked at me, he looked at Aurelio. His expression was worried as he spoke. "I only ask you both a great favor—please, we have to maintain in absolute confidence everything we discuss here today and are going to do. We can't share this with anyone, especially not here, and whatever happens we take it to our graves. Not for my life, but for those of my wife and little boy, Manolito. If I can get that silence from you, that will represent the tranquility and peace to become once more the man I used to be. We don't even know who here is an informant for Che or Piñeiro. I can assure you that neither of them will stop for anything. They have no scruples and are capable of doing anything, killing anyone, especially with the power of the entire government behind them like they do. Anyone who gets in their way and creates an obstacle to their plans will end up dead."

I smiled. "For my part, I promise you that no one will know a single word of what we say or plan here today."

Aurelio said, "You've known me for a long time, Lieutenant. I would rather die than compromise you or anyone."

"Thank you," Mendoza said.

I said, "Believe me, I know exactly what you're talking about. I can assure you that the power Che and Piñeiro possess is not used for good, but for evil. I've been close to both of them and I saw only a few days ago Che blow his best friend's brains out in front of me just because he suspected him of betrayal. At that moment, Che showed me his true colors. Before you blink, someone's life is gone, and the body burned at the side of a road. Heaven knows what lie he told the victim's family; probably an invention about being killed on a special internationalist mission to bring down the Yankee capitalists. He even brought that man's family a medal for being a hero to the proletariat. That is the depth of his cynicism."

Both looked at me in shocked terror at my revelation of Che's true nature. They both shook their heads and murmured about how Che must be a demon. They crossed themselves. Mendoza said, "We have to be very careful with everyone even here. Everyone in general, because these individuals are masters of blackmail, deceit, and bribery. They know well how to intimidate anyone. I advise you not to trust anyone from this point on."

I replied, "Don't worry about it. This will not be discussed with anyone until I complete my investigation. If I find the right individual that I believe will actually do something, I will put this file in their hands. If not, I will tell you everyone in this is rotten, all the way to the top. Either way, I will tell you the truth." I looked at Mendoza. "Well, why are you waiting on giving Corporal Aurelio the good news?"

"Yes, this is the most important thing of all. Corporal, how would you like to be my replacement in this place with a promotion to Lieutenant as Chief of this Precinct?"

Aurelio looked at Mendoza incredulously. Then he looked at me and smiled. I nodded in confirmation. He said, "Thank you very much, Commandantico."

"No, don't thank me. Thank the Captain."

Aurelio looked confused. "Captain?"

"Yes, Lieutenant Mendoza will no longer be a Lieutenant. You will be, and he will be Captain Mendoza, in charge of the Central District."

Aurelio looked at both of us and grinned. "Congratulations, Captain."

Mendoza said, "I'll give you the full details later. But it's important that nobody, without exception, knows that you will be my replacement until tomorrow, when it's too late to stop it." He pointed at me. "It's all the Commandantico's idea."

I added, "Not entirely. I began it, but you completed the thought. It's absolutely important that nobody, not even your wife, has any knowledge that all this until Lieutenant Mendoza makes the announcement in the morning. Get up early tomorrow morning, Aurelio, and when you get here you will start your new job. No more Corporal Aurelio, it will be the fledgling Lieutenant Aurelio."

He shot up out of his chair so rapidly he nearly knocked it over had he not grabbed the back of it. He ran over to me with a huge grin, arms open, with the intention of giving me another of those killer bear hugs. I jumped as if loaded by a spring, sending my chair clattering to the floor. I drew my pistol and trained it on him. "You stop right there!"

"What?" He stopped in absolute shock at the extremity of my reaction.

"Don't dare to hug me. My preservation instincts have kicked in. You didn't know, *carajo*, that Mendoza nearly suffocated me a few minutes ago."

Aurelio turned serious. "I wasn't going to hurt you—I just wanted to give you a hug. It was never in my mind the intention to hurt you."

I smiled as I held my hand high. "You don't understand. I still have, I think, a fractured rib from this gorilla's hug, and he nearly asphyxiated me. Please express your gratitude to me in another way."

He looked pleased. "I didn't know what happened before."

"That's why I pulled my gun, to get you to stop."

"Commandantico. You must have an extraordinary gift from Providence to make everyone around you happy."

Mendoza said, "You have no idea how true that is."

"Thank you very much to both of you. Like you said not too long ago, Aurelio, I was only doing my duty. The difference is that my job is with the Supreme Architect of the Universe. I answer to no one. I'll leave you guys so you can complete the circle and debrief each other about what will happen tomorrow. I'm pretty sure Aurelio has a thousand questions for you."

Mendoza got up and picked up the phone on his desk with his right hand. He dialed a number and a voice on the other side picked up. "Yes, Lieutenant?"

Montauk: The Lightning Chance

"Corporal, I want you to get two patrol cars with four officers each. Escort the Commandantico for as long as he wants until he dismisses you."

"I'm just going to my uncle's," I protested.

"Yes but allow me this courtesy. It's the least I can do."

"OK, thank you very much. I promise you that I won't use them for very long."

"If you need them again, just pick up the phone and you'll have that escort whenever you want." He opened his arms again.

"No, no killer bear hugs!"

"No, no—I just want to give you a gentle hug before you leave."

"I'll settle for a handshake."

After I said goodbye to them, I left the station. While Che and Fidel had escorts who were driving civilian cars and wearing civilian clothing, I had official cars with uniformed officers while I drove in a marked, official jeep. People stopped and stared as our procession drove past. The lights of the police cars attracted all manner of attention. People even came out of stores to watch us drive past.

Daniel said, "Commandante, I love this! I'm starting to feel important. I know I've felt that way a lot around you, but now I feel bigger than Fidel."

Cisneros said, "I have the same feeling. It's extraordinary how good it feels. I think we should circle around Havana a few times so everyone can see us! Just a little tour. This is good promotion for the Commandos. People look at us like we're celebrities!"

Daniel said, "Of course we're celebrities. Don't you see it? Look at the crowds wherever we go.

I said, "Be careful guys. Ego is the most powerful weapon of Satan."

At that moment, Che and his three Oldsmobiles drove by. The windows all rolled down as they gawked at who it might be. Che nearly broke his neck as he leaned out the window to look at us better. Che exclaimed, "Oh, it's the Commandantico!" He waved at us vigorously.

Daniel muttered, "Look at that moron!"

We continued to drive down San Lazaros Street toward one of the most important barrios in Central Havana. It occupied the area bounded by Calle Infanta to the west, Calle Zanja to the south, Calle Belascoáin to the east, and the Gulf of Mexico to the north, forming the western edge of Central Havana. This would be the district Captain Mendoza will be taking charge of the next day. It was the most important district in the entire capital: a fairly good bribe that Che gave to Mendoza. This side was officially named the Third District or District Number 8 that covered the eight kilometers of the Malecon along the sea wall. It included the neighborhood of the Vedado, where all the luxury hotels in the capital were built: the Capri Hotel Cabaret and Casino, Havana Hilton, the Riviera, and many others.

We had nearly reached the Malecon when a temporary seafood stand caught my attention as we passed by it. Many of these formed in empty lots in the capital, each with a different type of food. They could be there one day and gone the next. I thought I recognized the car of Yaneba's family, and it looked like they were in line to get served.

I said, "Daniel, slow down and turn around. Make sure you do it slowly so the cars in front and behind us realize what we're doing. I think I know somebody at that seafood stand."

Daniel started to slow down and reached his arm out to signal the car behind, beeped the horn to attract the attention of the lead car, and made a circling gesture. The other cars understood and stopped and turned with us. We pulled over and parked. I was not mistaken. They were by now seated at a table beneath an umbrella, plates in hand. As soon as Yaneba saw us, she stood up and started to walk towards the jeep. As she came, she called out, "I saw you pass by, but didn't know if you saw us!" She gave me a hug and a kiss on my cheek as I got out of the jeep.

I greeted her and could see that she was under emotional distress. I said to Daniel and Cisneros, "Order whatever you want. I'm going to go say hello to Yaneba's family." As I left, I said to the chief of the escort, "Hey, if you guys want to eat something, order whatever you want."

He smiled. "There's a lot of us!" he exclaimed.

"Don't worry about it. It will go on my expense account." I patted my skinny frame. "I can't put too much in this tank, anyway. Eat for me, and I'll get fat for you."

"Thank you, Commandante." He held his hand out to me. "It's a great pleasure to meet you. I'm Corporal Rodriguez."

"The pleasure is all mine," I replied. "Eat all you want and take your time. We'll be here for a while until my friend's family finishes their meal." I looked at my watch. "Oh, my goodness! It's already ten pm. Time flies when you're having fun!"

"Not when you're working," the Corporal said.

"I'm working, too. I just enjoy my work."

"OK, OK."

I hadn't realized how much time we had spent at the police station. No wonder my stomach was growling. I added, "We slept until late today, skipped lunch, and only had a light dinner, so I'm actually hungry."

Yaneba smiled. "Why don't you order something, then? This is the best seafood place in Havana. We eat here frequently."

Daniel said, "Why not a seafood cocktail? I don't think something more substantial will settle well at this time of night."

I smiled. "OK. But no picante or anything like that! Everything else: ketchup, lemon, onions, cilantro, and if they have them, green olives."

"OK," he said. "Go to your friend's family. I'll bring it to you when it's ready."

"Thank you very much."

Daniel politely asked Yaneba, "Do you want something for yourself?"

She shook her head. "I already have my food on the table over there. Thank you very much for asking, Daniel." She held her hand out to him. "My name is Yaneba."

Daniel took her hand. "Nice to meet you."

Cisneros smiled from the table where he was sitting, already eating from the largest size seafood cocktail he could get. He made sure to be the first in line so he could eat first. Yaneba and I walked to the table where her family, including her younger sister, Elena sat eating their meal. As we walked over, she said, "Don't touch the subject of my uncle's trial unless they do. Everyone is devastated. The sentence came out today, and he's been sentenced to death before the firing squad. He'll be shot in a few days."

I shook my head, my face showing clear distress at that news. I spoke in a very low voice. "In what prison is he being held?"

"In La Cabaña."

Figure 44 La Cabaña

"When will they execute him?"

"We don't know the exact date. We only know it's two or three days from now." She asked in curiosity, "Why are you asking this? You know very well that after someone is sentenced to death in this regime it's impossible to do anything for that person. Anyone who tries to intervene risks being executed as well according to the new revolutionary laws."

"Just remember in this life nothing is impossible, especially when you have the good will of the Supreme Architect of the Universe in your favor. Besides, many things can happen in two or three days. You have to have faith and never, never let fear take it away from you. Don't give Satan a chance to become even more powerful and strong with you. You cannot ever abandon your faith, or it gives evil forces greater power. Don't forget, Satan represents the evil forces of the bad in the world; God represents the noble and good in everyone. For that reason, Satan never will be ever able to prevail. And in the end it won't matter how many battles he wins; we will send him to eternal fires of Hell in the final battle, where he'll be locked up burning every day and never come back to us again."

Yaneba smiled a little. "You know something? That is the thing I admire the most about you and why I like you so much. You cannot deny that you are an eternal optimist."

"Well, I think we should leave this conversation for another place and time. We're getting close to your table."

"Thank you for reminding me."

Montauk: The Lightning Chance

We got to the table and I noticed that her parents received me with a different kind of attitude: more friendly and accepting. I didn't know what she had told them, but it felt a lot better than the cold shoulder I received from them at the Capri. It was hard to understand, but nothing in this world affects my personality more and wounds my feelings deeper than unjustified rejection. They didn't know me well, just superficial greetings when we saw each other in the neighborhood. I didn't think it was fair to evaluate someone just because of how they dressed or the cars in which they drove. Because of my uniform, they prejudged me for being a communist.

We finished the delicious seafood cocktails. The sign they had up at that establishment clearly stated in large navy-blue letters on the white background, "Seafood cocktails with the famous oysters from Sagua La Grande." This place being advertised was a little town in the province of Santa Clara reputed to have the sweetest seafood along the entire coast. Of course, that place was well-known all over the island. We stood up and I said goodbye to her family, and she asked her parents for permission to walk all the way back to the jeep.

On the way back, I asked, "What is the full name of your uncle?"

She looked at me askance. "Bejasmin Cesar Loubus." She kept her eyes locked on mine. "Please, don't even let it cross your mind to do anything crazy. There's nothing anyone can do to stop or delay a death sentence. Only God."

I smiled slightly. "I have very good and close relations with Him and His Son Jesus. Maybe He can intervene for your uncle."

She shook her head. "Please, I beg you—don't do anything crazy that could put your life in danger as well and wind up in the firing squad, OK? I couldn't live with the guilty feeling that happened because of me." She squeezed my right arm as her mother started to call her. They had already loaded into their car. She leaned in and gave me a kiss on the cheek. She held up a finger admonishingly. "Remember what I told you." She ran off to rejoin her family.

Daniel started the jeep and we drove with our police escort to the Hilton Hotel. As we arrived, the same commotion was caused with all the lights. People came out of the hotel to gawk at us, including the valet attendants. We stopped all activity at the hotel for people to see who was arriving. This courtesy was only offered by protocol to international diplomatic personnel. All the attention was enjoyed by Daniel and Cisneros every second. I, on the other hand, felt uncomfortable. It didn't seem very prudent. It attracted more attention to me than was normal and could awaken feelings of jealousy in other leaders in the revolution, with which I had already had some unpleasant experiences. As soon as we pulled in, I dismissed the escort. I asked Daniel for the keys and gave my appreciation to Corporal Rodriguez. I said to Daniel, "You and Cisneros go up to the room and watch TV or whatever you want. My day isn't finished yet—I still have a few things I need to do, and I have to do them by myself."

I said goodbye to them and went to the phone booths in the lobby. I went into the cabinet and closed the door before dialing a number after making sure I was secure and alone. A voice on the other side said, "Hello?"

"I'm sorry to call you this late. This is your nephew, Julio Antonio."

"Yes, I recognize your voice. Is everything OK? Don't worry about the hour, I hadn't gone to sleep yet."

"Yes, everything is OK. I need to talk to you immediately. I need your advice on something extremely important that cannot wait until tomorrow."

"Very well. I was just reading a book. Everyone else is already asleep. Come over and meet me in the clubhouse. I'll call the guard at the security booth to let him know you're coming so he doesn't have to call us to admit you."

"OK. I'm leaving right now. It will only take me a few minutes to get there."

"All right, see you in a little while."

I said goodbye and hung up. I had left the jeep practically at the hotel door so that the valet could keep their eyes on the car for security purposes. Indeed, as I came out, the chief of the attendants gestured towards his eyes. "I've been keeping my eyes on it."

I motioned him over to me. "Come here." I handed him a tip and drove off toward El Nautico. I pulled up to the gate, and the guard on duty signaled me to keep going as he raised the barrier. As I passed by him, he saluted me with a big smile on his face.

I drove to the clubhouse where I had since infancy come for birthday parties and other family events with all my cousins in the family. All of those memories flooded my mind as I pulled up. It was a time when everyone was in harmony and we celebrated with typical Cuban pulled pork, yuca con mojo, plantain bananas, and arroz congri. Those were beautiful, happy moments during which everyone completely forgot all political differences and gathered together to discuss them

Montauk: The Lightning Chance

intelligently in a civilized manner without any insults or disrespect. It crossed my mind that all that might stay in the past. The new reality of the revolution that cost so many innocent young Cuban lives brought with her the most perverse hatred and feelings of revenge that had slowly infected like a contagious disease a great majority of the Cuban people. It probably would stay for a long time and prolong that hatred that Satan created between people for many decades.

When I arrived at the clubhouse, Uncle Emilio signaled to me. He stood beneath one of the umbrellas on the patio outside the building. I parked the jeep and walked towards him, waving my right arm. I didn't know if he could see my smile in the darkness. I walked in that beautiful star-filled night that looked like it had been painted by a master with perfect distribution in that immense space. As I got close to him, he took the pipe he was smoking out of his mouth and gave me a big hug. I felt his care and love, but also felt a mixture of gratitude and pride that he knew he hadn't lost me but gotten me back. Now I was part of his ideological work. I was, in truth, never too far from him spiritually. All I had done, without knowing it myself, was to embark on the most important project in my life using only his knowledge and the basic principles he had taught me to perform a very serious, exhaustive investigatory mission. My objective was to find the truth behind all those leaders of the revolution, who said to the public one thing vastly different from what they had planned for the future of the country. Their intention was to catch everyone by surprise, especially useful fools like my loving father. His was the heart they would break to the point that he would never trust in any politician for the rest of his life.

After we embraced and sat down at the quaint table and chairs with comfortable cushions, I noticed two big steaming mugs on the table. He saw my glance and pushed one of the mugs towards me. He said, "That is for you." He picked up the other one and took a sip of the hot chocolate. "Close to the ocean, especially in these early morning hours, it can get to be very cold."

I smiled. "Thank you. You didn't have to do this."

"For me it is a pleasure, my nephew." He smiled. "Do you still like hot chocolate, as I remember?"

I smiled mischievously. "Yes, and of course if you baptize it with Grand Marnier, that will upgrade it tremendously."

He clapped his left hand to his forehead in mock dismay. "My God, forgive me for initiating my nephew to that liquor."

I interrupted. "Not liquor—Grand Marnier."

"God, please forgive me for that."

"You should thank God for that precisely." He looked at me in surprise. "After you introduced me to it, but not only for that but also for your very savvy and smart advice that one drink is a relaxing sedative, but the second could be deadly. When I tell you what happened in the past 48 hours, if we have the time after what will be a long conversation, I think you'll not just be very proud of your nephew but also fascinated to know that the famous writer, Ernest Hemingway, has placed on his list of famous cocktails our last name."

"How is that? By the way, I'm proud of you no matter what, you know that."

"Well, you'll be even prouder then. I suggested to him when he offered me a daiquiri that since the orange is a relative of lemon and lime to make a cocktail based on that and orange juice. He tasted it and loved it so much that he named it daiquiri a la Marmol."

My uncle took the pipe out of his mouth and laughed. "You won't believe what I'm about to tell you."

"I'll believe anything you say. I have complete trust in you."

"Well, the first thing is that what you said before should be in a book or a movie. The second thing is the tremendous coincidence. When I told you I was reading a book, it was one of his, *A Farewell to Arms*."

I shook my head and grinned. "Maybe too many people believe in coincidence. I don't know if you do or just said that. But I'm completely convinced from my past experience that every single thing, without exception that happens around us in all the universe is predestined, and all we can do is minimize the effects or lessen the impact. But we can never avoid it."

He looked at me. "I have the same opinion. Everything is already written before we're born. The irrefutable proof we have of that is before our eyes today."

"What is that?"

"The result is that we've spent nearly all our lives, my friends and I, trying to avoid happening has occurred with this revolution. It was predestined to be stolen by Satan from the real revolutionaries, the Cuban people." He took a sip thoughtfully as his face grew serious. Mug still in hand, he continued, "We cannot avoid it. Like you said before, maybe we can give it a twist and change its destiny in the process. It happened, but maybe we can detour it along an alternate route." He took another drink. "It will be very interesting the next time I prepare a hot chocolate and experiment with a shot of Grand Marnier. If this results in something so delicious as the cocktail you just told me about, we will add it to your list and call it the result Chocolate a la Marmol."

"You can take credit for that. You're a del Marmol, too. I don't want to under any circumstance to end in the hands Satan through one of his oldest tricks to control us: our egos."

He raised his left hand and tapped my arm with an expression of conviction in his voice. "Ha, ha, ah—no, no, no, no. That will never work with you. You are too intelligent to let anyone conquer you with that old trick. Like the old song says," and he started to sing a line from the old song "Vanidad." "*Vanidad con las alas doradas yo que pensava reir y ahora me pongo ha llorar.*[47]"

My uncle appeared to be in a very good mood. He smiled and said, "I'm tone deaf. Your musical ability is another quality of yours that I admire. Even at your young age, you have composed several pieces. I believe that gift comes from your Mima's side. We del Marmols are more in the sciences rather than the arts. Most of us are tone deaf, especially when it comes to music. On your other side, your Mima is not only an excellent pianist but also a beautiful mezzo-soprano. She has an angelic voice, even though your father never allowed her to develop that lovely gift from God. Maybe it was because of his insecurities. Your mother used to be the most beautiful and extraordinary woman I ever met, not only with physical beauty but also in her soul. Your father might not have wanted to take the chance of losing her if someone took her away from him." He smiled. "I don't blame him. He was extremely lucky. He found a diamond in the tiny town of Guane, Pinar del Rio. It's logical that she would be his treasure and he would want to protect her. Verena could compare to any actress in the movies; no one could touch her." I could tell he was giving me his true feelings. He smiled. I was very proud of my mother and loved her to death, and I could see that he had sincere admiration for her. That also made me feel good as her son because he admired her both as a woman and as a human being. Not only her gifts and physical talents but also her morals and spiritual values.

He took another sip of his hot chocolate, and I did so as well. He said, "I will be meeting with Canen, Mr. Xiang, and Doctor Sayas-Bazan in the early afternoon tomorrow to discuss some matters of priority and other important things that have transpired recently. Why

---

[47] Vanity, with your golden wings I think I will be laughing and now I have no choice but to cry.

don't you give me a very quick brief of what you considered so important over the last 48 hours? Then we can go through whatever you have in mind that you want to consult with me at the end, and I can give it my full attention. I know you have an urgency to bring up that plan, and I imagine, since I know you so well, that you are being very prudent and considerate with everyone around you. That is why you want to consult with me with whatever is worrying you. That must be something of such extreme importance that it is probably life or death since you cannot even wait until tomorrow morning and are here at this very moment."

Figure 45 Julio Antonio's Mima

CHAPTER 16: THE FORTY-EIGHT HOURS DEADLY DEBRIEFING

I replied, "You're completely on target. I want you to forgive me for contradicting you." I raised both of my arms high with a sad expression. "I believe that it will be more appropriate and prudent to start it the other way around, covering the most important thing first, in case we get interrupted unexpectedly at least we'll already have covered it. It's the only reason why I'm here bothering you so late at night."

He smiled at me. "There's no doubt in my mind that you were born a leader in whatever you do. Even in this small debriefing you know how to turn things around to make your point come through, even with a perfect and logical explanation of why it has to be the way you want."

I smiled back. "I'm sorry. That was not my intention at all. I don't want to come across like a power freak."

He raised his right arm high. "No, no—you don't have to apologize, my nephew. You have nothing to be sorry for. I know precisely that this is not your intention—power over me is not in your mind. It's something natural in you, and to be honest with you extraordinary, that you do in a spontaneous reaction because your mind works that way. It's fascinating. You may have the worry that the subject you need to discuss with me could suffer and lose its importance if we relegate it to the end. I understand. It's a perfectly natural worry and your instinct says to make it the first thing. That is why we should talk about it immediately. Is that not the way you're thinking?"

I nodded. I was embarrassed at possibly having overstepped my authority. "Remember, you're the chief of this tribe. All of us around you should do as you suggest and believe it is best."

He stopped me before I finished. He said in a firm tone, "No, no, Julio Antonio del Marmol. You are right. When you are right, I'll say it again, you have nothing to apologize for. You should be proud of your character and personality. It shouldn't matter who is your boss, who is in charge, or who is over you for whatever you do. This is an excellent quality you possess, not only for intelligence but for everything else. You have to use logic, diplomacy, be firm, and do what in your judgement is best to do. Others, even those above us in our hierarchy, don't possess the precious gifts you have. If you obey routine rules, it can cost you your life as well as those that you have under your wing."

I listened very carefully, respectfully not interrupting him. I kept all my attention on his words, holding his eyes with mine as I followed him. He continued, "You should never accept others' criteria or ideas that you consider wrong or erroneous. Discuss it with diplomacy but reject it with firmness and conviction. Maintain your points of view over the table without giving up on your standards. I want you to remember, my nephew, that your brain is capable of doing things in such an enormous way no one else is able to comprehend or has ever seen in anyone before. You have the mental capacity at least 100% above all the studies that have been researched over the past hundred years. This will surprise you, though I've told you a little before, what you can do with your mind. Don't let this scare you or intimidate you; it is the most precious gift that only a few beings like you receive directly from the Supreme Architect of the Universe for whatever reason. I'm very sure it is for a great purpose and I hope I can live to see the results. It will make me very happy. By the way, remember you never are a bother to me. It doesn't matter what hour you call, especially when it's an emergency like now."

I nodded. "Thank you."

"Well, what do you have in mind in such an emergency that you need to consult with me? It must be extremely different and dangerous for you to have this need. I know you have a mind that can resolve any problem."

I looked at him and passed my left hand over my face, forehead down to chin. I yawned a little. "I'm sorry about that yawn. Even though we woke up very late today, we didn't shut our eyes at all last night. The most relaxing and comfortable sleep is during the night and never gets replaced even if you sleep all day long. Let me tell you about that a little later. Let's go to the subject of what is really happening. The uncle of one of my best friends, Yaneba, is Bejasmin Cesar Loubus."

My uncle exclaimed, "Oh! What is going on with him?"

"You know him?"

"Yes, and I told him to be very careful because their group has been penetrated. I even gave him the name of the penetrator and that it could lead to death for all of them. He is a very great man, but he has a hard head. I advise you that if you ever get involved with this girl, be very careful because hardheadedness is a family trait."

"No, nothing like that. She's just my friend."

"Well, what about him?" he asked curiously.

"He got arrested not long ago and has been sentenced to death by firing squad. It will take place in just a few days."

He looked at me in curiosity. "That is very sad. I hate to tell him now that I told him so. People never listen until they have the problem in their face. It's a tremendous tragedy to lose his life so young at the hands of a cowardly traitor. Many people have been arrested and executed by the firing squad for months now. You've seen that for yourself. My question is, and please help me to understand, what is your emergency with this individual's death sentence? I understand it's very unfair and another injustice committed against our people, like thousands of others, but it's been happening all over the island."

"The biggest difference in this case is that this particular individual has the same purpose very similar to mine. He is in the same cosmic cycle. After I carefully reexamined everything, I decided I wasn't going to let him die. I would get him out of prison, whatever it costs me."

Uncle Emilio leaned back in his chair and held both hands up to slow me down. "Whoa!" He looked in my eyes and saw my determination. "How do you plan to do this? This is almost impossible."

"I haven't completely figured it out yet, but I believe, thinking about the conversation you and I had with your friend Canen, he might, with his high military rank in the Regular Army be my best accomplice in this 'crime'." Uncle Emilio smiled and shook his head. "He communicated with me the other day that he's been reassigned to be the General Prosecutor of the Revolutionary Tribunals; he might be able to help us without compromising his position or blowing his cover. I just wanted to figure out how we can get this man out alive somewhere, somehow, as soon as possible."

My uncle put both hands to his face and wiped them down. After a few seconds of thoughtful silence and taking a long drink of his mug of hot chocolate, he asked, "This individual is of such importance to you to the point of risking the lives of Canen and yourself, the most valuable and reliable assets I have had for a very long time?"

"Yes. With your help and Canen's, I'm pretty sure we can take this to a fruitful ending without difficulty. I've already studied how to get him out of Cuba, which is the most difficult part of the whole thing, thanks to the tremendous number of informants the government has created through the psychological terror they've created via the firing squads."

Figure 46 Canen and His Decorations

Uncle Emilio leaned back and lit his pipe. "I like your optimism. But you can tell me if you don't mind what kind of sources or contacts you have at your disposition to tell me you can get this man, a fugitive from the law sentenced to death, out of the country?" He shook his head and smiled slightly. "I would love to have that contact in my network. It could come to be very useful for me if that moment arrives in the same circumstances."

"I don't have any problem revealing my contact, and the name of it is *Pilar*."

Montauk: The Lightning Chance

He looked at me in confusion. "You have to be very careful with the ladies. They're the number one cause for the majority of spies ending up in jail or the cemetery."

I smiled and shook my head. "It's not a woman."

He looked at me in greater surprise. "A man with the name Pilar?"

I smiled and shook my head more vigorously. "The name is that of the yacht of your favorite author. When I explain in detail later and all the stuff that has transpired in the past forty-eight hours, you will understand perfectly how I came up with this plan to save this man who is like a brother to me. You will see how brilliant the plan is. The most important thing to me is to know for a fact that I can count on Canen's help. That will make things a lot easier. Everything else," I added with conviction, "will be very simple. With the enormous amount of money, gold, and other commodities that I have at my disposition, it will be very easy to bribe the prison guards at La Cabaña without exposing Canen's double identity."

Uncle Emilio took both his hands and clapped them to his head in confusion. He squinted his eyes shut. "Now I start to believe I made a severe mistake in allowing you to impose your conditions, no matter how much I celebrate your talents. I should have started the way I wanted to get my debriefing first. I'm completely lost with what you're saying. Now you're talking about gold and other commodities, and I don't know what you're talking about."

I smiled. "Remember what you repeated to me practically since I was born? Patience. It's a great virtue to those who manage to contain and control their curiosity as well as those who listen calmly all the way to the end of a story without interrupting the narrator. They are able to digest it better and enjoy the denouement. The great recompense is knowing in luxurious detail everything the narrator has in his mind that he is trying to communicate to us. They leave the questions, if any, patiently until the conclusion of the final act."

My uncle shook his head. "Ah, this kid!" He started to laugh. He was quiet for a few seconds and leaned back in his chair. With a huge smile he said, "You have all the reason in the world, and it's very clever of you to use my own words to kick me in my butt to convince me to shut up and calm the curiosity that is consuming me. It's OK." He took a long draw on his pipe. He exhaled the smoke. "Go ahead and proceed. I promise I won't interrupt you another time unless you ask me a question."

"Here comes my first question. Do you really think Canen will be in the disposition to help?"

He replied with conviction, "I assure you that Canen, even at risk to his own life if necessary, will use all his efforts to help and save the life of your brother who is maybe from another planet or your cosmic clone."

I smiled. "We always make fun of those things we don't understand."

My uncle grew serious. "No, you misunderstand me. What I said is not at all a joke or making fun of you."

I raised my right arm high. "Life itself is the greatest cosmic joke and possibly the biggest experiment in all the humorous things that happen in the world. How do you think that I cannot understand you? I only said that before to screw around with you a little. Changing the subject completely, I will have a meeting at the end of the week with Ernest Hemingway. Do you want to come and meet him? I will be able to introduce you to him if you want."

He raised both hands in strong negation as he shook his head. "No, it would not be smart or prudent, not just for me but for you as well. There's a possibility this man is a great patriot but he also could be a double agent as a spy or at the worst, an opportunistic mercenary; if not why the hell has this famous, renowned writer associated with these political delinquents?"

"I believe, after your meeting tomorrow with Canen and the others, I maybe could obtain from you a more affirmative and exact decision how we can channel and develop the plan to rescue Bejasmin from prison. But we've come to the moment to update you with all that has happened in the last forty-eight hours. It's best to start from the beginning, after my debriefing with you and Canen here."

My uncle leaned back and took a long drink of hot chocolate. "I'm all ears and very anxious to hear all the details. Like you said, from the beginning. You've been giving me bits and pieces and driving me crazy for over an hour. I'm all ears."

I smiled. "OK. Let's start at the beginning. After I left your house the other day, we drove straight to the Capri to have lunch." After another two hours, I had finished covering the details of my story. My uncle's head was spinning.

He said, "I cannot believe you did all of this in just a couple of days!" His expression was admiring. "You've really been very busy." He massaged his forehead with his fingers. "My God!"

Montauk: The Lightning Chance

"Now you will understand why I've been yawning so much."

"The next thing I will do in the first hours of the morning is have my contacts in the intelligence community run a complete check on Hemingway. You need that report on him before you meet with him at the end of the week. That way you'll know what waters you're swimming in."

"OK, that sounds smart."

"You will be the best spy that ever existed, just due to your natural gifts and talents. Additionally, that is the position God has put you into. It's unbelievable how much you've discovered and done in such a short period of time."

"Well, there was quite a bit of help from the Gentleman of Paris and his team of insurrectionists. My friends Daniel and Cisneros also helped tremendously."

"Yes, I know—but you directed the whole thing! You're the leader, remember. Knowing your intelligence, I'm sure you haven't shared a single thing with any of them what you're doing with us." He twiddled the pen I had given him between his fingers. "All this evidence here—oh, my God! I met you at exactly the right moment when you came to me. This is Divine intervention."

I smiled. "You must be kidding me. That will be committing suicide prematurely, and I will break all the records in stupidity that ever existed in intelligence!" I shook my head. "Absolutely not! I will never reveal to anyone what I'm doing with you."

He looked at me proudly and clapped me on the shoulder. "I know. I had to ask you anyway."

"I can assure you that I have a small list of names that keeps growing and growing as the days and hours pass that will be not reduce and have a great possibility to become bigger with future intelligence warriors. All of them could help accomplish obtaining fresh intelligence straight from the source. We will use it to destroy them. If we're not capable of collapsing this system they've started, at least we will continue to keep it in check for many years to come. I'm prepared to give a huge migraine to all these double zeroes and diabolical political delinquents."

He looked me in the eyes. "You know, many spies exist in our community and in other agencies, as a matter of fact, both friends and enemies. The most difficult to find in this business of espionage is finding the master spies. They are exceedingly rare to find, like precious stones you find once in a while a red diamond, the rarest color of diamond in the world, the Moussaieff red for instance. You are that diamond, Julio Antonio. A master spy who hasn't even had the time yet to be properly trained, and you have conquered and made a network of spies. That is an invaluable prize for any international intelligence agency. By the way, how did you discover that the Gentleman of Paris is working with us? This is something I wanted to ask you." I smiled and raised the hand with my ring and showed it to him. He looked at me without understanding. "All these rings are different." I removed the ring without saying a word and put it on my thumb and held it out to him. He lit his lighter.

I said, "Look at the border of the ring."

"I don't see what you're seeing. There's nothing strange along the border."

"I don't think you understand. I'm referring to the decoration on the ring's side." He lit his lighter and examined it again, scrutinizing both sides of the facing. I said, "Do you see the little design surrounded by gold on the border? I know that's the container the needle uses to release the dose of poison. Though, that little detail covers that golden circle for anyone who is observant enough like me, it only takes a few minutes while a person is talking for the finger to uncover it and you can spot it. I saw it, and I will grant you it's a tiny detail, but it told me that the resemblance between the ring you gave me and that of the Gentleman of Paris', added into the details of the conversation he and I had, gave me the first clue that it was a 75% chance that he was working with you or for the same team." He shook his head mutely. I said, "Either that or he stole it from somebody who was working with you guys."

He looked at me incredulously. I was getting used to that look from people. "You never cease to amaze me! No one who has worn these rings for all these years has ever noticed that detail. I know it's difficult to find someone like you, and it's going to be very difficult for someone like you to work with our enemies, but thank you very much for bringing that detail to me. It could cost somebody their lives if your cosmic clone has the same gift as you and happens to work with our enemies."

I smiled. "I can guarantee you that it will be very difficult, more difficult than to catch lightning in the sky with your hand."

He smiled. "That will be very difficult, my nephew. I believe it will be extremely important for you to come back tomorrow night to be able to discuss all the details of your plan. Bring with you some samples of the treasure. Canen will be able to use those to show to the soldiers that he wants to try and bribe to partake. I will assure you it will motivate their covetousness. They will do whatever they need to get it, even at the risk of their own lives, but they will no longer care. Even we can lose our lives."

I checked my wristwatch. I looked back at him. "Where is your optimism, my uncle? Remember faith and goodwill moves mountains. How can we not move a simple iron gate?"

He stood up and embraced me. He murmured in my ear. "Don't ever lose your optimism. Maybe you cannot move mountains, but I assure you that you can conquer many friendly hearts and you can also produce chills and terror to the minds of our enemies. Of that I am absolutely sure. Tomorrow, at eight pm. Is that OK?"

"Yes. That will be fine." I looked at my watch again. "It's almost 2 am, and I had better get going. We still need some time to rest, and I don't want to fall asleep at the wheel."

"OK. I'll arrange the meeting with the others."

"Thank you."

"You don't have to thank me. It's a pleasure." He waved it away.

We said our goodbyes and I walked to the parking lot. As I started to walk towards the jeep, I began to hear a buzzing in my ears like a train whistle. It grew louder and I heard it in both ears. I put the key in the ignition, and it got even louder. I hesitated. It was like I had an insect buzzing in both ears that crawled into my head. It had started light but grew stronger the closer I got to the jeep. Now, inside it, it was like an alarm or a whistle on a pressure cooker releasing steam. After a few minutes of indecision, I smiled to convince myself that I was being paranoid. I started the jeep. I breathed a sigh of relief and smiled slightly. The strange buzzing had not gone away, though. I thought that, perhaps because it was so late and I was lacking sleep, it might go away after a good, solid night of sleep. I tried to optimistically convince myself because I didn't want to add another worry to the others that already crowded my brain.

Dr. Julio Antonio del Marmol

Figure 47 Nautico Gate

As I drove off in the direction of the entrance the buzzing increased to the point of being intolerable. Now I was getting worried. I stopped around one hundred and fifty feet from the gate. The buzzing grew a little quieter as the vehicle halted. It decreased to a much more comfortable level as I observed this, perhaps to fifty percent. The minute I started to drive forward, it blasted back to full intensity. I stopped again, and it diminished in the same way. I thought about this as I looked at the guard's shelter. I looked at my watch as I tried to assimilate what was going on; it was exactly the same time as when I left my uncle. The second hand had not moved.

I thought perhaps the guard had fallen asleep. I could see the lights inside the shelter were dimmer than before. I wondered what the reason for all of this was. I put the jeep in gear once more, and the buzzing increased yet again. I stopped again, not having moved more than a few feet. I shook my head to try and get rid of the buzzing. As soon as I stopped again, the buzzing reduced once more. I was disturbed. I could not understand. I decided to go ahead and move forward, but even before I put the jeep in gear and removed my foot from the clutch, a male voice yelled in my ears in an echoey manner, "Stop! Stop! Stop! Stop!"

I felt an intense chill all over my body from my feet all the way up to my head. It was like a strong, cold ocean wind, followed by an electrical shock. I nearly stood up in my seat in the convulsions. At that moment, I saw beneath the spotlight at the shelter a man dressed in a paramilitary outfit violently burst out of the shelter with a machine gun in his hands. He raised it up to open fire in my direction.

That same current that seemed to bring me up with the freezing breeze took me to the roof of the jeep. I grabbed the middle support

Montauk: The Lightning Chance

bar for the tarp with my hands and swung my feet forward to brace them with the front support bar where the windshield joined it. I pushed myself into the tarp covering the jeep. I was sucked in by that strange force to hold me there. A fraction of a second later a rain of bullets sprayed all across the windshield from one side to the other, shattering it into tiny shards and spraying the seats with the broken glass. I heard another burst of machine gun fire and what was left of the windshield was destroyed. Then a third burst, but this one sounded like it was discharged into empty air.

I heard three popping sounds that could have been silenced followed by three yelps of pain as someone got shot. I was completely frozen in my position. That serious electrical force kept me glued to the canvas. I made no effort to hold myself there—it was like I was weightless. I trained my neck around to see what was going on around me. I felt like I was in my mother's womb once more, being held in place. I could see flashlights bobbing towards my way.

A voice that might have been the Gentleman of Paris inquired, "Commandantico, are you OK? Where are you?" I didn't answer. "We are your friends. You don't have to worry—all your enemies have been put down."

I heard Solitario's voice yell from farther off. "The jeep is empty!" He had apparently already been in here and I hadn't noticed. "He must have left it and escaped before these guys started shooting. After that hail of bullets, nobody could still be in that vehicle and live."

I heard a little sound beneath me and looked down and saw Macarena[48] opening the door and climbing into the front driver's seat. She looked up and saw me. "You can come down. All you have here are friends."

I looked down at her and smiled at her cute but dirty face, under which she held her flashlight like a ghost. I released one hand and held a finger to my lips. She got out of the jeep and yelled, "Jose Maria! The Commandantico is alive! He's here in the jeep!"

Solitario's voice said, "No, that's impossible! I looked everywhere in that jeep. It's completely empty!"

Jose Maria asked, "Did you look into other dimensions? Maybe you looked in one where he's not currently located."

They came over and opened the doors. All the flashlights shone on me and I winced in the sudden glare. They looked at me in awe as

---

[48] Maca's full name

they saw me clinging to the bars in a fetal position. I had felt so protected and comfortable I didn't want to leave it. I looked at all of them, still blinking at the glare.

"Please take those lights out of my face." They put the lights down. I said to Jose Maria, "Thank you for your intervention."

"Do you need help getting down?"

"No, all I need is for you guys to get out of the jeep so I can land in my seat." They did, and I let go of my feet and stood on the seat. I let go of my hands and slid into it. I got out and they crowded around me to hug me. I followed them to the three masked men the Gentleman of Paris had taken down.

He said to Solitario, "Take off their masks so we can identify them."

I recognized one of them as a member of Piñeiro's escort. That didn't surprise me; I knew what they were capable of doing, and remembered I had bruised Piñeiro's ego a few days ago at the hospital. In the end, these three men had received punishment from the hands of people they had never imagined would be their executioners.

The Gentleman of Paris handed his sophisticated sniper rifle that had two scopes on either side—one for night vision, one for daylight—to Solitario. He said, "You know where to put it—in the back seat and cover it with blankets."

Aleida, the mezzo-soprano, came over to me and put her arm around my shoulders. "I'm very glad you're OK, honey. We already cleaned up the broken glass in your jeep. You can sit there without any problems. Maca helped me."

"Thank you very much, all of you."

Jose Maria said, "You should leave at once. Don't worry about anything else. We'll take care of all of this." He gestured to the bodies. "We'll feed the sharks with them. More victims of the diabolic cult of international communists. Arise ye workers from your slumbers, arise you slaves and poor of the world and the ones who have no bread."

I shook my head and gulped. I clenched my jaw in anger and a sad expression as I tried to maintain my serenity. I had to control my emotions at the realization of how close another disciple of the Devil, Piñeiro, had come to assassinate me. I said, "More life lost. Even though they're my enemies, and all for the political ambitions of unscrupulous men who want to silence us, steal our freedoms and rights, and destroy and take away the goodness in all of us."

They nodded and said almost in unison, "You're right."

Montauk: The Lightning Chance

From a distance we could hear the police sirens. I said goodbye to the others and jumped into the jeep. I could see in the rearview mirror that they dropped the bodies in Jose Maria's bus and then rushed to get out of there, leaving behind only one man—the real guard in the shelter. He was tied up, blindfolded, and gagged. Fortunately, he was still alive, but Gentleman of Paris didn't want to untie him. He just whispered in his ear, "Don't worry—everything will be OK. We got the bad guys. Just wait patiently until the police arrive."

Jose Maria showed me once more that he is completely a professional. He explained to me later that we could never leave a witness behind who could identify any one of us even though we're the good guys. That way we never have to answer any questions posed by the local authorities that we could not answer. During my return to the Hotel Hilton I passed many police cars heading in the opposite direction. I looked into the rearview again and saw the lights of the Gentleman's bus following me with the rest of his team. I breathed a sigh of relief and my breathing became more peaceful and tranquil. I continued my travel to my destination.

When I arrived at the hotel the young attendants all questioned me when they saw the shattered windshield on my jeep. One said, "What happened, Commander? Did you have an accident?"

"Oh," I replied, "one of those turkey vultures ran into my windshield as I was driving along the Malecon. Don't worry about it—this will be replaced in the morning. We'll send it to the military equipment maintenance."

I said goodbye to the young men and walked towards the elevators. They wished me a good evening. I entered the elevator and pushed the button for my suite. A few minutes later I walked into the suite and smiled. The snoring of those two giant friends of mine sounded like a train. I was glad that we had three separate rooms. I didn't think I would be able to sleep with all that noise. I quietly walked over and shut the doors of their rooms.

I sat down at the dining table and wrote a note instructing them not to wake me up in the morning since I had gotten in at 4 am. After breakfast they should take the jeep to get the windshield repaired and I would give them details later what had happened. I went into my room, utterly exhausted. The past two days of adrenaline rush was finally hitting my body that screamed for a few hours of rest.

I slept well, and the next day I awoke earlier than I expected. I looked at my watch and saw that it was only 10 am. I went to the bathroom to discharge my strategic weapon and empty my bladder. I repeated to myself, "Well—4 to 10. I slept six hours, that should be good enough." I wanted to convince myself that I didn't need any more sleep. I got into the jacuzzi and after a relaxing, hot bath to open my pores, I got out and took a very cold shower to close them up and clean the impurities of my skin. I took a clean, freshly pressed uniform the hotel had left in my closet, dressed, took my uniform hat, and then went down to get some breakfast.

As I entered the cafeteria the maître d surprised me by asking me to allow him to bring me something he knew I would like. I said, "I like surprises. Go ahead and bring it to me."

I was glad I did that. He brought me everything I liked. A plate of fresh fruit cut into slices: strawberries, oranges, papaya. Another plate with chicken wings and bearnaise sauce. Another of prosciutto, black forest ham, pate of cognac and rosemary, and some slices of Brie cheese with anchovies on top. As a final touch he brought me a small fruit tartlet with mixed fruit, and he had already baptized it with Grand Marnier.

When I left the cafeteria, I was so full and satisfied but I felt my belly was about ready to burst. I had eaten more than I was accustomed to, but I felt happy. This great feast brought my optimism to high levels. I started to think about what I was planning to do. I had already conceived it, and knew that I would manage to save the life of the man I only ever saw in my dreams, but he was still somebody special with a tight connection to the angels who had protected me ever since I was in my mother's womb. I wondered who could not be grateful to anyone who had been watching your back even before your birth.

As I thought about all these things I walked through the lobby of the huge hotel, thinking to take a taxi. I had not seen my friends and thought that the errand to replace the windshield had come to be a little complicated or taking more time than predicted. I had almost reached the glass doors at the hotel's entry when I heard a feminine voice behind me.

"Commandantico!" she yelled.

I turned and saw the beautiful girl at the desk with lovely short black hair and large green eyes. She held a piece of paper in her right hand that she shook to catch my attention. I raised my right hand and waved to her as I smiled. I turned and walked to her. Her name was Elisa. I had several conversations on different occasions with her before, and it seemed to me that she had a huge crush on Fidel. She had asked

Montauk: The Lightning Chance

me whenever the opportunity presented itself to introduce her to him. This young, beautiful girl had studied medicine at the university and worked at the hotel to pay for her schooling. She had no idea what kind of monster she was so infatuated with. Unfortunately, I could never tell her or warn her about her mistake. Perhaps it was because of all these things she looked for the opportunity to talk to me and be around us to such an extreme that she would send chocolate and flowers up to our suite all the time with a card reminding me of my promise. Every time I saw these gifts I would smile at her persistence.

This time, as I walked towards her, I shook my head a little as I wondered what she held in her hand this time. I realized that one should never assume because most times the assumption was wrong. She only had two different phone messages. One was from Daniel and Cisneros informing me the jeep would not be ready until late in the afternoon since no windshield was available in stock. They would have to order one from Matanzas, close to Veradero. The other message was from my uncle, letting me know that the meeting had become an emergency due to rapid changes in events. Instead of 8 pm, the meeting would be at 2 pm.

I checked my watch and looked at the time he had called me. It appeared he had called me 10:30, a half hour after I had woken up. It was strange that while I was in the jacuzzi and taken my shower that I had not seen the blinking red light on the phone indicating I had a message. I tried not to be paranoid and considered that the front desk might have had a busy morning. I removed the incident from my mind and decided to use my new contacts instead of using a taxi as I saw a security guard pass by. Most taxis in Cuba had by now been recruited by the G-2, the secret state security for the new government. These individuals sent reports in on who they took and where. Given that they reported directly to Manuel, Piñeiro Losada, that was the last thing I wanted to do right now. Though I had no direct proof he had sent those men to harm me, there was an extraordinarily strong possibility that those guys had been sent by him in retaliation for my humiliation of him.

I thanked Elisa and walked to the telephone cabinets by the lobby restrooms. I locked myself in one and dialed a number I had memorized. A masculine voice answered, "Good afternoon, Municipal Police, Pablo Rodriguez. How can I help you?"

I said, "I'm the Commandantico. How are you doing?"

"Oh, great Commandantico. It's great to hear from you," he said happily. "Do you remember me?"

"Of course I do. How did those seafood cocktails settle?"

"Very well. Thank you so much again. You're a great trooper."

"You're very welcome. No problem. I like to make people happy."

"What can I do for you, Commandante?"

"My jeep is in for repair. I had an incident with a turkey vulture that decided to land on the hood of my jeep. His head broke the glass of my windshield. I need to do several things today and I have no escort or vehicle, since my guys took the jeep early this morning to the headquarters mechanics."

He said very happily, "Oh, no—no problem. You stay there. I'll be there in a little while with an escort of three cars for you."

"That's not necessary."

"Oh, the new Chief of this station, Aurelio Gonzalez, assigned me to be his personal escort before he left an hour ago. He told me that if you, for any reason needed me, leave someone in my place and attend to your call."

"That is very nice. Thank him for me when you see him."

"Are you in the same hotel?"

"Yes, I am."

"Very well. Don't move. Wait for me in the lobby and I'll be there in a few minutes."

"Thank you. I'll be waiting for you right here."

"OK. There it goes! See you in a few minutes."

I hung up and sat down in one of the comfortable chairs in the lobbies. I picked up an issue of *Life* magazine. I noticed that Fidel was on one of the first pages and took up around five pages with photos of the parade following the victory of the revolution. I didn't know it if my spy instincts, even though I wasn't fully trained, or my natural instincts from my cosmic connections, but a tall man wearing thick reading glasses, elegantly dressed in a brown suit and matching hat that had a bandana of brown and rose color which matched the rose color of his shirt caught my attention. He also wore a matching tie of brown and rose diagonally traversing it. It caught my attention; I was used to people staring at me because it was uncommon to see a kid as young as I with long hair like a guerrilla with the freedom fighters with such a high rank on his epaulettes. There was also the obvious wearing of the .38 pistol on one side of my belt and the massive Commandos knife on the other side. What really attracted my attention was when I normally looked at ordinarily curious people they would smile and wave to me in a friendly

Montauk: The Lightning Chance

manner. This man, however, tried to hide his face by turning away from me. It looked like he didn't want to be recognized. Because of what had happened the previous night, I discretely unsnapped the peace bond over my pistol that secured my pistol in the holster so it would be clear if I had to draw it if needed.

A few minutes later I saw on the other side of the glass doors three police cars that appeared to be my escort pull up. They parked in front of the entrance and I saw Rodriguez get out of one of them. I stood up. I saw the man stand up at the same time, like he was imitating me. He started to walk over to me as I paused. At that moment, corporal Rodriguez, surrounded by several policemen, entered the lobby with a smile on his face. I was frozen, my hand on my pistol. I did not want to turn my back on this strange man. He walked over to me briskly. I was surprised because someone who intended harm to me wouldn't be so obvious. I didn't want to have to shoot him to defend myself, which was my only option at that point. I prayed to God to not let the situation deteriorate to that point. I tried to lock eyes with him, but he kept looking at the floor.

Finally, he raised his head a little and I got a glimpse in his eyes. I saw no hatred or aggressiveness that I would expect an assassin to have in his countenance. I could also see him take his right hand and reach for something inside his jacket. I locked eyes with him and turned to present my left side towards him, hand still on my pistol as I half drew it. If he intended to shoot at me, I wanted to present him the smallest profile as a target possible. At this point, I concluded that I would not need to use my pistol as he looked me directly in the eyes. I knew now I could freeze him mentally, so I released my grip on the half-drawn pistol and let it slide back into the holster. I had only wanted to telegraph to him that I was prepared for an aggressive move.

Corporal Rodriguez yelled, "Be careful, Commandantico!" He drew his own pistol and yelled at the man, "Put your hands where I can see them, or I'll shoot!"

The man was extremely scared. He snatched his hands out of his suit and held them up. His right hand held a pipe, which he had apparently been pulling out.

I raised my left hand high. "Don't shoot! This man is unarmed. He has no intention of harming me or anyone else."

Rodriguez didn't want to take any chances. He ordered two of his men to search him to make sure he was clean. After they frisked him without finding a weapon, it was revealed the man was an insurance agent. Another man confirmed to Corporal Rodriguez the man's identity. It turned out that this third man and the other guy recognized each other and had stood up at the same time. I thought what an extraordinary coincidence, maybe a little drill, not even a real fire, that the man who was meeting his friend at the hotel would stand up at the same time and that they happened to be seated with me in the middle. I was completely uninvolved in their transaction. I believed that incident showed that I had to continually keep my eyes open from now on. I thanked Corporal Rodriguez as he apologized to me with a long face.

"You have nothing to apologize for," I told him. "I was exactly thinking the same thing. One day I'll tell you why. I might have sent you the wrong signal with my own hand on my pistol. You probably received it and acted accordingly."

He scratched his head. "One question I wanted to ask you. How did you know he was unarmed and harmless, even though you thought the same as well?"

We walked through the door and got into the cars as I responded. I pointed to my eyes. "I could read his eyes. I saw that he was not a threat."

Rodriguez nodded and gave me a half smile. "I believe you, Commander. The things I've heard about you before from everyone and now from Lieutenant Aurelio, I have no doubts that you are not an ordinary human being."

I put my index finger to my lips. "Sh." I pulled my fingers across my lips in a zipper motion with a small smile."

He saluted me. "Where are we going?" He walked around and sat down in the front passenger's seat.

"To the Prime Minister's office."

"Did you hear that?" he asked the driver.

"Yes," the driver said. We drove off, carefully navigating through the crowd of onlookers including the valets and their captain.

We drove to Fidel's offices in the Vedado. He had taken a complete block, sealed off at either side with tanks and machine guns installed on amphibious vehicles. These offices were part the beginning of the appropriation of private property. The new Prime Minister and Commander-in-Chief, Fidel Castro, used the trust the people had entrusted in him and the revolutionary leaders to restore the democracy taken from them by Batista. Now that he was in power, Fidel once related to us, his closest friends, the entire block he had codenamed "4X."

Montauk: The Lightning Chance

When he was a student at Havana University, this block held the most opulent residences in the entire Vedado area. All the multi-millionaires lived there in the capital. One particular residence was built in the center of the block. According to his story, he was forced back then to drive an Oldsmobile that was falling apart. The bumpers were tied on with wire hangers because he didn't have the money to have them properly rewelded, and the upholstery was held together with Scotch tape. he had paid $50 for it and his friends would see him coming, they would say he was like the city spraying for mosquitos his car smoked so badly. He dreamed when he drove around the block of one day owning that house. His female friends at the university didn't care about that—they cared about his beautiful dreams. He was forced to drive such a beat-up car because his father had stopped his allowance, which had been his means of living as a student. When that ended, he lived off politics and being a hitman to eliminate all possible rival factions.

He filled their brains with Utopian pipe dreams and brought them to that block in front of the house. He would point and tell them that after they were married, that was the house they would live in. He said not one single girl he brought there ever would refuse having sex with him inside his disgusting Oldsmobile. He called it 4X because he never passed it more than four times before he obtained the virginity of these girls with those promises. The commotion of this activity was so loud that the security guard, summoned by complaints about the noise, got to know him by name.

After the triumph of the revolution, he decided to take over not just his dream house but the entire block. The first assignment he gave Piñeiro was to make life so miserable for the homeowners to get them to abandon their property and leave Cuba. Then he could take over those expensive residences those people had spent so much sweat from their brow to obtain; He didn't stop there. He told Piñeiro to find that "son of a whore" of a security guard the worst prison in Cuba and stick him there for a long time.

As we arrived at the Prime Minister's office of 4X, I was deep in my thoughts remembering these conversations during which Fidel bragged before the entire entourage. I understood, even at that young age, why all these men hated society, why they followed Satan's disciples so loyally, and why they wanted to destroy everything they get their hands on. We passed by one of the security guards. The first car in the police escort spoke with the guard, gesturing back to us in the second car. The guard, recognizing me, raised the barrier and signaled the escort through. As we passed by, he saluted me.

We drove into the parking area. I said to Rodriguez, "I don't think we'll take long here, but if you need any refreshment, let me know."

"Don't worry about it, Commander. Do what you need to do, and we'll wait for you here."

I walked into the most beautiful office of the entire capital. It was also one of the best-decorated with beautiful marble floors and runners of expensive Turkish carpets. I said hello to Gladys, Fidel's personal secretary, receptionist, and all the other things Fidel needed. She was a beautiful, tall, slim brunette with beautiful long amber hair and large blue eyes. She bore a resemblance to the American movie star Lauren Bacall. She always joked with me that I was supposed to hurry up and grow up so she could marry me. Every time she said that, I couldn't help but blush in embarrassment. She loved doing that to me. I was unaccustomed to such a direct approach from a beautiful woman fully seven years older than me. She was the daughter of one of the ministers, a personal friend of Fidel's who came from a family of Greek descent. This girl looked like a princess and her sultry, heavy-lidded eyes made her more mysterious. When she looked at you with such intensity and said what she did to me all the time, it gave me goosebumps and tensed all my muscles.

She said to me, "How are you doing today, handsome?" She grinned. "You didn't bring me any flowers today?" She asked. "I've heard you brought Rita chocolate and flowers. What about me?"

My lips tingled. I had to get out of there quickly—she was too much of a distraction to me. I thought to myself, *You cannot, Julio Antonio del Marmol, let this woman distract you from what you are here to do. Don't let the picture out of the frame and maintain focus on your plans.* I already knew what we were going to do, and I couldn't waste a minute. I went into the hallway of that huge residence turned into offices. I walked into what was once the laundry room. Now a sign in the corridor read in red letters on a white background, "*Quarto de Desahogo*.[49]"

I knew that this room served for the excess classified documents and memos that were no longer considered relevant. They stored them here until they could be destroyed. Every week a truck came to take a load to be incinerated to prevent them from being used to damage the government and expose the things they didn't want to come to public

---

[49] Spare room

Montauk: The Lightning Chance

light. I approached the door and opened it. I took a quick look through the boxes and plastic bags, making sure that I assessed and checked the back door the truck pulled up to to receive a load. I noted how many locks it had and whether they had bolts or not. Like I thought before, maybe I could come back at night and do what I had in mind. But I abandoned it when I saw how difficult the door's security would make things.

I closed the door behind me and went to the library. I walked into the large area and said hello to Rita, the attendant of the library, among other things. She smiled in satisfaction at seeing me. "Commandantico, thank you so much for the lovely roses and exquisite pastries you sent."

"You are very welcome. Not just for the flowers. The pastries are the favorite of my Mima, and you remind me so much of her for your nobility and gratefulness."

She smiled and melted. "No matter how young you are, you are a true gentleman. There are a lot of men in this world but there are very few like you. Gentlemen are hard to find."

I smiled and thanked her for her compliments. I continued into the library into the extreme back of it, far out of her eyes. I took one of the books and sat down. I glanced at the title and noted that it was *How To Make a Forgery*. I glanced through the book for the information I needed in order to move my plan forward. Rita was a woman in her mid-forties or early fifties. She was in very tight with Fidel Castro and his "first ring." She was supposedly the direct cousin or second cousin of the most powerful woman in Cuba, Celia Sanchez.

Figure 48 Celia Sanchez

Dr. Julio Antonio del Marmol

Celia was Castro's most loyal confident from the Sierra Maestra, where the root of the revolution had been created. She was also his mistress. Whatever Fidel asked for, he got from her. She was a loyal trooper and tremendous asset to him not only through her loyalty but also the intelligence she possessed. What she lacked for in beauty she more than made up for in intellect and good heart. Celia proved to be smarter than the rest of them because silence conquered the power no one else had in Cuba using the power a woman has over a man. Rita was her agent inside and reported to her daily. I would see Rita frequently in the office speaking with her for hours after everyone left. Celia Sanchez was like a ghost that frightened the high leaders of the revolution even more than Fidel Castro did, because everyone knew whatever Celia said is what went. The only time Fidel Castro contradicted her is when he wanted to execute Huber Matos.

The two of them were old friends and even though Castro had never liked Matos when Celia introduced the two men, he remained pleasant, well-mannered, and honest. Huber also didn't like Castro much. It took only a brief conversation for him to read the personality of the egotistic liar. He warned Celia that Castro would hurt her feelings deeply one day. Celia, being the loyal friend to both men, tried to smooth things between them whenever they clashed. Celia also understood that they could work together but they could not be always in the same company; Matos was a genuine leader with solid morals while Fidel was the reverse. It took Huber a short time to earn by his own merits and bravery in combat to get the highest promotion to Commander in the rebel army, though the last thing Castro would have wanted was to make Matos his equal in rank.

Huber forgot over time the initially unpleasant introduction. Castro, however, never forgot that Matos didn't sympathize or agree with certain ideas he had expressed. He resented that and bottled it up in his mind for many years. Castro ordered the Marxist indoctrination of the troops, and Commander Huber Matos wrote a letter to Fidel as a friend—even though no friendship existed. He asked and pled with Castro to stick to the promises made to the Cuban people since it had provided them the financials and support of the population. He reminded Castro that the commitment was not just to restore freedom to Cuba, but to democracy. I was in the office when that letter was presented to Castro by Celia. The screams could be heard a block away as Castro threw a tantrum, calling Matos the worst traitor the revolution ever had. As I listened to this unfold, I was tremendously disappointed

Montauk: The Lightning Chance

to see the big man who was supposedly adored by the Cuban people to be so resentful and filled with hate against someone who had fought by his side during the revolution. It was also the first time I saw Celia remain on her feet. She said, "You are *not* going to execute Matos. If you do, I will not only leave you, I will leave Cuba and go into exile. I will not be an accomplice to what the revolution does: devour her own sons."

Everyone in that office believed that they would truly break up that day. Castro blinked and bowed to Celia's wishes since he didn't want to lose his right arm. He compromised by promising to leave the decision to the tribunal, but he insisted Huber had to be punished so that no one else followed his example. He needed to teach the other officers that those who disobeyed orders would face serious consequences. He deceptively convinced Celia of this and calmed her down. According to him, he had urged the tribunal to give them the max, but he told Celia that though the tribunal had sentenced Matos to 30 years he had lowered it to 20. I don't think Celia was ever fully convinced of this; but she accepted it since she had at least gotten away with keeping Matos from being sentenced to death. That was her primary goal. I believe this incident taught Celia the dark personality of her lover. I believe she got one of the greatest deceptions that she never recovered from until her death. When she died, some people in the government said that it was the first time they had ever seen Castro cry in public. I believe that the tears he shed over her death were just a façade for public consumption. She had dedicated almost all her life and was his accomplice in all the crimes he committed against the Cuban people without ever getting a single bit of recognition from her chauvinist partner for all her sacrifices.

I had two books on the table near the end of the library where I was seated. The first one was the book on how to make forgeries and how to detect them. The other one was a book on astrology, which was a decoy in case anyone came by for me to cover up what I was really planning to do in the next forty-eight hours that I had in order to protect Yaneba's uncle Bejasmin's life. I had had been provided the information when he was to be executed, and I wondered what might be going through his mind as he sat in that cell counting the minutes he had left in his life. A strong, powerful tremor went from my feet into my brain. I found that I had made mental contact with him. Wow, what a rush!

I closed my eyes tight and breathed deeply. I whispered, "Bejasmin—don't worry about it. I'll get you out of that place alive.

Please, be patient. Help me; ask Jesus with all our heart and His Father to not abandon us."

Like a TV had been turned on, I could see his face before me as well as where he was seated on his single bunk bed. His face had two tears rolling down his cheek of happiness and hope. I heard his voice in my ear, "Who are you, please?"

I started and opened my eyes in shock. I hadn't expected him to actually hear me. As soon as my eyes opened, the TV turned off and his image disappeared. After I recovered from my surprise, I remembered my uncle had told me the day before that I should not fear these things that my brain could do. On the contrary, I should face it and try to learn to use it for good, so I closed my eyes once more to try and establish that contact again. I found the smiling face of Bejasmin, like someone had switched the TV on once more. This time, he seemed to be able to see me as well, like it was a two-way video feed. He waved at me with his right hand. "Who are you?"

I waved back at him with my right hand. "Don't worry about who I am. You have to have faith and trust. Right now, right here, I'm working to get you free and to a safe place where no one will touch you again."

He nodded. "Thank you very much. God bless you and Jesus keep you by His side."

"Thank you, brother."

I heard a voice next to me. It was Rita. "Julio Antonio. Commandantico. Are you OK?"

I opened my eyes in shock, and the image of Bejasmin faded once more. I saw Rita next to me, concern and worry in her face. "You were talking to somebody. It sounded like your brother."

I immediately rushed to cover the book I had in front of me. Apparently, she had heard me speak to somebody. I must have raised my voice above the whisper without realizing it. She hadn't seen anyone else enter the library, and I was the only one there. I had to come up with an explanation quickly. "I'm sorry. Che had me very busy last night until quite late hours. I haven't closed my eyes all night. It's possible what while I was studying these books, I fell asleep. Believe me, you're not the first person to tell me that I talk in my sleep."

Rita looked at me seriously for a few seconds. It occurred to me that I might have committed an indiscretion when I was speaking with Bejasmin that might give me away. I felt better when she smiled in her usual, friendly way. "I think you had better go and take a long nap after lunch. It's not good for you to deprive your body of sleep. That's the most important nutrient for the brain. That's why people will even fall asleep while driving and kill themselves."

I smiled as I realized I had nothing to worry about. I picked the books and stood up. "OK. I've almost finished. Let me put these books away and go to the bathroom to wash my face and refresh my brain with cold water so that I don't fall asleep again. I don't have to worry about driving because I have the police escort driving me around while my jeep gets repaired. I'll follow your advice and go back to the hotel after lunch and take a long nap."

She held her hands out. "Give me the books and I'll put them away."

"Under no circumstance. I didn't come here to add to the work you have to do already."

She smiled and shook her head. "I always tell Celia and Fidel that you not only are a well-mannered young man but also that you have qualities that adult men don't have that we have daily encountered here. To the extreme of some of them using the restroom without even bothering to flush the toilet, leaving bowel floating there for the next person to see. Truly disgusting!"

I shook my head. "I cannot understand how some individuals can conduct themselves in that way." I made a disgusted expression and she responded in kind.

She said, "These men probably grew up in a pig farm."

"Probably," I replied with a nod. "I believe a lot of them are around the capital lately. But we have to be patient; we should try to teach them not only for their own health as well as ours."

She smiled incredulously and shook her head. "I don't know. I don't know." She didn't sound optimistic about teaching them as she evidently lost her patience a long time ago and didn't want to deal with these people who frequented the place now and their lack of manners. She raised her hand dismissively.

A couple of navy officers walked into the library. I used the distraction to quickly put the books back on the shelves, waved to her, and got out of the library. In my rush, I pretended to leave my military Commandos cap on the table. I went to the storage room. This time, I walked in and closed the door behind me. I quickly inspected the boxes and found one marked with the "Ministry of the Interior, Classified G-2. Orders and Memorandums, Commander Piñeiro, Personal and Confidential." I took the box and went to the Document Depository at the end of the room. I sat down on some of the boxes there, hidden behind the stacks but at an angle where I could keep both doors in sight, the one that went inside as well as the outside door the delivery trucks used.

After a little while of going through documents, I was lucky in that very shortly I found the ones I needed: some that were signed by Piñeiro addressing problems to Fidel that bore the official logo of the Ministry of the Interior with his signature and seals. I took more than one just in case I needed to combine them with what I had planned. I opened the buttons on my shirt and stuck them inside, making sure they lay flat on my belly. I had no excuse for being in this room. When I decided to leave, when I was about to open the door, I heard the clacking of a woman's high heels on the marble floor outside. I flattened myself against the wall behind the door since I had no time to conceal myself better. I turned my head to avoid getting hit by the door when it opened. I was so tense that I even held my breath lest it give me away.

The door opened and Gladys' voice asked, "Commandantico? Are you in here?" I didn't answer. I realized that one of the envelopes in the box I had put back was hanging out of it from beneath it between two boxes. I tensed even more and grimaced. The other boxes were very carefully organized, and it was obvious someone had been rummaging around in there.

The room wasn't completely dark, but there were certainly shadows, which was likely why I hadn't noticed that before. It was right in front of Gladys when she opened the door. When I didn't respond, she turned the lights on, and she noticed it. I saw her beautiful nyloned legs as she walked in and picked the envelop up. She looked at it curiously. She saw the logo for the Ministry of the Interior, opened the box, and put it inside. She turned back towards the door, turned the lights off and left. As soon as the door closed, I breathed a soft sigh of relief as I shook my head in distress. That tiny detail I had overlooked led to many people being executed as traitors to the revolution.

I opened the door slowly. After making sure no one was in the corridor, I walked briskly to the men's bathroom. I double locked the door and breathed more freely. I pulled my pants down, removed the papers and put them inside my underwear, resting on top of my penis. That way, if anyone patted me on the belly, they wouldn't find anything. I put my pants back on, washed my face to refresh some of the adrenaline rush aftereffects I was experiencing, grabbed one of the beautiful, thick white towels whose initials and crest belonged to the family that previously owned the house and dried my face. As I did so, I could tell it was a quality towel and expensive towel. I looked at the navy-blue crest embroidered on the towel and shook my head. I thought how Fidel, the hit man, hired by corrupt politicians managed to even steal the towels of these people. In the rush to save their lives, they had to leave even the most personal things behind.

I left the bathroom. When I got to Gladys' desk, she stopped me. "Where the devil have you been? I've been looking for you everywhere."

"Are you sure you looked everywhere? Did you look in the men's restroom?"

She looked at me in surprise with an unhappy expression. "In the men's restroom? What kind of woman do you think I am? No decent lady would ever snoop in the men's restroom. That's not a place for a decent woman."

I smiled. "Well, there you go. That's why you didn't find me, because that's where I was. I went there as soon as I left Rita in the library. By the way, what is your emergency that you were looking for me everywhere? Were you going to invite me to lunch?"

She shook her head, her serious expression returning to the pretty smile she usually gave me. "I believe you're the one who is supposed to invite me to lunch or dinner, not the other way around." She produced my uniform cap from behind her desk. "Are you going to reward me for this? Rita came after you because of it. I told her you hadn't passed my desk, so she left it here for you to make sure you wouldn't go crazy trying to find it later."

I raised my right arm and saluted her. "Thank you very much. You are an angel from the sky. To be honest with you, I didn't even notice I had left it behind. It makes my hair sweat too much. It may be a regulation I wrote myself; I didn't want to break protocol and give my officers a bad example. We leaders have to be examples all the time to the others. Even if I don't wear the hat, I should at least have it in my hand at all times." It occurred to me as I spoke to her that she suspected I was snooping around the offices. Those who are guilty always assume the worst. When she returned to her normal behavior, however, I realized she didn't think I was doing anything wrong. To make sure I left a friend behind me, I added as I left, "By the way, in reference to dinner or lunch, you tell me what day or time, and you decide for me what you want, I'll take you to the Hilton as an expression of gratitude, and dinner or lunch will be on me."

She looked at me in surprise and gratitude. "Oh! I was just kidding, but I'll take you up on that one day." She stood up and walked around her desk to give me a noisy kiss on my cheek. "You are truly a gentleman. That's hard to find these days. That's why I keep telling you to hurry up and grow up because I want you to marry me."

"Wait a minute—I'm supposed to be the one to ask that." I blushed again. "Gladys, you always make me blush when you talk of marriage. I'm too young for that!" I believed that she enjoyed seeing me blush.

Figure 49 Carlos III

We said goodbye and I walked to where my police escort awaited me. I asked Rodriguez to take me to Carlos III and Infanta. Rodriguez repeated it to the other drivers. "I'll give you more specific directions when we get there. We're going to my uncle's house on Carlos III." I guided them there and told Rodriguez that I would be back in a few minutes. "I'm going to say hello to my relatives and pick up some things."

I used my key to the side gate so that I didn't disturb my uncle or give them a panic attack at the sight of all the police cars in front of their house. I made as little noise as possible when I opened the gate and went around to the back where the treasure was stored. I picked up some portfolios I had left there before. I pulled my pants down, retrieved the documents and hid them there, and took three bars of gold stamped in the middle with 18K. I put the three bars and the documents into the portfolio and returned to the police caravan. I said, "Let's go to the Interior Ministry, to Piñeiro's office."

Rodriguez looked at me in surprise. Thinking he hadn't heard me correctly, he said, "The Ministry of the Interior/?"

"Yes, the office of Commander Piñeiro."

"OK, Commandantico." He repeated the orders and the caravan went into motion.

I wanted to finish cooking all my plans before meeting with my uncle and his associates. I wanted to have all the details in hand so that I could expose my ingredients to them in an effective way. Then it would be both more concrete and productive.

Since the beginning of the revolutionary tribunals, everyone was terrified by the G-2 and their repressive apparatus that was comparable to the Soviet's KGB. That is why even mentioning the Minister of the Interior to Corporal Rodriguez caused him to hesitate slightly. He pretended he hadn't heard me clearly, but the reality was that most of the firing squad executions in Cuba had been done by this sinister secret police force. Some people pretended to be your friends and displayed disaffection to the new extreme Left wing ideas with the purpose of proving the disloyalty of anyone to the government, whether those being entrapped were high ranked officers in the Army, police, or any other branch of the government. It was fair to say if you were condemned of any violation of the new laws of the revolution you had less chance of surviving to be declared innocent than a sheep in a giant cage locked in with very hungry lions. All Cubans had to thank Sergeant Batista, who turned himself overnight into a general and the next day changed into a dictator. This gave an excuse for the members of the communist party to penetrate all the different parts of the government and steal the democratic revolution out of the hands of the Cuban people, right before their eyes.

Dr. Julio Antonio del Marmol

Figure 50 Cell in Villa Marista

As we approached Piñeiro's office, I said to Rodriguez, "When we get there, bring with you the whole entourage of police officers."

That wasn't in my plan at the beginning, but I wanted to improvise since I had the opportunity of having all these men with me to walk into Piñeiro's office. I doubted he would be there, but if he was, when he saw me come in with all the police around me, he would raise no objection to what I wanted to do. If he was there, I would move to Plan B and I would show him that I had more power than he had, since I had the sympathies of Fidel and Che.

We walked in the door. Like every government building, two uniformed soldiers were on guard in complete fatigues and gear, fully armed, representing the new era of intimidation. They greeted me and saluted respectfully. They didn't bother asking me for any ID. They handed us visitor's badges to clip onto the flaps covering our pockets and told me where Piñeiro's office was located.

We entered the elevator and went to Manuel Piñeiro's headquarters. A lady, slightly overweight, in her mid- to late forties with heavy thick reading glasses introduced herself the moment I walked in with my entourage. She jumped to please me. "It's a great honor to meet you in person. I've seen you many times on TV with the Maximum Leader. My name is Juanita Odio. Commander Piñeiro is out of the city and won't be back for several days." I smiled. That was music to my ears. I wondered at the lady's last name. Odio was also the Spanish word for "hate," which was perfectly suitable for Piñeiro's personal secretary. The top leaders of the revolution ordinarily liked to have beautiful secretaries, like the typical male chauvinists they were. It occurred to me that since she wasn't attractive that Piñeiro probably gave her the position because he liked her last name.

I asked, "May I use the typewriter? I want to leave a long message for Manuel."

"Of course, Commandantico!" she replied enthusiastically. "You can use his office if you want. He's not here, and I know he'll be delighted to find that you came over to spend some time with us."

"Thank you. I need some privacy anyway."

Corporal Rodriguez and the policemen sat down in the reception area while she opened Piñeiro's private office to let me in. She said, "If you need anything, punch this button on the intercom and I'll come right away."

"Thank you. You're a very good secretary." She smiled and left, closing the door behind her and leaving me alone in the office. I could hear her establishing a conversation with Rodriguez. He later told me some pieces of it, but from what I could hear it appeared that she was born in the same town in the Oriente Province as he was. She had grown up, but they had never known each other. It looked like they had established a good connection.

I was glad the Corporal had come with me, because they distracted her with their conversation, and she would not realize how long I spent in the office. It was the perfect alibi. I pulled the documents with Piñeiro's signature and stamps out of my briefcase and sat down. I used his own letterhead on white paper to type out the transfer orders for the prisoner Bejasmin Cesar Loubus from La Cabaña Prison to the Ministry of the Interior to be processed and interrogated one final time before his execution on the direct orders of the Prime Minister Fidel Castro Ruz. I cut what the papers I brought that already had his identifiers and signature and attached them to the bottom of the orders I had just typed out. I took this document and went over to his personal photocopier and made a copy of my new document. I looked at it carefully to make sure no line across the page was visible and then compared it to another of the documents I had brought with me. The match was perfect.

I wrote another note to Piñeiro by way of greeting that I had stopped by his office to apologize to him had I in any way or manner offended him. It was not my intention and we all worked together under the same ideals with the same goals to create this beautiful socialist revolution. I signed it and put the forgery away in my briefcase and left my note out. I pushed the button on the intercom. I asked Juanita where the envelopes were so I could leave my note in a sealed container, as it was personal and confidential.

She said, "I'll be there in a few minutes. They're in the wall cabinet." She came in pulled out a set of keys and unlocked one of the cabinets. I could see that it also contained the various stamps and seals. I realized that the only thing I needed that wasn't in there was his signature, since it had everything else. She took out a couple of envelopes. "In case you make a mistake, here's an extra one." She left and I locked the door. I took several envelopes out of the cabinet and put them in my briefcase—in case I needed them in the future. I sat down at the typewriter and addressed the first one "To Whom It May Concern," pulled out the forgery, folded and inserted it into the envelope, and replaced in my briefcase. Then I addressed the second one "To Manuel Piñeiro, from Commander Julio Antonio del Marmol." I inserted my note, sealed it, and placed it on his desk.

I got up and calmly left the office. I didn't show any rush to get out of there. I said goodbye to Juanita and left in the company of my police escort. We left our visitor tags at the lobby of the building and left. I checked my wristwatch and saw it was about 1:30 pm. We walked to the patrol cars and Corporal Rodriguez told me a little about the chat he had with Juanita. It turned out he knew all her family, though he had never met her. He asked me where we were going next.

"To the Nautico," I replied

"Did you hear that? Nautico." Rodriguez turned to me. "Miramar?"

"Yes, around that area."

I said, "We're going to my uncle's house, my father's brother. He's a brilliant, intelligent man, a doctor specializing in obstetrics and gynecology."

When we got to the security barrier, the guard didn't hesitate to open the bar and signaled us inside. Apparently, too many police cars had passed through there recently and he was easily impressed. We parked by the Nautico clubhouse. I said, "After I finish my meeting with my uncle, I want to take all you guys to the Hilton for a nice, rewarding lunch."

"Commdantico, there's too many of us! I don't want to be a burden to you; we're just doing our job."

"I insist. I'll feel better if you have a great meal with me when we're done here."

He acquiesced. "Thank you very much. You're very generous." "The revolution is very generous."

Figure 51 Nautico Clubhouse

We exchanged smiles and I walked to the clubhouse. I saw my uncle sitting beneath the umbrellas on the beach, basking in the sun with Canen and Mr. Xiang, even though I was about twenty minutes early. When I got there and we exchanged cordial greetings, Canen was the first to ask nervously, "Why the hell are all these police cars with you? What's going on?"

I replied with a smile, "That signifies the power of persuasion. It's extraordinary what it can do when you learn to use it properly." They looked at me curiously since I hadn't replied directly. "OK, let me give you a little debrief. The new chief of the police station where they took the guy who tried to rob me at the liquor store the other day, when I was buying a bottle of Grand Marnier for Ernest Hemingway, has been promoted to Captain by Piñeiro and Che. I'll give you more details later, because this is a long story. You guys have better things to do than to listen to all my rites of passage as a beginning spy. I'll share everything with my uncle, and when he has more time, he'll tell you."

Canen spread his hands in protest. "Oh, man! You're just giving us the previews of the movie."

"Well, this individual in his gratitude to me offered me an escort anytime or anywhere I needed one. I can use his personal entourage. When I was leaving this place last night, I had a tiny encounter by the guard shack that nearly cost my life." I pointed at my uncle and he nodded. Clearly, he knew already. "Thank God all that happened was that the windshield on my jeep was shattered by a shower of bullets. I'm assuming who it was that was behind it, but that someone tried to remove me from the world of the living and send me to the land of the dead."

Uncle Emilio raised his right hand. "Yes, yes. The Gentleman of Paris already debriefed me in detail early this morning. I will put you guys in the picture later. Right now, though, we should give all our attention and listen to your plan. I cannot figure out how you propose to extract this man from prison, especially avoiding anybody getting hurt or taking the lives of any of us."

The attendant of the club approached us. I shut my briefcase at once and put it on my lap beneath the table. He had a small notebook in his hand and a pen and asked, "What would you gentlemen like to eat or drink?"

Everyone was silent for a moment. My uncle said, "Order whatever you want. This is my treat. Today you are my guests."

They ordered different drinks and food. I thanked him for his courtesy and ordered an orange juice, explaining my promise to the escort regarding lunch at the Hilton, since they had been with me since early in the morning. After the attendant left, I pulled my briefcase up and put it on the table. I opened it and pulled out the documents signed by Piñeiro. I handed it to my uncle, who read it and passed it to Canen, who then passed it to Mr. Xiang. They all looked at me in disbelief.

Mr. Xiang asked, consumed by curiosity, "How the hell did you manage to get Piñeiro sign this document?"

Canen shook his head. "After what your uncle has told me about you and what you've accomplished in the last forty-eight hours, when I have had only one single short debrief with you, I won't be surprised if you told me that you took that document out from under the very nose of Piñeiro himself."

I looked at him seriously, but slightly surprised at the comment. It was close to the truth. I looked him in the eyes and understood he had simply made an extraordinary guess. I smiled and nodded. "I don't think even you understand how close you are to the truth. You made me think for a minute that either you have been following me or you sent someone to do so."

Canen replied, "No. I would never do that to my friends. I would do that only when I have doubts about somebody. But as your uncle says, believe but verify. About you, however, from the very minute I met you I had no doubts that you truly are the real sugar cane juice, not the one they sell in bottles."

Montauk: The Lightning Chance

"Thank you very much for your trust in me. But you gave me the same positive reading. That means that you and I are on the same cosmic alignment. It's very possible that maybe some way around the line we will come to be in the same family circle."

He replied, "That's very possible. I have three sisters, and one of them has your first name: Julia."

I smiled. "Interesting coincidence! I have three sisters as well, but none of them is named Canena." Everyone smiled at my jest. "Well, later on I will give you the long version if my uncle gets too tired. Don't forget to ask me. Let me say how I got this document. The truth is that this is not real—it's a forgery. But only the contents. All the rest, including the paper watermark, is real and from Piñeiro's personal office. What I need from you, Canen, more than anything, is at least four regular Army uniforms. I need two rank insignia: one Captain, one Commander. This will complete my plan because I intend to walk this man out of jail through the main door and the front gate in plain view of everyone, late tonight or early tomorrow morning. I discovered that Piñeiro is out of the city, and I want the Gentleman of Paris to come with me and dye his beard and hair red. I believe with a little cleanup of his hair and some makeup if I saw him in the backseat of one of those Oldsmobiles he would come to be the perfect double for Piñeiro. Just in case something goes wrong with your contact inside the prison, I don't think anybody will dare to say no to that devil, the Redbeard."

Canen asked, "Where the hell will you get those Oldsmobiles? Only the leaders have access to those now, especially the black ones."

I said, "Very simple—the car collection of Che Guevara. I not only have access but also authorization to use any car whenever I need it."

Mr. Xiang shook his head and rubbed his forehead. "I cannot get over this kid! Good job, good job! You earned the trust of the Devil himself!"

I smiled. "I don't know if that's good or bad, Mr. Xiang."

"No, no—that is very good, very good. It's almost impossible to obtain his trust. The Devil believes in nothing, not even himself. That is why I say it's such a good job. What you achieved is almost impossible."

"Thank you very much for your recognition of my little talent." I pointed at my uncle. "All I've done, really, is follow his advice and methods. I believe I have to share whatever compliment you give me with him. I think that's more appropriate. I don't want to inflate my ego—remember, that's one of the Devil's temptations."

Emilio smiled. "That is another of your good qualities. Your humility. But I believe that the best pupils surpass their teachers. I never have to repeat the same thing to you more than twice."

Canen said, "Well, it's true that for the past few days since you have joined our clandestine cell, we've advanced by almost fifty percent our capacity for the tremendous amount of information that we've been accumulating, just taking into consideration only that which you provide for us."

I replied, "Yes, it's not about me. I'm not trying to put myself down, but it's the tremendous access I possess inside the guts of these people."

Canen said, "Give yourself a little credit, OK? Not everyone your age can maintain the cool to get away with what you've done."

Emilio said, "Don't forget his natural gifts he was born with. That is extremely important."

Two waiters came over with the food. I put the briefcase on my lap under the table once more. They served the food and drinks the others had ordered. I was the only one with any papers, and I didn't want to call attention to it in case anyone there was an informant. After they served us and left, Canen said to me, "In a few hours you will have the uniforms in your uncle's hands. Not only the official rank insignia but also a pair of plain uniforms."

"Yes. I need some people to wear them like guards for the officers. I'll call my uncle in a couple of hours to make sure he has them."

Emilio said, "Why don't we save time and I'll call you and leave a message? I'll say that I have the book by Hemingway you asked me for."

I pulled the briefcase back up onto the table. I took three bars of gold out of it. I placed them one on top of the other on the table, and my uncle rushed to cover the stack with a napkin embroidered with the Nautico club logo. He turned to Canen and asked, "How many do you need?"

"I only need one. It's more than enough—it's worth a lot of money. Since we have a different plan now, this guy doesn't need to share it with anybody. He was going to split it with the people who pick up and drop off the laundry. Now we only need to take care of him. I love this plan—it's a lot better and involves a lot less risk. This document the Commadantico brought with the order for release will exonerate my contact of all responsibility. He had been planning to have the laundry people put the prisoner in the truck of inmate uniforms from the dirty clothes early in the morning on its daily run. This has zero risk to him. By the way, the individual who will be in charge of the operation that you or whoever is going to talk to is the chief of the cell block. He is the only officer authorized, especially after normal hours of work, eating, or exercise to move prisoners. His name is Captain del Valle. Whoever you put in charge of this operation should directly contact this man. Those individuals who are sentenced to death are maintained isolated from the rest of the inmates. Your plan is the best because you won't have to pass through the general population."

Emilio asked me, "What do you want me to do with these two extra bars of gold you brought?"

"Use it however you find necessary for our cause. There's a lot more where those came from. It will be very useful in the future for the same purpose we're using this one right now."

Canen asked, "What are the sizes of uniforms you need?"

"About your size. These individuals that will be helping me in this plan are around 6 foot 6. They're huge."

"OK. I measure 6'6" and a half. I can use my uniforms. I have plenty. All I have to do is locate the insignia for the Commander. We can use one of my Captain's bars. This won't be difficult at all. Just give me a couple of hours, OK?"

I smiled. "If everything goes the way I expect, tomorrow morning very early we'll save one more life from the nails of Satan. A great man, Bejasmin Loubus, will be far out of his reach."

Mr. Xiang asked Canen, "Is there any time in particular that will be best for your contact to do this operation?"

He shook his head. "No, no. In reality, he said to me that any time is good. Of course, late at night always the illicit is a lot more convenient and appropriate. In the shadows of the night it is a lot more difficult to remember facial structure and details of anyone, which makes sense. They're sleepy and tired, so their brains don't function with the same clarity as in the plain light of day."

Mr. Xiang nodded. At the same time, he took a bite of one of the egg rolls on his plate. "Ha! That's true, Canen, unless you're dealing with bats or vampires who sleep during the day and come out to eat at night."

I said, "Let's hope that these guards aren't either bats or vampires." I stood up. "I think we've covered everything. I should get going. I have a lot to do and prepare still for tonight. I don't want to break my promise to these great police officers that are escorting me and made my life a lot easier in Piñeiro's office today. Unless you have nothing else to debrief me with?" They shook their head as they ate. "Well, guys, I'm getting hungry and I don't want to watch you guys eat any longer. I'll feel sorry for myself and order something here, breaking my promise. I know for sure you have other things to discuss and debrief each other on."

I said goodbye to them and started to walk towards the police cars and the men I considered my buddies. They had patiently waited for over two hours. I thought that if they deserved a good lunch before, now I had no doubts at all that lunch would not be enough. They deserved a good, exquisite dinner as an extra reward for that long wait. I hadn't thought that the meeting would go so long.

I jumped into one of the patrol cars. We left the Nautico towards Fifth Avenue, passing by the luxurious residences of the Miramar community. A little while later we arrived at the Hilton and I could see my jeep was parked in the same place I usually parked it almost by the front door. I got out of the patrol car and walked over to it, followed by Rodriguez to look at the windshield. They did a fantastic job at the mechanical pool. They not only replaced the glass; they replaced the entire front of the jeep that had been damaged by the bullets. The new, shining rubber surrounding the windshield made the jeep look better than ever. I thought how God worked in mysterious ways. I shook my head as I was very pleased with the job.

Rodriguez said, "Boy! That jeep looks brand new!"

The attendants came over to us. "Looking good, eh?" one of them said.

I smiled. "Yes. I'm very happy with how surprisingly good it looks." I said goodbye to them and entered the hotel with my police friends. The valets looked at me in admiration. Rodriguez, likewise, felt proud to be with me as he held his head up high as we walked into the lobby. Heads turned as we entered; even Elisa noticed us and waved to me cheerfully. We walked to my favorite place, the gourmet Cafeteria and Catering. The maître d as soon as we walked in recognized me. Noticing the large number of police coming in with me, waived his right hand to me from the back. He gestured to me that he would seat us immediately if we could be patient and wait just a little while.

Montauk: The Lightning Chance

The place was completely full. Most of the foreigners were Russians from the embassy and many Chinese and Vietnamese from the consulate. I nodded and waved back. The maître d clapped twice and called a few waiters over without speaking to disturb anyone there—even though everyone was paying attention to all the policemen standing at the entrance. He pointed to various locations wordlessly and his men went to the back door into the kitchen. Like an orchestra conductor, the maître d's men followed his direction and moved a Spinet piano to one side, replacing it with three tables which they immediately set and then brought in chairs for all of us. All the policemen clearly were enjoying being the center of the spectacle. The professionalism and speed of the staff was amazing and quite a show to watch. The maître d pointed where he wanted things set and brought in a silver bucket filled with ice and a napkin. He then brought in wine and water glasses. Without wasting a second, I looked at my watch. It took them less than five minutes before he waved us back with a smile on his face.

Everyone there watched the parade walk between the tables. I said to the maître d, pointing at my watch, "Not even five minutes! Your efficiency exceeds the most demanding extremes from the culinary ethics. You've managed to sit and prepare this table in a record time of less than five minutes."

The maître d replied, "Thank you very much, Commandantico, for your good taste and lovely words. They stimulate us to continue serving with the greatest pleasure and makes us feel proud to be better and more efficient at our job."

I nodded and grinned. "Thank you very much because a beautiful compliment can only be paid back by another compliment full of joy and gratitude."

He smiled again and bowed his head to all of us. He asked, "Do you want to order from the menu, or as you sometimes like to do, allow me to surprise you and your friends with the most exquisite variety and refined recipes of high cuisine?"

I squeezed my chin with my left hand for a second and thought. I turned to Rodriguez. "What do you guys prefer? You can order from the menu like people commonly do, or we can, since my friend Rolando frequently does as a special courtesy to me, bring us the most exquisite dishes that the master chefs prepare daily as variety for distinguished preference customers like us? Do you prefer that or the menu?"

"For me, I love to be surprised!" The other men nodded their assent.

One of them said, "I don't even understand this menu, it has so many strange names. I think it's better we get surprised."

Rolando smiled. "That is a good choice, gentlemen! This man has a taste for haute cuisine!" he added with a gesture towards me.

Time passed and our drinks were served by different waiters. A large jar of freshly squeezed orange juice got set down on the table next to me. They knew my preferences very well by now. I thanked Rolando for remembering my favorite drink. Later, they served our meal with a tremendous variety of dishes. Each that arrived could seduce the most demanding palate. The first one was fresh seafood: jumbo shrimp, sliced calamari, clams, oysters in their shells on top of ice, nova lox, thinly sliced Swiss cheese, Gouda cheese, green olives with pimento filling. These platters of fresh seafood were filled with a bowl of cioppino, a form of bouillabaisse, served cold. All of the dishes were heavy in tomato sauce, because these were Italian dishes that originally came from San Francisco, brought to Cuba by an Italian American chef.

More exotic dishes kept arriving. The friends of the policemen, mostly peasants recruited by the revolutionary governments who came from poor families, had never seen in their lives both that quantity and quality of food. This gourmet food fascinated them, especially with the sauce surrounding the platters with small containers of dipping sauces: tartar, bearnaise, cashew hot sauce with horse radish, and so on. The next main platter came with cold meats: ground beef with mixed nuts (a special kind of meatloaf in Cuba), mortadella, salamis, pate, with all kind of crackers and toasted sourdough bread, slices of baguette garlic bread with olive oil. In the end, this became a feast for them.

I watched them enjoying the food, as I did as well, and thought that I was glad that I had eaten nothing with my uncle and his friends save for the orange juice. It stimulated my appetite and allowed me to indulge now in the things I really liked. I asked, "So far, how are you guys doing? Do you like it?" Some of them had mouths full and gave me a thumbs up.

One of the guys said, "I wish I could afford to come here for every meal of the day!"

Rodriguez said, "With your salary, son, you couldn't even afford breakfast here every day. I myself couldn't afford it." He turned to me. "Look. I've already had to unbuckle my belt, hoping I'll have a little more room to eat a little more. I don't want to leave any food on the table and don't think it would be proper to take it home, and I can't even swallow a grain of sugar or my stomach will bust."

Montauk: The Lightning Chance

"Don't worry about," I said. "This is on the revolution. If you want to take some home, tell Rolando to wrap it up for you."

They looked at me aghast. "Really?!"

"Yes. It's already paid for, and these guys bring us more than we can ever eat. Are you sure you don't want dessert?"

They shook their heads, clearly more than full themselves. I signed the check Rolando brought to me, giving him a generous tip. I said to them, "Stay here and eat in peace. Rolando, wrap up whatever they want to take with them, and send my compliments to the chef for all this great food."

I said goodbye and walked towards the elevators. I took one and pressed the button for the floor our suite was on and went to reunite with Daniel and Cisneros. When I opened the door, I could hear both of them snoring like freight trains. They had ordered room service from the carts and had already had a sumptuous lunch. I woke them up. I said, "Well, well, well—if Fidel saw this he would call you bourgeois." I saw a couple of bottles of beer. "Even though you guys are large in size, you're still minors. You shouldn't be drinking alcohol. You're going to get me in trouble as well as yourselves."

"We're sorry, Commandantico," they said.

"It's OK. I had a couple of daiquiris with Che and Hemingway the other day."

I sat down at the dining table and explained the plans I had and how we would put them in motion. I finished my debriefing and we left the hotel. We went to the compound of the Gentleman of Paris. As I arrived there, he was waiting for us outside. Clearly, my uncle had already contacted and updated him. He was not in his normal interplanetary vehicle but a regular navy blue and white 1951 Buick. We exchanged greetings and chatted about the final details for a few minutes, we separated. He was going to CMQ channel to pick up a couple of old friends who were TV actors. One of them played one of the main roles in the Zorro series, Modesto Burdom; the other one, Francisco Blanco, played the close associate of Zorro. Tonight, they would play the personal assistants to Piñeiro that would have the heavy burden of dealing with the captain in charge of the prison. I was to take Daniel and Cisneros with me to Che's mansion in Boca Siega to get the two Oldsmobiles that served to complete our disguise and develop the whole operation. Everyone would be convinced that the supposed Redbeard was indeed sitting the back seat without any doubt. The operation would soon be ready to put in motion: the rescue of Bejasmin Cesar Loubus. We called it Operation Green Moon.

The story of the Cuban Lightning and his experiences relating to the Montauk Project continue in *The Lightning and Montauk: Reality vs. Fiction*

Montauk: The Lightning Chance

Other Works by Dr. Julio Antonio del Marmol

The Zipper: The Cuban Lightning
Cuba: Russian Roulette of the World
ISIS: The Genetic Conception (Lack of Judgement)

<u>Rites of Passage of a Master Spy Series</u>
Cuba: The Truth, the Lies, and the Coverups
The Havana Conspiracies
The Dark Face of Marxism
The Deadly Deals
The Evil Rituals
JFK: The Unwrapped Enigma

<u>Forthcoming Books</u>
The Lightning and Montauk: Reality vs. Fiction
The Lightning and bin Ladin: Genetic Trail of the Lightning

www.ingramcontent.com/pod-product-compliance
Lightning Source LLC
Chambersburg PA
CBHW031958220426
43664CB00005B/60